£30·00

OXFORD ENGLISH MONOGRAPHS

MELODIOUS TEARS

The English Funeral
Elegy from
Spenser to Milton

DENNIS KAY

CLARENDON PRESS · OXFORD
1990

Oxford University Press, Walton Street, Oxford OX2 6DP
Oxford New York Toronto
Delhi Bombay Calcutta Madras Karachi
Petaling Jaya Singapore Hong Kong Tokyo
Nairobi Dar es Salaam Cape Town
Melbourne Auckland
and associated companies in
Berlin Ibadan

Oxford is a trade mark of Oxford University Press

Published in the United States
by Oxford University Press, New York

© Dennis Kay 1990

British Library Cataloguing in Publication Data
Kay, Dennis
Melodious tears: the English funeral elegy from
Spenser to Milton.—(Oxford English monographs).
1. Elegiac poetry in English—Critical studies
I. Title   821.0409
ISBN 0-19-811789-2

Library of Congress Cataloging-in-Publication Data
Kay, Dennis.
Melodius tears: the English funeral elegy from
Spenser to Milton / Dennis Kay.
p.   cm.—(Oxford English monographs)
Includes bibliographical references.
1. Elegiac poetry, English—History and criticism.
2. English poetry—Early modern, 1500–1700—
History and criticism.   3. Funeral rites and ceremonies
in literature.   4. Death in literature.
I. Title.   II. Series.
PR539.E45K38   1990   821'.040903—dc20   89–71150
ISBN 0-19-811789-2

Set by Hope Services (Abingdon) Ltd
Printed and bound in
Great Britain by Bookcraft Ltd
Midsomer Norton, Bath

CONTENTS

ABBREVIATIONS

Unless otherwise indicated, references to classical texts are to editions in the Loeb Classical Library. References to Shakespeare are to the text in *The Riverside Shakespeare*, ed. G. B. Evans (Boston, 1974). The usual abbreviations are used for the titles of Shakespeare's plays, and for Sidney's works; i.e. *AS* for *Astrophil and Stella*. *OA* for *The Old Arcadia*, and *NA* for *The New Arcadia*. For ease of reference, titles of *STC* books are normally given in the form of that catalogue.

DNB	*Dictionary of National Biography*
ELH	*Journal of English Literary History*
ELN	*English Language Notes*
ELR	*English Literary Renaissance*
ES	*English Studies*
JMRS	*Journal of Medieval and Renaissance Studies*
MLR	*Modern Language Review*
MP	*Modern Philology*
N&Q	*Notes and Queries*
PLL	*Papers on Language and Literature*
PMLA	*Publications of the Modern Languages Association of America*
RES	*Review of English Studies*
RQ	*Renaissance Quarterly*
SEL	*Studies in English Literature, 1500–1900*
SLI	*Studies in the Literary Imagination*
SP	*Studies in Philology*
STC	Short-title Catalogue
TSLL	*Texas Studies in Literature and Language*
YES	*Yearbook of English Studies*

INTRODUCTION

I'd like to begin with the events of two consecutive days in the spring of 1559, the first spring of Queen Elizabeth's reign. Henry Machyn, a London undertaker, recorded two contrasting funerals in his diary. On 6 April, at St Clement's Without Temple Bar, the funeral took place of Lady Cary, a woman of about 30 who had been married first to Sir William Walsingham and then to Sir John Cary. Machyn notes the quantity of candles and banners displayed in the church, and that the ceremony concluded with 'masse and or communyon'. The account indicates that there was nothing unusual or remarkable about what occurred.[1]

On the following day, Machyn scribbled a description of a funeral in Cheapside. There are gaps in his version—the name of the dead woman being the most notable—but his mounting incredulity in encountering the novel phenomenon of a Protestant funeral is obvious enough:

ther was a gret compene of pepull, ii and ii together, and nodur prest nor clarke, the new prychers in ther gowne lyk ley [-men,] nodur syngyng nor sayhyng tyll they cam [to the grave,] and a-for she was pute into the grayff a [collect] in Englys, and then put in-to the grayff, and after [took some] heythe and caste yt on the corse, and red a thynge . . . for the sam, and contenent cast the heth in-to the [grave], and contenent red the pystyll of sant Poll to the Stesselonyans the . . . chapter, and after thay song *paternoster* in Englys, boyth prychers and odur, and [women,] of a nuw fassyon, and after on of them whent in-to the pulpytt and mad a sermon. (p. 193)

What struck Machyn was the disruption of accustomed order. The new preachers, 'in their gowns like laymen', were indistinguishable from the company of people; the congregation seemed to him to be assembled indiscriminately, mingling ranks and sexes both as they walked in procession and as they prayed. Perhaps because English rather than Latin was used, he could not tell which chapter of the Epistle to the Thessalonians was read; and to him the Lord's

---

[1] *The Diary of Henry Machyn, Citizen and Merchant-Taylor of London, from A.D. 1550 to A.D. 1563*, ed. J. G. Nichols. Camden Society, os, 42 (1848), 193.

Prayer was the *'pater-noster'* even in his native tongue.[2] For the same reason, perhaps, he records merely that one of this assembly 'red a thynge'—some sort of prayer over the body—and then that one of them 'made a sermon'. Confronted with these shocking sights and sounds, Machyn's system of note-taking seems to have broken down. He could not record what was happening before his eyes.

The culture of pre-Reformation Europe has been characterized as 'a cult of the living in the service of the dead'.[3] At the simplest level, the sheer number (in excess of two thousand) of chantries in England, and the evidence from wills, testifies to the immense importance attached to praying for the repose of the souls of the deceased.[4] With the Reformation, everything changed: in Keith Thomas's words, 'Protestant doctrine meant that each generation could be indifferent to the spiritual fate of its predecessor'.[5] Other scholars write that death was no longer the focal point of life, that a wedge had been driven between the living and the dead.[6]

With the Reformation the Requiem Mass, with its potential for infinite repetition, endless accumulation, disappeared. The chantries closed.[7] Nothing the mourners might do or say would be held to

---

[2] See the brief account of revisions in the Book of Common Prayer in Clare Gittings's important and detailed study, *Death, Burial and the Individual in Early Modern England* (1984), 40–2.

[3] A. N. Galpern, *The Religions of the People in Sixteenth-Century Champagne*, Harvard Historical Studies, 92 (Cambridge, Mass., 1976), 20 (see also pp. 21–35).

[4] See K. L. Wood-Legh, *Perpetual Chantries in Britain* (Cambridge, 1965), 304–5; Gittings, *Death, Burial and the Individual*, 19–35. Quite apart from the wish of some testators to have large numbers (sometimes many thousands) of masses said for their soul, the expenditure involved in funeral observances could be immense: Gittings remarks that 'Perhaps the most striking feature of all the details concerning the cost of burial in late medieval England is the level to which expenditure on the funerals of the aristocracy had risen by the late fifteenth and early sixteenth centuries' (p. 25).

[5] Keith Thomas, *Religion and the Decline of Magic* (2nd edn., Harmondsworth, 1973), 719–21.

[6] 'La vie cessait de chercher dans la mort son point de perspective' (L. Febvre, *Au Cœur religieux du XVI͏ᵉ siècle* (Paris, 1957), 58); see the informative chapter, 'Funerals and Faith', in Gittings, *Death, Burial and the Individual*, 39–59. Four important studies of attitudes to death are: P. G. Stannard, *The Puritan Way of Death: A Study in Religion, Culture and Social Change* (Oxford, 1977); M. Vovelle, *Mourir autrefois* (Paris, 1974); P. Ariès, *Western Attitudes Towards Death*, tr. P. N. Ranum (1974); and his *The Hour of Our Death*, tr. H. Weaver (Harmondsworth, 1983).

[7] The standard modern account is A. Kreider, *English Chantries: The Road to Dissolution*, Harvard Historical Studies, 97 (Cambridge, Mass., 1976), esp. pp. 5–92. In the words of W. K. Jordan, 'the most shattering and irreversible action of the Reformation in England was the proscription of prayers for the repose of the souls of the dead' (*Edward VI: The Threshold of Power* (Cambridge, Mass., 1970), 181).

influence the fate of the soul of the deceased.[8] The focus of funeral observances shifted radically towards the secular. Ceremonies became, on the one hand, representations of the status of the deceased at the time of death and, on the other, expressions of the reaction of the survivors. Great attention was paid to the orders and degrees of mourners at these funeral solemnities, which became so elaborate and took such a long time to organize that the body would either be embalmed or buried privately in a separate ceremony.[9] For the nobility, funeral arrangements were 'the tribute of a deferential society to the dignity of a title': in the words of Weever, 'Decent buriall, according to the qualities of the person deceased, with attendants of kindred and friends, is an honour to the defunct'.[10]

The question of what constituted 'decent' burial was inevitably controversial. In the words of Shakespeare's Lafew, 'Moderate Lamentation is the right of the dead; excessive grief the enemy to the living' (*AWEW* I. i. 51).[11] Richard Braithwait, for example, advocated 'decencie' in funeral observances, conscious that 'there is a vaine-glorie euen in death'.[12] But others thought simplicity could be overdone; Camden complained that 'some of especiall note amongst vs, neglecting the last duty eyther vpon a sparing or a

[8] In Hugh Latimer's words: 'When one dieth, we must have bells ringing, singing, and much ado: but to what purpose? Those that die in the favour of God are well: those that die out of the favour of God, this can do them no good.', *Sermons by Hugh Latimer*, ed. G. E. Corrie, Parker Society (1844), 305.

[9] R. Huntington and P. Metcalf, *Celebrations of Death: The Anthropology of Mortuary Ritual* (Cambridge, 1979), 163–5; on embalming, see Gittings, *Death, Burial and the Individual*, 29–30, 87–8. Some wills show testators (usually, but not invariably, female), facing the prospect of evisceration with alarm. Hence the fashion for private burials and for lifelike effigies which could be used in the public procession. See Lawrence Stone, *The Crisis of the Aristocracy 1558–1641* (Oxford, 1965), 379; Thomas, *Religion and the Decline of Magic*, 722; E. H. Kantorowicz, *The King's Two Bodies: A Study in Medieval Political Theology* (Princeton, NJ, 1957), 421; R. Giesey, *The Royal Funeral Ceremony in Renaissance France* (Geneva, 1960), 85.

[10] Stone, *Crisis of the Aristocracy*, 572; John Weever, *Ancient funerall monuments* (1631), 25.

[11] Spenser likened the 'despairful outcries and immoderate wailings' of the Irish to the unrestrained mourning of the Egyptians at Joseph's death (*A View of the Present State of Ireland*, ed. W. L. Renwick (Oxford, 1970), 55–6); Renwick points out (p. 204) that Spenser probably meant to refer to Jacob, and recalled the Geneva Bible, Gen. 1: 3, 'The Egyptians bewailed him seventie dayes', with its marginal note, 'They were more excessive in lamenting than the faithful'.

[12] Patrick Hannay, *A happy husband. To which is adjoyned the Good Wife, by R. Braithwait* (1618), D1r; see also Braithwait's *Remains after death: including divers memorable observances* (1618), and Stannard, *The Puritan Way of Death*, 97–122.

precise humour, are content to commit to the earth their parents, wiues, and nearest vnto them *in tenebris* with little better than *sepultura asinorum*.[13] The substance of the argument was hardly novel: it recalls, obviously enough, the usual Lollard wish for unostentatious burial, and it had been fully rehearsed in Erasmus's colloquy *Funus*.[14] But commentators returned to it repeatedly; the issue was never resolved, and provided inexhaustible matter, an open-ended subject of discourse. Each ceremony would need to be judged against an idea of 'decencie', each celebration of a unique individual was required to be correspondingly unique, particular.

It is important to stress this new particularity—and the problems that were acknowledged to be involved in achieving it. Translated into the sphere of literary responses to death, it is a theme that runs through this book. Some elegists, as shall be shown, confined themselves to a role that was essentially heraldic; like the heralds, they saw it as their function to ensure a respectful celebration of the status the deceased had enjoyed when alive.[15] But more sophisticated writers—and those about whom I shall have most to say are Spenser, Sidney, Donne, and Milton—recognized that the elegist faced in an especially well-defined way the problem of fitting words to the special requirements of an occasion and of arguing for uniqueness both for the subject and for the elegy. The parallel with the situation of the sonneteer is evident, and will be developed later in these pages. To put it very baldly, just as the sonnet was an aggregative form, in which practitioners defined their individuality against their predecessors, so with the elegist. After all, the elegy—and especially the pastoral elegy—had from ancient times been recognized as a form in which consciousness of tradition, repetition, translation, and imitation was inseparable from innovation and invention. The habitual elegiac protestations of sincerity, inexpressibility, uniqueness, and individuality are suggestively analogous to the performance of many speakers in sonnet sequences. Such

---

[13] William Camden, *Remaines of a greater worke concerning Britaine* (1605), ii. 28.

[14] See K. B. McFarlane, *Lancastrian Kings and Lollard Knights*, ed. G. L. Harriss (Oxford, 1972), 210–20; *The Colloquies of Erasmus*, tr. C. R. Thompson (Chicago, 1965), 357–72 (refs. to Erasmus's other writings on death are given on p. 358).

[15] On the role of the heralds, see Stone, *Crisis of the Aristocracy*; Gittings, *Death, Burial and the Individual*, 166–87. Machyn's *Diary* records (pp. 209–10) the obsequies of the French King Henri II, and describes a large assembly of heralds; in the entry for 6 Sept. 1559, he records of another funeral that 'the chyrche and the [street] was hangyd with blake with armes; *and master Clarenshux sett them in order*' (p. 210: my italics).

matters, obviously enough, are closely related to the opposition—authoritatively developed in Erasmus's *Funus*—between plainness and ostentation in preparing for, celebrating, and experiencing death. And just as death could be understood as a performance to be evaluated, appreciated, and admired, or condemned, so with reactions to it.[16] As the elegy became an increasingly widely attempted form, this inexhaustible controversy became an inescapable context for most elegiac writing, and acquired, as might be anticipated, significant religious and political dimensions.[17]

No less crucial to the development of the funeral elegy was the example of the funeral sermon, the innovation which, within weeks of being remarked by Machyn, had become, according to the evidence of his diary, common practice.[18] The preacher's task was set not by literary convention but by the occasion; in a sense, he performed the ancient role of professional spokesman for a grieving community.[19] It was an important part of his function to dramatize, to represent, the process of coming to terms with death; his performance had a primary, human consolatory purpose. A second, related purpose arose from treating the death of an individual as an example to others: the preacher's job was to locate the exemplary matter in his subject and then to broadcast it for the edification of the survivors.[20] And, as with the sermon, no matter how many practices and conventions and clichés accumulated, the funeral elegy was essentially a form without a form, a performance in which a high value was attached to individuality (of speaker as much as subject), invention, and improvisation, a genre defined by its occasion.

The neo-Latin elegy was an established medium for the

[16] The authority on this subject is Stephen Greenblatt. See his *Sir Walter Ralegh: The Renaissance Man and his Roles* (New Haven, 1973), esp. chs. 1 and 2, and his fuller development of the topic in *Renaissance Self-fashioning: From More to Shakespeare* (Chicago, 1980), *passim*.

[17] See below, Chs. 5 & 6 for examples.

[18] See Machyn's *Diary*, 201, 211, etc. and index, s.v. 'Sermons'. For a statistical survey, see Gittings, *Death, Burial and the Individual*, table 4, p. 240.

[19] As Margaret Alexiou asserts, 'The lament for the dead is essentially functional' (*The Ritual Lament in Greek Tradition* (Cambridge, 1974), 3; on professional mourners, see pp. 10–23). See also R. Garland, *The Greek way of Death* (1985), 121, and below, pp. 41–5.

[20] See B. K. Lewalski, *Donne's Anniversaries and the Poetry of Praise: The Creation of a Symbolic Mode* (Princeton, 1973), 73–141. For some remarks on sermons in general, see Patrick Collinson, *The Religion of Protestants: The Church in English Society 1559–1625* (Oxford, 1982), 48–51, 257–64.

exploration and expression of aspects of the complex relationships between Renaissance humanist culture and the past. But that is another subject. The vernacular funeral elegy as it developed in Renaissance England was, like the funeral sermon, defined, structured, by its occasion more than by generic expectations or prescription. Formally, as I have claimed, the funeral elegy has much in common with the prayers spoken over the body—what Machyn called a 'thynge'—and the sermon, that were initially so novel, so unassimilable, to Henry Machyn, since from ancient times it has been associated with the period up to and surrounding burial (in contrast with the epitaph, which is connected, whether actually or fictionally, with the tomb). And because the elegist had a marked degree of freedom to improvise, to imitate, or invent, the elegy may be considered in some senses the quintessential Renaissance kind, in whose performance a high value was placed on those qualities especially prized in Renaissance theories of composition. As such it was a form which encouraged emulation and competition; it was also accessible to writers of all ages and abilities, and was for many of them evidently a kind of laboratory in which they learnt about composition. This observation applies with as much force to young men who grew into connoisseurs and patrons as to those with literary ambitions who declared their profession, or sought patronage, by using the elegy to show their virtuosity. For many writers, the funeral elegy was a medium for interrogating and comprehending principles of composition—a training in understanding the components of art and the disciplines of the craft.[21]

In the years before the Civil War, as the mass of surviving published and manuscript material demonstrates, the elegy was a form which any educated person would have wished to try, and it was a form in which most such people would have felt sufficiently competent to recognize and appreciate real distinction.[22] The

---

[21] Some of the most significant studies of the last dozen years have been: Terence Cave, *The Cornucopian Text: Problems of Writing in the French Renaissance* (Oxford, 1979), esp. 125–56; D. West and T. Woodman, eds., *Creative Imitation and Latin Literature* (Cambridge, 1979); two articles by G. W. Pigman III, 'Versions of Imitation in the Renaissance', *RQ* 33 (1980), 1–32, and 'Imitation and the Renaissance Sense of the Past: The Reception of Erasmus' *Ciceronianus*', *JMRS* 9 (1979), 155–77; T. M. Greene, *The Light in Troy: Imitation and Discovery in Renaissance Poetry* (New Haven, 1982), with a useful bibliography, pp. 312–13; and B. Vickers, *In Defence of Rhetoric* (Oxford, 1988).

[22] A series of appendices (below, pp. 233–264) includes several examples of elegies from the MS tradition.

almost instant effect of Donne's *Anniversaries* on a whole genera-
tion of young poets in 1612 is the most striking of many possible
examples. The present study charts the movement of the elegy in
England from the time when it was the province of professional
writers, the balladeers and chroniclers, to the time of *Lycidas*.
Elegy is a form that can be approached in terms of tradition,
influence, authority, the large questions raised by the individual
poet's relation both to his predecessors and to death itself, as
is exemplified in some distinguished recent criticism.[23] More
immediately relevant to this book is the fact that, as a form without
frontiers, the elegy appears to have constituted a species of poetic
activity that was especially receptive to the generic variety that has
come to be recognized as central to Renaissance principles of
composition.[24]

If writing elegies was one of the ways poets learnt to write in the
vernacular, it was also a way they learnt the discipline of fitting what
they wrote to highly particular occasions. As a consequence, it
became a means of learning about decorum, of investigating,
exploring, representing, analysing, anatomizing social relationships
on the occasion of the subject's death. Therefore, as well as writing
about individual poets as elegists, I shall also discuss in what
follows the literary responses to three particular deaths, of Sir
Philip Sidney in 1586, of Queen Elizabeth in 1603, and of Henry,
Prince of Wales in 1612.[25] But I hope to show further that the elegy

[23] Three important recent studies, which will be referred to on several occasions in
what follows, are Arnold Stein, *The House of Death: Messages from the English Renaissance*
(Baltimore, 1986); G. W. Pigman III, *Grief and English Renaissance Elegy* (Cambridge,
1985); and the more wide-ranging Peter M. Sacks, *The English Elegy: Studies in the Genre
from Spenser to Yeats* (Baltimore, 1985). See also Morton W. Bloomfield's thoughtful
study, 'The Elegy and the Elegiac Mode: Praise and Alienation', in Barbara Lewalski,
ed., *Renaissance Genres: Essays on Theory, History and Interpretation* (Cambridge, Mass.,
1986), 147–57.

[24] See Rosalie L. Colie, *The Resources of Kind: Genre Theory in the Renaissance*
(Berkeley, 1973); Alastair Fowler, *Kinds of Literature: An Introduction to the Theory of
Genres and Modes* (Oxford, 1982), *passim*, but esp. pp. 136–8, 181–3; J. A. Wittreich,
Visionary Poetics: Milton's Tradition and his Legacy (San Marino, 1979), 221–2, for a
valuable bibliography. Three important anthologies are Lewalski's *Renaissance Genres*,
Stephen Greenblatt's *The Forms of Power and the Power of Forms* (Norman, Okla., 1982),
and Kevin Sharpe and Stephen Zwicker, eds., *The Politics of Discourse* (Berkeley, 1986).
On frontiers, see Greenblatt's introduction to his *Representing the English Renaissance*
(Berkeley, 1988), xii–xiii.

[25] Gittings records the changes to the Book of Common Prayer in 1552, which had
the effect of drastically reducing the number of references to the name of the deceased,
although it is worth noting that the strict Calvinism represented by such revisions was

also, every bit as much as the sonnet, and for a longer period and to a wider extent, constituted a space in which writers felt encouraged to write introspectively, to make themselves their own subject.[26]

The process of secularization is neatly encapsulated in the words of one of Henry Machyn's fictional successors, when the 'tomb-maker' Bosola, in Webster's *The Duchess of Malfi*, observes that[27]

> . . . Princes images on their tombes
> Do not lie, as they were wont, seeming to pray
> Up to heaven: but with their hands under their cheekes,
> (As if they died of the tooth-ache)—they are not carved
> With their eies fix'd upon the starres; but as
> Their mindes were wholly bent upon the world,
> The self-same way they seeme to turne their faces.
>
> (IV. ii. 153–9)

tempered in the Elizabethan Prayer Book (1559), which also included prayers for the dead. See J. E. Booty's edition of *The Book of Common Prayer 1559* (Charlottesville, 1976) and I. Pullan, *The History of the Book of Common Prayer* (1900), 237–45.

[26] See Patricia Fumerton, ' "Secret" Arts: Elizabethan Miniatures and Sonnets', in Greenblatt, ed., *Representing the English Renaissance*, 93–133, and Joel Fineman, *Shakespeare's Perjured Eye: The Invention of Poetic Subjectivity in the Sonnets* (Berkeley, 1986). For the argument that the practice of Petrarchism constituted a training in poetic diction, see L. Forster, *The Icy Fire: Five Studies in European Petrarchism* (Cambridge, 1969), ch. v.

[27] Text from *The Complete Works of John Webster*, ed. F. E. Lucas (1927), ii. 97.

1. THE ENGLISH TRADITION OF ELEGY

While generalized laments—'elegy' in Gray's sense—have a lengthy history in English letters, the personal elegy appears first at the close of the Middle Ages.[1] And these pre-Reformation obituary verses may be classified under five headings.[2] The hierarchy properly begins with laments for monarchs: the model was Geoffrey de Vinsauf's archetypal threnody for Richard I.[3] Such poems, which praise their subject and proclaim the instability of human glory, tend to be virtuoso exercises in *amplificatio*. A poet showed his skill by avoiding repetition despite treating a subject exhaustively: as Geoffrey put it, 'varius sit et tamen idem' (*Poetria Nova*, p. 225). In the fifteenth century such techniques were increasingly applied to contemporary events.[4]

Then there were general considerations of the *de casibus* theme (like Lydgate's *Fall of Princes*), whose exempla served primarily to reinforce or illustrate general ethical propositions.[5] Similarly, political poems usually dwelt on issues rather than their named subjects: even the most dense and ingenious of them included catalogues of excellences and universalized meditations on the human condition.[6] The fourth category, the warning from the dead, was essentially, like the *transi* tomb, a *memento mori*: many manuscripts depict these warnings inscribed on scrolls issuing from

---

[1] The Old English elegies have been characterized as a 'compound of Teutonic melancholia and Christian utilisation of the *ubi sunt* motif' (S. B. Greenfield, 'The Old English Elegies', in E. G. Stanley, ed., *Continuations and Beginnings* (1966), 142).

[2] See the excellent discussion in R. J. Lyall, 'Tradition and Innovation in Alexander Barclay's "Towre of Vertue and Honoure"'. *RES*, NS, 23 (1972), 1–17.

[3] Geoffrey de Vinsauf, *Poetria Nova* (ll. 367–430), in E. Faral, *Les Arts poétiques du XIIᵉ et du XIIIᵉ siècle* (Paris, 1923), 210; J. W. H. Atkins, *English Literary Criticism: The Medieval Phase* (Cambridge, 1943), 91–118, 200–3. See also E. R. Curtius, *European Literature and the Latin Middle Ages*, tr. W. R. Trask (1953), 79 ff.

[4] For examples, see R. H. Robbins, *Historical Poems of the XIV and XV Centuries* (New York, 1959), 111–13, 176–80, and the pseudo-Skeltonic lament for Edward IV printed in *Pithy, pleasant and profitable workes of Maister Skelton* (1568), H1ʳ (also printed by Robbins, p. 159).

[5] R. Woolf, *The English Religious Lyric in the Middle Ages* (Oxford, 1968), 317–28; also Robbins, pp. 184–6, and D. A. Pearsall, *John Lydgate* (1970), 223–54.

[6] See Woolf, p. 78, Robbins, pp. 186–90, and V. J. Scattergood, *Politics and Poetry in the Fifteenth Century* (1971), 223–54.

or held by the deceased.[7] The fifth, most 'literary', kind, the allegorical dream vision, included masterpieces like the *Pearl* and *The Book of the Duchess*. They represented, at one level, an attempt to confront the problems posed by death and by the act of writing itself: they dramatized the gulf between human understanding and the perspective of eternity. But since they were inappropriate models for public elegies because of their private delicacy and intimacy, their influence (apart from Spenser's *Daphnaida*) was slight.

The early sixteenth century saw some influence of the *déploration* popularized by French *rhétoriqueurs*: Alexander Barclay's 'Towre of Vertue and Honoure' combines dream allegory with some pastoral elements to generate, in the words of a modern commentator, the 'effect of contemplation, of the . . . thinking-through of a complex moral problem'.[8] By and large, however, the public, declamatory fifteenth-century styles survived with few modifications into the Tudor age of Gascoigne and Churchyard, the world 'defined by the court, the prison and the scaffold', whose most typical product was the *Mirror for Magistrates*.[9]

While traditional poets continued in the manner of Lydgate, humanists found the terse copiousness required by the epitaph more to their taste.[10] Nevertheless, the humanist cult of the individual, which informed the vogue for verisimilitude in portraiture, perhaps explains a poem like Surrey's lament 'Wyatt resteth here', which appears to embrace particularity.[11] The *blason* of Wyatt's body and virtues occupies 38 lines (paralleling the subject's age), and the poem's very ingenuity constitutes a compliment to one in whose head 'wisdom misteries did frame' (p. 28).[12]

Surrey is an exception. Most Tudor public poets responded to

[7] J. Huizinga, *The Waning of the Middle Ages*, tr. F. Hopman (Harmondsworth, 1972), 134–46; Woolf, pp 309 ff.; D. Gray, *Themes and Images in the Medieval English Religious Lyric* (1972), 176–220.

[8] Lyall, 'Tradition and Innovation', 12.

[9] Emrys Jones, *The Origins of Shakespeare* (Oxford, 1977), 193.

[10] The standard account is still H. H. Hudson, *The Epigram in the English Renaissance* (Princeton, 1947), 1–21, 145–69. See also D. H. Parker, 'The Literary Epitaph in the Seventeenth Century', B.Litt. thesis (Oxford, 1970), 12–57.

[11] For an account of the humanist interest in the portrait, see John Pope-Hennessy, *The Portrait in the Renaissance* (Princeton, 1966), *passim*.

[12] *Henry Howard, Earl of Surrey: Poems*, ed. E. Jones (Oxford, 1964), 27–8: see A. Fowler, *Conceitful Thought* (Edinburgh, 1975), 25–30, and C. W. Jentoft, 'Surrey's Five Elegies: Rhetoric, Structure, and the Poetry of Praise', *PMLA* 91 (1976), 23–32.

an important event like their predecessors: by generalizing.[13] As an idea of style, *amplificatio* was challenged by *copia*, but the delight of readers in full and sententious treatment of themes remained constant. Though *poeta* gradually lost ground to *vates*, the attitudes and ambitions of Churchyard's fellows approximate more to those of Lydgate than to those of Spenser and Daniel. By Drayton's day the jigging rhymes of these Tudor writers were considered old-fashioned.[14] But they had in their time represented a search for the humanist ideal of the long heroic line. Based on clusters of small units or short lines, the two main forms, the 'poulter's measure' and the 'fourteener' were held, whatever their other qualities, to be especially memorable, and pedagogically highly useful.[15] Ironically it was this very mnemonic impulse, alongside an understandable wish to load verses with ornament, that made these measures sound less like a stately procession of long lines than a jumble of smaller phrases and formulaic padding. The greater the art, the greater the apparent bathos and fragmentation, as the parodies of the forms indicate. Yet, despite the scorn, the Tudor style had value in teaching, as a 'poetry of social gesture', and as a vehicle for morally serious writing (such as Spenser's 'July' eclogue).[16] Chapman and Drayton were after all to employ such measures in epics, and Shakespeare's Jupiter was to be summoned by them in *Cymbeline*.

Parodies of the mode attack metrical inflexibility, intellectual shallowness, low diction, bathos, and crude verbal ornament. But some writers could dignify serious matter through an apparent conquest of metronomic regularity, and capitalized adroitly on the medium's resources. Consider an anonymous elegy on Sidney, written in a language far removed from shepherds, popular balladeers, or pretentious flatterers.[17] Devices commonly reiterated

[13] See Thomas Whythorne's vivid account of his response to the death of his employer William Bromfield in 1563: *The Autobiography of Thomas Whythorne*, ed. J. M. Osborn (Oxford, 1961), 143–4.

[14] '... had they | Liv'd but a little longer, they had seene, | Their workes before them to have buried beene': Drayton, 'To My Most Dearely-loved Friend Henery Reynolds Esquire of Poets and Poesie', ll. 76–8, in *The Works of Michael Drayton*, ed. J. W. Hebel, 5 vols. (Oxford, 1931–51), iii. 228.

[15] Whythorne, for example, composed verses when offered advice on winning the esteem of women: 'becawz I wold print the substans of this saing the deeper in my remembrans, I mad it thus in meeter' *Autobiography*, 77 (orthography modernized).

[16] See L. G. Black, 'Some Renaissance Children's Verse', *RES*, NS, 24 (1973), 1–16.

[17] Text from *The Poetical Works of Edmund Spenser*, ed. J. C. Smith and E. de Selincourt (Oxford, 1912), 559–60. The elegy is attributed to a 'friend' of the subject: the most likely candidates are Fulke Greville and Sir Edward Dyer. R. M. Sargent

ad nauseam are employed selectively. The first line—'Silence augmenteth grief, writing encreaseth rage'—links verbs by sound, and opposes 'silence' and 'writing', 'grief' and 'rage'. Alliteration may be confined to the first half of a line—'Now sinke of sorrow I, who liue, the more the wrong'—or to the second—'Farewell to you my hopes, my wonted waking dreames'. In the usual 'padding' position, where phrases like 'alack the day', 'I dare well say', might be expected, the poet places intensifiers, such as 'the more the wrong'. He distributes stock devices, such as multiple repetition, for local effect. Since he is sparing with his resources, even the most commonplace, their effectiveness is not progressively devalued. Thus repetition, for example, is employed dramatically to mime the shock of loss: 'Sidney is dead, dead is my friend, dead is the worlds delight'. The poem's density, metrical variety, and avoidance of formulaic cliché combine to make the ending a surprise, as the speaker is shown finally yielding to the towering pressure of bereavement. And in this envoy, the poem is itself redefined as an artefact, fixed to the tomb in a final gesture:

> Now rime, the sonne of rage, which art no kin to skill,
> And endles griefe, which deads my life, yet knowes not how to kill,
> Go seeke that haples tombe, which if ye hap to finde,
> Salute the stones, that keep the lims, that held so good a minde.
>
> (37–40)

The solemn progress of the verses, as in many elegies, expresses both the inevitability of mortality and the capacity of art to depict it: and the speaker's professed struggle with his medium explicitly parallels his wrestling with grief. This poem impressively accommodates twinned yet contrary impulses: to lament and to comprehend a meaning in death. It is an arresting example of what might be achieved by an intellectually and artistically sophisticated writer in the scorned Tudor mode.[18]

---

rehearses the arguments (initially proposed by Malone) for Dyer's authorship in *At the Court of Queen Elizabeth: The Life and Lyrics of Sir Edward Dyer* (1935), 211–13: see also John Buxton, 'Shakespeare's *Venus and Adonis* and Sidney', in J. Van Dorsten, D. Baker-Smith, and A. F. Kinney, eds., *Sir Philip Sidney: 1586 and the Creation of a Legend* (Leiden, 1986), 105. The poem has also been proposed as an influence on Milton. See R. Jungman, 'Greville as a Source for *Lycidas*, lines 8–9', *Sidney Newsletter*, 4 (1983), 14–15.

[18] In Lewis's words, 'the very draff and scum of contemporary English poetry' (*English Literature in the Sixteenth Century Excluding Drama* (Oxford, 1954), 109).

Thirty years earlier, Nicholas Grimald had shown himself to be the first recognizably 'modern' elegist. In his manner, lively and innovative, the ingenious, particularizing pose of the learned elegist first appears in English. His elegies were published by Richard Tottel in the first edition of *Songes and sonnetes* (1557); most were omitted from subsequent editions.[19] Conventional literary history knows Grimald as a reactionary, as the archpriest of the 'Drab' age, whose evident appeal to mid-century readers reflected their regrettable preference for humanist sententiousness over the Italianate manner of Wyatt and Surrey. But Grimald's verses were not influential because they were somehow less challenging; rather (like Wyatt's paraphrases and Surrey's translations) they played a role in creating a vernacular medium for serious writing.[20] Courthope justly compared Grimald's allusive pedantry to the work of Cowley's generation, and Rollins's carping at Grimald's 'heavy-footed classicism' and 'uncourtly tone' similarly identifies qualities which locate Grimald in what is, after all, a major English tradition.[21]

Admittedly, Grimald is more like Cleveland than Donne, and he does sometimes collapse into bathos. An instance is the elegy on Lord Mautravers, 'translated out of doctor haddons latine':

> From yeres twise ten if you in count wil but one yere abate:
> The very age then shall you finde of lord Mautravers fate.[22]

But his avowed sensitivity to questions of style (expressed, for example, in the preface to *Christus redivivus* (1542)), indicates a degree of artistic self-consciousness and the application of ingenuity in resolving stylistic problems. From this distance, of course, it is difficult to distinguish experiment from incompetence:

[19] I will refer to the unique Bodleian copy of the 1st edn. (of which there is a facsimile published by the Scolar Press (Menston, 1970)). The edn. by H. E. Rollins, *Tottel's Miscellany 1557–1587*, 2 vols. (Cambridge, Mass., rev. edn. 1965) is cited as Rollins.

[20] See John N. King's thoughtful account of the 'measured elegance' of Grimald's verse in his *English Reformation Literature* (Princeton, 1982), 242–4. David Norbrook, on the other hand, argues that the studied generality and avoidance of topical controversy (whereby Tottel's selection presents Wyatt 'not as a Protestant humanist but as a courtly lover') of Marian verse renders it more cautious, indeed duller, than the 'exuberant populism' of Edwardian writing: *Poetry and Politics in the English Renaissance* (1984), 58.

[21] W. S. Courthope, *A History of English Poetry*, ii (1897), 151: Rollins, ii. 106.

[22] Sig. P1ᵛ: Lewis called the piece 'loutish' (*English Literature in the Sixteenth Century*, 238).

> Man, by a woman lern, this life what we may call:
> Blod, frēdship, beauty, youth, attire, welth, worship, helth & al
> Take not for thine:
>
> (sig. Oiii^r)

Is the enjambment intentional? Does the entire work dramatize a struggle with grief through a self-conscious struggle with form? We cannot know. And Grimald could compose metronomically, as in his first poem on Sir James Wilford. But the next version of the subject, translated from Beza, presents consolation achieved through a neat turn:

> But sins that heaven this Wilforde goste dothe keep,
> And earth, his corps: saye mee, why shol they weepe?
>
> (sig. Oii^v)

This pair of poems, with their hyperbolic expressions of grief (translated from humanist sources), are capped with epigrammatic consolation. Likewise with an epitaph on a woman who died in childbirth, who 'In yielding worlds encreas took her decaye' (sig. Oiii^r), where the terse brevity of an epitaph captures well the paradoxical or contradictory elements inherent in the subject.

A second pair (sig. Oiii^r–iiii^r) commemorates two brothers. The first poem, whose 52 lines may express the completion of a temporal cycle, invests its subject with some specificity of detail, alluding to his blindness. There are three sections, approximating roughly to Roman prescriptions (the speaker initially dismisses Thalia's 'feastfull layes' but ends by asking her to renew them when his 'chered muse . . . Her doolfull tunes . . . stayes') but the components of praise and lament are hard to distinguish, and consolation seems to reside primarily in the overtly circular structure, which presumably implies some sort of regeneration. The subject is a *puer senex*, with a 'mindefull brest', and qualities that made him 'Woorthy to lyue old Nestors yeres', and suggested that he 'wold be our schooles ornament, one day'. He was also amusing—'more pleasant Plautus neuer was'—and Grimald's special friend: 'An other Grimald didst thou seem to bee'. It is from this friendship that the speaker's most furious complaint arises, and it leads immediately to a spurning of futile lament:

> O Chambers, O thy Grimalds mate moste dere:
> Why hath fell fate tane thee, and left him here?
> But whereto these complaintes in vain make wee?

Such woords in wyndes to waste, what mooueth mee?
Thou holdst the hauen of helth, with blisfull Ioue
Through many waues, and seas, yet must I roue.
Not woorthy I, so soon with thee to go:
Mee styll my fates reteyn, bewrapt in wo.

The last contrast, between Chambers in heaven and Grimald dying daily on earth, structures the remainder of the poem, which, according to Rollins, shows 'more feeling than is usually found in Elizabethan elegies'.[23] It is followed by a very different piece, a tersely argumentative epitaph on Chambers's brother. The style seems deliberately lowered:

Why, Nicolas, why doest thou make such haste
After thy brother? Why goest thou so? To taste
Of changed lyfe with hym the better state?

And it ends with a laconic, ostentatiously restrained flourish:

If our farewell, that here liue in distress,
Auayl, farewell: the rest teares do suppresse.

The opening lines of Grimald's longest and most ambitious elegy, on his mother, are in the same contentious vein:

Yea, and a good cause why thus should I playn,
For what is hee, can quietly sustayn
So great a grief, with mouth as styll, as stone?

(sig. Oiiii^r)

Classical precedents for filial lamentation are adduced, the catalogue concluding with Grimald himself. A second lengthy section is a biographical *narratio*—one of the few sources of information about the poet's life—that ends with the speaker struggling to find some means to make permanent his mother's name if he cannot revive her. He is led to meditate on the suitability of verse as a memorial:

Haue, mother, monumentes of our sore smart:
No costly tomb, areard with curious art:
Nor Mausolean masse, hoong in the ayre:
Nor loftie steeples, that will once appayre:
But waylfull verse, and doolfull song accept.

[23] Rollins, ii. 243. The unidentified subject may be the brother of one N. Chambers who proceeded BA from Christ Church in 1547/8.

By verse, the names of auncient peres be kept:
By verse, liues Hercules: by verse, Achil:
Hector, Ene, by verse, be famous still.

(sig. Pi^r)

As ever in Grimald's most self-conscious work, the alliteration is selective, the caesura varied, repetition and parallelism are artful, and classical allusions apt. Further, the professed equivalence of verse and monuments directs attention to its triptych form, whose central narrative with its domestic style contrasts vividly with the formal, classical quality of the briefer outer sections. The narrative, a species of *epanos*, is preceded by *threnos* and followed by *paramythia*.[24] This form is conveyed numerically or architecturally (it aspires, the poet claims, to outdo a 'Mausolean masse'): Grimald embeds within his work traces of physical organization, of a plan to shape the song into a physical monument, 'areard with curious art'.[25]

Grimald's elegies demonstrate sensitivity to generic requirements and decorums: though his style may anticipate Cleveland, his neoclassicism prefigures Jonson. Innovatively, he introduced personal and particular elements into the wailing of a 'funerall song' and the terseness of an epitaph. At the same time, he worked within the native heroic mode, applying the resources of Tudor verse to serious subjects.[26] Grimald never mixed his two voices: only rarely (as in the elegy on his mother) do they appear in different sections of the same poem. The 'conceited' register, characteristic of his epitaphs, looks forward to metaphysical wit. His humanist pretensions coincide with predominantly stylistic experiments, such as his pioneering development of blank verse. Grimald, as these brief remarks have indicated, was no reactionary. He was the first

---

[24] For a helpful consideration of these terms, see O. B. Hardison, *The Enduring Monument* (Chapel Hill, 1962), esp. 113 ff.

[25] The poem contains 99 lines, disposed into units of 22 (lament), 49 (praise), and 28 (consolation). Twenty-two is the number appropriate to chastity and to the alphabet (with obvious panegyrical suggestions of completeness and comprehensiveness): read as 11 couplets it enacts the limit of mourning imposed on the Spartans by Lykourgos. Forty-nine, 7 squared, is the perfection of earthly perfections, and the product of the gifts of the Holy Spirit and the virtues, with connotations of musical harmony. Twenty-eight, as a perfect and pyramidal number, is a monument in its own right. Ninety-nine is the product of 11 and 9 may have further panegyric implications. See A. Fowler, *Triumphal Forms* (Cambridge, 1970), 3–10, 34–7, 177–89, etc.

[26] Grimald took both an antiquarian and a reforming interest in the English literature of earlier generations: see King, *English Reformation Literature*, 243, 297–9.

English writer to use the elegy as a medium for virtuoso experiment. His skill, his 'curious art', which combined sensitivity to the resources of convention with responsiveness to its potential for experiment, found full expression in his striking set of commemorative poems. Whoever revised Tottel, however, disagreed.

It would be a grotesque—but hardly unprecedented—distortion of literary history to write an account of the English elegy that ignored Thomas Churchyard and the other public elegists of his generation. Churchyard (?1520–1604) was the most prolific, and typical, Elizabethan elegist. He was also the only poet of his time (Spenser apart) to be granted a state pension. Yet posterity has dismissed him utterly. Even he was modest enough about his writing, his 'trifles'—'the best banquets I can make to my friendes, is but bare Tragedies, Epitaphes, or such bitter fruite as fewe doe feede on, and many takes no taste in'.[27] His commemorative verse is essentially public in character, designed for a wide audience of questionable literacy: and official approval of his efforts presumably explains his life pension of 18d. (later 20d.) per day (from about 1596–8).[28] There are times when he claims to be an apologist for the established order: '. . . before all other thynges (except the honouryng of Prince and publike state) a true writer ought of duetie, to haue in admiration and reuerêce, the valliaunt Soldiours, and men of worthy value'.[29] Inadequacies of style and want of invention were to be justified by this function, and by the poet's 'desire to do well':

But though the harmonie be not so sweete and delicate, as is to be wished, the desire to do well, is the instrument onely, that maie bryng suche delite, whiche maie for euer purchase good acceptation. And for that to the art of Musicke and harmonie, belongeth seuerall sortes of partes, to make good concordance, I haue tuned all my notes and songes worthie the hearyng, into one kind of voice and order . . . where many a piece of descant is to

[27] From the Preface to *A feast full of sad cheare* (1592), sig. A2ᵛ. For a more sympathetic view of one of Churchyard's laments, see William Schutte, 'Thomas Churchyard's "Dollfull Discourse" and the Death of Lady Katherine Grey', *Sixteenth Century Journal*, 15 (1984), 471–87.
[28] M. H. Goldwyn, 'Notes on the Biography of Thomas Churchyard', *RES*, NS, 17 (1966), 1–15: 'A note on Thomas Churchyard's Pension', *N&Q*, NS, 21 (1974), 89.
[29] *A generall rehearsall of warres* (1579), sig. **iijᵛ. The volume is more commonly known as *Churchyardes choise*. Of his subjects, Churchyard (sig. *iiᵛ) observed: 'I can not want good store and copie of causes to write of in this crooked age, where no thing is straight and vpright but a noble mynde, that neither stoupes to the mutabilitie of fortune, nor boweth doune to the wickednesse of this waiward world'.

bee seen (and some iarres maie happen of misliking of discordes) yet a nomber of partes soundyng together, maie couer the faults and imperfectiõs of an ignoraunt Musition.[30]

It is clear that he saw himself in the Lydgate tradition of poet-as-compiler:

> . . . finding myself vnfurnished of learning, and barely seene in the artes liberall, & farre vnfit to touch or treate of Diuinitee . . . looking into mine owne strength, I sawe me most ablest and apt . . . to bring foorth some acceptable worke, not striuing to shewe any rare inuention (that passeth a meane mans capacitie) but to vtter and reuiue matter of some moment knowne and talked of long agoe . . . [31]

These disclaimers define Churchyard's social role: not for him the 'expert readers' with their 'quicke capacitie' to whom Timothy Kendall, for example, addressed his work.[32] He published elegies on public figures throughout his career, probably starting with the Earl of Pembroke (d. 1570) (laments for Henry VIII and Edward VI are unlikely to have been Churchyard's juvenilia), and finishing with Archbishop Whitgift who died, shortly before Churchyard himself, in 1604. A comparison of the two elegies reveals surprising differences. Indeed, a survey of Churchyard's elegies seems to indicate the poet's dim awareness of the English Renaissance going on around him.

Yet Churchyard's resources were undeniably limited. His repertoire of poetic material for praising the dead is easily summarized. For political subjects he adopted the stance of the balladeer typical of his earliest, Langland-inspired, flytings.[33] Mourning Lady Lennox he summons 'noble dames of greatest birth . . . to see how fleshe and blood must fall': in this high style, with its ballad tone and obligatory list of ancestors, the portrayal of the deceased is generally public.[34] Sidney, for example, is a patron and a soldier, who left 'a world of weeping eyes'. It is 'chiefly Prince and publick weale / / who waies his worth aright. | A secret sigh or two they steale / / in thinking on this Knight'.[35] Inexpressibility is

---

[30] *A pleasant laborinth called Churchyardes chance* (1580), sig. ai[v].
[31] *A sparke of frendship and warme goodwill* (1588), sig. B1[r–v].
[32] Phrases taken from the title-page of Kendall's *Flowers of epigrammes, out of sundrie the most singular authors* (1577).
[33] See King, *English Reformation Literature*, pp. 247–51.
[34] *Churchyardes chance* (1580), sig. A1[r].
[35] *The epitaph of Sir Philip Sidney* (1587), sig. A4[v]–B1[r].

frequently announced, with Churchyard's disclaimers ranging from hysteria—'I had rather crie and rore, and shrillie houle and yell'— to grave formulae: 'To write of Henryes reigne, a true discourse to tell:| A world of wit it would containe, . . . '.[36] Having thus gathered his audience, and apologized for his shortcomings, the speaker usually proceeds to embark on a crude *blason*.

The catalogue of Edward VI's qualities (face, head, tongue, heart, ear, wit, zeal, and hand) concludes with a simple complaint at the death of this compendium—'Helas the while, our Lanterns light is gon'. The image had appeared earlier in the poem:

> Full dimme and darcke
> Is now that sparke:
> That whilome was, the staie of Englands boaste.[37]

Robbed shrines (ironically enough, in Edward's case) and quenched lamps abound.[38] In the elegy on Lady Bagnall, for example, the past happiness of Newry—'of this sweet sainct the shrine'—is contrasted with its present state as 'the soile of sighes and sobbs'.[39]

No Tudor poet shunned sententiousness, and Churchyard was no exception. Death as a subject ideally suited their tastes: it is the moment when good and evil stand finally revealed in their true colours; as an occasion it invites considerations of human life in terms of the cycles of nature, of death as a harvest; and it suggests contrasts between physical ageing and celestial happiness. The location of this last, in almost all of Churchyard's elegies, is Abraham's bosom. One example may stand for all of them:

> Wherefore dere freends, yt reads these lines, be sure his soule is well:
> And he through christ doth triumph still, on dreadfull death and hel.
> And sitts as safe in Abrams breast, as babe in mothers lappe:
> Moste glad are Adams offspring all, that meets sutche blessed happe.[40]

Occasionally a specific audience is identified ('worthie wiues' are urged to listen to the elegy on Mrs Blount), enabling the speaker

---

[36] *A reuyuing of the deade by verses that foloweth* (1591), sig. A3ʳ (on Henry VIII).

[37] *Churchyardes choise*, sig. Eeiiᵛ–iiiʳ: a similar figure was used of Sidney in the *Epitaph*: 'His bountie blased like Torch by night | and dimde their Candles all, | And staynd both lampe and Lanterne light | where sparkes from flame did fall.' (sig. A4ʳ).

[38] Of Sir Nicholas Bacon, Churchyard wrote: 'Out of our goodlie golden Ryng, is falne a precious stone'; and of Sir William Courtenay, 'The shrine is robbde, the saincte is fled, where ye were wont to staie' (*Churchyardes chance*, sigs. A1ᵛ, A2ᵛ).

[39] *Churchyardes chance*, sig. 4ᵛ.

[40] *Churchyardes chance*, sig. 5ᵛ.

pointedly to contrast life and death—'As you that mourne, are cladde with blacke, in white her soule doth shine'.[41] Elsewhere the audience is summoned to participate in the funeral ceremonies:

Come weepe with me, & shew thereby, some signe of your great trothe.
For I haue lost a freend, and for his sake I vowe,
To plant my penne vpon his tombe, and rest from writyng now
Till I his like maie finde, which hardly shalbe don:[42]

In the 'Envoy' to the poem on Sir Christopher Hatton, Churchyard for once doffs the public mask, and claims primacy of grief: 'Who mourneth more than he that made this verse? | To whom good turnes, this lord did often send'. The work suddenly becomes dramatic—'Come noble Guard, and kneele before his herse . . .' —as the speaker invites servants and retainers to join him:

Come fall in rank, that doth your Captain knowe.
And trayle your staues along hard stony ground.[43]

Churchyard, who shows an uncharacteristic metrical variety and flexibility in this piece, evokes a sense of vivid movement, of solemn ceremony; he conjures its sounds—the staves rattling on the cobbles, the grim shout 'La mort', the thump of the 'dolefull drum'.[44] From the same material so unimaginatively treated in the elegy on Sidney, Churchyard manufactures a poem of moving richness, almost Spenserian in its sonorous repetition, stately in its rhyme royal. The equally impressive elegy on Whitgift also uses the decasyllabic line: perhaps he saw a formal distinction between heroic 'high style' commemorative poems written in long lines and a more personal, more specifically elegiac, form.

Churchyard's topoi of praise are somewhat unsophisticated. Clusters of hyperbolic comparisons appear to reflect a naïve delight in exotic names rather than a scholarly concern for apt similitudes. The Earl of Pembroke (possibly the last great statesman to be illiterate) was 'sure a man in deede, | That well might ryse from

[41] *Churchyardes chance*, sigs. 5^r, 1^r.
[42] *Churchyardes choise*, sig. Eiii^v.
[43] *A reuyuing of the dead*. sig. B2^{r-v}.
[44] Perhaps Churchyard recalled the account of the funeral of Argalus in Sidney's *Arcadia* (1590), Book III, ch. 12: '. . . with all the funerall pompe of militarie discipline, trayling all their Ensignes vpon the ground, making his warlike instruments sound dolefull notes' (ed. Feuillerat, p. 426).

Troyians race, and honour Hectors seed'.[45] The qualities praised are generally public, the most frequently cited being liberality. Lady Lennox had been 'a noble hart where bounties budds, did blome and beare good fruite', while Lady Bagnall had been 'A spring of larges streames'.[46] Churchyard's celebration of generosity, maintained throughout his career, can hardly be unconnected with his lifelong quest for a patron.[47] Generically, the assertions of intimate knowledge of the deceased are related to the particularity and specificity of reference that had appeared in the elegies of Surrey and Grimald.[48] The subject of one of the poems addresses Churchyard thus: 'Thou hast . . . for fauours sake, praise'd some thou didst not knowe; | I was thy freende, wherefore in verse, my course of life doe showe'.[49] Since epideixis and history are traditionally associated, such showing of the 'course of life' is unquestionably an explicitly panegyric act.[50] And biographical or historical *narratio* as a component of praise distinguishes the longer public funeral verses from the compendious brevity of the humanist epitaph: one sought comprehensiveness, the other density. The former is typified by the poem on that 'famous soldierlike king' Henry VIII, 'A King that made Kings stoup, and held them all in awe'; the King's diplomatic and military triumphs are listed, and the rattling verse leaves the reader with a store of choice epithets to apply to the subject.[51]

Churchyard's critics, beginning with Drayton, have been insensitive

[45] From the broadsheet *The epitaph of the Honorable Earle of Penbroke* (1570). On Pembroke's probable illiteracy, see Michael Brennan, *Literary Patronage in the English Renaissance: The Pembroke Family* (1988), 26. Master Archer of Kilkenny had been 'A *Toby* to his children all, yea *Iob* for happy state'; of Sir Nicholas Bacon, Churchyard wrote: 'Ne *Tulles* toung, nor *Petracks* penne, nor stoute wise *Catoes* vaine. | Maie not surmount the philed phrase, and reche of Bacons hedd' (*Churchyardes chance*, sigs. 5ᵛ, 1ᵛ).

[46] *Churchyardes chance*, sigs. 1ʳ, 4ᵛ.

[47] See *A feast full of sad cheere*, where we learn that Worcester's hospitality had extended to 'each degree', that William Holstock had been 'free and francke at boord', and that Bishop Underhill had combined generosity with frugality (sigs. B1ʳ⁻ᵛ, B3ᵛ–C1ʳ). For other instances, see *Churchyardes chance*, sigs. 4ʳ, 6ᵛ.

[48] Some examples: on the Earl of Essex, 'I haue lost a freend' (*Churchyardes choise*, sig. Eiiiᵛ): on Lady Lennox, 'Her life my gaine, her death my losse, her fauour helpt my state . . . ' (*Churchyardes chance*, sig. 1ʳ): on the Earl of Pembroke, 'I lost a friend' (*Epitaph*).

[49] *Churchyardes chance*, sig. 6ᵛ.

[50] Curtius, *European Literature and the Latin Middle Ages*, pp. 82 ff., 155 ff.: Hardison, *The Enduring Monument*, pp. 155–82; Brian Vickers, *In Defence of Rhetoric* (Oxford, 1988), 52–64.

[51] *A reuyuing of the dead.* sig. A3ʳ⁻ᵛ.

to his occasional efforts to rejuvenate his muse by emulating writers of the younger generation.[52] There are variations and experiments in his work, and they do imply some slight response to contemporary developments. The achievements of Spenser and Daniel seem to have led him to cultivate a new and specifically artistic pride in his role—by the 1590s he writes as a man performing a national duty.[53] Literary ambition had surfaced even earlier. Two elegies in *Churchyardes chance* (1580) stand apart from everything else in the volume for their uncharacteristically innovative disposition of commonplace matter. The first, on Sir William Pickering (the courtier, diplomat, and, briefly, suitor to the Queen), is cast as a narrative (sig. A3ᵛ). The speaker on his 'quiet couche' is woken by news of a catastrophe (later revealed as Pickering's death) by 'worlds reporte', who 'badde sluggishe muse awake' in order to compose 'mourning matter newe'. Fame catalogues the active and contemplative virtues of Pickering ('A *Tully* bothe with penne and tong'), and sadly notes the lack 'in these drousie dayies' of men of his stamp, who 'from the Gods, the rarest gifts possesste'. The dramatic expression of the wholly conventional relationship between Fame and her mouthpiece, the poem's narrator, is a major innovation for Churchyard.[54] A similar process occurs in the poem on Sir John Constable (sig. 6ᵛ). The speaker, walking meditatively, 'waiying well with equal paies, the weight of yearthly mould', is surprised by a 'sadd, and priuie voice', eerily emanating from a 'shroudyng sheet . . . In hollowe Caue, or vaute of stone'. The voice (Constable's) instructs him to 'looke to true report, . . . Tymes cheef daughter', setting aside all 'fonde affects, whiche leades the penne amis', and recalling their friendship. This said, he vanishes, leaving Churchyard primed to write. The fiction, a common enough medieval device, dramatizes and articulates the poet's elegiac functions. And in some of his works, Churchyard seems to aim for 'skilfull heads and scannyng minds' with a degree of self-

---

[52] To Lewis, Churchyard 'continued to write Drab all through the age of Gold' (*English Literature in the Sixteenth Century*, p. 265): John Buxton noted Churchyard's efforts, but concluded that he was 'too old to change his style' (*Sir Philip Sidney and the English Renaissance* (3rd edn., 1964), p. 193.

[53] M. G. Brennan, 'The Literary Patronage of the Herbert Family, Earls of Pembroke, 1550–1640', D.Phil. thesis (Oxford, 1982), 71–4: also his *Literary Patronage in the English Renaissance*, 78–81, 208–9.

[54] The poet, as historian, describes the process by which his text came into being: 'Whęn Fame had told her tale, I cald for paper streight: | And in such verse as here you reade, I put these words of weight' (A3ᵛ).

consciousness that shows him more than simply a 'great meterer', as Drayton put it.

But the public manner is the staple of his work. *A reuyuing of the deade* (1591) begins with pieces on Henry VIII and Edward VI, and in 1593 Churchyard revised his *Legend of Shore's Wife* after thirty years, 'not in any kind of emulation, but to make the world knowe my device in age is as ripe & reddie as my disposition and knowledge was in youth'.[55] There are some instances of a more 'modern' manner alongside this public voice. An example is the poem on Hatton, whose intimate and private conclusion was noted above. The first part of the poem more conventionally mourns 'A mightie man of great account', whose fall exemplifies honour's fragility ('like a candle out it goes, and quickly steales away').[56] Similarly the deathbed scenes in Churchyard's later elegies display a new and intimate dramatic vividness—however commonplace the material:

As lyfe got laude, so he at death, to friends and children said,
O babes before I yeeld vp breath, and Pilgrims part be plaid,
I blesse you all, and giue my goods among you as I may,
Then in the bed shrunke downe his head, and went like blaze away.
The good he did in his accounts, where soule now pleading is,
He feeles, where heauenly ioy surmounts, all kind of earthly blis.[57]

The medial rhyme that is such a feature of this passage was to become one of the more obtrusive ornamental techniques of Churchyard's later years. Another is the inversion of the order of the fourteener's components:

But God that all doth see, and giues man grace and gift of pen,
Of late hath moued mee, with verse to honour worthy men.[58]

Another feature is the appearance of verbal 'wit', usually involving puns on the subject's name. Thus we read of Walter Mildmay's

---

[55] *Churchyards challenge* (1593), sig. S4ᵛ. See S. M. Pratt, 'Jane Shore and the Elizabethans: Some Facts and Speculations', *TSLL* 11 (1970), 1293–1306, and King, *English Reformation Literature*, 247.
[56] *A reuyuing of the dead*, sig. B1ᵛ–B2ᵛ.
[57] *A feast full of sad cheere*, sig. B4ʳ (on William Holstock); in the same volume (sig. C1ʳ) a similar picture is painted of the last moments of Bishop Underhill: 'Full long before his leaue he tooke, and life made his last end, | Vnto the heauens did he looke, and praied with a friend. | And when the pangs of death arose, as sicknes did increase, | He held vp hands and eyes did close, and went away in peace.'
[58] *A feast full of sad cheere*, sig. B2ʳ.

'milde showe', are told that '*Walter Mildmay* water brought', before, at the point of death, '*Mildmay* mildly fell asleep'.[59]

Churchyard's final funeral poem features an extended quibble on a name:

> *Whitegift* his name, great gifts of God he had,
> Won worthy fame, as white & black now shoes,
> His presence made, full many people glad,
> Always got friends, and still reclaymed foes,
> Held liberall house, and kept a Lordly trayne,
> Fed rich and poore, with all God sent and Gaue,
> Hoorded not vp, nor lou'd no greedy gayne,
> Knew that all we, shall carry nought to graue,
> But shrowding sheet, good name, & true renown,
> That winnes from hence, an euerlasting Crown.[60]

The poem is crammed with the usual formulae, and, inevitably, the Archbishop hoped 'to sleepe in *Abrahams* breast' (sig. B4ʳ). But this solemn and dignified piece, which combines the entirely predictable with some more modish touches, shows the resilience—and the virtues—of the Tudor elegiac tradition, as its most celebrated practitioner brings his career to a close with a performance of stiff but far from unimpressive dignity.

Of Churchyard's contemporaries, George Whetstone is perhaps the most notable. His elegy on the Earl of Sussex begins in a solemn vein:

> Whylom of *Macedon*, the mighty King,
>   By *Homer* pend, Achylles life did reade,
> Homer aliue, and Alexander dead:
> Desire of Fame, Contempt of life so bread,
> And trueth to say, mans life is but a breath,
> When *Fame* outliues, *Enuie*, *Time*, and *Death*.[61]

Whetstone saw his role as the instrument of fame, charged with the task of immortalizing his subjects' reputations (the Earl of Bedford's life, for instance, he would make appear like 'Dyamonds set in Bras'): and he recalled three reasons why the ancients

---

[59] *A reuyuing of the dead*, sig. B1ʳ. Bishop Underhill receives similar treatment: 'Sate I not safely *Vnderhill*, (in calmie vale below) . . . Now Vnderhill lyes vnder ground, knit vp in sheete full short' (*A feast full of sad cheere*, sig. B4ᵛ).

[60] *Churchyards good will* (1604), sig. B2ʳ.

[61] *A Remembraunce of the life, death, and vertues of Thomas, late erle of Sussex* (1583), sig. A3ʳ.

remembered the dead: 'that Obliuion should not bury the vertues, with their bodies . . . that the Auncestors noble Monuments might be presedents of honour to their posteritie: and therefore, it was not improperly sayd, that the histories of Time, were a second life, and tooke awaye a great part of our feare to dye'.[62] This is the poet as historian and moralist, in the tradition of the *Mirror for Magistrates*: 'Cronicles of good mens actes', Whetstone declared, are the 'guydes of wel doing', and he significantly classed his elegies as 'remembrances'.[63] The *Rocke of Regarde* (1576) employs the *Mirror* technique of putting 'tragedies' into their subjects' mouths, and the earliest of his elegies, on 'the wel imployed life, & godly end' of George Gascoigne (1577), does likewise. The main part of the poem is a life of the subject. Then Gascoigne, in surprisingly chirpy mood, rehearses the provisions of his will, before performing an exemplary death:

> In this good mood, an end woorthy the showe,
> Bereft of speech his hands to God he heau'd:
> And sweetly thus, good *Gaskoigne* went *a dio*,
> Yea with such ease, as no man there perceiu'd,
> By strugling signe, or striuing for his breth:
> That he abode, the paines and pangs of death.[64]

Good men, hypocrites, careless livers, courtiers, merchants, lawyers, prelates, and 'Readers in generall' are exhorted to 'leaue unsure, for certaine things to take': the poem ends with a sonnet/epitaph, and the Ovidian tag, 'nemo ante obitum beatus' (*Metamorphoses*, iii. 136–7). Having become thus established, this pattern was followed in the rest of Whetstone's (increasingly sententious) 'remembrances'. The personal details of his subjects were generalized and directed to similar exemplary purposes. The address from the deathbed was commonly an amalgam of improving sentences culled from a stock even smaller than Churchyard's, and the focus is invariably public. Thus Sir Nicholas Bacon:

> His head was staied, before his tounge did walke,
> His eyes did search, the simple sutors harte:
> He trusted teares, farre, more then filed talke . . .[65]

[62] *A mirror of treue honnour and christian nobilitie* (1585), sig. Aii[r–v].
[63] *A Remembraunce of the . . . erle of Sussex*, sig. A2[r].
[64] *A remembrance of the wel imployed life, & godly end, of George Gaskoigne, esquire* (1577), sig. Biii[v].
[65] *A Remembraunce of the worthie and well imployed life, of . . . Sir Nicholas Bacon* (1579),

More pretentious is the stiffly pompous poem on Sidney ('A perfect Myrror for the followers both of Mars and Mercury'): unlike those who had (like Churchyard) rushed intemperately into print, Whetstone claims he had been 'headfull' to produce a considered record of a peerless man:

> The cause is showne, why he desired Life,
> For publique good: but to our common woe:
> Our sinnes did drawe, and sharpe the fatall knife,
> His vitall threade, to cutte and shread in two,
> That his sweet soule, might forth of Prison goe,
> Which forthwith flewe, to Abraham his brest,
> Where now it raynes, and still shall liue in rest.[66]

Whetstone was even less responsive than Churchyard to contemporary literary developments: and his occasional variations accentuate his limitations. Where Churchyard's deathbed scenes had sought authority from some (no doubt fictional) particularity of detail, Whetstone's deaths are uniform in style and matter. His range is from pomp to hysteria, and his stolid high style embodies the survival of the aesthetic of an earlier age. His tiresome *gravitas* is consistent with his view of his poetic ambition: 'English Historiographers which haue quiet recorse vnto the Muses, are bound to eternise the memories of the good maiestrates disseased'.[67]

Of the other 'drab' poets, Turberville, with his artfully cultivated lowness of diction, is an obvious contrast with Whetstone's pretentiousness, but Barnabe Googe is perhaps even more worthy of note.[68] He seems to have attempted in his epitaphs a fusion or

---

sig. B3ʳ: the figure of Bacon sums up his experience of life pithily: 'From office and, from honours trouble come, | Nemo beatus, ante obitum', (sig. C1ʳ). Whetstone's Sussex used similar terms: 'I wish men would this moral Rule but heede: | *The end is that, that maketh Fortune good.* | Ten thousand times he would contemplate thus: | *Nemo ante obitum beatus*' (sig. B3ʳ).

[66] *Sir Philip Sidney, his honorable life, his valiant death, and his true vertues* (1587), sig. C2ᵛ.

[67] *A remembraunce of the precious vertues of the right Honourable and reuerend Iudge, Sir James Dier* (1582), sig. Aiiᵛ.

[68] Two examples of Turberville's art from *Epitaphes, epigrams, songs and sonets . . . etc.* (1567) must stand for the rest. First his version of the inexpressibility topos: 'If teares could tell my thought, | or plaints could paint my paine, | If dubled sighes could shew my smart, | If wayling were not vaine' (77ᵛ): second, an account of how he came to write an elegy and what its purpose was: 'At point to ende and finishe this my Booke, | Came good report to mee, and wild me write | A dolefull Uerse, in praise of *Author Brooke* | That age to come lament his fortune might' (143ᵛ).

correspondence of subject and style. He could produce the thumping rhythms of the balladeers when writing of a death in battle:

> A bluddy Butcher byg and blunt,
> a vyle vnweldy knaue,
> With beastly blow of boysterous byll
> at hym (O Lorde) let dryue.[69]

Yet he mourned Virgil's translator, Phaer, in a very different, and altogether more literary, manner: restrained use of alliteration and a sprinkling of apt classical allusion reinforce the argument that 'Virgils verse hath greater grace | in forrayne foote obtaynde' (sig. Ciii^v). Googe's elegy on Grimald (in heroic couplets) was printed as four-line units, a method of presentation that produced some oddities, dividing individual lines thus:

> Behold this fle-
> tyng world how al things fade . . . [70]

But there is in his elegies, as in his work more generally (which includes translations of Montemayor's pastoral eclogues), a sense of poetic experiment, a movement away from the fourteener and a perception of the possible interplay of matter and manner.

These Tudor poets operated in a tradition where the poet was a maker, a compiler; a figure charged with the task of recording and commemorating public celebrities and their acts. They are the direct descendants of the political poets of the previous century, and of the sententious poetic historians like Lydgate. The notion that funeral verse might constitute a showcase for a poet's personal talents would have seemed indecorous to them: none indulges in self-display. Only Churchyard regularly attempted to individualize his subjects. And while there are purely 'literary' touches, these writers valued matter and sentence: artfulness was to be prized only if it combined panegyric aptness and effective instruction. As Churchyard put it:

> The quick I fawne not on, the dead may none dispise,
> Speake well of those are gone, is likt among the wise.

---

[69] *Eglogs, epytaphes, and sonnettes* (1563), sig. Ci^r–v.

[70] While the short lines may be merely a printer's act void of literary meaning, J. Thompson praised 'a sound of mastery like that of George Herbert's short lines' (*The Founding of English Metre* (1961), 67).

The quick must die or droope, as fairest flowre in field.
Vnto the strongest troope, the weakest force doth yield.
So to the vertuous sort, that leaues good name behind.
I yeeld but true report, to call the dead to minde.[71]

[71] *A feast full of sad cheere*, sig. C1[r].

2. THE ELEGIES OF SPENSER AND SIDNEY

Both Spenser and Sidney appear to have grasped from the outset that the funeral elegy (especially the pastoral elegy) is an essay in poetic tradition, that, as ancient writers and many later commentators recognized, 'pastoral poems are made of other pastoral poems'; and they conceived of a tradition immeasurably more elevated and more ancient than anything seen in England before.[1] Just as much as with every other literary kind they attempted, the elegy was rediscovered, reinvented, and transformed by the age's most formally innovative writers. The elegy itself—or even the very act of writing—is a central concern of each of their laments. Both poets, as I hope to show, appear to use the form in highly self-conscious ways.

The funeral elegy, occasioned as it is by death, by the incontrovertible demonstration of the fact of mortality, is a very ancient pastoral form. It naturally dwells on continuity, change, loss, and memory, and does so in ways that necessarily bring to the fore the very purpose and value of art itself.[2] It can be a stark examination of the proposition that 'Art rescues men from the trials of their lives'.[3] Both writers set their elegies in the pastoral, a mode understood by theorists and practitioners in the Renaissance to be hospitable to many genres, a vehicle for literary experiment where

[1] The phrase is cited from D. M. Rosenberg, *Oaten Reeds and Trumpets: Pastoral and Epic in Virgil, Spenser, and Milton* (Lewisburg, 1981), 18. The very application of the term 'elegy' to a funeral poem is exceptionally rare before Spenser: the Alexandrian and Roman pastorals upon which Marot and Spenser based their eclogue/elegies were not written in elegiac metre and therefore not elegies in their original form. As Weitzmann observed, 'Spenser was the first poet of note to apply the name to a chant of personal grief' (F. W. Weitzmann, 'Notes on the Elizabethan "Elegie" ', *PMLA* 50 (1935), 439–40). See also A. L. Bennett, 'The Principal Rhetorical Conventions in the Renaissance Personal Elegy', *SP* 51 (1954), 107–26: U. Kuhn, *English Literary Terms in Poetological Texts of the Sixteenth Century* (Salzburg, 1974), s.v. 'elegy'.

[2] See Peter M. Sacks's eloquent study, *The English Elegy* (Baltimore, 1985). Sacks defines his project as using the study of the elegy 'as a perspective from which to reexamine the connections between language and the pathos of human consciousness' (p. xii).

[3] R. Colie, *Shakespeare's Living Art* (Princeton, 1974), 252. See also Colie's earlier observation that the pastoral elegy 'offers a marvellous rationale for death . . . it provides the pattern for the pastoral relation of man to nature, of creation to inspiration . . .' (p. 248).

artistic, as well as ethical and political controversies could be dramatized.

NOUEMBER

The *Nouember* eclogue of *The Shepheardes Calender* (1579) is, with Sidney's *OA* 75, the earliest pastoral elegy in English. Like the ancient *Lament for Bion* it consists of fifteen sections, but its immediate model was Marot's *Complainct de Madame Loyse de Savoie* (1531).[4] It is a typically Spenserian blend of the familiar and the novel, with his usual manipulation of the reader's assumptions and expectations, yet the contexts that are provided—by locating the elegy within a conversation between two shepherd-poets, and by furnishing the reader with E.K.'s gloss—offer helpful guidance.

The eclogue beings with a request from Thenot that Colin Clout should perform, as his habit had been, 'songs of some iouisaunce', ending his Muse's silence (caused by 'loues misgouernaunce'). Thenot proposes that Colin's work will secure 'endles souenaunce' | Emong the shepheards swaines', whether it be in praise of his mistress or of Pan. Colin's reply indicates that he has been stirred to action: but he argues that amatory and religious verses have their own seasons and that decorum dictates his subject. His argument is an ancient one:

> Thilke sollein season sadder plight doth aske:
> And loatheth sike delightes, as thou doest prayse:

but the language he uses fixes his enterprise firmly in a native tradition. After all, *Troilus* had opened with the conjunction of 'sory chere' and 'a sorwful tale', a 'woful vers': and there is surely a recollection of the beginning of the *Testament of Cresseid*:

> Ane doolie sessoun to ane cairfull dyte
> Suld correspond and be equivalent:

where the speaker describes writing in the teeth of howling gales and hailstorms.[5] Should the imperatives of decorum fail to move

---

[4] For an account of the correspondences between *Nouember* and its models, see *The Works of Edmund Spenser: A Variorum Edition*, ed. C. O. Osgood and H. G. Lotspeich (Baltimore, 1943), vii. 404–16.

[5] *The Poems of Robert Henryson*, ed. D. Fox (Oxford, 1981), 111, 358.

him, Thenot is told, he himself is well fitted to compose 'light virelayes, | And looser songs of loue'.

Thenot's reaction to such instruction announces the exemplary nature of Colin's performance, and proclaims the value of poetic tradition for practitioners of the art

> . . . better learne of hem, that learned bee,
> And han be watered at the Muses well:
> The kindlye dewe drops from the higher tree,
> And wets the little plants that lowly dwell.

He then offers an appropriate subject for a song of 'sorrowe and deathes dreriment', namely the death of Dido, the matchless daughter of the 'greate shepehearde'.[6] In return for performing this service for Thenot (who asks him to 'bewayle my wofull tene'), Colin will receive material reward: a lamb for the poem, whatever its quality, and the guarantee of 'greater gyfts for guerdon' if the piece is up to the standard of his love-complaints. So the first English elegy is set up for us, as a social exchange, the utterance of a professional commissioned to articulate the grief of a patron in terms which conform to the decorums of subject and season and at a level of art comparable to the poet's best in other genres. The notion of literary hierarchy is reinforced deftly by Thenot's brief expression of grief—

---

[6] Inevitably, there has been much speculation as to the identity of Dido. Some hold, with T. G. Rosenmeyer in *The Green Cabinet: Theocritus and the European Pastoral Lyric* (Berkeley, 1969), 119–20, that she is purely fictional. M. H. Parmenter, on the other hand, identified Queen Elizabeth as Dido, in his article, 'Spenser's "Twelve Aeglogues Proportionable to the Twelve Monethes"', *ELH* 3 (1936), 190–217. P. McLane proposed Dido's death as an allegory of the Alençon marriage negotiations in *Spenser's Shepheardes Calender: A Study in Elizabethan Allegory* (Notre Dame, 1961), 47–60. H. Cooper considered the poem a model to be followed in the event of Elizabeth's death (in her *Pastoral* (Ipswich, 1977), 208). Luckily for Spenser, the Queen herself, who was understandably sensitive on the matter, did not, as far as may be deduced, share Cooper's view of the elegy. For more detail, see H. Woudhuysen's unpubl. D.Phil. thesis 'Leicester's Literary Patronage: A Study of the English Court 1577–82' (Oxford, 1981), 192–206; Norbrook, *Poetry and Politics*, 59–90 (esp. 85–7); L. A. Montrose, '"The Perfect Paterne of a Poete": The Poetics of Courtship in *The Shepheardes Calender*', *TSLL* 21 (1979), 34–67, '"Eliza, Queene of Shepheardes", and the Pastoral of Power', *ELR* 10 (1980), 153–82, 'The Elizabethan Subject and the Spenserian Text', in P. Parker and D. Quint, eds., *Literary Theory/Renaissance Texts*. (Baltimore, 1986), 303–40 (esp. 318–23), and his full-length study *In Mirrors More than One: Elizabeth I and the Figurations of Power* (Chicago, forthcoming); P. Berry, *Of Chastity and Power: Elizabethan Literature and the Unmarried Queen* (1989); J. N. King, 'Spenser's *Shepheardes Calender* and Protestant Pastoral Satire', in Lewalski, ed., *Renaissance Genres*, 369–98, and A. Patterson, *Pastoral and Ideology: Virgil to Valery* (Oxford, 1988), 118–32.

> For deade is Dido, dead alas and drent,
> Dido the great shepehearde his daughter sheene:
> The fayrest May she was that ever went,
> Her like shee has not left behinde I weene.

It is against such conventional lines that Colin's achievement is about to be measured, and it is by Thenot's literary standards that the piece is to be judged—at least within the world of the *Calender*. It is perhaps instructive to turn straight to that judgement:

> Ay francke shepheard, how bene thy verses meint
> With doolful pleasaunce, so as I ne wotte,
> Whether reioyce or weepe for great constrainte?
> Thyne be the cossette, well hast thow it gotte.

At the simplest level, Colin has succeeded in pleasing Thenot enough to gain his lamb, so we can assume that Thenot recognizes the skill of the piece he has heard. But its meaning appears more problematic for the audience within the poem. Thenot calls the elegy 'verses meint [mixed] with doolful pleasaunce', and pronounces himself uncertain as to whether tears or rejoicing be the proper response to it. Yet both men, we will recall, had earlier appeared to agree on the fitness of doleful verses to the season and subject. So Thenot's journey in the eclogue has taken him from seeking poetic recreation to requesting an elegy to this state of mixed joy and sorrow. The conclusion, giving the lamb to Colin and urging,

> Vp *Colin* yp, ynough thou morned hast,
> Now gynnes to mizzle, hye we homeward fast—

indicates the conventional conclusion to pastoral *otium*, the resumption of action, and implies that Thenot has been consoled, that the elegy has achieved its practical objectives of cheering its audience and securing reward for its author.

So much for Thenot, the primary audience. E.K., on the other hand, has no lamb to offer and no occasion of grief. Indeed he acknowledges in his headnote that the identity of Dido is 'secrete, and to me altogether vnknowne'. His estimation is more unequivocally aesthetic: again in the headnote he asserts the poem's outstanding quality, claiming that, as well as outstripping its model (Marot), it is also superior to 'all other the Eglogues of this booke', the entire

Calender.[7] So even before the eclogue begins, and before the conversation which precedes the elegy, the authoritative voice of E.K. has alerted us to the mysterious subject and to the high art of what we are about to encounter.

We are presumably meant to note that, when Thenot offers the lamb, he is conforming to ancient pastoral practice, even though he is himself utterly ignorant of the fact.[8] E.K. does not make that particular point, but he takes pains to show that beneath the homely rusticity of the diction (which he habitually glosses) lies a text which is highly conformable to the classical elegy. He tells his reader who the Furies, the Fates, Melpomene, Philomel are, and reveals the traditional association of Cypress with funerals, as well as the meaning of Nectar, Ambrosia, and Elysium. More prosaically, we are told what biers and hearses are.[9]

Apart from noting the *epanorthosis* in the third stanza of the elegy, E.K. restrains his interest in rhetorical figures, concentrating instead on simple glossing, or on explaining metaphors. Thus 'mantled medowes' is glossed: 'for the sundry flowres are like a Mantle or couerlet wrought with many colours'. But there are few attempts to use the notes to justify the extravagant praise of the headnote. He tells us that the comparison of man's life to the fading of the 'flouret' is a 'notable and sententious comparison A minore ad maius', and praises the complaint at the 'trustlesse state of earthly things' as 'a gallant exclamation moralized with great wisedom and passionate wyth great affection'.

Taken together, the comments of E.K. and the words and actions of Thenot are valuable guides to the elegy that Colin

---

[7] See H. Berger, 'Mode and Diction in *The Shepheardes Calender*', *MP* 67 (1969), 140–9. More generally, on the self-consciously encyclopaedic inclusiveness of Spenser's volume and its implications, see M. McCanles, 'The Shepheardes Calender as Document and Monument', *SEL* 22 (1982), 5–19; R. S. Laborsky, 'The Allusive Presentation of *The Shepheardes Calender*', *Spenser Studies*, 1 (1980), 29–67: J. Goldberg, *Voice Terminal Echo: Postmodernism and English Renaissance Texts* (1986), 38–40, 168–9. On generic mixture in the *Calender*, see A. L. Deneef, *Spenser and the Motives of Metaphor* (Durham, NC, 1982), 17–27, and W. Iser, 'Spenser's Arcadia: The Interrelation of Fiction and History', in M. Spariosu, ed., *Mimesis in Contemporary Theory: An Interdisciplinary Approach*, i. *The Literary and Historical Debate* (Philadelphia, 1984), 109–40.

[8] Thus Theocritus 1. 23–4, 'And if you will only sing as you did when you were competing with Chromis from Libya, I will give you a goat'. This and other precedents, from Virgil (*Eclogues* 5, 81), Boccaccio's *Admeto*, and Sannazaro's *Arcadia* to Marot's elegy, are noted in the *Variorum*, vii. 406.

[9] For a more ironic reading of some of E.K.'s comments, see Sacks, *The English Elegy*, 49–50.

speaks. But neither is especially authoritative—Thenot cedes authority to Colin and E.K. undermines himself with his errors and his failure to note many of the poem's more striking features.[10] The third reader—that is to say, the reader of the *Calender*—is left to find additional qualities to admire and emulate.

Let us consider the remarkable first stanza, and try to look at it with the eyes of one of its early readers.[11] The first line would have been instantly recognizable as a broken-backed alexandrine wholly characteristic of Tudor verse:

> Vp then *Melpomene* thou mournefulst Muse of nyne,

but what follows is, in context, a surprise. Rather than another alexandrine or a fourteener, we find a decasyllabic line which itself departs from convention by being broken in the middle:

> Such cause of mourning neuer hadst afore:

and perhaps its oddity is accentuated by the use of the cosily familiar device of alliteration. Having started with this slight disturbance, Colin appears to settle into a regular pattern in the three following lines:

> Vp grieslie ghostes and vp my rufull ryme,
> Matter of myrth now shalt thou haue no more.
> For dead shee is, that myrth thee made of yore.

These lines fit Gascoigne's prescription that the caesura in decasyllabic lines should occur after the first four syllables, and alliteration connects them with the poem's opening.[12] But the pattern is no sooner established than broken. Recalling Thenot's 'deade is Dido, dead alas and drent', Colin sings

---

[10] See F. Whigham, 'Interpretation at Court: Courtesy and the Performer–Audience Dialectic', *New Literary History*, 14 (1982–3), 623–39.

[11] The entire stanza is cited by William Webbe in *A Discourse of English Poetrie* (1586) as 'a verie tragicall mournefull measure': G. G. Smith, ed., *Elizabethan Critical Essays* (Oxford, 1904), i. 271. Webbe's notice of the elegy comes as the culmination of an account of the progressively more complex forms Spenser has employed in the *Calender*. On the elegy's 'fusion of aesthetic and spiritual preoccupations', see A. Hume, *Edmund Spenser, Protestant Poet* (Cambridge, 1984), 53–5.

[12] Gascoigne recommends the caesura 'be placed at the ende of the first foure sillables' in a decasyllabic line. He also opposed the potential for 'forgetfulnes or carelesnes' that could arise from metrical variety within a poem: 'euery yong scholler can conceiue that he ought to continue in the same measure wherwith he beginneth': *Certayne Notes of Instruction* (1575), in Smith, ed., *Elizabethan Critical Essays* i. 54, 49. To Sacks, however, the quatrain is 'highly stilted and theatrical', and reinforces his sense of Colin's performance as a 'set-piece' (*The English Elegy*, 49).

> *Dido* my deare alas is dead,
> Dead and lyeth wrapt in lead:

where the shift to a stress pattern is heavily emphasized and leads to the apostrophe 'O heauie herse'. Yet suddenly the length of line increases in a witty self-reference:

> Let streaming teares be poured out in store:

which itself seems to burst out of the restrictions of the preceding lines (and, pointedly, alliterates with none of them). The common metaphorical twinning of tears and elegies informs the stanza's concluding refrain: 'O carefull verse'.

This first stanza, as William Webbe recognized, is a remarkable demonstration of Spenser's art. It shows him combining low diction with learned allusion, homely and primitive verse forms with a striking variety of metrical effects. There could hardly be a more eloquent illustration of the potential of the vernacular than this mixture of naïveté and sophistication, and the familiarity of its elements (at least to Thenot, who would recognize the Tudor mode, and to E.K., who can identify Melpomene) enables the reader to discover the innovations Spenser creates, and to discern method in an experimentation that might well have seemed chaotic, anarchic to readers of Gascoigne's generation.[13]

The rest of the elegy is simpler, with each part more obviously fulfilling a particular generic requirement. After the second stanza, with its rather aggressively old-fashioned rusticity and repetition, Spenser one by one reproduces most of the conventions of the classical pastoral elegy.[14] Colin, who after all began by summoning a Muse to mourn, is perhaps designed to recall Theocritus in his lament for Daphnis, and he follows his models to create a 'summons to mourn' (63 ff.), a catalogue of the effects of Dido's death on nature (83 ff., 123 ff.), a procession of nymphs (143 ff.), and the transformation of lament into consolation (163 ff.).

November, the eleventh month, is traditionally associated with the commemoration of the dead. Further, the connection of the number eleven with mourning goes back to Sparta in the time of Lykourgos, when eleven days became established as the period of

---

[13] In contrast with Drayton, for example, the fourth eclogue of whose *Idea. The Shepheards Garland* (1593) is a lament for Sidney, closely based on the *Nouember* eclogue.

[14] See the *Variorum*, vii. 399.

mourning (and in the *Iliad*, 24. 665, etc., Achilles assures Priam that the Greeks will not harass the Trojans until the twelfth morning after the death of Hector).[15] In accordance with these ideas, presumably, Colin's elegy consists of eleven stanzas of lament followed by four of consolation. The difference is signalled conventionally by the altered refrain ('O heauie herse . . . O carefull verse' becoming 'O happy herse' and 'O ioyfull verse'): and we should note that the refrain was itself 'the most common formal element in the pastoral dirge'.[16] The significance of four is doubtless related to the high status it enjoyed in Pythagorean theory—largely because it contained the decad and therefore all other numbers, but also for other sorts of comprehensiveness (the seasons, the elements, and so on) and concord.[17] The numerological sense of the elegy as a whole, then, augments the basic, simple pattern of lament followed by consolation. In effect the concluding stanzas express the idea of wholeness, of inclusiveness, implicitly 'explaining' Dido's death as part of an ultimately harmonious system. The fact that lament is less dismissed than encompassed perhaps explains Thenot's reference to the elegy as 'verses meint | With doolful pleasaunce' and his uncertainty as to whether tears or rejoicing would be the fittest response to it. The concluding sense of the poem is not that art obliterates grief, that an elegy can instantly persuade the bereaved that the dead have exchanged earthly struggle for heavenly bliss. Instead it seems to propose the capacity of art to comprehend death, to provide a context for it: the paradox is that art, conventionally opposed to and threatened by the operation of time, is here employed to argue for an ultimate purpose in the passage of persons and seasons. Such a meaning is eminently suitable in the setting of the *Calender*, and also fits the

[15] Plutarch, *Lykourgos*, 27; M. Alexiou, *The Ritual Lament in Greek Tradition* (Cambridge, 1974), 17, 109, 211; A. Fowler, ed., *Silent Poetry: Essays in Numerological Analysis* (1970), 171.

[16] Rosenmeyer, *The Green Cabinet*, 118. Greek precedents include Theocritus 1. 127 and Moschus 3. 115–25. Presumably the greater metrical regularity of the final four stanzas is designed to express the speaker's acquisition of a sense of consolation. Sacks observed that 'The words are not strikingly original, . . . but they do suggest an access of power'; *The English Elegy*, 50.

[17] The number 4 is immensely rich in numerological meaning. Guy le Fevre de la Boderie, in his introduction to the French transl. of *De harmonia mundi totius* (1579), explained that the Pythagorean *tetrakys* contained the decad and therefore all numbers (cited in C. Butler, *Number Symbolism* (1970), 58–9). See S. K. Heninger, *Touches of Sweet Harmony: Pythagorean Cosmology and Renaissance Poetics* (San Marino, 1974), 151–6, 158–76, 329–35.

month of November. Conclusively, in context, it is a meaning apparently accepted by Thenot, whose final words ('Vp *Colin* vp, ynough thou morned hast, . . . hye we homeward fast'), like the ending of *Lycidas* or of *Twelfth Night*, assert the necessity of continuing, of resuming action.

It is salutary to recall just how early this elegy is. In the context of 1579 it is an extraordinary piece. Where Churchyard and Whetstone specifically disclaimed artistic ambition, and proclaimed the priority of matter over manner in their 'remembrances', Spenser created in Colin a poet in whose writing praise and ingenuity were inseparable, where ornament was integral to meaning, innovation and inspiration to sense. Indeed, the elegy dwells upon the nature and function of art as a vital part of its procedure.[18] Colin combines and in a sense reconciles the roles of public and private poet, since he performs a professional operation while at the same time laying claim to a laureate status which is also acknowledged (in their different ways and with different emphases) by Thenot and E. K. Spenser, in the person of Colin, adds himself to a poetic tradition. This he does explicitly by adopting the name Colin (Marot's name for himself) and in taking as his own Marot's emblem ('La Mort n'y Mord'—death bites not), as well as by reproducing in English most of the conventions of the classical pastoral elegy and tempering some of the more extreme elements of his source. This act of faith in the continuity of a living artistic tradition is more than presumption on the part of a fledgling laureate. The stress on continuity also has a profoundly consolatory implication, which exactly matches the poem's central argument. And, in addition, it is a manifest invitation to others to follow suit, as he had followed Marot: the poem shows Spenser at his most exemplary, and indicates that, in Digby's words, 'our NORTHERN climate may give life to as well tempered a brain, and as rich a mind as where the sunne shineth fairest'.[19] With its first appearance in the English Renaissance, the pastoral elegy, and by implication any elegy with artistic pretension, had established as a central principle

[18] G. W. Pigman argues that 'Spenser shifts the emphasis from the death of a person to the disappearance of beauty and virtue from the world. Dido's death is an emblem of earthly transience; this is what Spenser is lamenting, not Dido the individual . . . The reassurance of the afterlife . . . makes mourning for Dido problematic': *Grief and English Renaissance Elegy*, 83–4.

[19] Sir Kenelm Digby, *A discourse concerning Edmund Spenser*, in BL MS Harley 4153; text from R. M. Cummings, ed., *Spenser: The Critical Heritage* (1971), 148.

the necessary conjunction of praise, invention, and participation in a vital tradition. As such, it is consistent with the ambitious project of the *Calender* as a whole. It might indeed be thought to embody it.[20]

SIDNEY'S ARCADIAN ELEGIES

From the same early date are the elegies on the supposed death of Basilius in the first version of Sidney's *Arcadia*. Sidney takes care to give his reader guidance, to establish the context of these compositions. His narrator sets the scene:

Therefore, after the ancient Greek manner, some of them remembering the nobility of his birth, continued by being like his ancestors: others his shape which, though not excellent, yet favour and pity drew all things now to the highest point; others his peaceable government, the thing which most pleaseth men resolved to live of their own: others his liberality which, though it cannot light upon all men, yet all men naturally hoping it may be they, makes it a most amiable virtue: some calling in question the greatness of his power, which increased the compassion to see the present change (having a doleful memory how he had tempered it with such familiar courtesy among them, that they did more feel the fruits than see the pomps of his greatness). All with one consent giving him the sacred titles of good, just, merciful, the father of the people, the life of his country, they ran about his body tearing their beards and garments: some sending their cries to heaven: others inventing particular howling musics: many vowing to kill themselves at the day of his funerals: generally giving a true testimony that men are loving creatures when injuries put them not from their natural course, and how easy a thing it is for a prince by succession deeply to sink into the souls of his subjects—a more lively monument than Mausolus's tomb. Lastly, having one after the other cryingly sung the duke's praise and his own lamentation, they did all desire Agelastus, one notably noted among them as well for his skill in poetry as for an austerely maintained

---

[20] On the basis of the elaborate apparatus of the *Calender* as a book—emblems, woodcuts, notes, envoy, and so forth—Montrose observes that 'in such print-specific genres, Elizabethan texts manifest a tendency toward the elaboration rather than the effacement of their status as social—not merely literary—productions . . . That we conveniently date the beginning of the Elizabethan literary renaissance from the publication of *The Shepheardes Calender* is the measure of its success: our project of canon-formation has already been prescribed by Spenser's', 'The Elizabethan Subject and the Spenserian Text', 320. See also S. K. Heninger, 'The Typographical Layout of Spenser's *Shepheardes Calender*', in K. J. Höltgen, P. M. Daly, and W. Lottes, eds., *Word and Visual Imagination: Studies in the Interaction of English Literature and the Visual Arts* (Nürnberg, 1988), 33–51.

sorrowfulness (the cause of which, as it were too long to tell, so yet the effect of an Athenian senator to become an Arcadian shepherd), to make an universal complaint for them in this universal mischief:[21]

Sidney's prescription is a remarkable piece of antiquarianism. He signals his general source immediately by referring to obsequies 'after the ancient Greek manner', and it will be useful to note some of the details he gives.

Let me begin at the end with the role of Agelastus: he is what Garland terms a 'dirge expert', whose function is to express in artistic form the grief which family and friends are too distraught to articulate.[22] The best ancient example is the *prothesis* of Hector, where Andromache leads the wailing of kinswomen while professional singers perform mournful compositions (*Iliad*, 24. 720–3). In the *Odyssey*, Achilles' kinswomen, the ocean nymphs, mourn uncontrollably whle the Muses perform the role of the leaders of the dirges. They sing antiphonal laments which stir the entire assembly to tears (24. 58–62). There appears to be a distinction between the two types of funeral lament, and the terms used in Greek are *góos* for the family's cries, and *thrênos* for the more polished elegy.[23] Clearly these expert performances could be elaborate, and Solon's proscription of them seems to reflect a desire to curb ostentation in lament and to simplify funeral ceremonies so that they could not be used as an occasion for political demonstrations.[24]

What happens in Sidney's text conforms to ancient precedent fairly exactly—although we should remember that the subject of the lament is neither Hector nor Achilles: even if we have failed to guess that he is not dead, we might be justified in finding the event not a little incongruous, as the narrator seems to.[25] Basilius is mourned by a succession of individuals, who, we are told, praise his

---

[21] *The Countess of Pembroke's Arcadia (The Old Arcadia)*, ed. J. Robertson (Oxford, 1973), 283–4. All subsequent refs, unless otherwise specified, are to Robertson's edn.

[22] P. Garland, *The Greek Way of Death*, 121.

[23] See Alexiou, *Ritual Lament*, 10–23, 102–8, 210–11; Garland, *Greek Way of Death*, 28–31; J. Griffin, *Homer on Life and Death* (Oxford, 1980), 44–9, 72–6, 81–143.

[24] Plutarch, *Solon*, 21. 4; Garland, *Greek Way of Death*, 26–34; Alexiou, *Ritual Lament*, 14–17.

[25] Two of the best accounts are M. A. Dana, 'The Providential Plot of the *Old Arcadia*', SEL 17 (1977), 39–57, and W. R. Davis, 'Narrative Methods in Sidney's *Old Arcadia*', SEL 18 (1978), 13–33; both are reprinted in D. Kay, ed., *Sir Philip Sidney: An Anthology of Modern Criticism* (Oxford, 1987), 83–123.

noble birth, his shape, his peaceable government, and liberality.[26]
The application to Basilius of these conventional topoi of praise for
a good governor is decidedly questionable, but the narrator justifies
the performance by proposing that humans naturally wish to think
well of people and that most had reason to hope that Basilius was as
they described him. At another level, the whole exercise is a model
of royal mourning, and the rehearsal of its conventions therefore
essential to its exemplary status.[27] It is typical of Sidney that
Agelastus (whose name signifies that he is 'not laughing') is an
elegist by temperament as well as by profession, and that behind his
public role lies a personal sorrow which is merely hinted at: there is
thus a limit to the extent to which the truth of the circumstances
can devalue his verses, which spring as much from his inner grief as
from his professional commission. He therefore presents a contrast
with Colin Clout in *Nouember*.

Repetition, echo, what might be termed musical effects, are
authorized by the Greek context Sidney takes such pains to
establish. But the artistry with which they are deployed is distinctly

[26] Aristotle, *Rhetoric*, 1. 9, is the most important source. Some later examples. From
Sir Thomas Hoby's transl. of Castiglione's *The Book of the Courtier* (Everyman edn.,
1928): 'I will have this our Courtier therefore to bee a gentleman borne and of a good
house. For it is a great deal lesse dispraise for him that is not borne a gentleman to faile
in the actes of virtue, then for a gentleman. If he swerve from the steps of his ancestors,
hee staineth the name of his familie' (pp. 31–2) . . . 'therefore will I have him to bee of a
good shape, and well proportioned in his lims, and to shew strength, lightnesse and
quicknesse, and to have understanding in all exercises of the bodie that belong to a man
of warre' (p. 40). From Sir Thomas Elyot, *The Boke Named the Governor*, ed. S. G.
Lehmberg (Everyman edn., 1962): 'nothing is more honourable, or to be desired in a
prince or nobleman, then placability' (p. 115) . . . 'liberality (as Aristotle saith) is a
measure, as well in giving as in taking of money and goods. And he is only liberal, which
distributeth according to his substance, and where it is expedient . . . liberality taketh his
name of the substance of the person from whom it proceedeth; for it resteth not in the
quantity or quality of things that be given, but in the natural disposition of the giver' (p.
130). See also Angel Day, *The English secretorie* (1586), 220–1, and the catalogue of
Tudor topoi of praise in D. L. Peterson, *The English Lyric from Wyatt to Donne*
(Princeton, 1967), 53–76. A valuable collection of information on ancient epideictic
literature is in *Menander Rhetor*, ed. D. A. Russell and N. G. Wilson (Oxford, 1981), esp.
pp. 170–9, 200–7, 331–6, 346–50; see also B. Vickers, 'Epideictic and Epic in the
Renaissance', *New Literary History*, 14 (1982–3), 497–537, and *In Defence of Rhetoric*
(Oxford, 1988), 52–64.
[27] See the important accounts in E. Kantorowicz, *The King's Two Bodies: A Study in
Medieval Political Theology* (Princeton, 1957); R. Giesey, *The Royal Funeral Ceremony in
Renaissance France* (Geneva, 1960); R. Huntington and P. Metcalf, ed., *Celebrations of
Death: The Anthropology of Mortuary Ritual* (Cambridge, 1979). For some Sidneian
examples see *Miscellaneous Prose*, 134 (nobility); *NA* 180 (shape); *OA* 358 (peaceable
government); *NA* 16 ff. (liberality).

post-classical.[28] The first of Agelastus' poems, and the one designed 'to make an universal complaint' for the Arcadians, is a sestina; this highly sophisticated composition (in a form which Puttenham said would 'try the maker's cunning' to make it 'sensible') constitutes an assertion of the value of art when humans are faced with a circumstance that both challenges reason and calls into question consoling assumptions about the existence of order and meaning.[29] On the other hand, there is no suggestion of consolation. The first stanza begins and ends with 'wailing', and seeks to justify lamentation for the 'causeful sorrow'; indeed, the poem as a whole concludes with a distinctly gloomy recapitulation of the repeated words:

> Since sorrow then concludeth all our fortune,
> With all our deaths show we this damage public.
> His nature fears to die who lives still wailing.

We see here the typical paradox of the sestina, in presenting an image of artistic triumph which actually depicts, or at least strongly suggests, a mind unable to escape from preoccupation, tormented by unrelieved obsession.[30] Sidney makes more of this quality in the double sestina (*OA* 71) in which Strephon and Klaius bewail the absence of Urania, but the suggestion is present in Agelastus' poem.[31] And when Agelastus is finished the response of the Arcadians indicates no great change in their state of mind: 'They did with such hearty lamentation disperse among those woods their resounding shrieks that . . . their voice, helped with the only answering echo, came to the ears of . . . Philanax'. The absence of consolation is consistent with the idea that the elegy is properly associated with the period of the *prothesis*, and thus primarily with the shock of grief.[32] Agelastus' sestina, whose context is heroic rather than pastoral, stands therefore in obvious contrast to Spenser's consoling pastoral elegy.

[28] See J. Hollander's graceful and suggestive study, *The Figure of Echo* (Berkeley, 1981), *passim*.

[29] George Puttenham, *The Arte of English Poesie*, ed. G. D. Willcock and A. Walker (Cambridge, 1936), 87.

[30] Ringler proposed that the 'monotonous sevenfold repetition of the same six words is appropriate to a song of mourning' in his edn., *The Poems of Sir Philip Sidney* (Oxford, 1962), 416.

[31] See A. Fowler, 'Sestina Structure in *Ye goatherd Gods*', *Conceitful Thought*, 38–58.

[32] Garland, *Greek Way of Death*, 26–31; Alexiou, *Ritual Lament*, 6, 11–12.

In the Fourth Eclogues, however, the situation is somewhat changed. The Arcadians, believing Basilius to be dead, retire to a mountainside to escape the political confusion, the 'garboils' and riots which threaten the stability of their country (327). They are joined by three foreigners, Strephon, Klaius, and Philisides. The Fourth Eclogues consist of six poems. In the first four, the newcomers lament their misfortunes, and their separation from the objects of their love. Then, and in an apt setting of pastoral retirement, of comparative *otium*, Agelastus 'rather cried out than sang' a second lament, this time a pastoral elegy (*OA* 75, p. 344). [33] Together with *Nouember* this is the earliest English pastoral elegy. Like Spenser's, it is furnished with a full context, and its model is relatively modern.

The general pattern and many particular details derive closely from the eleventh eclogue of Sannazaro's *Arcadia*, where Ergasto mourns his beloved Massilia. [34] Common to both poems are the summons to nature to mourn, the invocation of Philomela and Echo, and the contrast of mortality with regenerative forces in the natural world. But there is one crucial difference, and it is with this difference that an account of the elegy must begin. Sidney has Agelastus modify Ergasto's pathetic fallacy throughout. For example, instead of describing the sea as nature's tears, he fastidiously urges, 'Let all the sea thy tears accounted be': instead of charging the earth miraculously to shroud itself in black ('Et tu, terra, depingi nel tuo manto | I gigli oscuri et nere le viole'), he asks more modestly, 'Upon thy face let coaly ravens swarm'. [35] In looking at the skies as night falls, Agelastus concludes that 'well (methinks) becomes this vaulty sky | A stately tomb to cover him deceased'. The focus, then, is on the response of the speaker: nature is not

---

[33] In the 1590 *Arcadia* the poem was 'roared out' by 'one accounted good in that kinde, and made the better by the true feeling of sorrow' (*NA* 498). Sidney makes more explicit in this later text a generic connection between elegy and uncontrolled grief, and associates elegy directly with the funeral ceremony. As in *OA*, the mournful temperament of the speaker is stressed.

[34] See *Poems*, ed. Ringler, 419–21, and *OA* 477, for comments on parallel passages. For a text of *Arcadia*, use M. Scherillo's edn. (Turin, 1888): a useful transl. is *Arcadia and Piscatorial Eclogues*, tr. R. Nash (Detroit, 1966). Two important recent studies of Sannazaro in relation to tradition are D. Quint, *Origin and Originality in Renaissance Literature* (New Haven, 1983), 43–69, and W. J. Kennedy, *Jacopo Sannazaro and the Uses of Pastoral* (Hanover, 1983).

[35] Agelastus appears to anticipate Rosenmeyer's remark that 'when Sannazaro initiated the Renaissance . . . pastoral lament, he abandoned all caution' (*The Green Cabinet*, 113).

reversed, but the leader of the dirge interprets natural phenomena as a reaction to his subject. Where Sannazaro proceeds to consolation, to comfort after extreme perturbation, Sidney presents us with an Agelastus trapped (albeit self-consciously) within an obsessive grief.

The poem is built on its refrain—'Your doleful tunes sweet muses now apply'—into which Sidney cleverly builds the 'ai' with which the hyacinth records its mythically tragic origin ('O hyacinth let ai be on thee still').[36] The refrain disposes the material into nine sections—presumably an allusion to the muses the refrain conjures. Where Spenser had changed the refrain to signal consolation, Agelastus' words remain as fixed as the hyacinth's badge of grief.

The poem falls broadly into three parts: a 'summons to mourn', a comment on the transience of human life, and a complaint at the consequences of Basilius' loss.[37] But the whole is cast in terms of the familiar topoi of inexpressibility, where the speaker simultaneously declares his individual inadequacy to deal with subject and proclaims that the whole world (or nature) expresses it.

At one level, the poem is an exemplary pastoral elegy, as *Nouember* is, rehearsing in English the major elements of the form, and giving guidance both to those who would read and those who would emulate it. Its use of refrain, to choose the most obvious example, was clearly to be influential on Drummond (in *Teares on the death of Moeliades*) and through him Milton (in *Lycidas*). But the *Old Arcadia* is set in a world where irony, especially dramatic irony, is endemic. Thus, while it is possible to argue that the absence of consolation represents a conformity with ancient practice and a deliberately 'pagan' touch, the reader is also faced with the nature of the speaker as an obsessive melancholic to whom consolation is temperamentally alien.[38] And Basilius is in any

[36] Recalling the same device in Moschus, *Lament for Bion*, 5. 5 ff., and Ovid, *Metamorphoses*, 10. 215.

[37] Many elegies invest their centre with significance, as will be illustrated in later chapters. The central line of this poem (italicized here) may mark the low-point of the speaker's performance: 'And if, O sun, thou ever didst appear | In shape which by man's eye might be perceived, | *Virtue is dead, now set thy triumph here.* | Now set thy triumph in the world, bereaved | Of what was good, where now no good doth lie; | And by thy pomp our loss will be conceived' (p. 347). See Fowler, *Triumphal Forms*, 23–33.

[38] As Ringler puts it, Sidney 'is writing a lament by a pagan shepherd for a pagan ruler who did not have the consolations of Christian immortality' (Sidney, *Poems*, 419). See also V. Skretkowicz's brief remarks in his edn. of *The Countess of Pembroke's Arcadia (The New Arcadia)* (Oxford, 1987), 577–8.

case not dead.[39] So there are ironies in Agelastus' version of inexpressibility:

> The style of heavy heart can never fly
> So high as should make such a pain notorious.

Agelastus' disordered and rebellious attitude to nature—

> Ah, let us all against foul nature cry:
> We nature's works do help, she us defaces.

—shows the truth of his identification with Basilius, whose inner failings had spread to his subjects and his country. Consequently, entirely conventional aspects of lament are charged with an extra significance; as in the final section:

> His life a law, his look a full correction;
> As in his health we healthful were preserved,
> So in his sickness grew our sure infection;
> His death our death. But ah, my muse hath swarved
> From such deep plaint as should such woes descry,
> Which he of us for ever hath deserved.

Agelastus, in attempting to articulate the grief of the Arcadians, has succeeded in unconsciously identifying the root of their problem, their corporate participation in their ruler's delinquency.

Agelastus, like most sonneteers and most elegists who followed him, presents his own rough, uncontrollable style as a mirror of his inner state:

> One word of woe after another traineth;
> Ne do I care how rude be my invention,
> So it be seen what sorrow in me reigneth.

This is the problem of writing he addresses: how accurately or adequately to convey the sense of his own feelings. Basilius' qualities, the impact on the natural world, the laments of the Arcadians, are all essentially, inescapably, manifestations or confirmations of his own predicament. 'O notes of mine, yourselves together tie', he cries, 'With too much grief methinks you are dissolved', and his own personality as figured in the poem provides one sort of continuity between the elegy's components. He regards

---

[39] Indeed, K. Duncan-Jones additionally suggests that Amphialus, the subject of the elegy in the revised *Arcadia*, might well have been somehow restored to life had the work been continued: in her edn. of *Sir Philip Sidney: Selected Poems* (Oxford, 1973), 211.

his task as 'to teach the world complaint', and Sidney furnishes the
reader with an artful version of hysterical repetition and wailing. He
makes Agelastus' uncertainty a central feature of the poem, but
deploys it in sophisticated ways. The tension between artless
wailing and poetic craft is expressed in a particular musical effect,
that of the echo. Echoes and reverberating or antiphonal laments
are a version of ancient practice, and as such are to be expected.[40]
And Agelastus, again in keeping with his models, is an artist, a
specialist, whose words are to be tied together and are designed to
articulate and direct grief. Where the sestina had been structured
on repetition, here the repeated sounds are meant to seem more
violently mournful, less susceptible of disposition into artistic
symmetries:

> O echo, all these woods with roaring fill,
> And do not only mark the accents last
> But all, for all reach not my wailfull will;
> One echo to another echo cast
> Sound of my griefs, and let it never end . . .

The first two lines are self-referential: the 'accents last' are both the
sound of the preceding paragraph and, presumably, the repeated
words of the sestina. But the sense of these echoed sounds is utter
and inconsolable mourning, at least as far as Agelastus is
concerned. His argument is based on the notion of inexpressibility,
that so great is the grief for Basilius that conventional artistic
inventions are completely inadequate, and the cries of the
mourners are perpetual. But, as so often, echo has an instructive
role to play. The pattern of linking rhymes ('dissolved/revolved/
resolved', 'killeth/spilleth/filleth', and 'deceased/oppressed/re-
dressed') counterpoints Agelastus' argument. While there are
opposing sequences ('time/climb/crime'), the very existence of two
contrasting views of sequence, of time, of the course of events,
makes these linked words, and the musical devices within the poem
generally, a counter to the hysterical outburst Agelastus proposes

---

[40] Alexiou, *Ritual Lament*, 135 ff.; Rosenmeyer, *The Green Cabinet*, 94–5; F. W.
Sternfeld, 'Repetition and Echo in Renaissance Poetry and Music', in J. Carey, ed.,
English Renaissance Studies (Oxford, 1981), 33–43. For other accounts of the poem, see
M. Turner, ' "Where rooted Moisture Failes": Sidney's Pastoral Elegy (OA75) and the
Radical Humour', *ELN* 15 (1977), 7–10, and Robert E. Stillman, *Sidney's Poetic Justice.
The Old Arcadia, its Eclogues, and Renaissance Pastoral Traditions* (Lewisburg, 1986), 168–
70, 209–10.

and which he claims to be making. The result is that echo and musical effects (as in *AS* 44) imply a movement which the argument of the poem denies. Viewed out of context, the poem might be held to dramatize a contrast between a mourner trapped inside an apparently unbreakable circuit of grief, and an echo which instructively hints—in the conventional manner of echoes—that meaning, purpose, order may be discerned. In context, the fact that Basilius is not dead may explain Agelastus' inability to mourn.

His final lament is likewise void of consolation, although its polished art constitutes some sort of statement: as a rhymed sestina, it is another demonstration of the technical accomplishment of the 'dirge specialist'. Where the previous poem had been classed by the narrator as a song, this time we are told that Agelastus 'thus maintained the lamentation in this rhyming sestine, having the doleful tune of the other shepherds' pipes joined unto him' (p. 349).[41] The substance of the elegy is the destruction of Arcadia, and the directionless and grieving state of those who survive their duke. But the performance of the poem suggests another sense: instead of shrieks and groans from the mourners, the harmony of pipe music is heard. Instead of a poem which has to be asked to bind its own elements together, we have a piece which is rhymed, in which the syntactical patterns are few and repeated, and where the rhyme-words (initially deployed ababcc) resolve themselves into couplets by the sixth stanza:

> Let tears for him therefore be all our treasure,
> And in our wailful naming him our pleasure.
> Let hating of ourselves be our affection,
> And unto death bend still our thoughts' direction,
> Let us against ourselves employ our might,
> And putting out our eyes seek we our light

And the final stanza, with its medial rhymes, is even more explicitly paradoxical, as an obviously artful rejection of art, as the rhyme words are repeated in the order in which they had originally appeared:

> Farewell our light, farewell our spoiled treasure:
> Farewell our might, farewell our daunted pleasure:
> Farewell direction, farewell all affection.

---

[41] Alexiou, *Ritual Lament*, 131–6.

When *Arcadia* first appeared in 1590, many of the more sophisticated ironies would have been inaccessible to most readers: after all, they were encountering the elegies within the revised text, the *New Arcadia*. While originally written as laments whose flaws and inconsistencies were part of an authorial design, they were presumably first read 'straight', as exemplary laments. They were not widely imitated, no doubt because they were explicitly fictional as well as technically very difficult to emulate; yet those who did follow them included poets of the highest quality, such as Donne, Drummond, and Milton. They had a more general importance in the history of the elegy, however, in that the very complexity and accomplishment of the pieces constituted a major divergence from the orthodoxy of the generation of Whetstone and Churchyard. And, even more important, the technical virtuosity was accompanied by a shift of focus, redirecting the elegy towards the speaker. Where his predecessors saw themselves as heralds, chroniclers, and moralizing historians, Sidney showed in his Arcadian elegies a speaker whose struggles with his art, and with his subject, mimed the grief he professed, both by temperament and commission. Sidney had introduced a new specificity, a particularity, into the funeral lament, which made the form, like the contemporary funeral sermon, one whose decorums were (like those of the sonnet sequence) predicated on the unique qualities of subject, speaker, and situation. But the response to Sidney's death in 1586—the first occasion of widespread and possibly officially sponsored elegy-writing—occurred in more or less total ignorance of Sidney's literary achievements, for his elegies were not available as models until the early 1590s, when they appeared in the revised *Arcadia*.

'VERSES VAINE (YET VERSES ARE NOT VAINE)': *DAPHNAIDA* AND *ASTROPHEL*

Anyone with access to Sidney's elegies in their original context would have recognized that his inspection of the 'problems of writing' led him generally to pessimistic conclusions, that art is ultimately pointless, or that it is at best an understandable human folly that can sometimes illuminate the labyrinth of contradictions and uncertainties represented by life on earth. Even in their first published settings, they were placed in a context that made it clear that consolation, especially Christian consolation, was not part of the programme of these avowedly pagan dirges. As such, therefore, these Arcadian poems stand in opposition to the consoling function of art as illustrated in Spenser's *Nouember* eclogue. And Spenser responded to the implications of Sidney's elegies, when faced with actual rather than fictional deaths. *Daphnaida* and the various laments for Sidney himself (culminating in *Astrophel*) constitute an attempt to depict, to advocate, and teach the role artistic invention can play when human wit is challenged to make sense of premature and unexpected death.

Where Sidney had gone to the ancient epics to mourn Basilius 'after the ancient Greek manner', Spenser found a source for *Daphnaida* much closer to home. Chaucer's *Book of the Duchess* had mourned Blanche, wife of his patron John of Gaunt; Spenser's imitation was occasioned by the death of Arthur Gorges's young wife Douglas Howard. Much of *Daphnaida*'s detail derives from Chaucer, and at one level Spenser's poem may be considered as a translation of an older classic into a more modern idiom.[42] But there is more to it than that. Chaucer's octosyllabics are replaced by a stanzaic form, for example, and the manifestly Greek flavour of the title—probably an allusion to the Daphnis mourned by Theocritus and by Virgil—represents a further move from the original, transforming a Gothic drama into an eclogue. More important is the question of consolation. In Chaucer we see a drama of consolation, a poem whose symmetries and patterns place the death of its subject in the framework of the order of nature, and imply meaning and purpose in the individual death. Spenser appears to end on a much less certain note: when the poet invites the bereaved man to stay with him 'till he were better eased | Of that strong stownd, which him so sore beset', his offer is declined:[43]

> . . . without taking leaue, he foorth did goe
> With staggring pace and dismall lookes dismay,

[42] There are three helpful recent accounts of the relationship of Spenser's poem to its source: D. Harris and N. L. Steffen, 'The Other Side of the Garden: An Interpretative Comparison of Chaucer's *The Book of the Duchess* and Spenser's *Daphnaida*', *JMRS* 8 (1978), 17–36; W. Oram, '*Daphnaida* and Spenser's Later Poetry', *Spenser Studies* 2 (1981), 141–58; Pigman, *Grief and English Renaissance Elegy*, 75–81, 150–2. See also Deneef, *Spenser and the Motives of Metaphor*, 42–50.

[43] Text from Spenser, *Variorum*, vii. 142. In what follows, refs. to Chaucer are to *The Complete Works of Geoffrey Chaucer*, ed. F. N. Robinson (2nd edn., Boston, 1957).

As if that death he in the face had seene,
Or hellish hags had met vpon the way:
But what of him became I cannot weene.   (558–67)

But meaning evidently lies in the poem's shape and symmetry.[44]
The introductory section consists of 28 seven-line stanzas. The
complaint consists of seven sections, each of 7 seven-line stanzas.
And then four stanzas conclude the piece, making a total of 81
stanzas, or 567 lines. These numbers seem to urge their
significance, and it is clear that Spenser's design is more elaborate
than the one he had constructed out of eleven and four in the
Nouember eclogue.

Twenty-eight is a perfect number. It is also the product of four
and seven, which is sometimes taken, as a combination of
mutability and order, to constitute fulfilment; and there are 28 days
in a lunar month. No less crucially, it is a pyramidal number, and
therefore particularly well suited to monumental and memorial
verse (Pietro Bongo proposed that the dimensions of Solomon's
temple were based on 28).[45] Thus 28 carries with it suggestions of
completeness and permanence; it implies a life whose proportions
were divinely ordained, perfectly proportioned, and a memorial
whose symmetries will withstand the buffeting of time. Spenser was
to use it in this way in *The Ruines of Time* and other elegists would
follow his example.[46]

Seven also corresponds to the number of notes in the musical
octave, the strings on a lute, the virtues, the gifts of the Holy Spirit,
and the planets. And it has a temporal dimension, of course, since
there are seven days in a week. Much more pertinent is the
conventional association of seven with man's mortal body, with

[44] For a similar assertion about *The Book of the Duchess*, see R. A. Peck, 'Theme and
Number in Chaucer's *Book of the Duchess*', in A. Fowler, ed., *Silent Poetry: Essays in
Numerological Analysis* (1970), 73–115.
[45] Fowler, *Triumphal Forms*, 176–7, 186–97; *Conceitful Thought*, 33–5.
[46] The passage in *The Ruines of Time* (400–9) runs: 'For deeds doe die, how euer
noblie donne, | And thoughts of men do as themselues decay, | But wise wordes taught
in numbers for to runne, | Recorded by the Muses, liue for ay . . . | Nor age, nor enuie
shall them euer wast. | In vaine doo earthly Princes then, in vaine | Seeke with
Pyramides, to heauen aspired' (*Variorum*, viii. 48). See M.-S. Røstvig, *The Hidden Sense*
(Oslo, 1963), 88; to Fowler's catalogue of elegies which employ 28 structurally
(*Triumphal Forms*, 188–9), add the final revision of Henry King's elegy on Prince Henry,
reproduced in app. B below. See also Deneef, *Spenser and the Motives of Metaphor*, 28–40,
who sees Spenser attempting to follow Sidney's prescriptions in the *Defence of Poetry*.

mutability, change, and loss.[47] Thus the poem is constructed out of units each made of seven lines, and it is elegiacally appropriate that the central lament should be based on further sevenfold repetitions, with seven numbered sections each containing seven stanzas. As such, the number chimes with and underscores the self-absorbed nature of Alcyon's grief. The speaker is shown trapped and rendered disfigured, unrecognizable, by the intensity of his mourning: he argues that Daphne has died merely to torment him, that the meaning of her death is fully achieved in him, wholly comprehended only by him. Indeed, as Pigman has observed, the central line in Alcyon's lament ('That with her lacke I might tormented be') appears to have been placed to epitomize—indeed to literalize—his self-centredness.[48]

Where seven is mutable, nine is immortal, heavenly, as in the House of Alma: 'Nine was the circle set in heauens place' (*FQ* II. ix. 22).[49] The whole of *Daphnaida* consists of 81 stanzas, or nine times nine, and as such represents perfection, circularity; with the added finesse that the units thus twice multiplied by nine are of seven lines each, so that it is as if the mutable seven were translated and subsumed within the harmony of nines. After all, the two numbers are traditionally twinned to achieve such effects. The base of the frame of Alma's house had been 'Proportioned equally by seuen and nine' (*FQ* II ix. 22), which adds a further notion, that of the climacteric, 63, a number whose structural importance in many Elizabethan texts has been fully demonstrated.[50] The poem as a whole contains nine climacterics, 9 x 63 lines, which presumably is meant to argue for a fitness in the death of Alcyon's wife, that it is the expression of higher orders and laws, in ways that are at present inaccessible to the understanding of the afflicted husband.[51]

---

[47] For a succinct account of the elegiac aptness of 7, see Fowler, *Conceitful Thought*, 33. I think it is reasonable to suppose that the present context excludes connections with the Deadly Sins.

[48] Pigman, *Grief and English Renaissance Elegy*, 78–9, 151–2.

[49] The antiquarian Henry Ferrers planned a prose history of England whose proportions were based on 9 and its multiples: see Fowler, *Triumphal Forms*, 4.

[50] Henry Constable's *Diana* (1592), Drayton's *Idea* (1619) and Sidney's *Astrophil and Stella* are the most celebrated instances. On Sidney, see T. P. Roche, '*Astrophil and Stella*: A Radical Reading', *Spenser Studies*, 3 (1982), 184–7 (repr. in Kay, *Sir Philip Sidney*, 223–5).

[51] See Thomas Wright's appendix to *The passions of the mind in generall* (1604): *A Succinct Philosophicall declaration of the nature of Clymactericall yeeres, occasioned by the death of Queen Elizabeth*, sigs. A3–C3.

Doubtless a similar sense resides in the use of squared numbers (4, 9, 49) throughout, whereby an impression of connectedness through number and proportion is the counter-argument to grief.[52]

Spenser's choice of Chaucer as a model provides another clue as to the species of consolation his poem was designed to afford. Behind each of the elegies is a personal relationship between a poet and his social superior: Chaucer and John of Gaunt, Spenser and Sir Arthur Gorges. And the way Chaucer integrated the relationship into the fabric of his poem—as he obviously had to, since the real Chaucer was giving a real poem to the real John of Gaunt on the death of his real wife—has some significance for an appreciation of Spenser's performance in *Daphnaida*.[53]

In the early stages of *The Book of the Duchess*, servants and their masters appear constantly. The poet identifies himself with the servants and personally apologizes to the man in black for troubling him in his sorrow:

> 'A, good sir, no fors,' quod y,
> 'I am ryght sory yif I have ought
> Destroubled yow out of your thought.
> Foryive me, yif I have mystake.'   (522–5)

The mourner courteously replies, 'There ys nothyng myssayd or do' (528), and the exchange between the fictional Chaucer and the fictionalized John of Gaunt establishes a framework of tact, of delicacy, whereby the poet starts from the desire not to offend or intrude, even if, like Joseph in Egypt (280), he is blessed with the gift of interpreting dreams and prophecies. We read of many servants whose office is to aid, console, and comfort. When the

---

[52] Pigman contrasts Daphne's words at the centre of the poem as a whole—'I goe, and long desired haue to goe, | I goe with gladnesse to my wished rest, | Whereas no worlds sad care, nor wasting woe | May come their happie quiet to molest; | But Saints and Angells in celestiall thrones | Eternally him praise, that hath them blest: | There shall I be amongst those blessed ones' (281–7)—with the way Alcyon's lament has placed himself physically as well as emotionally at its centre (*Grief and English Renaissance Elegy*, 78–9).

[53] This is not to ignore the importance of sources, of models, to each poet. D. W. Robertson reminds Chaucerians that 'We have hardly begun to understand the French sources': i.e. Froissart, Machaut, and the *Roman de la Rose* (B. Rowland, ed., *A Companion to Chaucer Studies* (rev. edn., New York, 1979), 408). For recent studies of some sources, see J. D. Burnley, 'Some Terminology of Reception in *The Book of the Duchess:*, *ELN* 23 (1986), 15–22; also A. Rooney, '*The Book of the Duchess*: Hunting and the "ubi sunt" Tradition'. *RES*, NS, 38 (1987), 299–314.

speaker cannot sleep, for example, he calls on one of his own
servants to fetch him a book to read (46), because he 'thought it
better play | Than play either at ches or tables' (50–1). In the story
which he reads, Queen Alcyone calls on servants to act as
messengers and to seek her husband (88–9). When she in her turn
falls asleep with the dream from Juno, she is picked up by her
women and placed in a bed (124–5): and then Juno orders her own
messenger to make the journey to Morpheus to retrieve Seys (132–
45). These, and further examples that might be cited, indicate the
ubiquity of the master/servant motif in the poem; and its immediate
effect is to place the conversation between the speaker and the man
in black in a context of comforting servants, of messengers who
bring consoling visions, fictions, books. Taken together, they turn
The Book of the Duchess as a whole into an offering, a gesture of
comfort. Chaucer's poem, while most obviously a model for
Spenser in its matter, is also a model as a gift, as a gesture or event.
The very fact of the borrowing seems to constitute a claim on
Spenser's part that his poem shares the qualities of all the consoling
ministrations of servants that Chaucer both depicts and mimics.[54]

Spenser uses structure as a species of consolation, as a
demonstration of the capacity of art to suggest meaning, order, and
purpose. There is a contrast with Sidney's Arcadian recreation of
ancient Greek practice, with the howls and shrieks of the observers
joined to the wailing of Agelastus. In Spenser's poem, each section
of Alcyon's dirge ends, 'Weepe Shepheard weepe to make my
vndersong': but the undersong that is made does not merely echo
or reinforce his intemperate grief. Rather it is a highly artful and
symmetrical assimilation of the dirge into a pattern charged with
consolatory meanings. As an object, as an artefact, the poem
possesses a status and an import which transforms Alcyon's request
for an echoing cry into a professional poet's exercise of the highest
powers of his wit to console his bereaved friend. And, within
Daphnaida, the consolatory structure springs from the relationship
between Alcyon and the community of shepherds whose spokesman
he is.

Such considerations prepare the ground for an examination of
Spenser's *Astrophel*, and the elegies printed with it in *Colin Clouts*

---

[54] While there are some masters and servants in Chaucer's sources, it is in *The Book of
the Duchess* that the topic plays a central, self-referential, defining role.

Come Home Againe (1595).[55] As with *Daphnaida*, Spenser's laments
for Sidney engage critically with the elegiac models and precedents
that might be found in *Arcadia*, with the added component that
Sidney's life and personality were to be treated alongside his ideas
and art. Spenser's highest compliment to Sidney is to transform
disagreement into panegyric.

References to Sidney as a writer are notably scarce in the elegies
published in the immediate aftermath of his death. Sidney was
mourned primarily as a national figure, a Protestant hero, whose
death came at a convenient moment in the political manœuvres
surrounding the execution of Mary Queen of Scots.[56] The *Astrophel*
collection, in contrast, comes from the period when Sidney's
reputation as a poet was becoming established, when his status as
an exemplary Christian knight was ennobling the profession of
letters.[57] Spenser, as the shaping intelligence of the collection,
seems to have taken some such development as his theme, turning
the act of compilation and presentation first into a strategy of
consolation and second into a demonstration of, and tribute to,
those characteristics of the subject that earlier elegists had perforce
failed to celebrate.[58]

Before considering the volume in detail, let us recall its contents.
The sequence begins with Spenser's own pastoral elegy, which
consists of three introductory stanzas, *Astrophel* itself (36 stanzas),
and the 'Lay' of Clorinda (18 stanzas).[59] Then come two poems by

[55] Spenser subtitles his poem 'A Pastorall Elegie': my texts of poems in the volume are
taken from Spenser, *Poetical Works*, ed. J. C. Smith and E. de Selincourt (Oxford,
1912). In dedicating the volume to Sidney's widow, he takes on the duties of the 'dirge
expert', becoming in some sense the equivalent of Sidney's Agelastus.

[56] See below, p. 68; for a brief account of Sidney's posthumous reputation, see
D. Kay, 'Sidney—A Critical Heritage', in Kay, *Sir Philip Sidney*, 3–41, esp. 4–25.

[57] The two most important texts are Harington's Preface to his transl. of the *Orlando
Furioso* (1591) and Nashe's preface to the unauthorized 1st edition of *Astrophil and Stella*
(1591).

[58] It has been suggested, for example, that the fact that *Astrophel* contains 216
(108 x 2) lines and the 'Lay', 108, is a complimentary allusion to the 108 sonnets of
Astrophel and Stella (Fowler, *Triumphal Forms*, 175). Further, the feminine rhyme (chiefly
in the praise of Stella (55–69)) would have been recognized as a demonstration of
Sidney's influence: since Sidney, as Harington remarked, 'not only vseth them, but
affecteth them' (Smith, ed., *Elizabethan Critical Essays*, i. 221).

[59] Arguments for Spenser's authorship of the 'Lay' (to which should be added the
evidence of a shared numerological compliment with *Astrophel*) are rehearsed in the
Variorum, vii. 500–5. I am persuaded by the arguments that have led Margaret Hannay
to include the Lay in her forthcoming edition of the Countess of Pembroke's writings.
The parallels with Spenser's other writings cited by the *Variorum* editors indicate that
she was the first of the Spenserian poets.

Lodowick Bryskett (one of which, 'The mourning muse of Thestylis' had been entered in the Stationers' Register on 22 August 1587), and a group of three pieces, already published in *The Phoenix Nest* (1593), by Matthew Roydon, Ralegh, and an anonymous friend, possibly Greville or Dyer.[60] As ever with Spenser, his art shows itself quite as much in overall conception, in the disposition of material, as in local detail, and his own contribution to the collection resides not only in the composition which heads the collection but also in the design of the anthology, the shaping intelligence which silently transforms the works which it might appear neutrally to reprint.[61] It should be noted that, while Bryskett subscribes his initials, Spenser is the only writer who declares his identity. Gone is the anonymity of *The Shepheardes Calender*, and the persona of Colin Clout is not invoked. It is as if he, as the professional, the 'dirge expert', were proclaiming his function as impresario, as the gatherer and organizer of more private laments. I shall consider the poems in turn, and then talk about their coherence as an anthology.

The immediate model for *Astrophel* is Ronsard's *L'Adonis* (1563), although both Bion's lament for Adonis and Ovid's *Metamorphoses* (x. 708 ff.) are, as elsewhere in Spenser, important sources.[62] No less significant is *Astrophil and Stella*, which, having appeared in 1591, had already become established as the exemplary sonnet sequence. Spenser's most notable departure from Ronsard is in tone. Ronsard is urbane, jocular, and his mythological figures are presented in a thoroughly human fashion: as Terence Cave observes, 'Venus abandons her divinity . . . to share the pastoral way of life . . . her passion, her lamentation, her ultimate inconstancy operate on a wholly mortal level, while the jealousy of Mars is identifiable with the psychological reflexes of the cheated lover'.[63] Spenser, on the other hand, is loftily serious, elevating human lovers rather than turning divinities into archetypes of thwarted lust.[64]

[60] See above, p. 11.

[61] Pigman writes of an 'overarching . . . structure' (*Grief and English Renaissance Elegy*, 152); see Deneef, *Spenser and the Motives of Metaphor*, 25.

[62] The text of *L'Adonis* is from Ronsard, *Œuvres complètes*, ed. P. Laumonnier (Paris, 1946), xii. 108–24; for details of Spenser's borrowing, see *Variorum*, i. 495–9.

[63] T. C. Cave, 'Ronsard's Mythological Universe', in Cave, ed., *Ronsard the Poet* (1973), 202–3. See also Cave's chapter on Ronsard in *The Cornucopian Text*, 223–70.

[64] See P. E. Bondanella and J. Canaway, 'Two Kinds of Renaissance Love: Spenser's "Astrophel" and Ronsard's "Adonis"', *ES* 52 (1971), 311–8, and Sacks's thoughtful account in *The English Elegy*, 50–62.

Of Astrophel's physical qualities, we are left to infer perfection of appearance from his active skills:

> In wrestling nimble, and in renning swift,
> In shooting steddie, and in swimming strong:
> Well made to strike, to throw, to leape, to lift,
> And all the sports that shepheards are emong. (73–6)

Ronsard's Adonis had been presented in much more frankly sensual terms, with his perfect beauty resembling the most peerless works of art:

> Un petit poil follet luy couvroit le menton
> Gresle, prime, frisé, plus blond que le cotton
> Qui croist dessur les coings, ou la soye subtile
> Qui couvre au renouveau la peau de la chenille.
> Ses levres combatoient les roses qu'au jardin
> On voit espanoüir au lever du matin,
> Qu'une jeune pucelle en son gyron amasse
> Avant que leur beau teint par le chaut ne se passe.
> Bref ce jeune pasteur est tout jeune & tout beau:
> Il semble un pré fleury, que le Printemps nouveau
> Et la douce rosée en sa verdeur nourrissent,
> Où de mille coulleurs leurs fleurs s'espanoüissent:
> C'est luy mesmes Amour!   (15–27)

The young hero Astrophel developed his combination of personal excellence and physical perfection 'With gentle vsage and demeanoure myld' (20), and exercised himself with 'faire' sports, and 'ioyance innocent' (25). He came to embody the virtuous conjunction of court and country virtues, seeming 'made for meriment, | Merily masking in both bowre and hall' (27–8). His poetic skill was expressed both in shepherds' dances and carols and in the composition of 'layes of loue' (31–5). This paragon, though admired by all, and wooed by many, was devoted to the service of Stella, whom he courted initially by his writings—'His thoughts, his rimes, his songs were all vpon her' (60)—and by the display of his physical prowess:

> Ne her with ydle words alone he wowed,
> And verses vaine (yet verses are not vaine)
> But with braue deeds to her sole seruice vowed.
> And bold atchieuements her did entertaine. (67–70)

As with both Chaucer's Troilus, and the Astrophil of *AS* 41, virtuous love inspires Astrophel to success in combat:

> In euery one he vanquisht euery one,
> He vanquisht all, and vanquisht was of none.   (77–8)

Ronsard's presentation of the Adonis story concentrates on physical desire; Venus laments with a shriek of hysteria, and the poet's conclusion, when the sobbing goddess abandons mourning as she finds consolation in the arms of Anchises, is characteristically worldly:[65]

> Telles sont & seront les amitiez des femmes,
> Qui au commencement sont plus chaudes que flames:
> Espointes de fureur, à la fin leur amour
> Comme une belle fleur ne se garde qu'un jour.   (365–8)

Spenser's speaker is more distant from the events he narrates: he adopts the role of spokesman for the bereaved community, for the family of the dead hero, and for the shepherd-poets to whom he dedicates the poem:

> To you alone I sing this mournfull verse,
> The mournfulst verse that euer man heard tell:
> To you whose softened hearts it may empierse,
> With dolours dart for death of *Astrophel*.   (7–10)

Further, he departs crucially from Ronsard in the treatment of the female lament that is the core of each performance. In Ronsard's poem, Venus weeps over the body of her dead beloved, recalling the delight she had found in him, and deploring her loss in an echo of the earlier description:

> La rose fuit ta levre, & au tour de ta bouche
> Ne vit plus ton baiser: toutefois je la touche,
> Morte je la rebaise, & sentir tu ne puis
> Ny mon baiser, ny moy, mes pleurs, ny mes ennuis.
>   He he, pauvre Adonis, tous les Amours te pleurent,
> Car aveques ta mort toutes delices meurent: (213–18)

This last couplet, which echoes Bion, becomes the refrain of her complaint and dominates the major part of the work (205–346).

But there are two female figures in *Astrophel*: Stella and the deceased's sister Clorinda. There is thus no single, exclusive focus on

---

[65] Bondanella and Canaway, 'Two Kinds of Renaissance Love', 312–3, 316.

a particular mourner, and Spenser divides his text to confirm the point. What is more, neither is remotely like Venus either in the tone or subject of her lament.[66] Another major departure from Ronsard resides in the treatment of immortality, of the lovers' relations after death, the memory that abides. The earlier poem is explicitly pagan, of course, and its intimations of ritual commemoration are from that pre-Christian, Greek rather than Roman, context. Ovid's account has Venus secure Adonis' annual return as a flower. In Bion, the tears of Cypris and the blood of Adonis are turned into flowers as they touch the earth. In *The Faerie Queene*, Spenser depicts Venus and Adonis trapped in a kind of provisional stasis, having staved off death without either achieving a final victory over it, or embracing it.[67] In *Astrophel* Spenser develops this idea, and indicates a comprehension of death as an occasion of the assimilation of the transient into the eternal, by having the lovers united in death, and transformed into a single flower.[68]

His narrative tells how Stella died of a broken heart over Astrophel's broken body: the account of her mourning is, compared to Ronsard, notably terse:

> His palled face impictured with death,
> She bathed oft with teares and dried oft:
> And with sweet kisses suckt the wasting breath,
> Out of his lips like lillies pale and soft.
> And oft she cald to him, who answerd nought,
> But onely by his lookes did tell his thought.   (163–8)

It is the pity of the 'Gods which all things see' that leads to the transformation of the lovers into a flower, which, by growing first red and then blue, figures Astrophel's story, and in whose leaves appears the mark of a star to commemorate Stella. Its sorrowful name, Penthia, is matched by its new, and equally sad, title Astrophel:[69]

[66] See M. O'Connell, '*Astrophel*: Spenser's Double Elegy', *SEL* 11 (1971), 27–35.

[67] J. Nohrnberg, *The Analogy of 'The Faerie Queene'* (2nd edn., Princeton, 1980), 520–68; K. Gross, *Spenserian Poetics: Idolatry, Iconoclasm, and Magic* (Ithaca, 1985), 181–209.

[68] On the basis of the contrasts between Clorinda and Stella, Sacks observes that 'In this progressive, oppositional structure, Spenser is . . . ensuring that the development of his poem enacts the work of mourning': *The English Elegy*, 57.

[69] See John Ford's play, *The Broken Heart* (long recognized as alluding to Astrophil, Stella, and their non-fictional counterparts) where Penthea dies of a broken heart. See K. Duncan-Jones, 'Ford and the Earl of Devonshire', *RES*, NS, 39 (1978), 447–52, and 'Sidney, Stella and Lady Rich', in J. Van Dorsten, D. Baker-Smith, and A. F. Kinney, eds., *Sir Philip Sidney: 1586 and the Creation of a Legend* (Leiden, 1986), 170–92.

> But thou where euer thou doest finde the same,
> From this day forth do call it *Astrophel*,
> And when so euer thou it vp doest take,
> Do pluck it softly for that shepheards sake.   (195–8)

Hinting at the conventional metaphorical twinning of verses and flowers, this suggestion that Sidney's immortality resides in a flower marked with the name Astrophel presumably alludes both to the recently published sonnet sequence (in terms which had, even by 1595, become habitual), and to Spenser's elegy itself.[70] As with *Daphnaida*, the status of the poem (or anthology) as a physical object, as the concrete expression of a relationship, is brought into prominence. Spenser did likewise in *Prothalamion*, the *Amoretti*, and in the *Epithalamion*, and it is fair to consider his emphasis on the physical, corporeal existence of his works as an essential part of his writing on occasional subjects, where the challenge to art is to celebrate a unique and necessarily irrecoverable event in terms which both do justice to its uniqueness and grant it some form of permanence.[71]

After the self-referential flower episode, Spenser's narrator describes the shepherds flocking to the scene of death, and forming themselves into a procession of mourners:

> And euery one did weep and waile, and mone,
> And meanes deviz'd to shew his sorrow best . . .

> But first his sister that *Clorinda* hight,
> The gentlest shepheardesse that liues this day:
> And most resembling both in shape and spright
> Her brother deare, began this dolefull lay,
> Which least I marre the sweetnesse of the vearse,
> In sort as she it sung, I will rehearse.

The placement of the funeral elegy proper, the 'dolefull lay', after the account of the subject's metamorphosis into a flower, is an apparent deviation from convention, although in the light of Spenser's performance in *Daphnaida* it is not wholly surprising that

---

[70] As early as 1592, Samuel Daniel observed that 'Astrophel . . . hath registered his owne name in the Annals of eternitie' and referred to Sidney's 'eternal songs' (*Delia: Contayning certayne sonnets* (1592), sig. A2; *Delia and Rosamond augmented* (1594), sigs. H5ᵛ, H6).

[71] Montrose, 'The Elizabethan Subject and the Spenserian text', 320; Sacks remarks that 'Spenser's achievement in *Astrophel* has . . . been won against and yet through his extreme awareness of his dependence on fictions': *The English Elegy*, 62.

a consolatory context should have been prepared for the lament: since we have already been told of Astrophel's immortality, the intensity of Clorinda's grief is confined to its occasion.

The lay itself is relatively straightforward. It is precisely half the length of the 'pastoral elegy' which precedes it, and its 108 lines presumably glance at *Astrophil and Stella*, but there are no suggestions of any more elaborate or arcane structural principles. The numerical compliment to Sidney is a silent demonstration of the sequence's survival, as well as of its capacity to structure subsequent writing.[72] What is more, within the context of the whole piece, Spenser shows a drama in which the shepherd-poets, led by Clorinda, mourn Astrophel, and the fact that the first lament is tacitly built on the framework of Astrophel's art illustrates a species of immortality that contrasts with that represented by the metamorphosis into a flower. Spenser reveals the consolation shepherd-poets may derive from art, and, crucially, from the continuities of literary tradition. As with all great elegies, the act of imitation becomes itself a primary strategy of consolation.[73] *Astrophel* does not merely announce Sidney's literary immortality: it seeks to prove it.

Spenser personally supervises the shift from a self-consciously literary, fictionalized lament in *Astrophel* to the personal dirge of the 'Lay', and brings the poem from a deliberately remote antiquity to a funeral present: from myth to an immediate sorrow. The 'Lay' enacts the ceremonies authorized by *Astrophel* and concludes by revealing their potential for consolation.

Clorinda's lay consists of sixteen stanzas, with two afterwards that are effectively narrative, and presumably spoken by the poet. Of the sixteen, eleven (as in the *Nouember* eclogue) are devoted to lament, ending with the line, 'Ay me, can so diuine a thing be dead?': consolation is inaugurated by, 'Ah no, it is not dead, ne can it die, | But liues for aie . . . '. The poem represents a dramatized education in accommodation to grief.[74] Clorinda initially seeks a sympathetic audience for her cries, but, finding none, turns inward:

---

[72] The anonymous *Alcilia* (1595) also contains 108 poems.

[73] See Cave, *The Cornucopian Text*, 35–77; Pigman, 'Versions of Imitation in the Renaissance', *RQ* 33 (1980), 1–32: T. M. Greene, *The Light in Troy: Imitation and Discovery in Renaissance Poetry* (New Haven, 1982), esp. chs. 1–4.

[74] The 5 stanzas remaining after the 11 of lament may relate to Spenser's structural use of 5 in other texts to suggest the Heraclitean principle of stability in change. See Fowler, *Conceitful Thought*, 85.

> Then to my selfe will I my sorrow mourne,
> Sith none aliue like sorrowfull remaines:
> And to my selfe my plaints shall back retourne,
> To pay their vsury with doubled paines.
> The woods, the hills, the riuers shall resound
> The mournefull accent of my sorrowes ground. (19–24)

As might be expected, her appeal for echo is answered by the opening words of the following stanza, before she embarks on a brief summons to mourn, urging the 'shepheards lasses' to turn their joy into sorrow, and to put aside Astrophel's songs because 'Death the deuourer of all worlds delight, | Hath robbed you and reft fro me my ioy' (49–50). Where Ronsard's Venus and Stella had embraced the bleeding corpse, Clorinda regards the flower that remains as 'but the shadow of his likenesse gone', and consoles herself with a vision of Astrophel's 'immortall spirit' in a characteristically Spenserian haven of immutable stillness (67–90), with echoes of the Garden of Adonis. She concludes by contrasting the soul's bliss with the miserable life endured by those 'wretches' who remain on earth, and identifies the subject of her mourning as herself:[75]

> Thus do we weep and waile, and wear our eies,
> Mourning in others, our owne miseries (95–6)

Astrophel and the 'Lay' demonstrate two contrasting elegiac strategies, fitting each to its supposed speaker. Where the mythological *Astrophel* had dwelt on the capacity of art to invoke the transformation of mortal life into the timelessness of ritual, the 'Lay' portrays immediate mourning transmuted into contemplation of eternity and, as its consequence, the frailty of humans. Stylistically, *Astrophel* is in a higher, more impersonal register, while the 'Lay' is full of the repetition, assonance, and metrical variety characteristic of Spenser at his most musical. Clearly the author imitates a sung dirge in the stanza once claimed to be 'unrivalled for melodiously suggesting that catch in the throat and breaking voice of sorrow':[76]

> Break now your gyrlonds, O ye shepheards lasses,
> Sith the faire flowre, which them adornd, is gon:

---

[75] See Rosenmeyer, *The Green Cabinet*, 206–31.
[76] P. Bayley, *Edmund Spenser: Prince of Poets* (1972), 77.

> The flowre, which them adornd, is gone to ashes,
> Neuer againe let lasse put gyrlond on.
> In stead of gyrlond, weare sad Cypres nowe,
> And bitter Elder, broken from the bowe. (37–42)

In these twinned poems, and in their relation to the rest of the volume, Spenser in effect invented the vernacular funeral anthology, and the Countess of Pembroke became the first Spenserian poet. He also established and sanctioned the variousness of elegy, and exemplified the diversity of forms which might be fitted to particular aspects of the range of functions an elegist might desire or feel obliged to fulfil. Having begun the collection by creating this principle of variety, and relating it to the processional aspects of the most ancient elegiac practice, he constructed a bridge between his own works and those of his fellows in the volume. When Clorinda ceases, Spenser introduces the mourning company (and we should remember that the volume itself is directed to such a company of shepherd-poets): the first is to be Thestylis—Lodowick Bryskett— with his 'mourning muse'. Then all the others:[77]

> And after him full many other moe,
> As euerie one in order lov'd him best,
> Gan dight themselues t'expresse their inward woe,
> With dolefull layes vnto the time addrest,
> The which I here in order will rehearse,
> As fittest flowres to deck his mournfull hearse. (103–8)

Recognisably Spenserian phrases effect the transition between his own elegy and the doleful lay of Clorinda. He establishes an equivalence between 'her' poem and those of Sidney's friends, who will be ranked 'in order lov'd him best'. Where Spenser had classed his own poem as a pastoral elegy, these others are generically similar and are 'lays', whose purpose is to express the 'inward woe' of their authors, to be fitted to the occasion ('vnto the time addrest'), and to be physically part of the funeral ceremony, as 'flowres to deck his mournfull hearse'. This last idea is based on the funeral adaptation of the commonplace verse/flowers parallel, whereby the pinning of elegies on a hearse was a literary

---

[77] The procession is organized on the basis of affection—'in order lov'd him best'— rather than kinship or other relationship. The pastoral fiction involves the establishment of an alternative order to the social procedures of quotidian society; it also carries with it the notion of community. See Rosenmeyer, *The Green Cabinet*, 154.

counterpart of decorating the hearse with flowers.[78] But there is an additional element that derives from the earlier claim that Astrophel has become immortal both by being turned into a flower and by leaving in his writings a permanent image of himself. By the use of these strategies of transition, Spenser turns a heterogeneous group of elegies in various modes into an ordered sequence, a miscellany into a procession.

Spenser's artful framing integrates Bryskett's poem so well that it appears to develop and expand the preceding pieces.[79] Spenser had omitted Mars from his elegy: Bryskett invokes the god and asks why he had failed to come to the assistance of his champion. And his account of Sidney's sister's grief also seems to be connected with Spenser's poem:

> If *Venus* when she waild her deare *Adonis* slaine,
> Ought moov'd in thy fiers hart compassion of her woe,
> His noble sisters plaints, her sighes and teares emong,
> Would sure haue made thee milde, and inly rue her paine:
>
> (128–31)

In keeping with its early date, however, is the emphasis on Sidney as a soldier. At a stylistic level, this is expressed by its location in the heroic register of Churchyard and Whetstone:

> *Aurora* halfe so faire, her selfe did neuer show,
> When from old *Tithons* bedd, shee weeping did arise.   (132–3)

More explicitly, Sidney's apotheosis culminates in his being led to a golden throne by Mars:

> . . . thy valour for to grace,
> A chaire of gold he setts to thee, and there doth tell
> Thy noble acts anew, whereby euen they that boast
> Themselues of auncient fame, as *Pirrhus, Hanniball*,

[78] A memorable example is *An Italians dead bodie, stucke with English flowers: Elegies, on the death of Sir Oratio Pallavicino* (1600), STC 19154.3. See also the Scottish anthology *Mausoleum: or the choisest flowres of the epitaphs on the death of Prince Henrie* (Edinburgh, 1613), STC 13160.

[79] Bryskett's poems are reworkings of Tasso, and as such are vehicles for the transmission of contemporary continental elegiac practice into English. See H. R. Plomer and T. P. Cross, *The Life and Correspondence of Lodowick Bryskett* (Chicago, 1927), 77–82; H. Smith, *Elizabethan Poetry* (Cambridge, Mass., 1952), 58–9; D. Jones, *Thomas Lodge and Other Elizabethans*, ed. C. J. Sisson (Cambridge, Mass., 1933), 245–53; see also the Introduction to *Lodowick Bryskett: Literary Works*, ed. J. H. P. Pafford (1972), and F. B. Tromley, 'Lodowick Bryskett's Elegies on Sidney in Spenser's *Astrophel* Volume', *RES*, NS, 37 (1986), 384–8.

> *Scipio* and *Caesar*, with the rest that did excell
> In martiall prowesse, high thy glorie do admire. (182–9)

Bryskett's second poem, *A pastorall Aeglogue*, has two speakers, Lycon and Colin. As in the *Nouember* eclogue, Colin is asked for an elegy. But Colin's reply is historically important, in that it prefigures the Spenserian movement. He tells Lycon, unsurprisingly, that grief engenders eloquence. He adds that such sincere grief gains force through being shared:

> Come let vs ioyne our mournfull song with theirs.
> Grief will endite, and sorrow will enforce
> Thy voice, and Eccho will our words report.[80]　　(32–4)

Yet the poem maintains a distinction between Colin, the laureate poet, and Lycon, the grieving friend, throughout: as in Spenser's elegies, the friend's sorrow is addressed to himself, here to '*Lycon* vnfortunate' (81). And he remembers details of the life he had known with his friend, recalling events in Sidney's youth (most notably when he remembers their journey to Italy—'Thou with him yodest: and with him didst scale | The craggie rocks of th'Alpes and *Appenine* . . . Still with the *Muses* sporting' (88–90)). It is the professional poet who takes a longer view, who argues for an immortality through verse:

> Loe where engraued by his hand yet liues
> The name of *Stella*, in yonder bay tree.
> Happie name, happie tree; faire may you grow. (125–7)

Lycon is consoled by a vision of the dead shepherd installed 'in heau'n with blessed soules' (136), the grave is adorned with flowers as tokens of 'the giuers faded state' (150), in a ritual to be repeated annually, so that his fame 'for euer may endure' (158).[81] The shepherds are recalled to their flock by sunset and imminent rain, returning to the world of *negotium* from pastoral *otium*. The relationship between the two men, between 'dirge expert' and

---

[80] As Agelastus had; see above, p. 45.

[81] The passage 'learndst shepheards honor may thy name | With yeerly praises, and the Nymphs alway | The tomb may deck with fresh and sweetest flowres; | And that for euer may endure thy fame' (155–8) may anticipate the conclusion of *Samson Agonistes*, where Manoa promises to erect for Samson a monument, shaded by evergreens and adorned with the hero's 'acts enrolled | In copious legend, or sweet lyric song, | Thither shall all the valiant youth resort, | And from his memory inflame their breasts | To matchless valour, and adventures high: | The virgins also shall on feastfull days | Visit his tomb with flowers' (1736–42): *Milton: Complete Shorter Poems*, ed. J. Carey (1968), 399.

friend of the deceased, fits well into Spenser's overall design, and its substance, a dramatized education in managing, articulating, and sharing grief, is of a piece with the rest.

More of a challenge to Spenser's imagination, perhaps, were the three poems from *The Phoenix Nest* (1593).[82] But, although only one is pastoral, each is a 'dolefull lay', and together they reinforce the complimentary implications of generic variety as well as imitating a procession which illustrates the ubiquity and intensity of mourning. The first is Matthew Roydon's 'Elegie, or friends passion, for his *Astrophill*', which is an allegorical lament that owes much to Chaucer and Spenser.[83] It opens in 'a circle . . . Like to an Amphitheater' (23–4), with an assembly of heraldic beasts (lion, unicorn, bear, stag), surrounded by a collection of named trees, populated by birds ('the airie winged people . . . Distinguished in od degrees'), notably the eagle, the dove, and the swan, and the phoenix in her cedar 'tombe of spicerie' preparing to 'take her dying flame' (7–42).

In the centre of this assembly is the mourner, whose narrative is the core of the elegy. The assembly urges him to reveal his inner torment and he obliges with an account of Astrophill's excellences, his love for Stella, his being favoured by Venus and slain by Mars (67–180). He claims the status of shepherd-poet for his subject by obvious Spenserian imitation—'You knew, who knew not *Astrophill*'. As in the Nouember eclogue, the shock of death is mimed by *paranomasia* and *epanorthosis*. The news of Astrophill's death precipitates universal lamentation. The dove mourns him as an example of faithful love (193–8), the swan's dirge argues that virtuous death is the key to eternal life (210–14), and the phoenix's funeral pyre is ignited. The narrator's eyes follow the eagle as it

[82] Text taken from H. E. Rollins's edn., 2 vols. (Cambridge, Mass., 1931). The anthology opens with a defence of Leicester's reputation, 'The dead mans Right (A3ʳ–A4ᵛ). D. E. L. Crane, in his Introductory Note to the Scolar Press facsimile of *The phoenix nest* (Menston, 1970), asserts that 'the Phoenix of the title was . . . Sidney' and speculates that 'the publication of Sidney's sonnets inspired R.S.' to assemble the anthology.

[83] Nashe, in his preface to Greene's *Menaphon* (1589), wrote that Roydon 'hath shewed himselfe singular in the immortall Epitaph of his beloued *Astrophell*, besides many other most absolute Comike inuentions (made more publick by euery mans praise, then they can be by my speech)': Nashe, *Works*, ed. McKerrow, iii. 323). Christopher Hill discusses Roydon, 'poet, mathematician, hermeticist' in relation to the Ralegh–Northumberland circle: *Intellectual Origins of the English Revolution* (Oxford, 1965, repr. 1972), 142 ff.

flies to report to Jove: the entire vision then leaves him and he is left to lament his loss alone, his tears putting an end to the physical act of writing.

Roydon's poem concentrates on the report of death, and on Sidney's death as a catastrophe that produces mourning. There is no sense of consolation. It is personal and dramatic in a way that Walter Ralegh's brief epitaph, which follows it, is not.[84] In part, such a distinction accords with the generic separation of elegy (associated with the death, with the funeral) and epitaph (associated with the erection of a monument, and implying a less emotionally coloured, more conclusive, response to death. Ralegh bases his poem on the topos of inexpressibility, even in its most celebrated lines (which seem—or are made to seem—to derive from Bryskett's poem)[85]

> That day their *Hanniball* died, our *Scipio* fell
> *Scipio*, *Cicero*, and *Petrarch* of our time,
> Whose vertues wounded by my worthlesse rime,
> Let Angels speake, and heauen thy praises tell.   (57–60)

Ralegh's poem, though not a *blason*, and rather less specific in its detail, is in the tradition of Surrey's epitaph on Wyatt. As the dedicatee of the entire volume, Ralegh clearly enjoyed a special status in the assembly of mourners Spenser gathered, but it is as Warden of the Stanneries that he mourns the Governor of Flushing: not for him, in this case, the pastoral fiction of a shepherd—poet mourning a fellow practitioner, nor yet the lamenting dirge of an elegy. His stiff and formal epitaph is predominantly in the public register of Tudor 'remembrances'.[86]

If the shepherd—poets to whom the volume was addressed wished to see an example of the emulation to which they were exhorted, here it was. And there is no doubt that they followed his example. With the *Astrophel* volume, Spenser invented Spenserian poetry.[87] From this collection his followers derived a clear and

---

[84] *Phoenix Nest*, ed. Rollins, i. 128–9.

[85] A. Latham, ed., *The Poems of Sir Walter Ralegh* (1951), xxix, xxxiv, xlv–liii; on the currency of the '*Scipio*, *Cicero*, and *Petrarch* of our time', see p. 98.

[86] Ralegh appears to declare that there had been little personal association with his subject: 'And I, that in thy time and liuing state, | Did onely praise thy vertue in my thought, | As one that seeld the rising sun hath sought, | With words and teares now waile thy timelesse fate' (9–12). For an account of the final poem in the anthology, see above, p. ooo.

[87] An excellent study of Spenserian poetry is Norbrook, *Poetry and Politics*, 195–214.

practical sense of the nature of poetic community, the value and possibility of poetic continuity, and the role and status of the laureate poet in relation to his fellows.[88] Spenser's performance as an impresario, as guide, and as the shaping intelligence whose own contribution frames, informs and reinterprets the efforts of his fellow mourners, established a significant precedent.[89] It became the model, as later chapters will show, for such writers as William Bedell (in compiling an anthology on the Lewkenors in 1606), Joshua Sylvester (compiling *Lachrimae lachrimarum* with contributions from Prince Henry's court in 1612/13), and for Milton, whose *Lycidas* concludes *Iusta Edouardo King* in an apparently conscious modification of the achievement of his 'original'. Spenser's collection was fitted to the diachronic and to the synchronic roles of elegy. Diachronically, it joined English verse to an ancient tradition, and enabled its followers and imitators in their turn to participate in that tradition. Synchronically, it expressed an idea of community (again through imitation of ancient models) which was to make the funeral anthology a vehicle for demonstrations of political, literary, familial, religious, and other shared interests. Further, there is a sense in which the generic variety of the anthology—with allegories, dirges, epitaphs, narratives, and so forth—could answer some of the major requirements of elegy better or more comprehensively than other contemporary forms. Such variety also carried an obvious panegyric implication, that the subject was so remarkable that no single form could do justice to it, and, indeed, that the more diverse an anthology, the more compendious the excellence of the subject.[90] In Chapter 4 I hope to show that it is not absurd to argue, on the basis of such reflection, that Donne's *Anniversaries* owes much more to Spenser's performance in *Astrophel* than has conventionally been supposed.

[88] See R. Helgerson, *Self-Crowned Laureates: Spenser, Jonson and the Literary System* (Berkeley, 1983), also D. Miller, 'Spenser's Vocation, Spenser's Career', *ELH* 50 (1983), 197–231, and J. Loewenstein, 'Echo's Ring: Orpheus and Spenser's Career', *ELR* 16 (1986), 287–302.

[89] Joan Grundy suggests that Spenserian pastoral 'delights . . . principally through its fiction' (*The Spenserian Poets* (1969), 94: see more generally pp. 82–93).

[90] There is an obvious analogy with the variety that came increasingly to be prized in erotic verse; in each case, the more various and diversely inventive the speaker's eloquence, the more authentic the sentiment behind it: the truer the poetry, as it were, the more it feigned.

3. ELEGIES ON SIDNEY (1586) AND ON QUEEN ELIZABETH (1603)

'The habit of elegy', claims Pigman, 'pervades Renaissance culture'.[1] To move from the poems of Spenser and Sidney to consider the response of elegists to two major public events—the death of Sidney in 1586 and of Queen Elizabeth in 1603—is to observe the period which demonstrates the aptness of such a remark. Elegy ceased to be the exclusive preserve of versifying chroniclers, and became instead a genre in which any writer could aspire to perform. Although Sidney died long before his own writings could have any influence beyond the tiny circle of those who knew him well, and although the political constraints of lamenting a monarch at the very moment of her successor's arrival from a foreign country presented challenges which may writers opted to avoid, it will nevertheless, I hope, become evident in the course of this chapter that the range, ambition, and focus of elegy were changing. The Tudor modes gradually became unequal to the task: they came to seem inadequate both as a medium for rehearsing the excellences of the subject and for considering, anatomizing, consoling the grief of the speaker.

The story of Sidney's reputation and cult is lengthy and complex.[2] His image at the time of his death and burial was of a national hero, a Christian soldier and patron.[3] The publication of his literary works in the 1590s led to a substantial modification of that image, and the conjunction of the religious, political, and literary values he was held to represent turned him into a figure who could be invoked as an authority, a privileged ideal, in political

---

[1] Pigman, *Grief and English Renaissance Elegy*, 43.

[2] See J. Buxton, *Sir Philip Sidney and the English Renaissance* (3rd edn., 1988), chs. 6 and 7; R. A. Lanham, 'Sidney: The Ornament of his Age', *Southern Review* (Adelaide), 2 (1967), 319–40; A. Hager, 'The Exemplary Mirage: Fabrication of Sir Philip Sidney's Biographical Image and the Sidney Reader', in Kay, ed., *Sir Philip Sidney*, 45–60.

[3] See the following articles in J. Van Dorsten, D. Baker-Smith, and A. F. Kinney, eds., *Sir Philip Sidney: 1586 and the Creation of a Legend* (Leiden, 1986); W. A. Ringler, 'The Myth and the Man', 3–16; S. Bos, M. Lange-Meifers, and J. Six, 'Sidney's Funeral Portrayed', 38–61; J. Gouws, 'Fact and Anecdote in Fulke Greville's Account of Sidney's Last Days', 62–82; J. Boswell and H. R. Woudhuysen, 'Some Unfamiliar Sidney Allusions', 221–37.

discourse for the best part of a century.[4] The cult of Queen Elizabeth was more elaborate, more complex, and perhaps more deliberately manufactured than Sidney's.[5] And, like Sidney, she came to be a focus for nostalgia and thence disaffection and satire within a few years of James's accession.[6] But this present chapter is primarily concerned with poems written close to the time of death, and with the way in which each event can be related generally to the history of the elegy.

'UNTO HIS FAMOUS LIFE AND DEATH A MARCIALL VALE' —ELEGIES ON SIDNEY

Sidney's lavish and spectacular funeral, of which a pictorial record survives on a scroll executed by Thomas Lant with engravings by de Brij, celebrated a man who 'in the cause of his god and true religion, and for the honour of his Prince and countrey, spared not to spend his blud'. Sidney was mourned as a Protestant champion, as a representative of a cause, more than as an individual.[7] His

---

[4] See my 'Sidney: A Critical Heritage', in Kay, *Sir Philip Sidney*, 3–41; and V. Skretkowicz's Introduction to his edn. of *The Countess of Pembroke's Arcadia (The New Arcadia)* (Oxford, 1987), pp. xliii–lii.

[5] P. Williams, *The Tudor Regime* (Oxford, 1979), ch. 11; S. Greenblatt, 'Invisible Bullets: Renaissance Authority and its Subversion', *Glyph*, 8 (1981), 20–61 (revised in his *Shakespearian Negotiations* (Oxford, 1988), 21–65); see also the standard accounts of the Elizabethan cult, notably E. C. Wilson, *England's Eliza* (Cambridge, Mass., 1939); D. Bergeron, *English Civic Pageantry, 1558–1642* (1971); R. Strong, *The Cult of Elizabeth* (1977); M. Axton, *The Queen's Two Bodies* (1977), as well as the important articles by L. A. Montrose, notably '"Eliza, Queene of Shepheards" and the Pastoral of Power', *ELR* 10 (1980), 153–82, and '"Shaping Fantasies": Figurations of Gender and Power in Elizabethan Culture', in S. Greenblatt, ed., *Representing the English Renaissance* (Berkeley, 1988), 31–64, and his full-length study, *In Mirrors More Than One: Elizabeth I and the Figurations of Power* (Chicago, forthcoming).

[6] For two recent accounts, see A. Barton, 'Harking back to Elizabeth: Ben Jonson and Caroline Nostalgia', *ELH* 48 (1981), 701–31 (also her *Ben Jonson: Dramatist* (Cambridge, 1984), 300–20), and K. Sharpe, *Criticism and Compliment* (Cambridge, 1987), 16–19. See also Chs. 5 and 6 below.

[7] Thomas Lant, *Sequitur celebritas & pompa funeris* (1587). John Aubrey was to recall seeing Lant's roll in Gloucester at the house of an alderman, who had 'contrived it to be turned upon two pinnes, that turning one of them made the figures march all in order' (*Brief Lives*, ed. A. Clark, 2 vols. (Oxford, 1898), ii, 247). The only comparable record of a non-royal funeral is the funeral portrait (possibly executed by a herald) of Sir Henry Unton (see R. Strong, *The Cult of Elizabeth* (1977), 84–110). In addition, Unton was, like Sidney (at whose side he had fought at Zutphen), the subject of a University funeral anthology, *Funebria nobilissimi equitis D. H. Untoni . . . etc.* (Oxford, 1596), which is

funeral seems to have been arranged at least in part to help maintain public order in the midst of the controversy surrounding the execution of Mary Queen of Scots.[8] And much of the commemorative literature concentrates on Sidney as a public figure: balladeers, for example, rushed to celebrate the dead hero, and presumably did so by rehearsing his ancestry and valiant deeds.[9] The three University anthologies mourn Sidney chiefly as an exemplary knight and as a patron.[10]

The public verse that survives, as might be expected, represents a continuation of the Tudor mode. The poems of Churchyard and Whetstone are of this kind, as already noted; so also with John Phillips, the Puritan writer of broadsheet laments and ballads.[11] Phillips, whose works include a *Balad intituled a cold pye for the papistes* (1571), follows the example of Whetstone (and *A Mirror for Magistrates*) by having Sidney address the audience of 'noble *Brutes*' on the lessons of his martyrdom: ('First God I sought in spirit and

'peppered with references to Sidney and his works': J. Boswell and H. Woudhuysen, 'Some Unfamiliar Sidney Allusions', in Van Dorsten, Baker-Smith, and Kinney, *Sir Philip Sidney*, 227.

[8] Sidney was buried on 16 Feb. 1587: Mary Queen of Scots had been beheaded 8 days earlier. See A. Hager, 'The Exemplary Mirage', in Kay, *Sir Philip Sidney*, 53–4.

[9] The Stationers' Register records the following: *SIR PHILLIP SIDNEYs Epytaphe that was of late Lord Gouernour of Fflushynge* (28 Nov.): *SIR WILLIAM HERBERTes SYDNEY* (16 Jan.); *The Life death and order of the funeralls of Sir PHILLIP SYDNEY knight deceased* (22 Feb.); 'a ballad of *the buriall of Sir PHILLIP SYDNEY*' (27 Feb.). *The sorrowfull sobbs and sighes of England* (8 Mar.) may be another lost piece on Sidney.

[10] The Renaissance funeral anthology in England seems to have been a phenomenon associated initially with Cambridge, although the fashion spread. The earliest examples are Thomas Wilson's *Vita et obitus duorum fratrum Suffolciensium, Henrici et Caroli Brandoni*, a collection on the death of Bucer, *De obitu . . . Martini Buceri . . . Epistolae duae* (1551), and Robert Dallington's *A booke of epitaphes made vpon the death of Sir W. Buttes* (1583 or 1584). The three Sidney vols. were edited by Alexander Neville (*Academiae cantabrigiensis lacrymae* (1587)), by John Lloyd (*Peplus* (Oxford, 1587)) and by William Gager (*Exequiae illustrissimi viri D. Philippi Sidneaei . . . etc.* (1587)). Texts may be consulted in A. J. Colaianne and W. L. Godshalk, eds., *Elegies for Sir Philip Sidney (1587)* (Delmar, 1980). There are some refs. to Sidney's writing: for a list see Kay, *Sir Philip Sidney*, 6. For some recent studies see J. W. Binns, 'William Gager on the Death of Sir Philip Sidney', *Humanistica Lovaniensia*, 21 (1972), 221–38; Norbrook, *Poetry and Politics*, 61–2; Pigman, *Grief and English Renaissance Elegy*, 52–9, 143–5; D. Baker-Smith, 'Great Expectations: Sidney's Death and the Poets', in Van Dorsten, Baker-Smith, and Kinney, *Sir Philip Sidney*, 83–103.

[11] John Phillips, *The life and death of Sir Philip Sidney* (1587). Phillips praises his subject for being 'to the learned liberall, to Sutors a great comfort', a point that was presumably aimed towards the Earl of Essex, the volume's dedicatee (who had also received the dedication of Phillips's *A sommon to repentance* (1584)). There is a brief account of Phillips's career and publications in the *DNB*.

truth to serue, | On him alone my hope and trust was set' (A3^v)).[12]
There is a lengthy diatribe against Spain and 'Incestuous Rome'
(A4^r) before the speaker, having described his own death and
funeral (the volume was entered on 22 February), takes his leave of
the mourners: 'Thus from my graue I bid you all adew . . . My tale
is tould, and I my race haue runne, | My bodie earth, my soule the
heauens hath wonne' (B4^v).

The title of Phillips's piece classes it with his poems on Lady
Margaret Douglas and on Sir Christopher Hatton: like Whetstone's
'remembrances' such works are typical of the mid-century elegy.[13]
Even Richard Barnfield, a sonneteer with a distinctive voice,
produced an utterly conventional, heraldic lament:

That *England* lost, that learning lou'd, that euery mouth commended,
That fame did prayse, that Prince did rayse, that Countrey so defended
Here lyes the man: lyke to the Swan, who knowing shee shall die,
Doeth tune her voice vnto the Sphaeres, and scornes Mortalitie.
Two worthie Earles his vncles were: a Lady was his Mother;
A Knight his father; and himselfe a noble Countesse Brother.
Belou'd, bewaild; aliue, now dead, of all, with Teares for euer;
Here lyes *Sir Philip Sidneis* corps, whom cruell Death did seuer.
He liv'd for her, hee dyde for her; for whom he dyde, he liued:
O graunt (O God) that wee of her, may neuer bee depriud.[14]

Like Whetstone, Angel Day claimed a degree of acquaintance with
Sidney, and with his writings.[15] He also modestly asserted his
inadequacy to do justice to his subject in a work 'which vpon a
sodain I haue penned, more answerable to mine owne good
intendment, then to the weight of his excellencies', and whose
theme is to be Sidney's 'Nobility, valour and worthiness' (A2^r).[16]

---

[12]In the dedication, Phillips had written, 'This Phenix sweet Sidney was the flower of
curtesie, who in his life time gaue a perfect light in his conversation to leade men to
virtue, the fruits whereof so glistered in the eies of mortall creatures; that by his example
they might both learne to feare God, to glory in sincerity, to abound in loyalty, and to
become carefull louers of their naytiue contrie' (A2^r).

[13] *A commemoration of the Ladye Margrit Duglasis good grace* (1578); *Vt hora, sic fugit vita;
a commemoration of Sir C. Hatton* (1591).

[14] Richard Barnfield, *Poems in diuers humours* (1598), E4^r.

[15] See Jean Robertson's introduction to her edn. of *The Old Arcadia*, p. xxxix, and D.
Kay, 'Sidney: A Critical Heritage', in *Sir Philip Sidney*, 6–7.

[16] Angel Day, *Vpon the life and death of Sir Phillip Sidney* (1587). The poem draws
upon the prescriptions for epideictic and consolatory writing published in his *The English
secretorie* (1586), 55–72, 200–21. It is dedicated to Walsingham, Sidney's father-in-law.

Sidney is praised in terms drawn from erotic verse and royal panegyric: he had been

> The very worke of all the *Muses* nine:
> The care of earth and skies, in one self twine,
> The rarest Tipe of courtly gentlenes:
> Adorned erst with them of noblenes.[17]   (A3^{r-v})

On the evidence of the two poems he wrote on Sidney, one an 'epitaph' which survives only in manuscript, the other a longer elegy printed in *Brittons bowre of delights* (1591), Nicholas Breton was classed by C. S. Lewis as a writer 'on the turn' from 'drab' to 'golden'.[18] There is no doubt that the speakers of the poems appear to claim a degree of intimate acquaintance with the subject which is unusual in Tudor verse ('My loue my lyfe my deare is deade'); and in the unpublished epitaph the loss is additionally presented in an approximation of Sidney's style:

> When he liued then I loued
> But my loue from lyfe remoued
> And dispayre discomforte geauinge
> What is this buy dyinge lyuinge.
> Livinge deathe, a sorrow suche
> Neuer creture knewe so muche.[19]

Both poems illustrate the amateur/professional tensions that frequently surface in Breton's work. In the shorter, private, piece, for example, Sidney is praised as a compendium, 'Reason, sence and learnings sweetinge | where the muses had their metinge'; in the longer, more public elegy, we learn that Sidney's 'onely ioy was honour of the fielde, | To conquere man, and make the captaines yeelde'.[20] As a fellow practitioner, Breton is perhaps surprisingly reticent about Sidney's art: his elegy resembles the sententiousness

---

[17] B. Lewalski points out that the topic of comprehensiveness was, at least as far as published texts were concerned, more common in royal panegyrics and elegies in the period before Donne's *Anniversaries* (see her *Donne's 'Anniversaries' and the Poetry of Praise* (Princeton, 1973), 19–38). Daniel, addressing Sidney's 'Angell Spirit', called him 'Compleat in all' (*The whole workes of S. Daniel Esquire in poetrie* (1623), M8^r).

[18] Lewis, *English Literature in the Sixteenth Century*, 480–1.

[19] Bodley MS Rawl. Poet. 85, fo. 26^v. See *Poems by Nicholas Breton (not hitherto reprinted)*, ed. J. M. Robertson (Liverpool, 1952), xxiv–xxv. Breton's main model is the Tenth Song of *Astrophil and Stella*, but he borrows from other Sidney pieces.

[20] *Brittons bowre of delights* (1591), A2^v.

of Ralegh's epitaph rather than the pastoral fiction of *Astrophel*.[21]
Indeed, an apparent delight in antithesis, paradox, and oxymoron
tends to invest each stanza with conclusions of epigrammatic
finality:

> To liue in death is but a dying life,
> To die in life, is but a liuing death . . .   (A2ʳ)
>
> I liue, oh liue, alas, I liue indeed,
> But such a life was neuer such a death.[22]   (A3ʳ)

Rather closer to *Astrophel*, both in organization and accomplish-
ment, is Francis Davison's *A Poetical Rapsody* (1602).[23] The volume
contains, for instance, an eclogue 'made long since upon the death
of Sir Philip Sidney', which is crammed with reminiscences of
Nouember and *Aprill*. When Thenot asks Perin why he is mourning,
he replies

> See how the flowrets of the field do spring,
> The Purple Rose, the lily white as Snow,
> With smell and colour for an Harvest King,
> May serue to make vs yong againe, I trow.
> Yet all this pride is quickly laid full low,
>> Soon as the root is nipt with northerne cold,
>> What smell, or beauty, can we then behold?   (i.36)

Perin and Thenot (in what would have seemed an unusual seven-
line stanza) debate which of them is fitter to perform an elegy: but
both recognize that the example of Colin Clout demonstrates the
meanness of the material reward they might expect—'Praise is the
greatest prize that Poets gaine, | A simple gaine that feeds them
ne're a wit' (i. 38). Eventually they decide that Thenot will play his
pipe to accompany Perin's performance of a 'sorry fit' composed
by Cuddy.[24] In a dozen twelve-line stanzas (loosely based on the
stanza of *Nouember*), Perin laments Willy (Sidney) primarily as a
shepherd-poet ('How often hath his skill in pleasant song | Drawn
al the water-nimphs from out their bowers . . . The learned Muses

---

[21] There are however a few neo-Spenserian passages: 'The trees are blasted, and the leaues do wither, | The daintie greene is turnde to duskie gray, | The gallant Uines are shrunke and gone togither, | And all the flowers doo fade and fall away' (B1ᵛ).

[22] There is also a text of this poem in Rawl. Poet. 85, entitled 'Amoris Lachrimae on the death of Sir P. Sidneye' fos. 27ʳ–34ᵛ.

[23] Refs. will be to the edn. *A Poetical Rapsody 1602–21*, ed. H. E. Rollins, 2 vols. (Cambridge, Mass., 1931).

[24] There is a text in MS Rawl. Poet. 85 ascribed to 'incertus author' (fos. 93ᵛ–98ʳ).

flockt to heare his skill, | And quite forgot their water, wood, and mount' (i. 40)), whose loss prompts reflections on the decline of the world, and on the way art is both powerless and unrewarded:

> Vnhappy skill, what good is got thereby,
> But painted praise that can no profite bring?
> If Skill could moue the Sisters three,
> Our *Willy* still aliue should be.   (i. 42)

Unlike *Nouember*, the elegy offers no vision of consolation: poetic immortality is merely hinted at, and the most the mourners can offer in the face of a hostile and degenerate world is the resolution to 'waile' their lost friend 'yeere by yeere' (i. 43). This bleak pastoral is followed by a group of four poems (attributed, like the preceding text, to 'A.W.') in classical metres on Sidney's death.[25] In the first, the poet notes that, by lamenting Sidney in the lasting marble of Latin and Greek, Cambridge had created an enduring 'Altar' for him. Following their example, he proclaims that he

> Wil make thy memory famous in after ages,
> And in these measured verses thy glory be founded,
> So be thy holy fauor, help to my holy fury.   (i. 189)

In the following piece, the author's expressed desire to render his commonplaces impervious to the ravages of time is augmented by a simple numerological conceit, where the poem's overall length of nine lines appears to underscore the reference to the Muses—'He liues eternall, with endlesse Glorie bedecked: | Yea still on earth hee liues, and still shall liue by the Muses' (i. 190). The speaker of the third poem adopts a tone of easy familiarity with the Muses, and feigns surprise that they should have abandoned their usual habitat for England; the reason being given to him, his jaunty manner evaporates and he rushes to join them:

> Ay mee! Alas, now I know the cause, now seeke I no further,
> Heere lies their glory, their hope, their onely reioycing.
> Dead lies worthy *Philip*, the care and praise of *Apollo*,
> Dead lies his carcase, but fame shall liue to the worldes end.[26]   (i. 191)

---

[25] There is a brief note of the poems in D. Attridge, *Well-Weighed Syllables: Elizabethan Verse in Classical Metres* (Cambridge, 1974), 207.

[26] Some passages in the poem read like text-book exercises in quantitative writing: 'Germany, France, Italy, Spaine, Denmark, Persia, Turkey, | India where Phoebus climes from the sea to the skie-ward, | India where Phoebus declines from skie to the sea-ward, | Tartary, Pole, Lettow, Muscouy, Bohemia, Norway' (i. 193).

The final poem in the group is thematically identical, and is perhaps chiefly notable for its Horatian tag, 'Dignum laude virum Musa vetat mori' (The Muse forbids a praiseworthy man to die. *Carmina*, IV. viii. 8), which it shares with the Oxford anthology *Peplus*[27] Although the phrase was not uncommon in such contexts, it is tempting to consider the poems in the *Rapsody* as being in some sense vernacular equivalents of the University elegies. After all, the second edition of the Cambridge anthology on Prince Henry in 1613 was to include a group of vernacular poems, and an English sonnet by King James VI of Scotland heads the Cambridge volume on Sidney.[28] In addition, the *Rapsody* pieces may be held to cohere sufficiently as a group to be considered as a sequence, although there is a marked contrast with the *Astrophel* collection in the relation of the pastoral elegy to the rest of the pieces; where Spenser's fiction embraces the other poems, and places them in a broadly consolatory context, the *Rapsody* elegy offers no consolation while the later poems blithely assert Sidney's achieved poetic immortality.

In 1593, Spenser's most notable follower, Michael Drayton, inaugurated his career with the publication of a pastoral anthology, *Idea: The Shepheards Garland*, subtitled 'Rowlands sacrifice to the nine Muses'. At every turn the volume invites comparison with *The Shepheardes Calender*, and there could have been little doubt in the minds of readers that Drayton was declaring his laureate, epic ambition, or that he was locating himself precisely within a particular tradition.[29] The fourth 'Eglog' is a lament for Elphin (Sidney), who had been for shepherds

> God of inuention, *Ioues* deare *Mercury*,
>   Ioy of our Lawrell, pride of all our ioy:
> The essence of all Poets diuinitie,
>   Spirit of *Orpheus: Pallas* louely boy.   (D4ʳ)

The reference to Orpheus claims kinship for Sidney (and through him Drayton) with the most ancient, semi-divine poetry, thereby

[27] The Horatian line may also be found on the title-page of Gabriel Harvey's *Smithus, vel musarum lachrymae pro obitu T. Smithi, equitis Britanni* (1578), and on that of the vol. of elegies on the death of Lord Hastings, *Lachrymae Musarum* (1649).

[28] For an account of the rise of the vernacular in University anthologies, see pp. 148–50 below.

[29] J. Grundy, *The Spenserian Poets* (1969), 74; see D. Norbrook, *Poetry and Politics*, 195–201, 207–9, etc., for connections between the political and artistic values and aspirations of the Spenserians.

extending the tradition invoked and celebrated in the poem beyond
Spenser, Virgil, and Theocritus. The characteristically Sidneian
figure of *climax* or *gradatio* is imitated. Astrophil is perhaps to be
recalled as the shepherds exchange hyperbolic expressions of
inconsolable grief:

> But all my words shalbe dissolu'd to teares,
> And my tears fountaines shall to riuers grow:
> These Riuers to the floods of my dispaires,
> And these shall make an Ocean of my woe.   (D4ʳ)

Consolation, when it arrives, is offered by Gorbo in the shape of a
'song of learned *Rowlands* making'. Drayton, in his pastoral
persona, produces an explicit recollection of what William Webbe
had called a 'verie tragicall mournefull measure' (see above, Ch. 2):

> *Melpomine* put on thy mourning Gaberdine,
> And set thy song Vnto the doleful Base,
> And with thy sable vayle shadow thy face,
>> with weeping verse,
>> attend his hearse,
> Whose blessed soule the heauens doe now enshrine.   (D4ᵛ)

Spenser's 'Kentish downes' are developed into full-blown pastoral
verisimilitude, prefiguring Drayton's abiding preoccupation with
the substance and fabric of English life and of the land itself.[30]
Shepherds play on rustic instruments, and in the eighth stanza
Rowland exhorts the mourning girls in English rather than
Arcadian terms:

> Come, Girles, and with Carnations decke his graue,
> With damaske Roses and the hyacynt:
> Come with sweete William, Marioram and Mynt,
>> with precious Balmes,
>> with hymnes and psalmes.
> This funerall deserues no lesse at all to haue.   (E1ᵛ)

The abrupt transition from lament to consolation, which occurs after
the sixth stanza, generates a 6:3 disposition of stanzas, miming the 2:1
harmony of the *diapason*, and implying thereby an underlying

---

[30] See R. Helgerson's important study, 'The Land Speaks: Cartography, Choro-
graphy, and Subversion in Renaissance England', *Representations*, 16 (1986), 51–85,
repr. in *Representing the English Renaissance*, 326–61; also Patterson, *Pastoral and Ideology*,
133–5.

pattern and meaning in the subject's life and death. In addition, Sidney is held to have escaped from mortality in two ways. First, wholly conventionally, his writings have ensured the permanence of his reputation:

> . . . Though thou hence be gone,
> In spight of death yet shalt thou liue for aye,
> Thy Poesie is Garlanded with Baye:
>> and still shall blaze
>> thy lasting prayse: (E1ᵛ)

In addition, as so often in pastoral, the mourned figure is asserted to be still a member of the pastoral community: although Rowland's life is presented as harsh, he is able, through the performance of the obsequies, and through maintaining the status of Sidney's art, to lay claim to fellowship with him. The heavenly apotheosis is expressed in emphatically pastoral terms:

> But see where *Elphin* sits in fayre Elizia,
> Feeding his flocke on yonder heauenly playne,
> Come and behold, you louely shepheards swayne,
>> piping his fill,
>> on yonder hill,
> Tasting sweete *Nectar*, and Ambrosia.   (E1ᵛ)

Even in heaven Elphin's life parallels Rowland's: he tends sheep, for example, and plays his pipe. Pastoral becomes by implication an ideal and potentially heavenly mode of existence (and thus of writing): through imitation and reiteration (whether of ceremonies, words, pastimes, or employment), those who are alive may both praise their distinguished predecessors and claim kinship with them.[31] And such reflections appear in the context of Drayton's youthful self-presentation as a disciple of Sidney and Spenser, as one who aspired to attain their standing through studious imitation of their art and diligent preservation of their values. But when Drayton came to revise the poem for his *Eglogs* of 1606, the optimistic resolution was purged: nostalgia had edged into satire.

---

[31] Thomas Watson's *Meliboeus* (1590), tr. by himself into English as *An eclogue vpon the death of Sir F. Walsingham* (1590), includes a vision of Sidney and his father-in-law soaring 'aboue the Sun' (C2ᵛ). Watson helpfully provides a key to his fiction: 'I figure England in *Arcadia*; Her Maiestie in *Diana*; Sir Francis Walsingham in *Meliboeus*, and his ladie in *Dryas*, Sir Phillipe Sidney in *Astrophill* and his Ladie in *Hyale*; Master Thomas Walsingham in *Tyterus*, and my selfe in *Coridon*'.

Specific references to the Drayton/Spenser/Sidney relationships are reduced in number and made less central. Sidney's death is presented as the passing of a golden age.[32] By 1606, as Joan Grundy observed, 'The idea of the shepherd . . . became virtually synonymous . . . with the old Elizabethan type of poet', and Drayton now records a decline since Sidney's day:

> when his fayr flocks he fed vpon the downs,
> the poorest shepheard suffered not anoy,
> now are we subject to the beastly clowns
> that all our mirth would vtterly destroy. . . .
>
> The groues, the mountains, and the pleasant heath,
> that wonted were with Roundelaies to ring
> Are blasted now with the cold northern breath
> that not a sheephard takes delight to sing.[33]

The established metaphorical connection between the pastoral life and the poetic vocation, transforming a company of swains into a community (whose scope was diachronic as well as contemporary) of like-minded poets, was strengthened by adversity, by external pressures. We may see the influence of the *Astrophel* anthology just as much as of *The Shepheardes Calender*, most particularly in the extraordinary spate of collaborative volumes such as *The shepherds pipe* (1614) and *The shepherds hunting* (1615). And Drayton came in the end to be seen as a personal link with a more heroic age, possessed of a voice that might rouse those who now regarded themselves as his followers. William Browne, in his commendatory poem to the 1622 addition to *Poly-Olbion*, wrote

> . . . All met not death
> When we entombed our dear Elizabeth.
> Immortal Sidney, honored Colin Clout,
> Presaging what we feel, went timely out.
> Then why lives Drayton when the times refuse
> Both means to live and matter for a muse?
> Only without excuse to leave us quite,
> And tell us, durst we act, he durst to write.[34]

---

[32] See Grundy, *Spenserian Poets*, 78–9, 94–8; Rosenmeyer, *The Green Cabinet*, 221, 229–30; Drayton, *Works*, v. 183 ff.

[33] Grundy, *Spenserian Poets*, 78; see also Ch. 6 below and R. F. Hardin, *Michael Drayton and the Passing of Elizabethan England* (Lawrence, 1973). Text from Drayton, *Poemes lyrick and pastorall* (1606), sigs. E8ᵛ, F1ʳ.

[34] Drayton, *Works*, ii. 393.

In the writings of Spenser, Drayton, and, to a much lesser extent, Breton, poetic responses to the death of Sidney mark a turning point in the history of the elegy. As has been indicated, most of the elegists were, for obvious reasons, unreconstructed practitioners of the Tudor mode, whose focus was exclusively on the public person of their subject, and whose work was frequently an undisguised appeal for patronage.[35] But Spenser's example had begun to attract followers, and they had effectively, even if on a small scale, inaugurated the fashion for elegy as a form within which praise could coexist with reflections on artistic tradition, on innovation and imitation, and through which issues could be explored that were at root cultural and political.

LUNA'S EXTINCT: ELEGIES ON THE DEATH OF QUEEN ELIZABETH

> But now, oh now, our mourning weedes are on,
> And many thousand blacks for her are borne:
> Which do demonstrate that *Eliza's* gone,
> For whose vntimely losse so many morne.
>   What these sad mourners are, good reader see:
>   And seeing reade, and reading, weepe with me.[36]

Michael Drayton, looking back in 1621 at the censure he had incurred for rushing to praise the new king in 1603, contrasted the shipwrack caused by his own forward pen with the pusillanimity he perceived in his contemporaries. To George Sandys he wrote that 'cowardyse had tyed up every tongue, | And all stood silent'.[37] It might be argued that the first part of Drayton's observation is as important as the second, and somewhat more accurate, for while a significant number of poets did write on the Queen's death (admittedly many fewer than had mourned Sidney or would mourn Prince Henry), every mourning tongue was 'tyed up', restrained by

---

[35] See Pigman, *Grief and English Renaissance Elegy*, 44, 141. A spectacular example is Nathaniel Baxter's *Sir Philip Sidney's Ouránia, that is Endimions song and tragedie*, which ('containing all Philosophie') has been described as a 'curious, discursive . . . hotch-potch' (Buxton, *Sidney*, 40). Endimion (Baxter) is reassured thus by Cynthia (The Countess of Pembroke): 'Cast feare away, Ile be thy Patronesse' (B4ᵛ). Then he embarks on an allegorical piece that is 'A subject fit for *Sydneyes* eloquence, | High *Chaucers* vaine, and Spensers influence' (C1ʳ).

[36] *Expicedium* (1603), B4ʳ.   [37] Drayton, *Works*, iii. 206.

the exigencies of a difficult, politically sensitive subject. Related to this point is the fact that the vernacular elegy was still a novel form, and that there were very few models for poets to follow in the spring of 1603.

The public mode of Churchyard and Whetstone still persisted, of course, and the nature of the subject would doubtless have seemed wholly appropriate to such stiffly formal treatment. The most Whetstonian of these 'remembrances' is Anthony Nixon's *Elizaes memoriall: King James his arrivall, and Romes downefall*; in it the three chief achievements of the Queen's reign are identified as the propagation of the word of God (sig. A4^r), the long peace (B1^r), and the 'plentie' of all things. Taken together, Nixon argues, they illustrate the truth of the familiar tag that 'Virtus post funera vivit' (B4^v). In the verse preface directed to his patron's widow, Nixon proposes the elegy as a demonstration of his accomplishment, reluctantly undertaken in the absence of a happier subject. Certainly what he wrote has the air of a dutiful exercise:

> This Virgin-Queene did rule fair Albion
> Twise two & twentie yeares, with great encrease
> Of peace, ioy, wealth, much honour & renowne,
> And then resigned vp her soule in peace,
> To him that gaue it an immortall crowne,
> In spite of thousands ten conspiracies
> Which Antichrist against her did deuise.   (C1^r)

The fiction of the poem is that it is an oration delivered as a prelude to funeral rites at the Queen's hearse: as such it firmly associates itself with the funeral ceremonies, and recalls those fifteenth-century political laments which were affixed as bills.[38] Like such poems, Nixon's is primarily an historical narrative and catalogue of the benefits of Elizabeth's reign.

Elsewhere, elements of the Whetstonian tradition are presented in ways that indicate some recognition of poetic fashion, and manifest some aspects of the interaction of literary and political values. An example is *The Lamentation of Melpomene, for the death of Belphaebe our late queene*, by T.W., where the traditional emphasis on narrative is given a modish Spenserian gloss. The author opens by admitting the impossibility of pleasing all readers:

---

[38] See Woolf, *English Religious Lyric*, 78, and Scattergood, *Politics and Poetry in the Fifteenth Century*, 22–33.

So diuers is the mindes of men: some will have this, some that:
Some verse, some prose: & some againe, wold haue they know not what.
Therefore I care not who finde fault, let who list laugh and scoffe:
Let him that likes it, reed the same: he that dislikes, looke off.

(Aii^r)

At one level these words can be understood as a version—of sorts—of the conventional strategies for establishing a community of mourners. But it should be noted that the test for membership of the group is aesthetic, and that the poet anticipates hostility.[39] We will see in later chapters that such combative exclusiveness was to become a staple of the elegist's persona within a few years of the Queen's death. Implicit in this development is the recognition that the certainty displayed by Whetstone and Churchyard in handling the genres in which they declared themselves to be writing is no longer available to elegists. The decorums of the Tudor elegy as understood by an earlier generation were clearly coming to seem inadequate to the task of dealing with an event whose meaning was extending beyond the merely narrative or ceremonial.[40] In this changed environment, the elegist was to become a rhetor, no longer simply a chronicler.

T.W.'s simple poem falls into two parts. In the first, Melpomene laments (Aiii^r) the death of the Queen (which is left for Fame to narrate), bewails the changed state of the world, and collapses into a swoon, crying 'Die hart with sorrow and eternall paine, | Vnless *Belphaebe* do reuiue againe' (Biii^r). At this point the poet himself takes up the narrative, relating how the Muses, having sent Terpsichore to cheer Melpomene, form themselves into a chorus and console their desolate colleague thus:

> . . . know, the Fates haue seated in her place,
> Though not a Woman, yet of heauenly race,
> A goodly KING, to be earthes Soueraigne:
> Which Iustice, Peace, and Vertue, will maintaine.   (Biii^v)

The poem thus concludes with the Muses 'Spending the time in wanton meriment', having won the recalcitrant melancholic Melpomene round to their perception of events. It represents, in

---

[39] There are obvious parallels with Spenser, most notably the Proem to Bk. IV, and last lines of Bk. VI, canto xii, of *The Faerie Queene*.

[40] See A. F. Marotti, *John Donne, Coterie Poet* (Madison, 1986), 178–83; more generally, N. K. Farmer, 'A Theory of Genre for the Seventeenth Century', *Genre* 3 (1970), 293–317.

its clumsy fashion, mourning and consolation displaced to an allegorical level, and shows Elizabeth depicted in death in terms of the fictions in which she had been expressed when alive. It draws attention to the personality of mourners (the poet and Melpomene), distinguishing them from the Muses as a whole and from those whose business is narrative or historical. As Spenser and Sidney had done, the poet locates the 'nature reversed' trope within the disordered consciousness of the grief-stricken speaker. In both aspects the influence of Spenser is observable, although the verse itself is stilted and crammed with commonplaces ('Her body was a Temple, where did raigne, | The true tipe of a vertuous sueraigne' (B1ʳ)).

As had been the case with Whetstone and Churchyard, the poets who wrote on Elizabeth's death rarely shunned such commonplace, and they seem to have shared their predecessors' ambition to be sententious and (therefore) memorable. The requirement to couple lament with praise of the new king seems merely to have given them more encouragement. Thus Robert Pricket: 'The Autums paste, now comes the springe, | The Queene God hath, God saue the king'.[41] A work that is in many ways typical is Robert Fletcher's *Brief and familiar epistle* (1603), which, we are told, was inspired by the example of Pricket's poem. The writer explains that he 'could not chuse but imitate, and therefore haue written a briefe Epistle to the vulgar, touching his Maiesties title. Secondly a meane Epitaph for her late Maiestie. Thirdly a fewe verses of reioycing after sorrow: And lastly, a prayer for the King, the Queene, and their children . . .' (A2ᵛ). Fletcher's 'Epitaph or briefe Lamentation' consists of seven six-line (ababcc) stanzas and opens with a neo-Spenserian flourish:

> Bewaile our greatest and most greeuous losse,
>   all mortall wights that on the earth do tread:
> Your honour, glory, beauty, turnde to drosse,
>   your wealth, your peace, your plentie, lapt in lead. (B1ʳ)

The poem brims over with elegiac clichés. We learn that Elizabeth had been 'a Flower in youth, | a *Iuno, Pallas, Venus*, in her age', and

---

[41] Robert Pricket, *A souldiers wish unto his soveraigne Lord king James* (1603), sig. C4ᵛ. Pricket's vol. was entered on 3 Apr. 1603; a prose work dedicated to James, *A souldiors resolution*, appeared shortly afterwards; in the following year he eventually published his commemoration of the Earl of Essex, *Honors fame in triumph riding*.

that death had 'turn'd her from the Stage'. The Muses, Apollo, Minerva, and all poets are summoned to lament: 'All Poets now, bring each a golden Pen, | and beautifie her hearce, each in his turne' (B1ʳ). The poem's most urgent message, that the Queen's final and most dazzling act of political brilliance had been to delay naming her successor until the moment of death, is fittingly saved for the last stanza:[42]

> O mirror then of Maiestie and power,
>   of wisdome and of woman-hood the best:
> That could conceele vntill her latest hower,
>   that we in her succession should be blest.
>   O Iewell rare, O Iem of greatest price,
>   Thy soule (with God) possesseth paradise. (B1ᵛ)

The poem, addressed like the rest of the volume 'to the vulgar', evidently participates in the attempt to establish in the popular mind the new king's legitimacy. As such, it admits of no uncertainty, and leads naturally into a group of mechanically antithetical verses whose unvarying inevitability seems designed to invest the succession with the inexorability of the movements of the seasons and the heavenly bodies:

> Our *Cynthia* in the euening set   **The**
> or after mid night tooke her rest: **Queene.**
> Dan *Phoebus* straight did not forget   **The**
>   to thinke his mansion must be blest.   **King.**   (B2ʳ)

The eloquent prayer that ends the volume includes a petition that 'as her late Maiestie like *Dauid* had conceiued to build the Temple, . . . So his Maiesty like *Salomon*, may fully finish and effect the same' (B3ᵛ). Fletcher played his part in the rapid propagation of James's self-image as the British Solomon.[43] Another work directed at a wide audience, the anonymous pamphlet *The Poores*

---

[42] Elizabeth's preparedness to perform an exemplary death and in some way to supervise her own posthumous cult appears to be signalled in Camden's account (in *The historie of the princesse Elizabeth*, tr. R. Norton (1630), Bk. I, 28–9), of the Queen's declaration of her marriage to the Kingdom and her perpetual virginity. She ended thus: 'Lastly, this may be sufficient, both for my memorie, and honour of my Name, if when I have expired my last breath, this may be inscribed upon my Tombe: "Here lyes interr'd ELIZABETH, | A Virgin pure untill her death." ' (cited in Montrose, 'The Elizabethan Subject and the Spenserian Text', 310).

[43] See G. Parry, *The Golden Age Restor'd: The Culture of the Stuart Court 1603–1642* (Manchester, 1981), 21, 24–35, 230–2, etc.; A. Patterson, *Censorship and Interpretation* (Madison, 1984), 80, 256.

Lamentation, is a significant early example of biblical poetics in the English funeral elegy.[44] The poet claims to act as spokesman for 'wailing wights that take delight to mourne' (A3ʳ): on their behalf he identifies the hand of God in the Queen's death, and connects her with biblical types ('Our *Abraham, Lot,* with *Ioseph* now is dead | And with our Queene their vertues wrapt in lead' (B2ʳ)).[45] Consolation is announced baldly: 'though our Queene *Elizabeth* be dead, | We haue a King that ruleth in her stead' (B2ᵛ), and the audience are urged to repent and obey their new ruler.

Numerous individuals writing in the spring of 1603 had, like Drayton, their eyes fixed more firmly on the future than the past. In several panegyric volumes, for example, brief laments for the Queen are given some space. In Samuel Rowland's *Aue Caesar* (1603), rejoicing at the arrival of the new monarch is briefly suspended while what looks like an address from the tomb ('within our marble armes, . . . ') is rehearsed. The little tripartite elegy in rhymed decasyllabics praises the Queen as Deborah and Judith (Aiiiiʳ) and concludes with an image of her 'seated in blisse' (Aiiiiᵛ); presumably the ensuing return to panegyric adds to such consolation the further assurance that the nation is in safe hands.[46]

In Joseph Hall's *The King's prophecie: or weeping joy* (1603) attention is directed to the predicament of those who experience the conflicting emotions occasioned by death and accession. The speaker asks, 'What Stoick could his steely brest containe | . . . from being torne in twaine | With the crosse Passions of this wondrous tide?' (A3ʳ). In contrast with his youth, when he was 'wont to find the willing Muse vnsought' and could confront single subjects with undivided reason, now he faces an army of passions, and writes 'tumultuous lines' to express those passions 'in Reasons silence' (A3ᵛ). Consolation is figured through the prophecy, heavily indebted to Virgil's Fourth Eclogue, in which, under James, 'we see | Faire Brittaine formed to a Monarchie' (A6ᵛ).[47]

---

[44] See B. K. Lewalski, *Protestant Poetics and the Seventeenth Century Religious Lyric* (Princeton, 1979), 35.

[45] The poem features some clumsy attempts to recreate Spenser's cadences: 'Gone is our Queene, whose life cannot be found, | gone is our Queene which always lou'd vs deare, | Gone is our Queen whose vertues did abound, | as by her care it often did appear' (B2ʳ).

[46] A work of similar stamp is the anonymous *Englands welcome to James* (1603), which includes a brief lament for the Queen at sig. A4ʳ.

[47] Parry, *Golden Age Restor'd*, 34–5; Patterson, *Censorship and Interpretation*, 58–73.

Hall's work displays a degree of artistic self-consciousness, and an apparent willingness to write about the task in hand. Some writers evaded the problem very simply. Arthur Gorges, for example, merely altered a few incidental details in an amorous sonnet of the 1590s; he was to engage in further recycling on the death of Prince Henry in 1612.[48] Likewise, Richard Johnson's *Anglorum Lachrimae: in a sad passion complayning the death of Elizabeth* (1603) applies previously written work to the new subject. Johnson's poem is a plagiarized version of Thomas Rogers's *Celestiall elegies of the goddesses and the muses, deploring the death of Ladie Fraunces countess of Hertford* (1598). But there are several pieces that indicate a greater ambition, and show that it was becoming possible to perform innovatively even on a most solemn and circumscribed public occasion.

Henry Chettle's *England's Mourning Garment* is a case in point.[49] The volume, as its full title might imply, is a pastoral anthology of prose and verse, whose generic variousness expresses its status as, in Chettle's words, 'a small Epitomie, touching the abundant Vertues of Elizabeth our late sacred Mistris' (Aiiʳ). The poem opens with a recollection of *Nouember*, as Thenot observes that Collin's demeanour is at variance with the spring:

> . . . thou look'st as lagging as the day,
> When the Sun setting toward his westerne bed,
> Shews, that like him, all glory must decay . . .   (A3ʳ)

Collin reveals that he laments both the death of Eliza and the inadequacy of verse to praise her: he notes the reticence of other poets, breaks his pipe, and collapses in a swoon. Again the example of Spenser is invoked:

> Yes, those that merit Bayes
> Though teares restraine their layes,
> Some weeping houres or dayes
>   will finde a time:
> To honor Honor still, not with a rural quill
> But with a soule of skil,
>   To blesse their rime.

---

[48] See *The Poems of Sir Arthur Gorges*, ed. H. E. Sandison (Oxford, 1953), 182, 238–9.
[49] The full title of the work, entered on 25 Apr. 1603, reads *Englandes mourning garment; worne here by plaine shepherdes; in memorie of their mistresse Elizabeth*. For a brief account of the poem, see H. Cooper, *Pastoral: Medieval into Renaissance* (Ipswich, 1977), 207–9.

> Aye me! why should I dote
> on rimes, on songs, or note,
> Confusion can best quote,
> sacred *Elizaes* losse,
> Whose praise doth grace al verse,
> that shal the same reherse,
> No gold neede decke her herse:
> to her al gold is drosse.   (A3ᵛ–A4ʳ)

When Collin revives from his trance he summons the company of shepherds and nymphs ('if it pleased them to lend attention, hee would repeat something of her, worth memorie, that should liue in despite of death' (A4ʳ⁻ᵛ)): and the ensuing lengthy disquisition concerning the Queen's ancestry, virtues, and actions is punctuated with a gradually decreasing number of questions from the predictably obtuse Thenot. Then Collin's fellow poets are urged to end their silence and join in mourning the Queen.[50] Collin sets an example with an elegy in the six-line stanza of *Astrophel*, which continues his Spenserian vein ('Death now hath ceaz'd her in his ycie armes, | That sometime was the sum of our delight' (D2ᵛ), and so forth). The poets are reminded of the contrast betweeen their present silence and their former eloquence: 'Nor doth one Poet seeke her name to raise, | That liuing hourely striu'd to sing her praise' (D3ʳ). Like most Spenserians, Chettle welcomed the accession of a poet-king ('the Muses trust'), in whose words as much as actions the virtues of Elizabeth might be preserved (D3ᵛ). Then Collin resumes his prose narrative, at whose conclusion the poets respond by displaying their communal grief.

Collin borrows a pipe from Cuddy ('who could neither sing nor play, he was so full of passion and sighs' (E4ᵛ)) to replace the one he had broken. Then in turn Collin, Driope, Thenot, and Chloris sing, invoking the aid of 'Muses and flowres and Graces', and engrave their verses on the 'lofty pine'.[51] The epitaphs are then recorded, in order like those of Sidney's mourners in the *Astrophel* anthology. After these verses is printed an account of the Queen's

---

[50] Including, apparently, Shakespeare, whose *Lucrece* is thought to be referred to in one stanza: 'Nor doth the siluer tonged *Melicert*, | Drop from his honied muse one sable teare | To mourne her death that graced his desert, | And to his laies opend her Royall eare. | Shepheard, remember our *Elizabeth*, | And sing her Rape, done by that *Tarquin*, Death.' See E. K. Chambers, *William Shakespeare: A Study of Facts and Problems*, 2 vols. (Oxford, 1930), ii. 189.

[51] See Rosenmeyer, *The Green Cabinet*, 202–3.

funeral procession (F2–3), followed by *The Shepheards Spring Song* to the King by the spokesman Collin (F4–G1) who is now in tune with the season, his grief having been expressed.

As a pastoral anthology, Chettle's volume owes much to its Spenserian predecessor. But it adds further elements of variety— prose narrative, a factual list of the order of the Queen's funeral procession, and so forth—as well as representing a step away from the full-blown fiction of Spenser's allegory. More typical of such fiction is Thomas Newton's sonnet sequence *Atropoïon Delion, or the death of Delia* (1603).[52] The allegorical narrative treats of the separation of Castitas from the Queen, and opens with a lament from the bereaved abstraction:

> Late I sad Angell in an Angels brest
> Inthroned sate in glory, state, and blisse,
> But now displac't to mourne my throne at rest,
> I see how brittle state, and glory is . . .   (A3ʳ)

The first part of the sequence is unified by each 'speaker' invoking the next in the final couplet: Atropos calls on Nature, who calls on death, who summons the Angels. At the centre of the sequence the movement halts with the utterances of the angels and of Fame, before Castitas resumes the account of the Queen's change of state and is followed by Nymphs, Heroes, and Doctors. These figures assemble at the tomb, which addresses them in turn (thus the Doctors hear a version of the *ubi sunt* motif—'what's her body now, whereon such care | Was still bestow'd . . . | Where are her robes?' (B4ʳ)). Castitas is advised to return, as one might have expected, to the (Spenserian) shepherds:

> There make a Chaplet of the sweetest flowers,
> That prettie pinked Groue or Dale doth yeeld:
> There shade thy temples in those templed bowers
> That canopize the hunters of the field:
>   And round about thee in the Springing Meedes,
>   The swaynes will finger Ditties to their reedes.   (B4ʳ)

---

[52] In keeping with its Spenserian machinery, the volume is dedicated to noted patrons of Spenserian writing, the Countess of Derby and her three daughters (A2ʳ⁻ᵛ): see Bald, *John Donne*, 110 ff.; C. C. Brown, *John Milton's Aristocratic Entertainments* (Cambridge, 1985), 13–26, 43–56, etc.; F. R. Fogle, ' "Such a Rural Queene": The Countess Dowager of Derby as Patron', in Fogle and L. A. Knafla, *Patronage in Late Renaissance England*, William Andrews Clark Memorial Library (Los Angeles, 1983), 3–29.

A further genuflection towards Spenser and Sidney is Newton's use of feminine rhyme (lamenting . . . contenting' (A3^v); 'attend her . . . ende her' (A4^r); 'prayse her . . . raise her' (B2^r)). And as the poem ends with the closing of the grave and the dissolution of the mourning company, Newton himself appears: he distinguishes between decorous and excessive lamentation, advising the assembly to 'weep slow with passion of the sight | But with a true remembrance of the minde' (B4^v), before they dry their eyes and prepare to welcome the new king.

Everything about this little sequence displays a notable degree of artistic ambition, as Newton draws upon the conventions of ancient and modern pastoral to create a procession of mourners and an allegorical anthology presumably designed to appeal to the taste of a distinguished patroness. A similar ambition, though in a somewhat different mode, may be discerned in John Lane's *Elegie*, a work which was, like *Atropoïon Delion*, carefully and elegantly printed by W. White.[53]

Lane's language and style is a pastiche of his major contemporaries, notably Marlowe, Drayton, and Spenser: he declares himself a lesser follower who has learned his 'Aprill song . . . by roate' (A2^r). It is an oversimplification to suggest that Lane's poem follows the provisions of Spenser's poetic will.[54] But the initial summons to mourn contains many Spenserian elements:

> Mine infant Muse, begins but now to creepe,
> Yet loe, already she has learnde to weepe,
> To weepe for her, from whose vntimely death,
> (Vntimely borne) she borrowes all her breath:
> And early learnes her prayses to rehearse,
> That with the fame of her immortall verse,
> A neuer dying life she may obtaine,
> And to her selfe a life of glory gaine.   (A2^v)

---

[53] John Lane, *An elegie upon the death of Elizabeth* (1603): entered 15 Apr. Lane's other published work, his first, is the satirical *Tom Tel-Troths message, and his pens complaint* (1600). He went on to compose pastiche and imitation of Chaucer and Lydgate (Bodley MSS Douce 170, Ashmole 53; BL MS Harley 6243).

[54] Cooper claims that although 'Spenser was dead . . . Colin had left behind the elegy for this occasion' (*Pastoral*, 209: she cites, as does F. Yates in *Astraea*, 61, the inaccurate text of Lane's poem in *Fugitive Tracts*, ed. W. C. Hazlitt (1875), II. ii). It will be apparent from the brief passages cited here that *Nouember* is echoed rather than closely imitated. See Patterson, *Pastoral and Ideology*, 121.

The Queen is mourned as 'Beta' (Drayton's name for her), and Lane's speaker appears to take the concept of community to include both a physical assembly of poets and the literary construction of a various style derived from many sources. But there is no doubt who has taught them how to mourn:

> Oh, come, and do her corse with flowres embraue,
> And play some solemne musicke by her graue,
> Then sing her Requiem in some dolefull Verse
> Or do the songs of *Colin Clout* rehearse.   (A3ᵛ)

As in *Nouember*, the tone shifts abruptly to consolation, with prophetic allusions to the Book of Revelation (B1ᵛ): and rejoicing at Elizabeth's installation as Queen of Heaven (B2ʳ): then James is praised as Solomon and, more improbably, as Gideon (B2ᵛ). But Spenser's chief importance was that he had created the pioneering demonstration of the potential of English verse for artful pastoral elegy as well as, more broadly, showing ways of relating the individual case of particular writers to tradition, and Lane's work represents an apparent aspiration to join that tradition, and to propagate the values, literary, political, personal, associated with it.

Likewise with Henry Petowe's *Elizabetha quasi viuens*, another mixed volume of sorts, where a prose account of the funeral procession, punctuated with verses, is accompanied by a group of eight funeral sonnets.[55] The work's combination of sonnets—a form conventionally associated with intimacy, with introspection (and defined by Petowe in the dedication as 'the formall manner of my priuate sorrowes' (A2ʳ))—with a bare record of a public ceremony is itself unusual.[56] It may be designed to echo the relation between the speaker and the water pageant in *Prothalamion*. Petowe himself conventionally apologizes for the belated appearance of 'this infant of mine artlesse braine' (A3ʳ), and notes that, while the major writers may be silent, the newer poets have taken Elizabeth's death as a signal to appear:

---

[55] The account of the procession is the same as that printed in *Expicedium*, a work formerly attributed to Lyly (*Works*, ed. R. W. Bond, i. 388, 358), but nowadays thought to be by Richard Niccols, whose elegy on Prince Henry, *The Three Sisters Teares* (1613), is considered below, Ch. 5. The author employs familiar topoi of modesty, and makes the usual complaint that the most distinguished pens are silent: 'Wher's Collin Clout, or Rowland now become, | That wont to leade our Shepheards in a ring? | (Ah me) the first, pale death hath strooken dombe, | The latter, none encourageth to sing' (B3ᵛ).

[56] The verses are repr. in *Harl. Misc.* x. 332–43, and in Nichols, *Progresses of Elizabeth*, iii. 615.

> Each moderne Poet that can make a verse
> Writes of Eliza, even at their Muses birth.   (A3ᵛ)

Petowe's sonnets display considerable skill and invention.[57] The poet-figure is initially, in keeping with the overall Spenserianism, an inconsolable melancholic whose grief cannot be assuaged by the assurance of the Queen's heavenly apotheosis. After exploring this problem in the course of several sonnets, the move to resolution and consolation is signalled briefly:

> She liues in peace whome I do morne for so,
> She liues in heauen, and yet my soule laments.
> Since shee's so happie, Ile conuert my woe
> To present ioy . . .   (B1ᵛ)

As if conjured by this inner transformation, 'Three thousand and od hundred clowds' suddenly darken the sky. It becomes apparent that the speaker has stumbled onto the Queen's funeral procession:[58]

> Like clowds they were, but yet like clowded men,
> Whose presence turn'd the day to sable night.
> They vanisht hence, note what was after seene,
> The liuely picture of a late dead Queene.   (B2ʳ)

His senses are ravished by the lifelike effigy—even a 'man of iudgement . . . would haue sworne and said, | To Parliament rides this sweet slumbring Maide' (B3ʳ).[59] This vision, far from inspiring a resurgence of grief, directs the speaker to find consolation in the Queen's immortality. The final sonnet moves rapidly into panegyric, as King James is invested with the imagery and magic of his predecessor:[60]

[57] On the basis of his *Hero and Leander*, Petowe is conventionally belittled, scorned as a foil to Marlowe and Chapman. Stephen Orgel, for example, calls his version of the subject 'inept and silly' in his edn. *Christopher Marlowe: The Complete Poems and Translations* (Harmondsworth, 1971), 7.

[58] For accounts of the funeral, see Niccols, *Progresses of Elizabeth*, iii. 614–52, and N. Williams, *Elizabeth, Queen of England* (1967), 353 ff.; the event is set in the context of other royal funerals of the period in Gittings, *Death, Burial and the Individual*, 216–34.

[59] Stowe commented of the effigy that 'the like hath not been seen or known in the memory of man' (*Annales* (1631), 815; also R. Strong, *The Cult of Elizabeth* (1977), 15). On effigies in general, see Giesey, *Royal Funeral Ceremony*, 80 ff.; Huntington and Metcalf, *Celebrations of Death*, 159–75; Muir, *Civic Ritual in Renaissance Venice* (Princeton, 1981), 263–77.

[60] Fully developed panegyric was deferred to Petowe's next publication, *Englands Caesar: His maiesties most royall coronation* (1603). On Elizabeth as Phoenix, see E. C. Wilson, *England's Eliza*, 372–3.

> *Luna's* extinct, and now behold the Sunne,
> Whose beames soake vp the moysture of all teares,
> A *Phoenix* from her ashes doth arise,
> A King at whose faire Crowne all glory aymes.   (B3ᵛ)

Apart from the obvious reminiscences of Spenser and Sidney—not least in the adoption of the role of the professional mourner, the 'dirge specialist' and the interpenetration of private grief and public performance, Petowe's poems also feature an element of musical imitation whereby the halting, jerky rhythms of the first sonnet, imitating excessive and undisciplined grief, give way to regularity, expressing the speaker's achieved resolution, in the final sonnet.

It ought to be clear, even from this necessarily terse survey, that, leaving aside the small number of wholly conventional broadsides and a few laments in the mid-century 'Tudor' tradition, the elegies written to commemorate Elizabeth represent a major departure in the royal elegy in England. The dominant influence, the presiding genius, is Spenser: not only in the deployment of elaborate fictions and allegories, but also in creating congenial, stimulating, and highly imitable models of the poet's role. On the other hand, the silence of the established writers cannot be ignored. No doubt the expectations reposed in James played a part. It might also be held that although the model of Spenser (and, to a degree, of Sidney) was a model appropriate to youthful declarations of laureate ambition, its posture of exile, self-questioning, opposition, and obliquity made it less appealing, perhaps less relevant, to the way in which the generation of Jonson, Daniel, Drayton, and the rest might have viewed the events of the spring of 1603. It was in the funeral verses of Donne, as I shall try to show in the next chapter, that an alternative elegiac mode was forged.

4. DONNE'S FUNERAL POEMS AND *ANNIVERSARIES*

> Teares are false Spectacles, we cannot see
> Through passions mist, what wee are, or what shee.
>   ('Elegie on the Lady Markham', 15–16)

The importance of Donne's *Anniversaries* in the history of the English elegy is immense, and an entire elegiac tradition (as later chapters will show) derived from them. In this chapter Donne's career as elegist is considered chronologically, and I hope to show that his funeral verses—most particularly those composed during the years 1609–14 when funeral elegies apparently constituted his major poetic occupation—represent a development from faltering imitation to generic innovation of the highest order of sophistication and accomplishment.

'LANGUAGE, THOU ART TOO NARROW': DONNE'S ELEGIES 1599–1609

Donne's earliest elegies are neoclassical in inspiration and form.[1] The first, 'Sorrow, who to this house scarce knew the way', probably mourns the death of the younger Thomas Egerton, through whose friendship Donne had been appointed secretary to the Lord Keeper.[2] The poet bore his friend's sword in the funeral procession in Chester Cathedral (27 September 1599): both men had been contemporaries at Lincoln's Inn and had gone on the Islands voyage.[3] For the Egerton household, the death represented an unwonted shock: a family that had seemed immune to the depredations of fortune was suddenly bereaved, and Donne's

---

[1] W. M. Lebans, 'The Influence of the Classics in Donne's *Epicedes* and *Obsequies*', *RES* NS, 23 (1972), 127–37.

[2] Text from H. Gardner, ed., *The Elegies and the Songs and Sonnets of John Donne* (Oxford, 1965), 26. On the occasion of the poem, see I. A. Shapiro, 'The Date of a Donne Elegy, and its Implications', in *English Renaissance Studies*, 141–50.

[3] A MS description of the funeral procession (BL MS Harl. 2129, fo. 67) is reproduced in R. C. Bald, *John Donne: A Life* (Oxford, 1970), 105–6. See Bald, 93–127, for an account of Donne's career in Egerton's service.

lament dwells on the impact of premature death at this domestic level.[4]

He starts with the topos of inexpressibility: 'strange' weeping makes grief tongue-tied, and the 'cold tongues' of the mourners must rely on Egerton's 'loud speaking workes' to speak his deserved praise. The poet's inarticulacy is mirrored in the repeated ejaculation, 'oh' (lines 2, 9, 23), and his first reflection on the death is about himself, using the conventional conceit of the deceased as the oak, the poet as the briar 'which by it did rise'. Hardly less conventional (nor indeed less implicitly mercenary) is the poem's second conceit, which derives from its subject's career as Essex's follower:

> no familie
> Ere rigg'd a soule for heavens discoverie
> With whom more Venturers more boldly dare
> Venture their states, with him in joy to share,
> Wee lose what all friends lov'd, him; he gaines now
> But life by death . . . [5]   (14–19)

The poem concludes with another commonplace, equating remembrance with progeny:

> His children are his pictures, Oh they bee
> Pictures of him dead, senselesse, cold as he.
> Here needs no marble Tombe, since hee is gone,
> He, and about him, his, are turn'd to stone.   (23–6)

The speaker is presented dramatically, with an obsessive, edgy manner that, together with the absence of consolation, locates the piece formally as an elegy or funeral song whose focus is on the immediate response to death, and whose composition (by a poet whom Donne takes pains to characterize) springs from the inarticulacy of the family of mourners.[6] More than that it would be

---

[4] As Shapiro points out, further disruption followed rapidly, in the shape of Essex's return (his party passed through Chester at the time of the funeral, returning to London in disobedience of the Queen's wishes), the illness and death of Lady Egerton, the Lord Keeper's remarriage, and Donne's affair with Ann More (Shapiro, 'Date of a Donne Elegy', 143–4; Bald, *Donne*, 107–15). The pressure of public events, as Bald (p. 106) notes, kept the Lord Keeper away from his son's funeral.

[5] A. F. Marotti, in *John Donne, Coterie Poet* (Madison, 1986), picks up the 'economically and politically significant' vocabulary of this poem, which he classes as an 'obvious act of clientage' (pp. 118–19).

[6] In the Henry E. Huntington Library, among the Ellesmere papers, are elegies,

unreasonable to claim for this (generally disliked) first attempt by Donne at the form.[7]

And to turn to the rest of his elegies puts the early experiment in the shade. In his middle years, Donne (like Spenser) composed occasional verses of assured virtuosity. The poet's desperate search for employment at the time provides some context.[8] In 1607 he sought a post in Queen Anne's household; in November 1608 Lord Hay unsuccessfully supported his candidature for a secretaryship in Ireland; in the following February courtiers gossiped that 'John Dun seekes to be preferred to be secretarie of Virginia'.[9] Repeated failure coincided with the first serious attempts (notably by Thomas Morton) to persuade Donne to consider ordination, and with his apparent preoccupation with reading extensively in canon law and religious controversy.[10]

In the Countess of Bedford Donne was fortunate to find a patroness to whom his intellectual and literary accomplishments were congenial.[11] He rejoiced that she had 'refined' him, and praised her as a living embodiment of Petrarchan ideals, as an epitome, encyclopaedia (or more typically 'mine') of virtues. For a few years he devoted his pen to her service, acting, as Bald remarked, as if he were her poet laureate.[12] Thus, when Lady

---

epitaphs, letters of consolation, and other pieces relating to the event, including poems by Egerton's chaplain Nathaniel Harris (EL 34/B56, 34/B19, 34/B57). I am grateful to Professor Patrick Collinson for drawing my attention to the importance of this archive.

[7] Lebans judged it to be 'brief, tentative, and experimental' ('Influence of the Classics', 128).

[8] See J. Carey, *John Donne: Life, Mind and Art* (1981), 20–93. Bald (p. 155) sums up Donne's life at the time as combining 'laborious hours of study and research' into 'problems of divinity and canon law', as well as displaying 'a certain Bohemianism in his leisure hours'.

[9] Donne, *Letters to Several Persons of Honour* (1651), 81–2; John Chamberlain, *Letters*, ed. N. E. McLure, 2 vols. (Philadelphia, 1939), i. 284.

[10] Izaak Walton, *The Lives of John Donne, Sir Henry Wotton, Richard Hooker, George Herbert and Robert Sanderson* (1675; World's Classics edn., Oxford, 1927), 32–5; R. B[addily], *The Life of Dr Thomas Morton* (1669), 98–9; W. Milgate, ed., *John Donne: The Satires, Epigrams and Verse Letters* (Oxford, 1967), lix–lx.

[11] See M. Maurer, 'The Real Presence of Lucy Russell, Countess of Bedford, and the Terms of John Donne's "Honour is so sublime perfection"', *ELH* 47 (1980), 205–34; B. Lewalski, 'Lucy, Countess of Bedford: Images of a Jacobean Courtier and Patroness', in Sharpe and Zwicker, eds., *The Politics of Discourse*, 52–77; P. Thomson, 'John Donne and the Countess of Bedford', *MLR* 44 (1949), 329–40; also Bald, 170–80, and Carey, *John Donne*, 77–81.

[12] Bald, 177: also P. Thomson, 'Donne and the Poetry of Patronage', in A. J. Smith, ed., *John Donne: Essays in Celebration* (1972), 308–23; M. Walters, 'Epistolary Verse and its Social Context, 1590–1640' (unpubl. B.Litt. thesis, Oxford, 1972), 80–5, 111–59;

Bedford's cousin, Bridget Lady Markham, died at Twickenham in May 1609, the event elicited a response from Donne.[13] He produced for his patroness both an elegy ('Man is the World, and death the Ocean') and a verse epistle ('You that are she and you, that's double shee').[14]

The elegy has been held to show 'a fully developed classical structure . . . in the manner of the earliest Roman funeral elegies', with the components (of more or less equal size) disposed in the unusual order lament, consolation, and praise.[15] The style of this rather pedantic exercise is notably uncertain, with qualifications, translations and glosses:

> Then our land waters (teares of passion) vent:
> Our waters, then, above our firmament,
> (Teares which our Soule doth for her sin let fall)
> Take all a brackish tast, and Funerall,
> And even those teares, which should wash sin, are sin.   (7–11)

But even if this poem is as 'frigid and artificial' as has been suggested (Bald, 177), it possesses significance in relation to Donne's maturing art as an elegist. Its argument, for example, is on an altogether more taxing intellectual plane than the Egerton elegy. Its affinities are with the verse letters, and it seems designed to 'pose and explore, on the occasion of a particular death, some general problem'.[16] Thus Donne appears to be stretching the province of elegy—as narrowly defined—beyond the expression of grief *tout court*. It might also be thought that this poem's blend of formality and impenetrable intimacy foreshadows his ambitious attempts to devise a non-pastoral (essentially latinate) funeral elegy

M. Maurer, 'Samuel Daniel's Poetical Epistles, Especially those to Sir Thomas Egerton and Lucy, Countess of Bedford', *SP* 74 (1977), 418–44; A. F. Marotti, 'John Donne and the Rewards of Patronage', in G. F. Lytle and S. Orgel, ed., *Patronage in the Renaissance* (Princeton, 1981), 207–34 (developed in *John Donne, Coterie Poet*, 202–32).

[13] Lady Markham's monument in Twickenham says she was 'inclytae Luciae, Comitessae de Bedford sanguine (quod satis) sed et amicitia propinquissima': cited by Bald (p. 177) and by Milgate in his edn. of Donne's *Epithalamions, Anniversaries and Epicedes* (Oxford, 1978), 177. All subsequent refs. to Donne's funeral verses are to Milgate's text, which will be cited as Milgate, *Anniversaries*.

[14] B. K. Lewalski, *Donne's Anniversaries and the Poetry of Praise: The Creation of a Symbolic Mode* (Princeton, 1973), 59–61; Marotti, *John Donne, Coterie Poet*, 223–5; for a text of the verse epistle, see Milgate, *Satires*, 94.

[15] Lebans, 'Influence of the Classics', 128; also his 'Donne's *Anniversaries* and the Tradition of Funeral Elegy', *ELH* 39 (1972), 545–59 (where he provides a slightly revised account of the poem's structural components).

[16] Lewalski, *Donne's Anniversaries*, 50.

that could be both domestic and serious. And the presumably conscious choice of a 'low', argumentative register is consistent with such a reading.[17] As in Spenser's later works, though in a different mode, ethical seriousness is combined with domestic familiarity in the exploration of the wider applications and meanings of a particular event. Further, the elegy should be read in conjunction with its companion-piece, the verse epistle, in which Lady Markham is proposed as a refutation of the 'forward heresie | That women can no parts of friendship bee' (57–8).[18] The latter poem is an intimately private work, addressed to personal loss, and suggesting a personal consolation—that Lady Markham's virtues, and the qualities of her friendship, survive in her friend. Set against this poem, the elegy becomes more general, more public, and perhaps more strongly confined to the period between death and burial (which would fix its composition to the period 4–19 May 1609).

As always, Donne did best when surest of his audience. He wrote (with few exceptions) to praise the dead and console the living as individuals or as members of family groups. Within that context, he challenged decorum and fashion in creating an innovatory non-pastoral funeral mode. Formally, he modified the examples of his Latin models, and set his writing in an argumentative register appropriate to conversation, satire, and the dramatic expression of inner turmoil. The tendency was to focus on the particularities of the speaker, the occasion, and the subject, in order to draw out more general implications. When wrenched from their domestic setting, these poems would risk appearing strange, inexplicable, and monstrous. Such a fate was to befall the *Anniversaries*, and indeed the first exercise in the new funeral manner was itself coolly received.

Cecilia Bulstrode, a close friend of Lady Bedford, died at Twickenham on 4 August 1609.[19] Donne's initial literary response

[17] See A. Fowler, *Kinds of Literature: An Introduction to the Theory of Genres and Modes* (Oxford, 1982), 70–1, citing Puttenham's *Arte of English Poesie*, iii, chs. 5–6, and R. Tuve, *Elizabethan and Metaphysical Imagery* (Chicago, 1947), 240–3.

[18] Milgate notes (*Satires*, 250), that most MS copies of the verse epistle class the poem as an 'elegy'.

[19] She seems to have suffered from some intermittent feverish illness: see Donne's letter to Henry Goodyer in *Letters to Severall Persons of Honour*, 215–16 (cited in Bald, 177, and Milgate, *Anniversaries*, 183). There is a report of her death in Sir James Whitelocke, *Liber Famelicus* (Camden Soc., 1858), 18. See Marotti, *John Donne, Coterie Poet*, 335.

seems to have been composed rapidly.[20] It opens with an apparent repudiation of the Holy Sonnet 'Death be not proud', as the speaker repents his earlier dismissal of death's power:

> DEATH I recant, and say, unsaid by mee
>   What ere hath slip'd, that might diminish thee.
> Spirituall treason, atheisme 'tis, to say,
> That any can thy Summons disobey.   (1–4)

With the argumentative force of his satirical voice, Donne's speaker catalogues instances which cumulatively establish the ubiquity of death's authority. Death is figured as a gluttonous monster, a 'mighty bird of prey' with 'bloody, 'or plaguy, or sterv'd jawes', and the speaker explains that it is the present occasion that has led him to recognize these truths.

> How could I thinke thee nothing, that see now
> In all this All, nothing else is, but thou.
> Our births and life, vices, and vertues, bee
> Wastfull consumptions, and degrees of thee.   (25–8)

Death's mistake, the speaker argues, was to fail to appreciate that Cecilia Bulstrode was a different kind of prey—'One whom thy blow makes, not ours, nor thine own' (36). Suddenly the tone of the poem changes from the lurid and allegorical mode, whose language and metaphors are essentially biblical, to a more argumentative register that leads back to the jeering scorn of death the elegy had begun by spurning. By snatching the victim hastily she was prevented from sinning, or inciting others to sin. Even the remote possibility that 'immoderate grief' would precipitate the mourners into death's clutches is removed: after all, their 'teares are due' (72), and weeping stimulates survivors to repent and to look forward to heavenly reunion with their exemplary friend.

Donne has obviously incorporated allusion into his elegiac method, and presumably sought to dignify his subject by reference to the Bible, to Seneca, to Plutarch, and to Augustine and

---

[20] Other writers who composed elegies included Ben Jonson (*Underwood*, xlix), Sir Thomas Roe (repr. in Grierson's edn. of Donne, i. 410–11): see A. Ribiero, 'Sir John Roe: Ben Jonson's Friend', *RES* NS 24 (1973), 161), and Sir Edward Herbert (*Poems*, ed. G. C. Moore Smith, 20–1). For standard accounts of Donne's poem, see A. L. Bennett, 'The Principal Rhetorical Conventions in the Renaissance Personal Elegy', *SP* 51 (1954), 107–25: Hardison, *The Enduring Monument*, 161–86; Lebans, 'Influence of the Classics', 127–32; Lewalski, *Donne's Anniversaries*, 51–2

Jerome.[21] His non-pastoral elegiac idiom combines Roman form
with Christian doctrine and consolation.[22] Though generally
classical, this poem's sense is governed by Christian commonplaces,
as in the conventional assimilation of the body/castle metaphor to a
spiritual context:

> . . . now thou hast overthrowne
> One whom thy blow makes, not ours, nor thine own.
> She was more stories high: hopelesse to come
> To'her Soule, thou'hast offer'd at her lower roome.
> Her Soule and body was a King and Court:
> But thou hast both of Captaine mist and fort.
> As houses fall not, though the King remove,
> Bodies of Saints rest for their soules above.   (35-42)

The concluding repudiation of death echoes the poem's horrific
opening section and obliges the reader to reconsider the poem as a
whole: in such reassessment the speaker's initial performance is
seen in a new light. Where it might on its own have seemed vivid
and terrifying, the poem's move to consolation makes it seem
instead irrational, extreme, ignorant. We can see that the poem
appears designed to enact a process of tempering immoderate
grief through consolations derived from scripture and the exercise
of the mind. It expresses lament followed by consolation. Praise of
the subject, however, is surely understood: she must be one of the
'Saints' because she has occasioned such a meditation. Everything
proceeds from the premiss of her excellence, even, perhaps, the
poem's implicitly panegyric circular structure.

The poem undoubtedly has an abstract quality. To Bald it was
merely 'unfeeling', and Lady Bedford was hardly more impressed.[23]
She seems to have written her elegy 'Death be not proud' in
response, and her poem is notable for its Calvinist thrust and for its
stress on the subject's youth. It leads up to a reaffirmation of its
original assault on death's pride, ordering death to

---

[21] Refs. are to Ezek. 14: 21; Rev. 6: 8; Seneca, *Consolatio ad Marciam*, 10. 5, 11. 3-4,
21. 6; Plutarch, *Consolatio ad Appolonium; Moralia*, 2. 121. For refs. to St Augustine and
St Jerome, see Donne, *Sermons*, ed. Potter and Simpson, iv. 54, iv. 52. See the full notes
in Milgate, *Anniversaries*, 183-7, and in Lebans, 'Influence of the Classics', 130-2, 137.

[22] In a sermon, Donne was later to cite St Jerome's commentary to 1 Cor. 15: 31, a
text central to an understanding of the elegy: '*Quotidie morimur, et tamen nos esse aeternos
putamus*, sayes S. Hierome; we die every day, and we die all the time' (Donne, *Sermons*,
iv. 52).

[23] Bald, 178; Marotti, *John Donne, Coterie Poet*, 223.

> teach this hymne of her with joy, and sing,
> *The grave no conquest gets, Death hath no sting.*[24]   (41–2)

Donne's reply opens with a version of the inexpressibility topos that seems to constitute some sort of acknowledgement that his earlier piece, with its virtuosity and challenges to decorum, had been clever rather than profound:

> LANGUAGE thou art too narrow, and too weake
> To ease us now; great sorrow cannot speake;
> If we could sigh out accents, and weepe words,
> Griefe weares, and lessens, that tears breath affords.
> Sad hearts, the lesse they seeme, the more they are,
> (So guiltiest men stand mutest at the barre)
> Not that they know not, feele not their estate,
> But extreme sense hath made them desperate.   (1–8)

This is familiar literary territory, albeit more common in an erotic or panegyric than a funeral context. These opening lines establish the relation of show to substance, seeming to being, as a central preoccupation of the poem. The theme is expressed in various ways. Thus the use of sententious semi-proverbial phrases ('great sorrow cannot speake') initiates a contrast in the speaker's performance between precept and experience, between received wisdom and the immediate reaction to bereavement.[25] Further (and with what degree, or tone, of self-reference we cannot know), the striking image of the mute culprit 'at the barre' introduces the topic of judgement, of evaluation, into the piece. The act of writing the elegy, then, is placed before the reader in a manner that is essentially dramatic. And like so many dramatic works of the period, its resolution implicates the audience. Cecilia Bulstrode's friends, just as much as the speaker of the poem, court 'guilt' if they mourn or if they fail to mourn: Donne explores the crisis that follows death, and presents the literary anxieties of the speaker as a version of the predicament of all the bereaved. He takes the convention of the elegist as spokesman for a grieving community to a new degree of intimacy and immediacy.[26]

While the poem embraces praise, lament, and consolation, it departs from ancient precedent by presenting Cecilia Bulstrode as

---

[24] Text from Milgate, *Anniversaries*, app. B (235–7).
[25] See M. P. Tilley, *A Dictionary of Proverbs in England in the Sixteenth and Seventeenth Centuries* (1950), s 664, 'Small sorrows speak, great ones are silent'.
[26] Lewalski, *Donne's Anniversaries*, 52–3.

an object of meditation, perhaps in response to the suggestion of her exemplary status in Lady Bedford's elegy. The speaker addresses not death but sorrow (identified in Matthew's Gospel as the harbinger of Christ's kingdom on earth), and employs alchemical terms to express her purity:

> She was too Saphirine, and cleare for thee:
> Clay, flint, and jeat now thy fit dwellings be;
> Alas, shee was too pure, but not too weake;
> Who e'r saw Christall Ordinance but would break? (21–4)

The 'nature reversed' topos is brought into line with the poem's meditative direction. Contemplation of the subject's untainted, other-worldly nature (rather than grief at her passing) does nothing to the weather or the landscape, but it transforms the understanding of the mourners:

> If we should vapour out, and pine, and die;
> Since, shee first went, that were not miserie.
> Shee chang'd our world with hers; now she is gone,
> Mirth and prosperity is oppression:
> For of all morall vertues she was all,
> The Ethicks speake of vertues Cardinall.[27] (29–34)

Such a transformation develops the stress on the gulf separating human from divine values and perspectives that had been apparent in the previous elegies, but the consistency of imaginative reference is a novelty. The erotic conceit of the subject's body as a citadel appears in a transformed—one might say transfigured—manifestation:

> Her soule was Paradise; the Cherubin
> Set to keepe it was grace, that kept out sinne. (35–6)

And the divine purpose is directly stated:

> God tooke her hence, lest some of us should love
> Her, like that plant, him and his lawes above,
> And when wee teares, hee mercy shed in this,
> To raise our mindes to heaven where now she is. (39–42)

Near the conclusion the speaker resumes alchemical terms in turning to the future:[28]

[27] There is a good brief account of this process in Milgate, *Anniversaries*, xvi–xx. For a more sceptical view of Donne's 'see-through women', see Carey, *John Donne*, 164.
[28] See E. Crawshaw, 'Hermetic Elements in Donne's Poetic Vision', in *Donne: Essays in Celebration*, ed. Smith, 324–48.

> The ravenous earth that now wooes her to be
> Earth too, will be *Lemnia*: and the tree
> That wraps that christall in a wooden Tombe,
> Shall be took up spruce, fill'd with diamond;   (57–60)

What is striking is that this projection of the speaker's current consoling insight (into the true nature of his subject) far into the future—to the reunion of body and soul at the Day of Judgement—involves real, physical transformations. It is less 'nature reversed' than the natural world ultimately corrected or transformed through contact with the crystal dwelling of the regenerate soul. Armed with these reflections, he returns to his role as spokesman for the company of mourners:

> And we her sad glad friends all beare a part
> Of griefe, for all would waste a Stoicks heart.   (61–2)

Donne has not posed as a 'dirge expert' on the Homeric model, but as something more like Montaigne's persona in the *Essays*. He has shown a speaker whose contemplation of the deceased and of the occasion has generated a series of 'findings' which may be shared with other mourners.[29] He moves from an adumbration of the inadequacies of language to a glittering 'poetic' image, contemplation whereof is implied to be conclusively consolatory. The subject of the elegy is not death, still less the deceased: rather it is the speaker's discovery of the authenticity of faith under trial. Commentators have remarked on the poem's unity of imaginative reference, and have associated the intense concentration of its metaphorical world with a Protestant tradition of meditation, of identifying the 'restored image of God in Man'.[30] And an essential component of the enterprise is a strain of hyperbole that goes beyond the first Bulstrode elegy. There the extended body/citadel metaphor had been diligently expounded (36 ff.): but it pales beside the later poem's identification of the subject's soul with Paradise and with the Burning Bush in the space of a few lines (35–6, 45–50). This second attempt to mourn Cecilia Bulstrode represents the creation of a new form of English elegy whose canons of decorum were based not on external, formal details but on an imaginative coherence whose purpose was consolatory and

[29] See Sherwood, *Fulfilling the Circle: A Study of John Donne's Thought* (Toronto, 1984), 114–16.
[30] Lewalski, *Donne's Anniversaries*, 108–41.

panegyric, and on a dramatized performance by the speaker that both demonstrated and advocated meditating on the essential, ideal, spiritual qualities of the subject rather than on more tangible attributes.

'THE BEST I COULD CONCEIVE': THE *ANNIVERSARIES*

Elizabeth Drury died in London early in December 1610. She was 14 years old. Donne, perhaps at his sister's instigation, wrote an elegy on the occasion.[31] The poem addresses the impossibility of confining 'such a ghest' as its subject within 'workes of hands' or 'the wits of men'. Even the most lavish tomb, whose 'every inch were ten escurialls' would be inadequate: what is more, it would have to face the intractable fact that 'Yet shee's demolish'd'.[32] As for elegies:

> Can these memorials, ragges of paper, give
> Life to that name, by which name they must live?
> Sickly, alas, short-liv'd, aborted bee
> Those Carkas verses, whose soule is not shee.
> And can shee, who no longer would be shee,
> Being such a Tabernacle, stoope to bee
> In paper wrap't; Or, when she would not lie
> In such a house, dwell in an Elegie?   (11–18)

Donne explicitly translates the Whetstone–Churchyard notion of the elegy as 'remembrance' into a new, and altogether more spiritual idiom. The focus is not the subject's fame but her soul, and the speaker is not a herald but a questioning, analysing intelligence. He examines a variety of consolatory topics in the course of the poem, notably those associated with youthful death. But the central proposition is that since Elizabeth Drury had been to the world as 'fine spirits' are to the body, 'which doe tune and set | This organ . . . which beget | Wonder and love' (27–9), her influence will persist. Every subsequent virtuous person will be 'her

---

[31] Bald, 240.

[32] Lewalski observed that Elizabeth Drury is mourned in terms of 'conventions of Petrarchan hyperbole and of panegyric celebrations of the ideal through a particular example' (*Donne's Anniversaries*, 222). See P. A. Parrish, '"A Funerall Elegie": Donne's Achievement in Traditional Form', *Concerning Poetry*, 19 (1986), 55–66, and his earlier study, 'Donne's "A Funerall Elegie"', *PLL* 11 (1975), 83–7.

delegate, | T' accomplish that which should have beene her fate'
(99–100), the idea with which the elegy ends:

> For future vertuous deeds are Legacies,
> Which from the gift of her example rise.
> And 'tis in heav'n part of spirituall mirth,
> To see how well, the good play her, on earth.   (103–6)

The poem proclaims no special intimacy. Nor does it provide
detail. But in its imaginative coherence and its argument (as well as
in the implicit characterization of the speaker through the normal
dramatic devices) it recalls Donne's recent elegies. Particularly
striking is the contrast between the opening of the poem, where the
piece seems to define itself as an elegy pinned to a tomb, as a
physical expression of mourning designed as part of the ceremonial
disposal of a body, and the conclusion, where the subject's example
survives in the lives of virtuous people on earth. The shift from
physical to spiritual memorials, from mutable commemoration to
an inspiration of 'spirituall mirth', epitomizes Donne's transformation
of the genre, and prefigures the achievement of the *Anniversaries*.

The elegy secured the dubious literary accolade of Sir Robert
Drury's approbation, and Donne was commissioned to compose a
Latin epitaph for the lavish tomb that was planned.[33] He also
embarked on the *Anniversaries*, which have been praised as 'the
finest long poems written in English between *The Faerie Queene* and
Paradise Lost'.[34]

Read in the context of his earlier elegies, the *Anniversaries*
provide further evidence of a desire to create a vernacular non-
pastoral elegiac idiom, quite distinct from the outmoded heraldic
laments, and from those of Spenserians or neoclassicists (whose
preferred form was the epitaph). The point of view of the poems
has been plausibly related to Protestant tradition, to the conception
of a regenerate soul as the restored image of God in man.
Meditative, imaginative coherence, rather than the formal disposition
of constituent parts, structures the poems and authorizes a degree
of flexibility and variety that shocked a few contemporaries and
excited many more.[35]

---

[33] Bald, 238–41.   [34] Milgate, *Anniversaries*, xxxiv.

[35] As well as Lewalski, *Donne's Anniversaries*, and Lebans's articles, 'Influence of the
Classics' and 'Donne's *Anniversaries* and the Tradition of Funeral Elegy', see R. Colie's
important and influential article, ' "All in Peeces": Problems of Interpretation in
Donne's Anniversary Poems', in P. A. Fiore, ed., *Just So Much Honor: Essays*

The *Anniversaries* were Donne's first major publication. His new readers evidently found the style and invention of the pieces exemplary, as the numerous imitations and borrowings attest.[36] Before the collected *Poems* of 1633, the *First Anniversary* (with 'A Funeral Elegy') was printed four times, and the *Second Anniversary* three times.[37] Outside the circle of his closest friends, Donne was 'from 1612 until 1633 the poet of the *Anniversaries*'.[38] It was from within that circle that criticisms, based on charges of impropriety and indecorousness, emanated.

Lady Bedford's displeasure elicited from Donne a feeble, faltering, and unfinished verse epistle by way of apology and explanation of his praise of Elizabeth Drury in terms which his patroness might have come to consider unique to herself or blasphemous or both.[39] To Goodyer he wrote that 'it became me to say, not what I was sure was just truth, but the best that I could conceive'; to Garrard he argued that, being unacquainted with his subject, he could not have 'spoken just truths', and instead took Elizabeth Drury as 'such a person, as might be capable of all that I could say'.[40] A similar exchange seems to lie behind Drummond's report of Jonson's conversation on the matter: 'that Dones Anniversarie was profane and full of Blasphemies that he told Mr. Donne, if it been written of ye Virgin Marie it had been something to which he answered that he described the Idea of a Woman and not as she was . . . '.[41] Two points emerge from these fragments. First, the implication that in other elegies Donne had written of

---

Commemorating the 400th Anniversary of the Birth of John Donne (University Park, 1972), 189–218; A. F. Bellette, 'Art and Imitation in Donne's *Anniversaries*', SEL 15 (1975), 83–96, and Marotti, *John Donne, Coterie Poet*, 233–45.

[36] Lewalski, *Donne's Anniversaries*, 307–70; A. J. Smith, ed., *John Donne: The Critical Heritage* (1975), 33–64.

[37] These early editions were all published anonymously.

[38] Milgate, *Anniversaries*, xxxiii.

[39] Donne's poem consists of a series of 'confessions': 'I confesse I have to others lent | Your stock, and over prodigally spent | Your treasure, for since I had never knowne | Vertue or beautie, but as they are growne | In you, I should not thinke or say they shine, | (So as I have) in any other Mine' (11–16). Text from Milgate, *Satires*, 104.

[40] Donne, *Letters . . . etc.*, 74–5 (Goodyer), 238–9 (Garrard): extracts of the letters are reproduced in Milgate, *Anniversaries*, xxxi–xxxii. Lewalski argues that the 'uneasiness expressed in these letters has to do rather with Donne's . . . sense that the role of professional poet is beneath him than with any qualms about the subject or the execution of the *Anniversary* poems' (*Donne's Anniversaries*, 307 n).

[41] Jonson, 'Conversations with Drummond of Hawthornden', in *Works*, ed. Herford and Simpson, i. 133.

each of his subjects 'as she was', and had uttered 'just truths', cannot have anything to do with narrowly biographical 'truth'. The suggestion is that elsewhere he had expressed the 'true'—abiding, essential—qualities in a manner consistent with the dual sense of 'just': 'righteous' and 'exact'. Such a gloss is consistent with his immediately previous practice. The second point is to observe the stress upon his own invention: the subject was 'capable of all that I could say' and enabled him to produce 'the best that I could conceive'.[42]

Elizabeth Drury, then, is the occasion, rather than the subject of the *Anniversaries* (whereas she had been both in the case of the elegy and the epitaph). The subject is both a theme, an idea ('the Idea of a Woman'), and a drama. The speaker's struggle with the task he has set himself, the way he pits his virtuosity against the task of apprehending and expressing the idea, is central to the poems. And it will be clear that such a foregrounding of the speaker's performance is closely related to the growing characterization of the speaker observable in the earlier elegies.[43] Further, the exercise is implicitly panegyric (as it had been in the case of Cecilia Bulstrode). Donne habitually represented a virtuous individual as a 'glass' through which heavenly order might be discerned: contemplation of the glass might illuminate issues deriving flatteringly from (as well as transcending) the particular person.[44] In such a context, as Donne was to argue later, hyperbole ceases to be hyperbole:

The world is a great Volume, and man the Index of that Booke; Even in the body of man, you may turne to the whole world; This body is an Illustration of all Nature: Gods recapitulation of all that he had said before, in his *Fiat lux*, and *Fiat firmamentum*, and in all the rest, said or done, in all the six dayes. Propose this body to thy consideration in the highest exaltation thereof; as it is the *Temple of the Holy Ghost*: Nay, not in a Metaphor, or comparison of a Temple, or any other similitudinary thing,

---

[42] As Donne was to put it in a sermon: 'You would scarce thank a man for an extemporall Elegy, or Epigram, or Panegyrique in your praise, if it cost the Poet, or the Orator no paines . . . ': *LXXX Sermons* (1640), 130.C.

[43] B. K. Lewalski, 'Donne's Epideictic *Personae*', *Southern Quarterly*, 14 (1976), 195–202; Marotti speaks of the 'technique of autobiographical self-reference customary in . . . manuscript-circulated coterie verse': *John Donne, Coterie Poet*, 294–5.

[44] In his sermons, Donne observed that we 'need such *Glasses* and such *Images*, as God shews us himself in the King' (*Sermons*, vii. 357), and he urged King Charles to 'make your selfe as a *Glasse*, . . . It was a *Metaphor* in which, your *Majesties Blessed Father* seemed to delight' (*Sermons*, vii. 72). See Milgate, *Anniversaries*, xix–xx.

but as it was really and truly the very body of God, in the person of Christ, and yet this body must wither, must decay, must languish, must perish.[45]

In this passage, from the funeral sermon on Sir William Cockayne (1626), Donne expresses himself in terms that appear to gloss his defences of the *Anniversaries*.[46] Consideration 'in the highest exaltation' leads to an apprehension of the physical not as a metaphor or type of Christ's body but as the thing itself 'really and truly'. And it is this 'consideration' that glosses the speaker's enterprise, 'the best praise that I could give': while he may begin by showing that ruin is 'witty'—poetic, metaphorical—his role is to educate his readers to a perception of the truths which the metaphors of the created world merely shadow. As Donne himself put it in a sermon of 1618/19, the Holy Ghost has identified those who are to preach, and 'put in them a care of delivering God's messages, with consideration, with meditation'.[47]

It was the printing of the *Second Anniversary* that gave the *First* its title, and signalled—albeit retrospectively—the creation of a new genre. There was no 'tradition of anniversary' as some have supposed. Puttenham had merely recorded ancient obsequies 'by custome continued yearly'; Scaliger (writing, of course, in a Catholic context) prescribed a gradual diminution in the component of lament in commemorative writings with the passage of time, and Ausonius perhaps advocated annual repetition of dirges in the Preface to the *Parentalia*.[48] But much more relevant is the contemporary vogue for 'anatomies'—a vogue that helps further to define the speaker's qualities and to associate the poems with Menippean satire and with complaints (with their *contemptus mundi*).[49] And the nearest thing to a model for these ambitious

[45] Donne, *Sermons*, vii. 271–2.

[46] Astrid Friis, *Alderman Cockayne's Project and the Cloth Trade* (1927), 224–81, gives an indication of why Donne might have felt the need to offer a defence of a man whose schemes included disastrous failures and dubious transactions. See Bald, 490, and Lewalski, *Donne's Anniversaries*, 210–12.

[47] Donne, *Sermons*, ii. 171 (on Ezek. 33: 32): delivered at Whitehall.

[48] Puttenham, *Arte of English Poesie*, 48; Hardison, *Enduring Monument*, 163. The Ausonius passage reads: 'O Dirge, so ready to do service with plaints for the dead, forget not thy yearly tribute to these silent ones—that tribute which Numa ordained should be offered year by year to the shades of our relatives, according as the nearness of their death or kinship demands': *Parentalia*, i. 59.

[49] J. Peter, *Complaint and Satire in Early English Literature* (Oxford, 1956), 9–13, 60–103; N. Frye, *Anatomy of Criticism: Four Essays* (Princeton, 1957), 298, 309–12; Lewalski, *Donne's Anniversaries*, 228–9; Fowler, *Kinds of Literature*, 118–19, 131, 238;

mixed-genre compositions is declared explicitly by Donne himself, where he associates his words with the great canticle of Moses in Deuteronomy 32, and justifies the poetic expression of his subject by reference to the biblical precedent. God instructed Moses

> . . . to deliver unto all,
> That song: because he knew they would let fall,
> The Law, the Prophets, and the History,
> But keepe the song still in their memory.
> Such an opinion (in due measure) made
> Me this great Office boldly to invade.[50]   (463–8)

At first sight, these words are among the most conventional in the *Anniversaries*, and, when taken with the conclusion of the poem, appear to represent a restatement of the justifications of their art found in Whetstone and Churchyard:

> Verse hath a middle nature: heaven keepes soules,
> The grave keeps bodies, verse the fame enroules.   (473–4)

But it is important to retain a sense of the biblical context of these remarks. Donne is claiming kinship with writings that are more than merely generically various and memorable: they are also, axiomatically, divinely inspired and as such exemplary.[51] Donne also implicitly derives from Deuteronomy a precedent for his anatomy of the death of the world and for his revelation of the wretched and ignorant postlapsarian state of humanity.

Of course the *Anniversaries* perform conventional elegiac functions, praising the dead and consoling the bereaved. But the speaker, who has been liberated from the fictional relationships between elegy

the chapter 'Bodies', in Carey, *Donne*, 131–66, and, more generally, F. Barker, *The Tremulous Private Body* (1984) and D. L. Hodges, *Renaissance Fictions of Anatomy* (Amherst, 1985).

[50] Donne's reading of the episode was the standard one of the age, and derived ultimately from St John Chrysostom (see Milgate, *Anniversaries*, 151–2; Lewalski, *Donne's Anniversaries*, 236–40). In a sermon, Donne observed that: 'when God had given all the Law, he provided, as himself sayes, a safer way, which was to give them a heavenly Song of his owne making: for that song, he sayes there, he was sure they would remember': *Sermons*, ii. 171.

[51] In Edward Leigh's words, 'The Book of the *Psalms, Job*, and the *Songs of Moses*, are the only patern of true Poesie' (*Annotations on Five Poetical Books of the Old Testament* (1657), sig. A6). Moses's songs are treated in George Sandys, *Paraphrase upon the Divine Poems* (1638). See the many refs. in Curtius, *European Literature and the Latin Middle Ages* (index, s.v. 'Biblical poetics'); B. Lewalski, *Protestant Poetics and the Seventeenth Century Religious Lyric* (Princeton, 1979); Fowler, *Kinds of Literature*, 146–7, 192.

and mourning, between epitaph and tomb, is authorized to be more general, more reflective. Since the subject's heavenly apotheosis is given, attention is directed to the poet and the reader, and the gulf separating the living from the dead is accentuated. The reader is challenged by a novel form, by compositions which, in the tradition of mixed-genre works, constantly invite and resist generic classification. Specifically, they anticipate the procedure of Donne's own sermons —a point that provides a helpful index of the relationship between speaker and reader in the *Anniversaries*.[52]

At one level, the structure of the poems is obvious: marginal notes and refrains signal the articulating points.[53] Yet few readings of the poems have resisted the temptation to seek to 'define' their structure, and Donne's flexibility, his 'opportunism', have perhaps been insufficiently appreciated.[54] After all, the refrain-units and sections are of varying lengths, and the poems are built on the premiss of the limitations of mortal comprehension: common sense urges caution in anatomizing an anatomy that cultivates the reader's recognition of inadequacy. And the speaker is disarmingly modest about his writing: he addresses the world:

> I (since no man can make thee live) will trie,
> What we may gaine by thy Anatomy.[55]   (59–60)

The matter of the *First Anniversary* is commonplace. But the style is not. Its first readers must have been struck by the appearance of a

---

[52] In Milgate's words: 'The only "genre" which can accommodate all the qualities to be found in the poems and which can include hymn, praise, condemnation, meditation, oration, satire, and vision, is, indeed, the sermon of the kind which Donne himself composed': *Anniversaries*, xl. See P. A. Parrish, 'Poet, Audience, and the Word: An Approach to the *Anniversaries*', in G. A. Stringer, ed., *New Essays on Donne* (Salzburg, 1977), 110–39.

[53] L. L. Martz, *The Poetry of Meditation* (rev. edn., New Haven, 1962), 211–35.

[54] As Lebans notes in a review of Lewalski, *Donne's Anniversaries* (*RES*, NS, 27 (1976), 346–50): 'major problems of interpretation have arisen from the progressive accumulation of theories designed to explain and to justify the Anniversaries . . . and, especially, from the tendency to displace the hyperbolic compliment to a more respectable intellectual plane'. Milgate (*Anniversaries*, xxxiv) cautioned that the *Anniversaries* may be 'rather simpler and at the same time more richly and flexibly imagined, than many modern discussions make them out to be'. J. Carey, commenting on the 'aerobatic extravagance' of the poems, judiciously observes: 'The whole affair had . . . only the most tenuous connection with Elizabeth Drury . . . The plan was to delineate "the best that I could conceive"—to drive his imagination to its limit' (*Donne*, 101, 103).

[55] Donne later referred to '*Solomons* Anatomy, and cutting up of the world' (*Sermons*, iii. 51).

way of treating serious subjects with pithy directness and intelligence. This was their first experience of Donne's poetic voice:

> There is no health; Physitians say that we
> At best, enjoy, but a neutralitee.
> And can there be worse sickenesse, then to know
> That we are never well, nor can be so?
> We are borne ruinous: poore mothers crie,
> That children come not right, nor orderly,
> Except they headlong come, and fall upon
> An ominous precipitation.
> How witty's ruine! How importunate
> Upon mankinde! It labour'd to frustrate
> Even Gods purpose; and made woman, sent
> For mans reliefe, cause of his languishment.
> They were to good ends, and they are so still,
> But accesory, and principall in ill.
> For that first marriage was our funerall:
> One woman at one blow, then kill'd us all,
> And singly, one by one, they kill us now.   (91–107)

Other qualities of the poems would have seemed innovative or challenging. Like some of Jonson's epitaphs, or Spenser's *Epithalamion*, Donne's work represented an explicit rejection of conventional views of the subjects appropriate to public verse. Further, its manner related to more intimate modes—such as the verse epistle—in which a 'lower', argumentative style was proper.[56] Milton was to effect a similarly disconcerting marriage of subject and style in *Paradise Regained.*[57]

The reiterated 'refrain and moral' passages ('Shee, shee is dead; shee's dead; . . . ') signpost the disposition of material within the poem: they further suggest a musical frame of reference which both connects the poems with Moses's song in Deuteronomy and implies that order, symmetry, and coherence may be derived from sounds as much as from sense or argument. Louis Martz proceeded from such observations to propose a five-part structure to the *First Anniversary* (each section comprising meditation, eulogy, and 'refrain and moral', flanked by introduction and conclusion): the whole being based on indebtedness to the

---

[56] In the verse epistles *To Mr T.W.*, Donne assessed his own performance as 'good prose, although the verse be evil' (*To Mr T.W.*, 'All haile sweet Poet', l. 27), and addressed one piece 'Hast thee harsh verse'; Marotti makes a similar point in *John Donne, Coterie Poet*, 36–7,   [57] Fowler, *Kinds of Literature*, 229, 259.

(essentially Catholic) 'meditative tradition'.[58] Others have argued that the passages of consolation in the *Anniversaries* resemble consolatory passages in funeral elegies, and that the poems are really just overgrown elegiac performances.[59] More obviously relevant, perhaps, was the virtuoso display of categorized learning characteristic of the 'Anatomies': such a context may help to grasp Donne's satirical thrust and studied avoidance of neoclassical generic purity. But readings of the *Anniversaries* since 1611 too frequently shrivel into such attempts to unlock them on the basis of some single generic key, or they reveal an occasionalist anxiety to 'discover' the 'identity' of the 'shee' of the poem. Donne created a novel manner of writing which, although it had its being in the control and disposition of various genre-systems, derived its vitality—and its meaning—from refusing exclusive allegiance.[60]

The aggregative, accumulative procedure of Donne's 'Anatomy' is that of the masterpieces of *genera mista* composition.[61] His achievement is to be measured more in terms of multifariousness and *copia* than of simple 'unity', and identified in the relationship between speaker and reader in their shared contemplation of the meaning of Elizabeth Drury's life and death. The poem's variety and amplitude are implied by the assured, philosophizing, argumentative confidence of the style, by suggestive accumulations of detail, and, most obviously, by reiterated words. These words ('Shee', 'All', 'Thinke') become charged with further import through repetition: they recall the continuo drone traditionally accompanying pastoral dirges, and maintain the fiction that the poem is a 'song' on the Mosaic model. In addition, they present themselves as topics of meditation, and thereby contribute to the cultivation of a sense of imaginative coherence specifically derived from the particular circumstances of the unique subject.

The poem's opening lament establishes the central terms of a contrast between earthly and heavenly perspectives. The distinction invites and structures simultaneous scrutiny of the subject and of

---

[58] *The Poetry of Meditation*, 211–48.

[59] Lebans, 'Donne's *Anniversaries* and the Tradition of Funeral Elegy', 559.

[60] R. Colie, *Paradoxica Epidemica* (Princeton, 1969), 396–429; ' "All in Peeces" ', *passim*. For a more recent development of these positions, that seeks to locate Donne's writing in the context of the arousal of a sense of the marvellous, see J. L. Klause, 'Donne and the Wonderful', *ELR* 17 (1987), 41–66.

[61] R. Colie, *The Resources of Kind*, 1–31; Fowler, *Kinds of Literature*, 107–8, 181–3, 254–5.

the reader's faculties (expressed initially in terms of literary experience). Related to it are Donne's habitual consideration of the relation of the particular to the universal, and his expression of the theology of the resurrection of the glorified body in terms derived from alchemy.[62]

The *Second Anniversary* opens with a series of explicit recollections of its predecessor. The speaker asks the 'Immortal Mayd' to 'be unto my Muse | A Father', since the only fame he can anticipate is 'To be hereafter prais'd, for praysing' her (32–5).[63] The theme of *contemptus mundi* reappears in the first occurrence of the refrain (where 'dead' has been tellingly replaced by the less immediate 'gone'):

> Shee, shee is gone; shee's gone; when thou knowst this,
> What fragmentary rubbidge this world is
> Thou knowst, and that it is not worth a thought;
> He honors it too much that thinks it nought.
> Thinke, then, my soule, that death is but a Groome,
> Which brings a Taper to the outward roome,
> Whence thou spiest first a little glimmering light,
> And after brings it nearer to to thy sight:[64]   (81–8)

From this point the poem grows generically further from the earlier 'Anatomy'. Its title, 'Of the Progresse of the Soule', and Hall's 'Harbinger', had prefigured such a development:[65]

> So while thou mak'st her soules Hy progresse knowne
> Thou mak'st a noble progresse of thine owne,
> From this worlds carcasse having mounted hie
> To that pure life of Immortalitie;
>
>   (27–30)

An additional distinction between the poems is implicit in the musical references with which each concludes.[66] The Anatomy had ended by claiming kinship with Moses's dying canticle to the

---

[62] See the second elegy on Cecilia Bulstrode, 'Language, thou art too narrow' (57–60), and Sherwood, *Fulfilling the Circle*, 81–3.

[63] An echo of Sidney, *Astrophil and Stella*, 35: 'Not thou by praise, but praise by thee is raisde: | It is a praise to praise, when thou art praisde' (*Poems*, ed. Ringler, 182).

[64] It seems to share Montaigne's view that 'Our religion hath no surer humane foundation, then the contempt of life', *Essays*, tr. Florio (1603), sig. E1ʳ.

[65] Text from Milgate, *Anniversaries*, 40; see also *The Poems of Joseph Hall*, ed. A. Davenport (Liverpool, 1969), 147.

[66] P. G. Stanwood, ' "Essential Joye" in Donne's *Anniversaries*', *TSLL* 13 (1971), 227–38.

Hebrews, a song inspired by God to fix the Law firmly in the mind of his errant people. The speaker in the *Second Anniversary*, on the other hand, identifies himself with a trumpet blown at God's command to summon the people to hear a proclamation (that is, Elizabeth Drury):

> Since his will is, that to posteritee,
> Thou shouldst for life, and death, a patterne bee,
> And that the world should notice have of this,
> The purpose, and th'Autority is his;
> Thou art the Proclamation; and I ame
> The Trumpet, at whose voice the people came.   (523–8)

In the *First Anniversary*, then, the speaker had claimed for himself a Mosaic role, the teacher transmitting—in palatable form—the wisdom of the Law to the people: in the second, he summons them to pay attention to a proclamation, which has been inscribed in his subject. Elizabeth Drury is no longer the occasion of meditation: she has become a text herself. Later in life Donne was to see the priest's office in similarly dual terms—the priest was both instrument and song, *tuba* and *carmen musicum*.[67] The shift in emphasis explains the stress in the *Second Anniversary* on the specific details of Elizabeth Drury's life. The topics under consideration are located in her: in her person they are resolved, particularized, unified. Accordingly, each section proceeds from the general to the particular. For example, when the speaker contrasts essential joys on earth (383–434) with those in heaven (435–46), he returns to his subject for authorization:

> shee to Heaven is gone,
> Who made this world in some proportion
> A heaven, and here, became unto us all,
> Joye, (as our joyes admit) essentiall.   (467–70)

Her apotheosis is classed as unclassifiable, unquantifiable ('he that names degree, | Doth injure her': 498–9): like the fourth Grace on Spenser's Mount Acidale (*FQ* VI. x) she augments that already perfect form, the circle (507–10). Yet alongside such conventional

---

[67] The scriptural resonances of this passage (as Lewalski (*Donne's Anniversaries*, 277–80) points out) are many and profound. Milgate (*Anniversaries*, 176) notes that the priests in Num. 10: 2–3, 10, were to summon the people by blowing silver trumpets. In a sermon of 1618/9, Donne, referring to Ezek. 33: 32, said (*Sermons*, ii. 166–70): 'And lo, thou art unto them as a very lovely song, of one that hath a pleasant voyce, and can play well on an instrument, for they hear thy words, but they doe them not'.

expressions of inexpressibility, the *Second Anniversary* provides the reader with more detail; more evidence is presented, in the course of this second demonstration, of the inadequacy of mortal understanding when confronted with the operations of the Godhead.

And much of this demonstration is carried out, mimed, in the language and style of the poem. The speaker explores the paradoxes generated by meditation on death, and seeks verbal approximations to the transformations a virtuous soul might anticipate. Although it possesses coherence by virtue of its thematic consistency and the essentially musical effects of repetition, the poem is stylistically a curious amalgam of the epigrammatic and the tortuous, with the speaker's language both supporting and enacting his arguments. Thus the sarcastic attack upon the fatuity of human systems of knowledge:

> Thou art too narrow, wretch, to comprehend
> Even thy selfe: yea though thou wouldst but bend
> To know thy body.   (261–3)

is expressed in regular, end-stopped lines which mockingly duplicate the certainties of human science. Thus:

> What hope have we to know our selves, when wee
> Know not the least things, which for our use bee?
> We see in Authors, too stiffe to recant,
> A hundred controversies of an Ant.[68]
> And yet one watches, starves, freeses, and sweats,
> To know but Catechismes and Alphabets
> Of unconcerning things, matters of fact;
> How others on our stage their parts did Act;
> What Caesar did, yea, and what Cicero said.
> Why grasse is greene, or why our blood is red,
> Are mysteries which none have reach'd unto.
> In this low forme, poore soule, what wilt thou doe?   (279–90)

When the speaker proceeds from his scorn of mortal ignorance to the celestial wisdom Elizabeth Drury has instantly acquired, he

---

[68] Donne's library included a copy of J. Wilde's edn. of *Augustanus: De Formica* (1615); see G. Keynes, *A Bibliography of John Donne* (4th edn. Oxford, 1973), L. 192, and the *First Anniversary*, l. 190, 'Be more then man, or thou'rt lesse then an Ant'. Donne also observed that '*Man*, who (like his owne eye) sees all but himself, in his opinion, but so dimly, that there are marked an hundred differences in mens Writings concerning an Ant', *Essays in Divinity*, ed. E. M. Simpson (Oxford, 1952), 14.

moves to a denser, more obviously reflective, style. The difficulty of expressing in words what she apprehends effortlessly is imitated (as elsewhere in Donne's work) by parentheses, hesitations, elisions, compressions, enjambments, and the like:

> Shee, who in th'Art of knowing Heaven, was growne
> Here upon Earth, to such perfection,
> That shee hath, ever since to Heaven shee came,
> (In a far fairer print,) but read the same:
> Shee, shee, not satisfied with all this waite,
> (For so much knowledge, as would over-fraite
> Another, did but Ballast her) is gone,
> As well t'enjoy, as get perfectione.
> And cals us after her, in that shee tooke,
> (Taking herselfe) our best, and worthiest booke.   (311–20)

The *Second Anniversary* was perhaps the first of Donne's poems to be composed with publication in mind, the first to be conceived outside a particular domestic context. Yet both *Anniversaries* are consistent with the developments in Donne's art that had been embodied in the second Bulstrode elegy: and the greater specificity of the *Second Anniversary* is a natural amplification of the matter of its predecessor.

In an apparent anticipation of renewed charges of indecorousness, Donne justifies pairing hyperbolic praise and an obscure subject by causing his speaker almost pedantically to explain the connection between Elizabeth Drury and each panegyric topos as it arises. And the speaker's opening performance prepares the ground for such a procedure by its precise and vivid dramatic characterization:

> Nothing could make mee sooner to confesse
> That this world had an everlastingnesse,
> Then to consider, that a yeare is runne,
> Since both this lower worlds, and the Sunnes Sunne,
> The Lustre, and the vigor of this All,
> Did set; 'twere Blasphemy, to say, did fall.   (1–6)

Here Donne sharpens the conventional funeral *epanorthosis*: the speaker introduces himself as linguistically fastidious, careful to distinguish the inappropriate finality of 'fall' from the implied regeneration of the more accurate and less heretical 'set'. There may be a self-referential element at work too: after all, this poem is a repetition, marking (as well as being) a second anniversary. Self-

awareness informs the deployment of reiteration, whereby themat-
ically crucial words are distributed in ways that explore and
augment their senses. The reiterated 'shee' in the fifteen lines
leading up to the refrain (65 ff.) operates in this way. 'Shee' is
immediately succeeded by the imperative 'thinke' which binds
together the sections classified in the margin as 'Contemplation of
our state in our death-bed', 'Incommodities of the Soule in the
Body', and 'Her liberty by death'. The poem seems to proceed by
metaphorical changes of key indicated by the modulation of these
drone-words (from 'shee' to 'thinke' to 'knowe' to 'shee' to 'up', and
so on), and the passages where the modulation occurs tend to
feature even denser bursts of reiteration. This process, of 'divisions'
upon the refrain, inevitably directs the reader to closer inspection
of both the subject and the poet's art. We consider, as it were, the
speaker's soul (or at least his understanding) alongside Elizabeth
Drury's—Joseph Hall, we should remember, complimented Donne's
'noble progresse' in the poems 'To that pure life of Immortalitie'.
From such a journey, within the context of the poem, the speaker
derives the authority to instruct his listeners:

> When wilt thou shake off this Pedantery,
> Of being taught by sense, and Fantasy?
> Thou look'st through spectacles; small things seeme great,
> Below; But up into the watch-towre get,
> And see all things despoyld of fallacies:
> Thou shalt not peepe through lattices of eies,
> Nor heare through Laberinths of eares, nor learne
> By circuit, or collections to discerne.
> In Heaven though straight know'st all, concerning it,
> And what concerns it not, shalt straight forget.   (291–300)

By making central to his poems the experience of the speaker,
Donne made creative use of his role as orator: he relocated the
topos of inexpressibility in the mind, and imagination, of the
elegist.[69] Struggles with expression mimed struggles to comprehend
the meaning of the subject's life and death: 'problems of writing'

---

[69] Lewalski, *Donne's Anniversaries*, 274–6; but see also Sherwood's persuasive
judgement of what he calls the depiction of 'the paradoxical intercourse between heaven
and earth' in *The Second Anniversary*: 'the soul's epistemological diet must necessarily
nourish the paradoxical elements in man's being. Taken together, the *Anniversaries* are
spiritual nourishment that enhances understanding of man's status in a corrupt world
and encourages the spiritual motions guiding his progress toward heavenly joy': *Fulfilling
the Circle*, 92.

became invested with the absorbing seriousness and importance they had held for Erasmus and Montaigne. It was such an internalization of one of the major components of elegy that clearly struck the first readers of the *Anniversaries* as both extraordinary and exemplary. At the same time, Donne's poems created a new model for the application of matter from the most elevated spheres of thought to essentially domestic concerns (as such, they perhaps suggested comparison with the recently published *Cantos of Mutabilitie*, where, for example, the landscape around Spenser's estate in Ireland was considered, wholly unironically, in terms of Ovidian myth).[70] Further, the remarkable generic variousness of Donne's poems had created a mode that was hospitable to the resources of hymn, meditation, and sermon, in which all artistic choices and emphases might be considered as part of the elegiac process and as an expression of the speaker's condition.

The elegies written on the death of Prince Henry testify to the rapidity with which the *Anniversaries* acquired exemplary status. The very number of poems which proclaim their indebtedness amply demonstrates the point.[71] Of course the charge of indecorousness could not apply in the case of Prince Henry, an event self-evidently important enough to elicit a poet's 'best praise'. Commentators have perhaps failed to grasp this point sufficiently. Ruth Wallerstein, for example, saw the influence of Donne's poems only in Tourneur's *Griefe on the death of Prince Henrie*.[72] Hardison, on the other hand, took the popularity of the poems as evidence that Donne's contemporaries found them 'traditional' and 'matter of course'.[73] What actually occurred was that the *Anniversaries* almost instantly became 'a model for praise and compliments . . . a touchstone for judging other poetic endeavours in panegyric and elegiac kinds'.[74] As Jasper Mayne was later to write:[75]

---

[70] See D. Cheney's account of Spenser's mythologizing the circumstances of his own life, 'Spenser's Fortieth Birthday and Related Fictions', *Spenser Studies*, 4 (1984), 3–31.

[71] The opening lines of Joshua Sylvester's elegy on the Prince seem to allude both to Donne's general pre-eminence as elegist and to Donne's own poem on the Prince, which appears in the same volume: 'How-ever short of Others *Art and Witt* | I knowe my powers for such a Part unfitt; | And shall but light my Candle in the *Sunne,* | To doe a Work shalbe so better Donne': *Lachrimae lachrimarum . . . etc.* (1613), sig. A2ʳ. See also Ch. 6 below.   [72] R. Wallerstein, *Studies in Seventeenth-Century Poetic*, 84–6.

[73] Hardison, *The Enduring Monument*, 163–70.

[74] Lewalski, *Donne's Anniversaries*, 308.

[75] Text from Milgate, *Anniversaries*, 93: see Lewalski, *Donne's Anniversaries*, 311, and S. Gottlieb, '*Elegies upon the Author*: Defining, Defending and Surviving Donne', *John Donne Journal*, 2 (1982), 23–38.

> Who shall presume to mourn thee, *Donne*, unlesse
> He could his teares in thy expressions dresse,
> And teach his griefe that reverence of thy Hearse,
> To weepe lines, learned, as thy Anniverse,
> A Poëme of that worth, whose every teare
> Deserves the title of a severall yeare.   (1–6)

THE INTERRED MUSE: 1614–1625

From 1611 Donne was the poet of the *Anniversaries*. Thereafter when he came to compose funeral verses he did so (as Jasper Mayne's words indicate) as the acknowledged master—indeed the inventor—of the form. The first such poem was his elegy on Prince Henry, discussed in the next chapter.[76]

No less pressing an occasion for Donne was the death of the young Lord Harrington, Lady Bedford's brother, on 27 February 1613/14.[77] Not yet 22, the 'most compleat yong gentleman of his age that this kingdom could afford for religion, learning, and courteous behaviour', died of smallpox at Twickenham.[78] He had been Prince Henry's companion, and had been presented to the Doge of Venice in 1609 as a potentially influential figure at the Stuart court.[79] Sir Henry Wotton said of him then: 'He is learned in philosophy, has Latin and Greek to perfection, is handsome, well-made as any man could be, at least among us'.[80] Harrington's piety and learning were eulogized by Richard Stock in a funeral sermon, and Thomas Fuller observed that he 'did not count himself privileged from being good, by being great'.[81]

Donne presents his elegy as his retirement from verse: the speaker addresses the subject's soul—

> Doe not, faire soule, this sacrifice refuse,
> That in thy grave I doe interre my Muse,

[76] Below, pp. 193–6.

[77] Bald, 280, 296–7; D. Novarr, *The Disinterred Muse: Donne's Texts and Contexts* (Ithaca, 1980), 102–3.

[78] Sir James Whitelocke, *Liber Famelicus*, 39; Bald, 276.

[79] A fine picture of the two boys at a deer-hunt has survived: it is reproduced in Milgate, *Anniversaries*, 66–7, and in Sir Roy Strong, *Henry Prince of Wales and England's Lost Renaissance* (1986), no. 24.

[80] L. Pearsall Smith, *The Life and Letters of Sir Henry Wotton*, 2 vols. (Oxford, 1907), i. 441.

[81] Fuller, *The Worthies of England* (1662), 130; Richard Stock, *The Churches lamentation for the losse of the godly* (1614), 61–94 (the vol. includes verse by several others, including Cecilia Bulstrode's lover Sir Thomas Roe).

> Who, by my griefe, great as thy worth, being cast
> Behind hand, yet hath spoke, and spoke her last.[82]   (255–8)

The elegy displays the same ample proportions as the *Anniversaries*, and resembles them in several ways. As in the *Second Anniversary*, for example, the speaker almost becomes a character in the work, inviting Harrington's soul to observe ('and with joy'):

> . . . mee to that good degree
> Of goodnesse growne, that I can studie thee,
> And, by those meditations refin'd,
> Can unapparell and enlarge my minde,
> And so can make by this soft extasie,
> This place a map of heav'n, my selfe of thee.   (9–14)

The early part of the poem dwells on the implications of 'unapparelling' and 'enlarging' the mind: we see the speaker's movement to self-knowledge through meditating on Harrington's death. He reports the effects of apprehending, however partially, the paradoxical qualities of the truths death teaches. Still addressing the 'faire soule', he says:

> Thou at this midnight seest mee, and as soone
> As that Sunne rises to mee, midnight's noone,
> All the world growes transparent, and I see
> Through all, both Church and State, in seeing thee;
> And I discerne, by favour of this light,
> My selfe, the hardest object of the sight.
> God is the glasse; as though when thou dost see
> Him who sees all, seest all concerning thee,
> So, yet unglorified, I comprehend
> All, in these mirrors of thy wayes, and end.   (25–34)

We are in familiar territory. God as a glass, the virtuous as mirrors or telescopes (with the usual anatomizing, satirical, exemplary

---

[82] The ceremony thus conjured may recall events reported to have occurred at Spenser's funeral, when other writers flung their pens into the grave: see W. Camden, *The historie of the princesse Elizabeth*, tr. R. N[orton] (1630), Bk IV (p. 135). Donne's lines ought to be read alongside his begging letter to Lady Bedford; 'hee which bestowes any cost upon the dead, oblige him which is dead, but not the heire: I do not therefore send this paper to your Ladyship, that you should thank me for it . . . your favours and benefits to mee are so much above my merits . . .', and so on (text from Milgate, *Anniversaries*, 196). In a letter to Henry Goodyer, Donne later complained that his performance, though it had moved the Countess to offer to write off his debts, had only brought in £30 (Donne, *Letters*, (1651), 218–19. Bald, 294–7; Thomson, 'Donne and Lady Bedford', 335–40; Novarr, *Disinterred Muse*, 102; Marotti, *John Donne, Coterie Poet*, 273–4).

implications), the reiterated 'all' (a theological commonplace of the period, 'part of a preacher's stock of erudite phrases'); all are recognizable components of Donne's elegiac mode.[83]

But this is a very polished and assured performance—we know that composition was slow and we can suppose that Donne's eloquent farewell to his art was carefully designed. The argument is smoothly presented, the speaker gliding from consideration of his own inadequacy and the possibility of profiting spiritually from contemplation of his subject's death to a meditation on the brevity of Harrington's life, concluding conventionally that longevity is no necessary part of virtue:

> Just as a perfect reader doth not dwell,
> On every syllable, nor stay to spell,
> Yet without doubt, hee doth distinctly see,
> And lay together every A, and B;
> So, in short liv'd good men, is'not understood
> Each severall vertue, but the compound, good;   (93-8)

The wit of 'doubt'—a letter in which the perfect reader may 'lay together', but will not pronounce, 'every A and B' (perhaps recalling Shakespeare's Holofernes (*LLL* v. i. 1–23))—deftly encapsulates the central notion of the speaker's refusal to engage in an anatomy of his subject.[84] He justifies his position in a way that suggests a generic distinction from the *Anniversaries*:

> I
> Should injure Nature, Vertue, 'and Destinie,
> Should I divide and discontinue so,
> Vertue, which did in one intirenesse grow.   (59-62)

The ensuing lengthy consideration of the soul's circularity opens with the familiar soul/compass metaphor; as in the clock image that follows, Donne draws extensively on emblematic conventions.[85] In so doing, he implicitly proclaims the indissoluble relationship between word, image, and idea that is itself the basis of his panegyric strategy in this poem. The final great image is that of the

---

[83] Lebans, 'Influence of the Classics', 130; Lewalski, *Donne's Anniversaries*, 128–9. She cites Calvin's *Commentary . . . upon the Epistle to the Colossians*, tr. R. V. (1581), 68. See also E. B. Gilman, *The Curious Perspective: Literary and Pictorial Wit in the Seventeenth Century* (New York, 1978), 167–203.

[84] See M. McCanles, *Dialectical Criticism and Renaissance Literature* (Berkeley, 1975), 54–117; Sherwood, *Fulfilling the Circle*, 116.

[85] J. Lederer, 'John Donne and the Emblematic Practice', *RES* 22 (1946), 199.

Roman Triumph, as the speaker attempts to justify the triumph accorded to his subject's soul.[86]

Points of articulation between the poem's governing conceits are not marked, as in the *Anniversaries*, by repetition and accumulated effects. The style here is noticeably less various, without antiphonic refrains, or the dirge-like reiterated 'drone' words. For example, the prelude to the triumph:

> Now I grow sure, that if a man would have
> Good companie, his entry is a grave.
> Mee thinkes all Cities, now, but Anthills bee,
> Where, when the severall labourers I see,
> For children, house, provision, taking paine,
> They 'are all but Ants, carrying eggs, straw, and grain;
> And Church-yards are our cities, unto which
> The most repaire, that are in goodnesse rich.
> There is the best concourse, and confluence,
> There are the holy suburbs, and from thence
> Begins Gods City, New Jerusalem,
> Which doth extend her utmost gates to them.   (165–70)

Donne exploits the rhetorical and metaphorical resources of the heroic couplet: conceits are reinforced by the metrical regularity. Cities and anthills, churchyards and cities, for example, are linked structurally as well as conceptually.

Surprisingly, in view of its valedictory conclusion, and the implication that it represented a summary of the speaker's eloquence, this poem has been little studied.[87] Yet, while not as revolutionary as the *Anniversaries* themselves, the 'Obsequies' exemplifies the qualities of the tradition of funeral verse that Donne inaugurated. Despite its polish, indeed, Donne's poem anticipates the writing of Cleveland and his generation, especially in its metrical regularity and tendency to antithesis (see especially lines 155–60, 223–8). The work illustrates Donne's classical non-pastoral elegiac mode. The final argumentative section, urging Harrington's entitlement to a triumph, blends classical and Christian matter, implying transcendence and apotheosis, but without the usual machinery of hermetic or alchemical allusion. The pagan references in the conclusion seem designed to reinforce

---

[86] See Milgate's article, 'Donne and the Roman Triumph', *Parergon* 1 (1971), 18–23.

[87] A rare exception is P. C. Kolin, 'Donne's "Obsequies to the Lord Harrington": Theme, Structure, and Image', *Southern Quarterly*, 13 (1974), 65–82.

the sense of Christian consolation; the poet's retirement (in which the poem itself plays a central role as part of a gesture) becomes a 'testimonie of love, unto the dead' simultaneously more valuable and less barbaric than the voluntary suicide of 'Saxon wives' and French 'soldurii'.[88]

Eleven years separate the 'Obsequies to the Lord Harrington' from Donne's final elegy. In 1625, Donne had been Dean of St Paul's for some three years, and had gained the confidence of the ageing King and of Buckingham. He had written little verse since his ordination, and had published some prose (mainly sermons). But the *Anniversaries* (republished in 1621 and 1625) kept alive his reputation as an elegist.[89]

In the 1633 edition of Donne's *Poems*, the elegy (which is classed as a 'hymn') on Marquess Hamilton is prefaced with Donne's letter to Sir Robert Carr: Carr's kindness is proposed as explanation for this disinterring of Donne's Muse.[90] Though not designed for publication, the piece shares many characteristics of the more 'public' of Donne's commemorative verses. After all, Hamilton, like Prince Henry and Lord Harrington, had lived a public life, in ways denied the female subjects of Donne's earlier poems.[91] Indeed, as a hymn addressed to the entire company of the saints, it is, though relatively brief, built on an immense scale. The structure is simple, as the hymn is disposed (as Grierson observed) into four syntactical units (1–8, 9–18, 19–30, 31–42).[92] In the first the speaker contrasts heaven's increase (which he cannot properly

[88] And Donne evidently intended to keep his promise: 'I would be just to my written words to my L.Harrington, to write nothing after' (*Letters* (1651), 197–8).

[89] Novarr, *Disinterred Muse*, 192–205.

[90] The text of the letter (taken from Milgate, *Anniversaries*, 209) runs: 'Sir, I presume you rather try what you can doe in me, then what I can doe in verse; you know my uttermost when it was best, and even then I did best when I had least truth for my subject. In this present case there is so much truth as it defeats all Poetry. Call therefore this paper by what name you will, and if it bee not worthy of him, nor of you, nor of mee, smother it, and be that the sacrifice. If you had commanded mee to have waited on his body to Scotland and preached there, I would have embraced the obligation with more alacrity: But, I thanke you that you would command me that which I was loath to doe, for even that hath given a tincture of merit to the obedience of, Your poore friend and servant in Christ Jesus, J.D.'. See Bald, 466–7, and Marotti, *John Donne, Coterie Poet*, 285 for details of Donne's relationship with Carr.

[91] And Chamberlain's remarks (27 Aug. 1617) suggest that Hamilton warranted a degree of hyperbole: 'I have not heard a man generally better spoken of then that marques, even by all the English insomuch that he is every way held the gallantest gentleman of both the nations' (*Letters*, ed. McClure, ii. 98).

[92] *Donne*, ed. Grierson, ii. 217.

discern) with earth's loss (which he can). He then lists those places and estates where the loss will be felt:

> The name of *Father, Master, Friend,* the name
> Of *Subject* and of *Prince,* in one are lame;
> Faire mirth is dampt, and conversation black,
> The *Household* widdow'd, and the *Garter* slack;
> The *Chappell* wants an eare, *Councell* a tongue;
> *Story,* a theame; and *Musicke* lacks a song;
> Blest *order* that hath him, the losse of him
> Gangreend all *Orders* here; all lost a limbe.   (11–18)

The third section explores the posthumous relation of body to soul, hinting at the horror of Hamilton's death—'All former comelinesse | Fled, in a minute, when the soule was gone' (20–1)—just as dissolved monasteries were instantly degraded 'Not to lesse houses, but, to heapes of stone' (24).[93] The speaker proposes that Hamilton's soul possesses the form of the body, dwelling in the 'sphaere of formes', where they may 'Anticipate a Resurrection' (26–8).[94] So that while his fame sustains his soul on earth, his form sustains his body in heaven. Simple consolation is offered in the confident assumptions that Hamilton is either already installed in heaven, or, as a Penitent, destined for it, whence he can help sinners left behind to achieve similar transformations:

> . . . let it bee
> Thy wish to all there, to wish them cleane;
> Wish *him* a *David,* her a *Magdalen.*   (40–2)

Generically, the hymn represents Donne's furthest departure from elegy, whether classical or native. Obviously enough, it is not addressed to grieving relatives but rather to the company of saints. It is removed from the fiction of funeral (and therefore from the epicede and elegy) and from the lapidary conventions of epitaph; it is more explicitly theological, though its theology is far removed from that of the earlier poems.[95] Actual grief hardly makes an appearance: the poem opens neither by questioning the fact of death, nor by searching for meaning in life, nor by proclaiming

---

[93] 'The *Symptoms* being very *presumptuous,* his head and body swelling to an excessive greatness; the hair of his Head, Eye-brows, and Beard, came off being touched, and brought the *Skin* with them': A. Wilson, *The History of Great Britain* (1653), 285.

[94] See Milgate, *Anniversaries,* 210; Sherwood, *Fulfilling the Circle,* 83–4.

[95] See Novarr, *Disinterred Muse,* 198–9.

inexpressibility. Rather the speaker (who now appears less like Montaigne than a somewhat pedantic scholar) enquires of the saints the precise nature of Hamilton's heavenly station:

> Whether that soule which now comes up to you
> Fill any former ranke or make a new;
> Whether it take a name nam'd there before,
> Or be a name it selfe, and *order* more
> Then was in heaven till now . . .   (1–5)

'I could wish a man of his yeares and place to geve over versefieng', wrote Chamberlain (though he conceded the poem was 'reasonable wittie and well don').[96] And few have argued with such a view: the piece is probably Donne's last poem, and it has seemed to many readers that his heart was not in the job: he would much rather, so the argument goes, have preached a funeral sermon. Nevertheless, there is much that is recognizable in it. As ever, Donne explores the gulf between the transient and the eternal, though here worldly things are presented either in a highly formal manner (as in the catalogue cited above) or through the transformed eyes of the subject's soul (39–42). A brief reference to the conventional notion of the abiding nature of fame (29) is set aside, as the speaker invites Hamilton to consider his mourning friends not as individuals, but as types of repentant sinners, as David and Magdalen. This, indeed, draws together and concludes the hymn's themes, since it had begun with a problem (is Hamilton *sui generis* or classifiable?) and had proposed that his loss was most keenly felt as an exemplary representative of various earthly roles.

Donne wrote about death throughout his career, and inevitably his elegies and *Anniversaries* tell only part of the story. The very process of dying evidently excited his imagination, much as other changes of state, transformations, and refinements did.[97] And the funeral poems (chiefly those from the years 1609–14) constitute at one level a dramatization of his own preoccupations at a critical stage in his life, when, for various reasons, the intellectual and emotional struggle to locate meaning in the fact of death seems to have exercised him strongly.

[96] *Letters*, ed. McClure, ii. 613.
[97] Lewalski, *Donne's Anniversaries*, 174–215; M. Roston, *The Soul of Wit* (Oxford, 1974), 184–97; Carey, *Donne*, 198–230; Sherwood, *Fulfilling the Circle*, esp. chs. 2, 3, 4; B. A. Doebler, *The Quickening Seed: Death in the Sermons of John Donne* (Salzburg, 1974).

The poems examined in this chapter display Donne's gradual construction of an idiom which might accommodate praise of the dead both with general philosophical and religious meditations and with dramatically enacted consolation. In tandem with a series of formal experiments, and related to them, Donne habitually explored, whether obviously or insidiously, those antitheses (life and death, time and eternity, individual and type, body and soul, and so forth) which could be generated by meditation on a particular death. His experiments with style led to the creation of a manner suited to argument (whether public or self-scrutinizing and interior), to the expression of ethical material, while expressing the contrasts in such a way as to embody the process of consolation— which was, of course, the immediate purpose of most of the poems. For the historian of the elegy, Donne's funeral verses constitute a highly significant development. He enlarged the repertoire of elegy, by moving towards increasingly inclusive and reflective forms and away from the immediate circumstances of death and burial.[98] Where an earlier generation of intellectual poets had struggled with the intractable Tudor metres and their inseparable baggage of formulae, the followers of Donne had before them vernacular models that were simultaneously innovative and based on reputable classical precedent. They had a new model of the poet's role, and a clear invitation to turn their admiration into imitation and emulation. Like Spenser, Donne gave a voice to a generation.[99] Unlike him, he achieved this initially—and primarily—through his funeral verses.

[98] For a later example of elegiac introspection, see R. Sargent, 'Poetry and the Puritan Faith: The Elegies of Anne Bradstreet and Edward Taylor', in W. Haslauer, ed., *A Salzburg Miscellany: English and American Studies 1964–84* (Salzburg, 1984), 149–60.

[99] D. Norbrook writes that Donne's 'public poetry, with its extravagant imagery of worship and self-abasement, has nothing in common with the Protestant pastoralism favoured by the Spenserians', but he concedes that 'This statement needs qualification, especially with regard to the "Anniversaries"': (*Poetry and Politics*, 200, 321).

5. ELEGIES ON THE DEATH OF PRINCE HENRY

Prince Henry's death on 6 November 1612 provoked an unprece-
dentedly intense, widespread, and unequivocal outburst of lamen-
tation.[1] The King withdrew to Theobalds, the Queen to Somerset
House: Foscarini reported that, even 'in the midst of the most
important discussions', James would cry 'Henry is dead, Henry is
dead': a little later Chamberlain noted how 'on Tewsday I heard
the bishop of Ely [Andrewes] preaching at court upon the third
verse of the 37th of Esay . . . pray solemnly for Prince Henry
without recalling himself'.[2] All Protestant Europe joined in the
mourning.[3] Never before had so many elegies been written on a
single occasion, by such a wide range of practitioners: poets of all
kinds, all (or most) religious and political persuasions. Those
who did, as what follows will show, included William Browne,
George Chapman, John Donne, William Drummond, Sir William
Alexander, Edward and George Herbert, Henry King, Joshua
Sylvester, John Webster, Cyril Tourneur, Thomas Heywood, Sir
Arthur Gorges, Sir Walter Ralegh, Thomas Campion, and George
Wither.[4] The only major writers who did not join in were Jonson,
Daniel, Drayton, and Shakespeare. This is not to mention the
almost innumerable pieces by lesser professional writers (such as
John Taylor the water-poet and the prophet James Maxwell), the
anthologies from each of the Universities, and the substantial

[1] E. C. Wilson, *Prince Henry and English Literature* (New York, 1946), Part III;
R. Wallerstein, *Studies in Seventeenth-Century Poetic*, 59–95.

[2] *C. S. P. Venetian*, xii. 449, 472; John Chamberlain, *Letters*, ed. N. E. McLure
(Philadelphia, 1939), i. 390, ii. 32.

[3] J. W. Williamson, *The Myth of the Conqueror, Prince Henry Stuart: A Study of 17th
Century Personation* (New York, 1978), 161–6.

[4] For an incomplete bibliography, see J. P. Edmonds, 'Elegies and Other Tracts on
the Death of Prince Henry', *Publications of the Edinburgh Bibliographical Society*, 6 (1906),
141–58; for fuller accounts, see two unpubl. doctoral dissertations, P. F. Corbin, 'A
Death and a Marriage: An Examination of the Literature Occasioned by the Death of
Henry Prince of Wales and the Marriage of His Sister Princess Elizabeth, 1612–1613'
(Birmingham, 1966), *passim*, and D. C. Kay, 'The English Funeral Elegy in the Reigns of
Elizabeth I and James I, With Special Reference to Poems on the Death of Prince Henry
(1612)' (Oxford, 1982), 171–319. See also Lewalski, *Donne's Anniversaries*, 312–26, and
Pigman, *Grief and English Renaissance Elegy*, 143–4.

quantity of material that survives only in manuscript, which inclused verses by such diverse figures as Sir Walter Aston and the future archbishop William Juxon, as well, memorably, as the anonymous epitaph:

> Who lies here? No man. No man. Truly no man.
> For to Prince Henry no man equal be can.[5]

'ELOQUENT, JUST AND MIGHTY DEATH': MOURNING PRINCE HENRY

Prince Henry's death represented a challenge for poets. The mourning for Sidney had been almost as lavish, but in 1586 vernacular elegies had essentially been the preserve of professionals: elegies by Sidney's intimates were published substantially later, and Sidney's reputation at the time of his death had been primarily that of a gifted soldier and diplomat. The death of Queen Elizabeth, as has been indicated, posed the obvious problem of reconciling lament with welcome for her successor. With Prince Henry the situation was evidently quite different—although of course implicit criticism of James's policy may be discerned in the militant Protestantism and politically charged Spenserianism of many of the elegies. In addition, many of the poems and anthologies contain pieces celebrating the marriage of Henry's sister Elizabeth to Frederick, the Elector Palatine. Sometimes the transition from lament to epithalamion is crude, as in the section in William Basse's volume entitled 'A morning after mourning'.[6] Other poets would dwell on the conjunction of joy and sadness. Peacham, for example, called his collection *The period of mourning* (a play on the double sense of 'period', both 'duration' and 'close') *disposed into six visions, together with nuptiall hymnes.*[7]

Before embarking on a survey of the elegies themselves, it is perhaps worth reflecting briefly on the question of genre. It will be recalled that the term 'elegy' had first been applied to a funeral lament by Spenser—before that it had merely denoted poems in elegiac metre—and although the usage was given further currency in the poem 'A funeral elegy' which Donne printed with the

---

[5] Bodley MS Rawl. Poet. 160, fo. 27.
[6] William Basse, *Great Brittaines sunnes-set bewailed* (Oxford, 1613), sig. C4[r].
[7] Henry Peacham, *The period of mourning, . . . etc.* (1613): see n. 97 below.

Anniversaries, the word in Elizabethan and Jacobean usage is habitually qualified by an adjective (such as mournful, lamenting, doelful, or funeral), as is common with many generic terms in the period (tragical history, tragical discourse, true tragedy, lamentable tragedy, and so forth). By 1631, however, Weever wrote of 'An elegiacal or sorrowful epitaph', which indicates that the funeral connotations had become dominant.[8] In Thomas Campion's elegy on Prince Henry, the implication is that the heroic couplet is the vernacular equivalent of the elegiac metre, and some other poets attempted to recreate the form in English. The subjects appropriate to the form included complaint—often love-complaint (like the elegies on brambles in *As You Like It* or Drayton's 'My life's complaint in dolefull elegies')—and moral, philosophical, satirical writing, as when Sidney in the *Defence* lists 'the lamenting elegiac' which 'bewails the weakness of mankind and the wretchedness of the world'.[9] Some elegists in 1612 were careful to qualify the term: thus we find Wither's 'elegies and songs of sadness' and Cyril Tourneur's 'broken elegie'.[10] Tourneur further explained—'It was the season for Elegies of this kind, when I wrote this; before His funeralls . . . I had no purpose (then) to haue it published'. The implication is that the elegy is the equivalent of the epicede or funeral song, designed to be sung over the body, and confined to the period before burial, after which the epitaph was (presumably) the more appropriate form. There may also be a connection with the Homeric practice of distinguishing between the formless and

---

[8] J. Weever, *Ancient funerall monuments within the united monarchie of Great Britaine, Ireland, and the islands adjacent* (1631), 8–9.

[9] 'Or is it the lamenting Elegiac; which in a kind heart would move rather pity than blame: who bewails with the great philosopher Heraclitus, the weakness of mankind and the wretchedness of the world; who surely is to be praised, either for compassionate accompanying just causes of lamentations, or for rightly painting out how weak be the passions of woefulness?' (Sidney, *Miscellaneous Prose*, ed. Duncan-Jones and Van Dorsten, p. 95).

[10] George Wither, *Prince Henries obsequies or mournefull elegies upon his death* (1612), D4ᵛ; Cyril Tourneur, *A griefe on the death of prince Henrie* (1613), A4ʳ. At the most obvious level, 'broken' means disjointed, fragmented, hoarse, dejected. It is also a musical metaphor, based on the notion that disruption may generate a superior form of harmony ('here is good broken music', says Pandarus in *Troilus and Cressida*, III. i: Shakespeare plays on the senses of broken on many occasions; see also *Henry V*, v ii. 234, etc.). More precisely, a 'broken consort' was a combination of instruments from various families, for example, strings and woodwind, and may be thought of here as making a connection between literary and musical expressions of generic mixture and inclusiveness—a kind of musical anthology.

hysterical weeping of the family over the body and the more artful and considered lament—at the same stage in the proceedings—from the 'dirge specialist'. Some of those who lamented Henry's death couched this consideration of genre and metre in terms of the characteristic Spenserian repudiation of Ovidian writing:

> . . . all our Elegies begot from passion,
> Come from rent hearts, and those that griefe proclaime.
> Confused thoughts the best conceits destroy,
> And are more harsh then when we sing of joy.[11]

'*To a* Trumpet *raise thy amorous* Stile', wrote Drummond: others professed to be restoring the elegy to its original variety of subjects by incorporating praise for King James and his family into a lament for Henry:

> . . . now, as elegie,
> Made at the first for mourning, hath been since
> Imployed on Love, Joy, and Magnificence:
> So this particular elegie shall enclose
> (meant for my Grief for HIM) with Joy for those.[12]

Others were clearly less happy about the problem of fitting a 'high style' subject, the death of a prince, into the middle to low style appropriate to elegy, especially the elegy derived from Donne. Others worry about the terminology, so pieces are classed as epitaphs, epicedes, equinoques, deplorations, anthems, groans, moans, sobs, sighs, garlands, lamentations, dirges. In addition, there are sonnet sequences, a song cycle, emblematic visions, tears, heroic couplets, rhymed octosyllabics, stanzas of varying degrees of complexity, lines of varying length; poems whose structural components are indicated by refrains, on the model of Sidney or Spenser or Donne. Some volumes are collaborative, others are anthologies by a single author. It is clear that there was no single form that was generally agreed to be capable of satisfying the demands—or exhaust the possibilities—of fitting a commemorative verse to its subject. And inevitably the selection of forms and styles was based upon considerations that were political and religious as much as aesthetic. Campion's repudiation of Donne's wit ('Law-eloquence we need not'), Sylvester's of Ovidian smoothness,

---

[11] Thomas Heywood, *A funerall elegie upon the death of Henry, prince of Wales* (1613), C1r.
[12] Drummond, *Teares on the death of Meliades* (Edinburgh, 1613), p. 105; Henry Goodyer in Sylvester's anthology *Lachrimae lachrimarum* (1613), F4r.

Browne's imitation of Spenser's *Shepheardes Calender*, Drummond's of Sidney, all have significance beyond the narrowly literary. The Prince's celebrated religious sternness underlies the anxiety of poets to produce what Goodyer called 'just plaintes', or what Donne called 'just lamentations'.[13]

It should also be remembered that the period just before Henry's death had added notably to the stock of material on which elegists might draw. The *Mirror for Magistrates*, for example, reappeared in 1610. Richard Niccols, one of its new editors, wrote a Spenserian allegory, *The three sisters teares*, on Henry's death. Then there was the publication of Shakespeare's *Sonnets* and of Spenser's *Mutabilitie* cantos in 1609, and, above all, of Donne's *Anniversaries*. Donne's influence was immense, and universally acknowledged. Joshua Sylvester, with a characteristically appalling pun, began his own elegy (introducing a collection that was to include Donne's poem on the Prince) thus:

> How-euer, short of Others *Art* and *Wit*.
> I know my powers for such a Part Vnfit;
> And shall but light my Candle in the *Sunn*
> To doe a work shall be so better Donne.[14]

Since the form of the elegy is frequently improvised, it may be seen as an expression, imitation, representation of its subject: certainly the cult of Henry structured the funeral verses written to commemorate him in a way that was to be echoed the following year by Middleton:

> every worthy man
> Is his own marble, and his merit can
> Cut him to any figure and express
> More art than Death's cathedral palaces . . .[15]

But while Henry's cult may have in some sense shaped the way it was celebrated and commemorated, there is no doubt that he himself had been in part fashioned by those who surrounded him,

---

[13] Recalling Spenser's designation of *The Faerie Queene* as 'matter of just memory' to distinguish it from trivial or false art, 'painted forgery . . . the aboundance of an idle braine': the double sense of the word 'just'—both 'exact' and 'righteous'—directs attention to the problems Prince Henry's elegists faced, of expending ingenuity without appearing trivial or sacrilegious.

[14] *Lachrimae lachrimarum*, A2ʳ.

[15] Commendatory verses to *The Duchess of Malfi*, 9–12.

those tutors and companions 'of quality and distinction' who were
put in place for his edification.[16] The influence of the predominantly
Puritan divines who attended him was considerable; Henry was a
'reverent and attentive hearer of sermons', who refused Catholics
admittance to his court, and kept a swear-box.[17] He also came to be
seen as the hope of militant Protestantism: Samson Lennard, who
fought beside Sidney at Zutphen, prayed, dedicating his translation
of Phillippe Mornay, 'that I may live to march over the Alpes, and
trayle a pike before the walls of Rome, under your Highnesse
standard'.[18] In addition, Henry's court displayed what Christopher
Hill called 'the congruence of Puritanism and science', as the
Prince (who supported such figures as Edward Wright the
mathematician and Thomas Lydiat the chronographer and cosmo-
grapher) showed an interest in learning of all sorts, with a manifest
fascination with its practical application.[19] Everything had a
purpose: thus Cornwallis tells us that Henry read history in order
'to inable his knowledge in government civill', and his taste for
neoclassical architecture was expressed in terms of a desire to
translate Vitruvian ideals into physical forms.[20] His literary,
musical, and artistic patronage were on a scale, and of a quality, to

[16] G. Parry, *The Golden Age Restor'd: The Culture of the Stuart Court, 1603–42*
(Manchester, 1981), 69–70; see also T. Birch, *The Life of Henry, Prince of Wales* (1760),
209–13; BL MS Harley 70007. There are accounts of Henry's upbringing in Wilson
(7–22, 45–64), Williamson (11–13), C. Hill, *Intellectual Origins of the English Revolution*
(Oxford, 1965), 214–6, and R. Strong, *Henry Prince of Wales and England's Lost
Renaissance* (1986), 7–70. The more important tutors were Adam Newton, Lord
Lumley, and Edward Wright. Works of advice dedicated to the Prince include
Willymat's *A princes looking glasse* (1603) and *A loyal subjects looking glasse* (1604) and
George More, *Principles for young princes* (1611).

[17] Sir Charles Cornwallis, *A Discourse of the most illustrious Prince Henry* (1641), A8ʳ;
Henry's chaplains are listed in Birch, *Life*, 209–13; see also Parry, *Golden Age*, 83–4,
Strong, *Henry, Prince of Wales*, 52–4. Divines who dedicated works to Henry included
Henoch Clapham, Hugh Broughton, Joseph Hall, Daniel Price, and Andrew Willett.
See Brennan, *English Literary Patronage*, 124–8.

[18] Phillippe de Mornay, *The mysterie of iniquitie: that is to say the historie of the papacie*
(1612), 3ᵛ; for similar passages, see Wilson, *Prince Henry and English Literature*, 29–30,
59–73, 100–16. Such texts are best exemplified by the anonymous *The French herald,
summoning all true christian princes to a generall croisade* (1611).

[19] Hill, *Intellectual Origins*, 213–19; Strong, *Henry, Prince of Wales*, 212–20.

[20] Cornwallis, *Discourse*, C4ᵛ. Historical works associated with the Prince are
numerous, the most important being George Hakewill's attack on regicides, *Scutum
regium* (1612), Drayton's *Polyolbion* and Ralegh's *History of the World*. The best recent
accounts of Henry's interest in art and architecture are Parry, *Golden Age*, 75–9, and
Strong, *Henry, Prince of Wales*. 86–137.

justify seeing him as 'the creator of a new aesthetic climate'.[21] Like most great Renaissance patrons, Henry was likened to Maecenas and invited to inaugurate a new golden age.[22] His court, 'intended by the King for a courtly college or a collegiate court', grew in size and influence as the Prince's standing increased.[23] James Cleland praised it as 'the true *Panthaeon* of Great Britain', an academy on the European model; Cornwallis remarked that 'He so distributed the day by dividing his houres into the service of God, to the apting of himself to the office he was borne unto . . . as no part of it could be said to bee in vaine bestowed'.[24]

Henry's status as Protestant champion grew markedly in the years following the death of Henri IV in 1610; the martial athleticism for which he had been renowned was thereafter increasingly praised as a token of a revival of chivalric excellence, and associated with the contemporary nostalgia for the perceived values of Elizabeth's court.[25] He became more closely associated with imperial expansion, and (initially under the guidance of Ralegh and Phineas Pett) with shipbuilding and colonial projects—including the plan to found the town Henrico (or Henricus or Henricopolis) which was to house a university and a 'College for the conversion of Infidels'.[26] Henry was more than a semi-mythical Prince of Troynovant: his connections with the Virginia and East

---

[21] Parry, *Golden Age*, 81; for more detailed accounts, see my 'English Funeral Elegy', 172–83, and Michael G. Brennan, *Literary Patronage in the English Renaissance: The Pembroke Family* (1988), 112–24.

[22] William Tooker, Dean of Lichfield, called Henry 'Maecenas of all the learned' in his *Duellum siue singulare certamen cum Martino Becano Jesuita* (1611), A3^r; see also *Luctus Posthumus* (Oxford, 1612), I3^v.

[23] Birch, *Life*, 97.

[24] James Cleland, *The institution of a young noble man* (Oxford, 1607), E2^r; Cornwallis, *Discourse*, C4^r.

[25] The picture of Henry as a Protestant champion in Henry Peacham's *Minerva Britanna* (1612), D4^v, is reproduced in Strong, *Cult of Elizabeth*, 187; see also Parry, *Golden Age*, 74–5.

[26] Ralphe Hamor, *A true discourse of the present estate of Virginia* (1615), E3^r. Pierre Erondelle wrote to Henry that 'poore Virginians doe seeme to implore your princely aide to . . . shake off the yoke of the divel' (Marc Lescarbot, *Nova Francia; or the description of that part of New France wh. is one continent with Virginia* Tr. P.E. (1609), I1^v. The most important source is *The Autobiography of Phineas Pett*, ed. W. G. Perrin, in *Publications of the Navy Record Society*, 51 (1918), 21–3, 30–2. See also Wilson, *Prince Henry and English Literature*, 22–4, 87–90; Williamson, *Myth of the Conqueror*, 49–55, and J. R. Mulryne, ' "Here's Unfortunate Revels": War and Chivalry in Plays and Shows at the Time of Prince Henry', in Mulryne and M. Shewring, eds., *War, Literature and the Arts in Sixteenth-Century Europe* (1989), 165–89.

India Companies, and with the Merchant Taylors, emphasize the practical and commercial foundation of his imperial interests.[27]

Even from this necessarily attenuated account the range of Henry's interests will be apparent, and, since the numbers of those in some direct or indirect client relationship with him were large, a great deal of commemorative material was naturally to be expected at his death, and much of what they wrote was conditioned by the Prince's image. That image provided elegists with more than a list of topics to treat of. After all, since the form of elegy could be improvised, it could itself be intimately connected with (and aspire quite literally to re-present) it subject. A natural starting-point is Henry's comprehensiveness, one of the most common topics of praise. When Alfonso Ferrabosco dedicated *Ayres* to Henry in 1609 he asked: 'to a composition so full of *Harmony* . . . what could be a fitter offering?'; and George Marcelline called Henry 'the *Index*, *Abstract* or *Compendium* of the very greatest Princes'.[28] Henry was figured as a combination of Xenophon's Cyrus and Spenser's Prince Arthur. In *The Olympian Catastrophe* Gorges calls him 'Natures quintessence . . . The Gods Epitome . . . The All of Glorye, and of worldlie blisse' (805–8)[29] Henry's inexhaustible compendiousness, his status as an encyclopaedia of excellences, became commonplace. John Davies of Hereford spoke of his 'Princely lookes composed . . . Of Venerable *grauity* and *grace*'; to Drayton he was the 'abridgement' of all greatness.[30] One convenient literary consequence for elegists was that an anthology becomes in such circumstances an implicitly panegyric form. When applied to a youthful subject, this compendiousness (which is a common feature of Petrarchist and theological writing) shades into the ancient funeral topos of the *puer senex*.[31] It comes in several versions. It

---

[27] See Hill, *Intellectual Origins*, 218; Birch, *Life*, 181–2, 96–7, 110–12. A voyager associated with Henry was Thomas Coryate, who dedicated to the Prince *Coryats crudities: hastily gobled up in five moneths travels* (1611). Henry was invited to sponsor colonies in Ulster: see T. Blennerhasset, *A direction for the plantation in Ulster* (1610).

[28] Ferrabosco, *Ayres*, A2[r]; George Marcelline, *The triumphs of King James* (1609–10), A2[r].

[29] Text from *The Poems of Sir Arthur Gorges*, ed. H. E. Sandison (Oxford, 1953).

[30] John Davies of Hereford, *The Muses-teares, . . . etc.* (1613), A3[v]; Drayton's phrase comes from *A paean triumphall* (*Works*, i. 481). See also *A Poetical Rapsody* (ed. Rollins, i. 305). The notion is a commonplace of Jacobean literature, of course: we might recall the assertion of Monsieur in Chapman's *Bussy d'Ambois* that 'in a King | All places are contain'd' (ed. N. S. Brooke (Manchester, 1964), I. i. 35–6).

[31] On the related topics of the classical and biblical text as cornucopia, of the Bible as a compendium and Christ as an inexhaustible library, see T. Cave, *The Cornucopian Text*

might be argued that those the gods love die young. Or that they were taken to prevent their falling into sin; or that they managed to live a full life in a brief space. Instances of all three are to be found in the Prince Henry elegies. Gorges's *Olympian Catastrophe* exemplifies the first, with a war between Venus, Bellona, and Minerva to claim exclusive rights in the British prince, and Chapman used the conventional image of a jewel glimpsed and snatched away—'Heaven open'd, and but show'd him to our eies, | Then shut againe, and show'd our Miseries'.[32] The second usually involves satirical reflections on the decadence and vanity of the Jacobean court. The third is articulated especially forcibly by Cyril Tourneur:

> As Humanitie now goes:
> HEE liu'd a *Man* as long as any does.
> For (onelie) in those *Minutes* that wee giue
> To *Vertue*, wee are *Trulie* said to liue
> *Men*, and no longer.[33]

In Greville's account, the young Philip Sidney had been notable for 'staiednesse of mind, lovely, and familiar gravity as carried grace and reverence above greater years'.[34] So with Prince Henry. To the Venetian ambassador he was 'ceremonious beyond his years'; to Boderie, 'none of his pleasures . . . savoured the least of a child'; though slow of speech, with a 'piercing grave eye' and 'terrible frown', he was 'gentle and easy to deal with', 'courteous, loving and affable'.[35] Likewise William Cornwallis, in his elegy in Sylvester's anthology, praised Henry as Alexander's superior:

> Wee need admire no longer PHILIP'S Sonne:
> Neuer was life in little better donne.[36]

(Oxford, 1978), 78–124, 171–82; also Lewalski, *Donne's Anniversaries*, 222–5; Wilson, *England's Eliza*, 360–1.

[32] Chapman, *An epicede or funerall song* (1612), B1ᵛ.

[33] Tourneur, *A griefe on the death of prince Henrie* (1613), B4ʳ; or, in Christopher Brooke's words, 'A princes Wisdom not in wrincles lies, | God measures not his Gifts by Age or yeares' (Brooke and Browne, *Two elegies, . . . etc.* (1613), C1ᵛ); or those of Robert Allyne: 'The ship sailes most that soonest gets her Port | He dies not soone that still on death is musing | Life's measur'd, not by time, but by times using': *Funerall elegies* (1613), B3ʳ.

[34] Greville, *Life of Sir Philip Sidney*, ed. Nowell Smith (Oxford, 1907), 6.

[35] *C. S. P. Venetian*, x. 74; Boderie is cited by Birch, *Life*, 75–6; the other comments are by Cornwallis (*Discourse*, B4ᵛ–B5ʳ), and by Bacon (*Works*, vi. 327).

[36] *Lachrimae lachrimarum*, E3ᵛ.

Henry's specific interests as a patron—in music, architecture, shipbuilding, for example, and his persona as a Protestant champion—expressed in pursuit of knightly skills and in the cultivation of a severe personal and religious discipline—were duly reflected in the laments. A simple example is the frequency of references to Henry on horseback (most notably in the elegies by Gorges and Hugh Holland (in *Lachrimae lachrimarum*), as well as the lengthy narrative in *The Two Noble Kinsmen* (V. iv. 48–85), where Pirithous describes how Arcite is fatally thrown from his horse at the moment of apparent victory)—an image, dense with chivalric and imperial meaning, that had been created for the Prince in the last few years of his life. It should be recalled that Henri IV had given to the young prince (who is known to have wished to appear on horseback in a masque) a riding instructor, in an act apparently calculated to proclaim the boy's role as the heir to the champion of Protestant chivalry and his assumption of the iconographic trappings of empire.[37] Campion wrote that

> though his yeeres were greene,
> Their fruit was yet mature: his care had beene
> Suruaying India, and implanting there
> The knowledge of that God which hee did feare.[38]

This Christian Alexander was characterized as another Cyrus, who might 'his shaddow spred | From siluer Ganges to *Sols* watrie bed' (recalling the Henricopolis project). To Sylvester the Prince had been

> The Churche's Tower, the Terror of the Pope,
> Heroik Henry, Atlas of our hope.[39]

But in many elegies, as will become evident, this topic of Protestant militancy found formal as well as thematic expression. Imitation and allusion locate Henry's story in the sphere of heroic literature, specifically in chivalric romance and masque. The form of a number of poems seems to derive from the Prince's military cult as fashioned by events such as the *Barriers*, *Oberon: The Fairy Prince*, and *Tethys Festival*. Henry had been celebrated as a second Arthur, the successor to Astraea, the ninth Henry and the ninth English

---

[37] Strong, *Henry, Prince of Wales*, 63–70; Williamson, *Myth of the Conqueror*, 111–12.
[38] The elegy prefaced to *Songs of mourning* (1613), in Campion, *Works*, ed. Vivian, ll. 49–52.
[39] *Lachrimae lachrimarum*, A2^r.

worthy. Where James established a cult of *rex pacificus*, Henry appeared in texts such as *Minerva Britanna* as a new Charlemagne, a warfaring Christian knight.[40] Drummond's *Teares on the death of Moeliades* invests Henry with his Barriers' name—an anagram of 'miles a deo'—God's soldier. Other elegists would relate him to Achilles, Hercules, Alexander, Caesar, Ajax and Cyrus, to Solomon, David, and Josiah, and to Arthur, the Black Prince, and all British kings: he was their 'epitome', destined to share their role in advancing providence.[41] As Sampson Price said after Henry's death: 'It was the *defence* of Religion, that made *David, Salomon, Josias, Constantine, Edward* the 6. Queene *Elizabeth*, and our late blessed *Henry* so honoured, that their names amongst all true hearted *Protestants*, are like a precious oyntment, their remembrance is sweet as hony, and as Musicke at a banquet of wine.'[42] The most extensive embodiment of this ideal is Sir Arthur Gorges's lengthy allegory, *The Olympian Catastrophe*, which includes an account of a tournament in which the Henry crushes the Prince of Antioch, a pagan swollen with pride: Gorges links the crusading matter of Ariosto and Tasso with the Spenserian matter of Britain, and ends with Jove looking forward to the young Charles as a second Charlemagne.

Henry became, inevitably, the focus for a series of exercises in 'Protestant poetics', not least, at the simplest level, because Lamentations (the paradigmatic biblical lament) was traditionally understood as a lament for Josiah (to whom Henry was frequently compared).[43] More general and more pervasive is the related presentation of Henry's death as divine retribution for the nation's sin. Many elegists (including, perhaps surprisingly, Donne) articulate an apocalyptic view of history, and seem to aspire (like James Maxwell) to a prophetic register, so that there is a sense in which the poet's voice or persona—which in an improvised form like the elegy is frquently presented as if it determined the nature of the composition—is itself formed in response to Henry's cult. It is only a step from specifically biblical modes to more generally Protestant kinds, or from speakers who appear to claim the role of prophet to

---

[40] Parry, *Golden Age*, 66–84.   [41] Brennan, *Literary Patronage*, 124–7.

[42] Sampson Price, *Londons warning by Laodicea's lukewarmnesse: A sermon* (1613), H2ʳ.

[43] See Lewalski, *Protestant Poetics*, 32–5, 69–70; the other biblical lament, David's for Jonathan, was hardly applicable to Henry (see Lewalski, *Donne's Anniversaries*, 28, who further notes Henry's identification with Christ). A good example of the parallel with Josiah is Daniel Price, *Prince Henry his first anniversary* (Oxford, 1613), D3ᵛ.

those who seek the elevated status associated with Spenser and Sidney. Thus, many of the elegies locate themselves explicitly in the chivalric mode of *The Faerie Queene* or the *Arcadia*. By quotation and allusion Webster, for example, establishes Henry's personality as an amalgam of the qualities of Sidney's Arcadian princes.[44] The six 'visions' of Henry Peacham's *The period of mourning* are crammed with Spenserian echoes. Henry, for instance, is a 'warlike impe . . . Ydrad of all for awfull Maiestie' and is 'hight Philocles'; his apotheosis recalls Calidore's vision on Mount Acidale, as the Prince is seen 'By one degree rais'd higher than the rest, | About whose brow an heavenly glory shone' (B3^r, C3^v). So it is too with Richard Niccols's *Three sisters teares*, where the Thames is presented as the Bower of Bliss:

> So many varying and so vaine delights
> Floating vpon that floud, I then did see,
> Such diuers showes and such fantastick sights
> That *Thames* the Idle-lak then seem'd to be.   (B2^v)

These realms of literary association affect the presentation of Henry himself, and provide a context for the common stress upon the Prince's 'Integrity of Life' ('fame's best friend', according to Webster (who borrowed the phrase for the last lines of *The Duchess of Malfi* from Cornwallis's elegy)). Cornwallis was happy to acknowledge that this boy, a 'Miracle of Nature', was no intellectual, not 'lip-learned' in 'pedant Arts'. But on the other hand 'Hee read men, in stead of Bookes', and

> his Iudgment knew
> The Latitude of things: and how to view
> The court and her Invisibilities.
> Which, seen, are not seen, often, by the Wise.[45]

In these lines, and in many other elegies, we encounter what Bacon called the 'piercing grave eye' and 'terrible frown' that enabled Henry, though slow in speech, to pierce the gaudy show of flatterers. In other words, an apparently genuine attribute of the historical Henry is inscribed within the elegies. But the process goes a stage further, as a result of the commonplace distinction

---

[44] See below, p. 166.

[45] In *Lachrimae lachrimarum*, E4^r. The phrase derives ultimately from the opening of Horace, *Carm.* 1. 22, 'Integer vitae . . . : see A. Gurr, *Playgoing in Shakespeare's London* (Cambridge, 1987), 83–4.

between those who are able (like Henry) to see through the veil of allegory, to recognize truth from falsehood, and the rest,

> Those baser mindes, unknowing, sensuall, rude,
> That measure contraries indifferently;
> Whose *Summum bonum* is their sleepe and food
> Preferring moments, to Eternitie.[46]

Only the hearts of men, William Browne and John Davies argued, were fit to house the Prince's virtues.[47] Such ideas are fundamental to Spenserian poetics. Consolation, a sense of the survival of the deceased, resides, as John Davies asserts, in the perpetuation of poetic communities: 'It is a kind of Ioy in case of *moane* | Not to be single' (B3ᵛ); and that community is made up of persons who recognize, in Davies's words, that '*Our* ALL's but *Nothing* than: For, that which IS, | Must be eternall' (B4ʳ). These people, who share the Prince's piercing eye, are naturally inclined to allegory, and to the prophetic, apocalyptic Spenserian modes. Such terms inform Gorges's address to his audience:

> But as for those, whom ignoranc so blinds,
> To count this Poeme Idle Ballatrye
> Because themselves with hood-winckt blunddringe mynds
> Cannot discearne a vailed mysterye.
> Bid such dymme sighted Owles goe learne againe,
> What morales *Æsops*-fables do containe.   (1189–94)

Even so emphatically non-Spenserian a poet as Donne was drawn to this manner when writing of Henry, whom he called King James's 'activ'st spirit to convey and tye | This soule of peace through Christianitie'. He went on:

> Was it not well believ'd, that hee would make
> This general peace th'eternall overtake?
> And that his times might have stretcht out so far
> As to touch those of which they emblems are?[48]

The variousness and distinction of the elegies—and indeed the very number of pieces produced and the range of writers who felt moved to produce them—is an expression of the breadth of the Prince's interests, of the universality with which his loss was

---

[46] Brooke and Browne, *Two elegies, . . . etc.*, B1ᵛ.
[47] See below, pp. 172, 176.
[48] Text from Milgate, *Anniversaries*, 33–8.

felt. Henry's court, these elegies seem to suggest, was not just the place 'where Vertue herself dwelleth by pattern, by practise, by encouragement, admonitions and precepts of the most rare persons in Vertue and Learning that can be found'.[49] More than that, it seems to have been taken as a microcosm of a virtuous commonwealth or court, and many of those who mourned its dissolution saw it as a personal loss even though their own connection with it had been slight or non-existent.[50] Donne's friend George Garrard, for example, explained: '(For This Man's Eye was neuer cast on Mee; | Nor could I dreame that euer it should bee): | Nor do I, with the fashion, *Mourne* in *Black*; | My *Sorrow's* in my Heart, not on my Back.' In Henry Burton's allegorical elegy, Henry's household thank their lord for generously providing for them, but say their greatest treasure is to be able to say for ever '*We were Prince* HENRY's *Followers*'.[51] A memorial volume, a sonnet sequence entitled *Great Brittans Mourning Garment* (1612), while dedicated to Sir David Murray and the household, was designed to have been 'Given to all faithfull sorrowfull subjects at the funerall' (A1ʳ), making it the equivalent of the 'blacks' distributed to clothe mourners.[52] Like Garrard, the author claims no special knowledge: he writes, 'I do but sound the accents of report | And sure report gives him a worthy name' (C4ʳ). Thus, while the court could claim primacy in mourning; 'none so well can sound his praise', as those 'that knew the upright treadings of his waies' (C4ᵛ), a great diversity of writers declared themselves compelled to write. Several presented their works with a show of diffidence, and only because, they claimed, others, better equipped, were silent. Christopher Brooke, 'In will (tho not in skill) strong as the best', offered his work as a foundation for others to build their monuments on.[53] Hugh Holland scorned those who were still too grief-stricken to write, 'His braine is idle | Who gives not vnto his teares the bridle'; while William Browne was more sympathetic:

> Alas! I see each one, amazed stands,
> Shallow FOORDS mutter, silent are the DEEPE:

---

[49] Cleland, *The institution of a young noble man*, E2ʳ.

[50] On the dissolution of the Prince's court and on its image, see A. F. Marotti, *John Donne, Coterie Poet* (Madison, 1986), 269–71.

[51] *Lachrimae lachrimarum*, C–D4ʳ (Garrard) and G2ᵛ (Burton).

[52] C. Gittings, *Death, Burial and the Individual in Early Modern England* (1984), 118–22.

[53] *Two elegies, . . . etc.*, B2ᵛ; see below, p. 169.

> Faine would they tell their griefs, but know not where,
> All are so full, naught can augment their store.[54]

Drayton was an exception. Perhaps his silence testified to the opprobrium he had endured for his panegyric on King James. But he could offer no explanation when he wrote his first funeral elegy in 1613:

> Since I knew ought time never did allow
> Me stuffe fit for an Elegie, till now:
> When *France* and England's HENRIE's dy'd, my quill,
> Why, I know not, but it that time lay still.
> ('Tis more than greatnesse that my spirit must raise,
> To observe custome I use not to praise;)[55]

A great deal of material in the elegies is commonplace, as might be expected. Most Renaissance princes were likened to Maecenas; most were praised for the comprehensiveness of their excellence, uniting the arts of war and peace, combining physical with spiritual perfections. Henry was no exception. It was possible for Sir Arthur Gorges, for example, to employ the same sonnet, with appropriate adjustments to the pronouns, to mourn Sidney in 1586, Queen Elizabeth in 1603, and Prince Henry in 1612—making the poem the literary equivalent of those generic tomb sculptures that were produced in studios and bought, so to speak, off the peg.[56]

---

[54] *Lachrimae lachrimarum*, D3^r; *Two elegies, . . . etc.* D4^r.

[55] From the elegy on Lady Clifton (1613); *Works*, iii. 219). In the context of Henry's death the silence of Spenser's most distinguished follower is much stranger than that of Jonson, though it is worth remembering that, of all the established poets with laureate pretensions, only Chapman wrote.

[56] Shakespeare's monument in Stratford, it has been noted, bears a generic resemblance to that of John Stow in London (see S. Schoenbaum, *William Shakespeare: a Compact Documentary Life* (Oxford, 1977), 309). On Gorges, see below, pp. 144–8. A poem on Prince Henry's death by Sir Walter Aston—which survives only in MSS (see app. D)—was modified to be applied to the death of King Charles in 1649. In the modification, the Aston poem had added to it the couplet: 'for that mischiuous and most vnhappie stroke | hath now all honest harts asunder broke'. 'Stroke' was—for understandable reasons—more usually applied to Charles than Henry—Denham in *Lachrymae Musarum* (1649) wrote of 'that impious stroke | That sullied Earth, and did Heaven's pity choke'. Indeed I might add parenthetically here that Henry's reputation does not seem to have been quite as unequivocally radical and aggressively Protestant as consideration of his cult might lead one to suppose. In manuscript miscellanies from the period leading up to the civil war, elegies on the prince seem increasingly to have been collected as private tokens of royalist taste and sympathy. And, surprisingly, perhaps, one of the most frequently encountered pieces is an elegant, neoclassical poem by William Juxon (see app. D). Its wide circulation indicates Henry's remarkable posthumous metamorphosis from Protestant hero to Laudian saint.

Henry's move from life to death is expressed as a transition from light to shade, from spring to winter, from bud to withered plant. Writers ask the familiar questions: 'Is he dead?', 'Are we dead?', 'Why did he die?'. The answer is usually couched in terms of providence or of Henry's being too good for the world. Blame is almost invariably attached to the sinful pride of Britain, which has provoked divine punishment. Grief is claimed to be universal, nature is disordered, reversed, and the community of Henry's family, household, court, and nation is dissolved. Henry's qualities are praised as being beyond praise, and shadowed by various images of worth and scarcity.

In the *Astrophel* anthology, Spenser had created a model of the poet's role as spokesman for the grieving community, and orchestrator, impresario, of their laments. Joshua Sylvester explicitly claims a similar status in his anthology of elegies from the Prince's court. So do Henry Burton, Christopher Brooke, and William Browne. And other writers adopted Spenserian poses too; both Wither and Peacham, for example, present themselves in the manner of the speaker in *Prothalamion*, wandering by the shore of a river in solitary grief. *Great Brittaines Mourning Garment* features echoes of Spenser: the anonymous author organizes a ceremony

> Strow Cypress, and pale violets on his tombe,
> And on his fair crest fixe a crowne of Bayes
> Immortal . . .   (A2ᵛ)

And, following the 'ancient Greek manner', and the model of Sidney's Arcadian elegies, he invites the select band of mourners 'so many friends so full of woe':

> And let thy heauiest Musick softly sound
> Vnto the dolefull songs that I recite;
> And euer let this direfull voice rebound
> Through the vast den: Ah ded is Britains light.   (A4ᵛ)

William Basse confines his audience to those who are prepared, like him, to restrain themselves in public, and reserve their lamentation to private gatherings: 'to you I therefore weep: to you alone | I show the image of your teares in mine'.[57] Basse weeps for them, proposing himself as the articulator of their woe. Niccols creates two voices: one is a member of the company of mourners

---

[57] *Great Brittaines sunnes-set bewailed*, A4ʳ.

who steps aside to make space for Niccols, as the professional, the specialist, to perform. The mourner says:

> But give I way to him, who knowes the way,
> And comes prepard to make the world to weepe,
> Since I want powr to think what I would say,
> Or say what I would thinke.[58]

Webster scorns the inadequacy of other poets whose 'waste elegies' are 'more base Then are the ragges they are writ on'.[59] The most distinctively characterized of these Spenserian spokesmen is Wither's, who repudiates the notion of physical community:

> And if it be a comfort in distress
> (As some thinke) to have sharers in their woes
> Then I desire to be comfortles.[60]

He claims 'I have not strived to seeme witty' (A3ʳ), and seeks 'a dull melancholy loneliness' to 'Fat my grief with solitarines' (A4ʳ). What he actually produces is a highly disciplined sonnet sequence of forty-five poems, many of which are addressed specifically to individual members of Henry's family. To Princess Elizabeth he says, 'now leave off thy teares in vain to shed, | For why? To spare them I have powr'd out mine' (B3ʳ). And the entire volume vividly illustrates a consoling counterpoint of structured formality with a highly dramatic protestation of unique and uncontrollable grief. Numerous poets are led to question the possibility of performing their duty, and thereby to dwell on the nature, scope, and ambition of their literary endeavours, on the capacity of their art to deal with the subject. Grief itself is put under the microscope: true and false lamentations are identified, the transience of mortal life acknowledged, and repentance frequently urged on the reader. Attacks on the nation's sin, assertions of the vanity of human wishes, and exhortations to repentance underpin a satirical thrust in many of the pieces, which take the anatomizing scalpel to society at large. Likewise the melancholy of grief leads, like other kinds of melancholy, to other anatomies (on the model of Donne's *Anniversaries*) as well as to the satirical, exclusive pose of the Spenserian poets.

---

[58] *The three sisters teares*, A3ᵛ.

[59] Webster, *A monumental columne, erected to the memory of Henry, late prince of Wales* (1613), C1ʳ.

[60] *Prince Henries obsequies*, A4ʳ.

But the distinction I may appear to have implied, between the commonplace and the artistically self-conscious, cannot be sustained. The elegy, however unsophisticated, is an essay in poetic tradition and an exercise in decorum. Thus Henry's image is expressed formally and structurally as well as thematically in the elegies, in response to the challenge of fitting art to the particular circumstances of an occasion. The elegist, like the sonneteer, was in a position where uniqueness and originality were conventionally defined against previous practice. Like the sonnet, then, the funeral elegy developed aggregatively, acquiring and modifying conventions, with poets writing consciously in emulation of each other, or in scorn of that emulation.[61] Donne's friend George Garrard distinguished himself from those 'hir'd to crie | And howle at every great man's obsequie': from those wits 'that closely wooe applause | By curious handling this sadd common cause', and from those who blot paper with their 'idle rimes' by 'striuing to outstrip each others braines'.[62] Inevitably the desire to put on a good show, to outshine others, brought some problems. The most manifest was a kind of panegyric inflation. Thus when George Wither scorned the 'fained stuff' of other elegists and launched into a praise of Henry as a Phoenix, he collided with a problem of celebrating the uniqueness of the reborn Phoenix in Prince Charles without compromising the King's equally pressing, and somewhat better established, claims to singularity: he advised Prince Charles to delay his rebirth.[63] Similarly in Richard Niccols's *The three sisters teares*, there is an abrupt transition when the poet seems to run up against the consequences of claiming uniqueness. So one stanza ends:

> For though thy losse be now laid out on beere,
> Forget him not, thou canst not finde his peere.

And the next begins: 'Except his royall Brother . . . ' (D4^r).

The most celebrated instance of panegyric inflation had been Donne's *Anniversaries*, to which George Chapman's *Epicede* is clearly a riposte. Where a 15 year old girl Donne had never met had been mourned in terms more commonly associated with royalty, Chapman reversed the process. He praised a prince by basing his

---

[61] e.g. See Cave's chapters on 'Imitation' and on 'Improvisation and Inspiration' in *The Cornucopian Text* (Oxford, 1978), 35–77, 125–56, and G. W. Pigman, 'Versions of Imitation in the Renaissance', *RQ* 33 (1980), 1–32; also pp. 5–7 above.

[62] *Lachrimae lachrimarum*, C–D4^r.   [63] *Prince henries obsequies*, B2^r.

poem on a Latin elegy on a 15 year old girl. Further, the name (Angelo Poliziano) of the author of the Latin source glances at the conclusion of Donne's elegy on the Prince,'I were an angel singing what you were'.[64]

Most elegists addressed the question of what consolation, if any, art had to offer. Since it could not assist the deceased, what purpose or meaning might it have? In some cases, the argument or the structure of a poem will assert a consolatory meaning, and will operate in counterpoint to the grief-stricken speaker. There are some examples of numerological consolation, where the physical components of a poem will be disposed in such a way as to imitate a monument or to embody the conceit of Henry's harmoniousness.[65] On the other hand, a studiedly disjointed style or a consciously fragmentary or uneven structure might mime either destabilizing grief or the irreversible catastrophe of the death. Thomas Heywood claimed that

> . . . all our elegies begot from passion,
> Come from rent hearts, . . .
> Confused thoughts the best conceits destroy
> And are more harsh than when we sing of joy.[66]

Webster apologized for 'the zealous error of my passionate Muse' (C2ʳ). This issue came to be associated with the topos of inexpressibility, an ancient elegiac commonplace, and with the developing vogue for self-conscious, often self-proclaimed sincerity.[67]

In the Prince Henry elegies, the image of the rules of art as chains, fetters, aggravating constrictions, is regularly found. Speakers conventionally present the passion of their grief as being in conflict with them. Since this topos is such a regular feaure of the drama of the period, it may have been employed by elegists as a

---

[64] See below, Ch. 4.

[65] Henry King's elegy on the Prince exists in three versions, of 18, 24, and 28 ll., incorporating revisions made over a period of some 40 years. Each version shows some evidence of numerological patterning, with the latest being the least intricate. See app. C.

[66] *A funerall elegie upon the death of Henry, prince of Wales* (1613), C1ʳ.

[67] It is perhaps worth recalling some of the better-known examples. John Daniel's song from 1606: 'Can doleful notes to measured accents set | Express unmeasured griefs which time forget?' (*Songs for the lute, viol and voice*, xiii); or Donne in his second elegy on Cecilia Bulstrode: 'Language, thou art too narrow, and too weak | To ease us now; great sorrow cannot speak'; or his letter to Sir Robert Carr with his hymn on the death of Marquis Hamilton: 'you know my uttermost when it was best, and even then I did best when I had least truth for my subjects. In this present case there is so much truth as it defeats all poetry'. See above, p. 120.

means of characterizing the speaker. To take three examples from Sylvester's *Lachrimae lachrimarum* anthology: George Garrard argued that it was foolish to try 'in a *measur'd* Verse | A *Losse* beyond *Dimension* to rehearse' (C–D4^r); Henry Goodyer questioned the power of 'poetik Magick' to bind 'Vnmeasur'd Griefs, in measure'd lines' (F3^r); and Hugh Holland asserted that 'True grief indeed, that cannot well be choaked | Will find a vent, and needs not to be cloaked' (D3^v). As Allyne put it, 'Mourning's a naturall motion in the heart | And scorns to be reformed by rules of art'.[68]

Writers of elegies faced the same problem as many sonneteers. Just as Sidney's Astrophil found himself torn between a compulsion to write and a conviction that writing anything other than Stella's name was futile, so elegists found themselves confronted with an obligation to write that made the act of composition seem worthless.[69]

Also like sonneteers is the elegists' tendency to talk about themselves, to display themselves to the reader as torn, divided, tormented. Henry Peacham described how mourning for Henry and celebration of Princess Elizabeth's marriage fought in his breast: 'like fire and water striuing for praedominancie', until he was 'enforced' to write 'euen to mine owne prejudice'.[70] Arthur Gorges ends his poem with what sounds like a conscious evocation of a sonneteer's plight:

> My Muse did want her selfe my sence was nume,
> My heart grew faint, my quicker power grew slow,
> Myne eyes weare dimme, my tongue was taken dumbe,
> My inke no longer from my penn would flowe,
>> For inke, tongue, eyes, power, hart, sence, muse, apawld,
>> Became thicke dumbe dymme, slow, faint nume, and stald.
>
> (1027–32)

In these passages, as in the lines from Wither cited earlier, may be seen extreme and eloquent instances of the focus of elegy being the poet himself: as such, of course, they correspond to an important feature of the traditional conception of elegy.

---

[68] Robert Allyne, *Funerall elegies* (1613). A2^r.

[69] J. Fineman in his study of Shakespeare's Sonnets, *Shakespeare's Perjured Eye* (Berkeley, 1986), arrives from a different direction at a not dissimilar connection between epideisis and the sonnet. As he puts it, 'praise . . . is what happens when mimesis and metaphor meet' (p. 3). See in particular his ch. II, pp. 86–129.

[70] *The period of mourning*, A3^v.

'ALL LOOKES BE PALE': ELEGISTS AND THEIR ELEGIES

Numerous elegies on the Prince survive in manuscript. Some circulated widely, others not at all; some derived from printed volumes, others from other manuscripts; most, though not quite all, are epitaphs.[71] While an appendix includes texts of a few of them, it is perhaps appropriate that the largest and most ambitious work, Sir Arthur Gorges's lengthy chivalric allegory *The Olympian Catastrophe*, which emanates from the centre of Henry's court culture, should be considered first among the elegies.

In the prefatory pieces to *The Olympian Catastrophe*, Gorges suggests that reason, wisdom, and the impending marriage with the Palsgrave have been the chief agents of consolation for the Queen and Princess Elizabeth. For himself, he offers his poem on Henry as his last work:

> So sings the Swann, when life is taking flight
> So sings my zeale, the noats that sorrow weepes
> Which Antheam sung, my Muse for ever sleepes.[72]

The speaker begins by declining to summon Melpomene, since his 'just plaintes' require no art to 'search the laborinths of deafest eares' (10–11).[73] His narrative—a version of the Judgement of Paris—opens with an account of how Bellona, Minerva, and Juno gathered to watch a tournament in which youthful knights would compete 'for honor and for dames' on the 'Olympion greene'.[74] We are told that the story will have a melancholy conclusion, which 'shalbe shew'd in place where it is due': but meanwhile attention is

[71] See H. H. Hudson, *The Epigram in the English Renaissance* (Princeton, 1947); D. H. Parker, 'The English Literary Epitaph in the Seventeenth Century', B.Litt. thesis (Oxford, 1972); for a printed anthology of epitaphs, see Andro Hart's compilation *Mausoleum; or the choisest flowres of the epitaphs on the death of Prince Henrie* (Edinburgh, 1613).

[72] All refs. to the text of *The Olympian Catastrophe* are to the edn. of *The Poems of Sir Arthur Gorges* by H. E. Sandison (Oxford, 1953)). Gorges, *Poems*, 138; in fact Gorges produced three versions of this poem (see pp. 81, 130), one of which (p. 130) was used by his son as a lament for Lord Hastings in *Lachrymae Musarum* (1649).

[73] For a full account of Huntington Library MS Ellesmere 1130 see Gorges, *Poems*, xlix–lviii; Sandison suggests the poem was originally compiled (using fragments that may be much earlier (liv)) as a work of advice to Henry in or around 1610; see also Strong, *Henry Prince of Wales*, 41, who remarks aptly that 'Gorges' poem reads like a handbook to the ideas and attitudes that motivated those who made up the Prince's household during the years 1610–1612'.

[74] Williamson observes that 'Significantly, Venus was replaced by a goddess of war, soft love never having been a part of Henry's myth' (*Myth of the Conqueror*, 184).

directed to a lengthy praise of chivalric pursuits, which stresses the manliness and exclusivity of knightly accomplishments.[75] There is a brief halt when a reference to the success of English archers in France under Henry V jolts the narrator into remembering his subject ('Henries very name, my sence distracts' (94)); but the account of the achievements of 'noble bloods in feats of Armes' continues until the appearance of a 'lovely springhald knight', a paragon of Stuart chivalry.[76]

A brilliant display of tilting at the ring is duly applauded by the onlookers; accepting the garland of victory, Henry proceeds to a banquet that lasts till nightfall. At night, the Prince sleeps only fitfully, and a squire sees 'A rainebowe . . . coullord like fire and blood'; when Henry wakes he recounts his own vision, a foretaste of Elysium, in which he had been advised thus: 'with speede prepare thy mynd; | For to this place the heavens have thee designed'. As might be expected in a setting so firmly located in the realm of chivalric romance, there then ensues a debate about the reliability of dreams: the persons of Ralegh and Gorges lurk beneath the fiction of the champion's servants. The discussion, medieval in subject, contemporary in its emphases, immediate in its application, concludes as the second day's exercises are announced: Gorges furnishes another lengthy equestrian word-picture of Henry to set the scene.[77]

Henry is presented as the 'quyntessence . . . Of arte, of Marte, of Venus, and of tyme': his first challenger is a courteous knight who runs three courses and loses them all (falling like a 'statelie battlement' (457) in the process). Gorges is led to meditate on the instability of fortune in war ('whereas Mars his Tennys balls doth tosse | No man cann wynne but by an others losse' (491–2)) while

[75] As often in such contexts, the democratization of warfare by the gun (a device that 'hath like might, | Shott by a dastart dwarffe, or hardie knight') is deplored; see C. Oman, *The History of the Art of War in the Sixteenth Century* (1937), 379 ff.; also M. Vale, *War and Chivalry: Warfare and Aristocratic Culture in England, France and Burgundy at the End of the Middle Ages* (1981), 129–46.

[76] The description is self-consciously Spenserian, and echoes the first appearance of Prince Arthur in *The Faerie Queene*, I. vii. 29 ff.: 'His owne attire was of Carnation hue, | With Orient pearles embrodred like a frett: | About his necke of silk a ribbon blewe, | Where hangs a George with diamonds besett: | His spur gold-hatcht, his buskynes spanish-white, | His left legg gartred, as St. Georges knight' (139–44).

[77] On the nocturnal rainbow, see Gorges, *Poems*, 234–5; *The Poems of Joseph Hall*, ed. A. Davenport (Liverpool, 1969), 149. Its occurrence is noted in *Eidyllia in obitum, . . . etc.* (Oxford, 1613), B3ʳ, and in Peacham, *The period of mourning* (1613), E3ʳ. An earlier instance is recorded in Baxter's *Ouránia* (1606), D4ᵛ.

the Prince prepares to encounter a new opponent whose immodest motto is 'Without Compare'. The conflict is briefer than the first one: the challenger precipitates his own downfall by straining to achieve an unfair advantage, to 'give more vigor to his hand', and Henry responds swiftly and sententiously, knocking him to the floor and commenting 'so prid will have a fall'. We then learn that the defeated knight had been the Prince of Antioch, and that his destruction represented the triumph of Christian chivalry over pagan deceitfulness (525–600). The result is that, after a few exercises at the Barriers, Henry (the 'North-bred starre') is confirmed as the chief knight of the assembly: the recollection abruptly brings to the speaker's mind the coincidence of triumph and death, as he shifts from the world of Ariosto, Tasso, and Spenser to the allegory on which the work is based, the conflict between the goddesses.

Each goddess predictably claims the greatest share in the Prince; but when Minerva leaves her colleagues still arguing, she meets Atropos, who wields a bloody knife and tells of Henry's death. Minerva reacts sententiously ('For arts grew fainte when this sweet prince was dead, | That in his life tyme them with bountie fed' (755–6)), and then returns to inform the others. They resolve to erect Henry's monument. Then follows a debate between Juno and Atropos, in which Juno represents the conventional 'why did he die?' element, while Atropos answers with an essay on the benefits of being dead:

> The Crowne he had, was but a type of care:
> The Crowne he hath is joyes eternall seale:
> That was but fleetinge, as earth's gloryes are:
> This Settles him in heavens aye-lasting weale: (847–50)

She also protests that she has deprived Henry of the possibility of slipping from his pedestal ('He lyv'd not to be tainted with disgrace, . . . at his best his soule I did divorce' (877, 882)): his passing therefore was 'most happie, that he was | Taken in tyme (when twas best tyme to take | Him)' and then installed above 'earthes planett changing moone' (967–72). When the goddesses dismiss Atropos and her 'all-anticipating-chat', they embark on an analysis of what has happened. Their deliberations are ended by Fame's report, speeding through the world, that 'The brave Prince is dead'. Astonishment spreads in Troynovant:

> Contemplate but Troyes greife when Hector fell
> And pensive Priamus and Hecuba . . .
>   You may conceipt the woe of Troynovant,
>   Of James, Anne, Charles, Eliza for theire want.   (1033–8)

The speaker expresses his own shock in a species of correlative verse:

> My Muse did want her selfe my sence was nume,
> My heart grew faint, my quicker power grew slow,
> Myne eyes weare dimme, my tongue was taken dumbe,
> My inke no longer from my penn would flowe,
>   For inke, tongue, eyes, power, hart, sence, muse, apawld,
>   Became thick dumbe dymme, slow, faint nume, and stald.
>   (1027–32)

Of all the mourners, Eliza displays grief most dramatically, tearing her clothes and hair, uttering a lament (of 26 lines), and resolving to spend the rest of her life in mourning with Philomel (1074).[78] But the narrator appears to recognize the futility, in practical terms, of elegy:

> But plaintes and teares no whit at all avayl'd,
> His *Genius* now hath scal'd eternity . . .
> And these laments theire want of him exprest,
> That findes no want of them wheare he doth rest.   (1093–8)

The three goddesses consider the complete withdrawal of their gifts from the earth but decide eventually to leave them in order to 'grace . . . a second Charlemayne', and beg Jove to grant this prince a longer life than Henry had enjoyed. Gorges ends his poem with Jove's far from discouraging response; he addresses the goddesses:

> Youre favorite: was myn: and for that cause,
> I tooke him from the earth, and from you all
> By death, the Seargeant of my death-lesse lawes
>   I tooke him thence, to give him heere his meed,
>   For earthes base pompe, his vertue did exceed.
>
> And as for Charlemayne your Minnion now,
> For whom your gracefull guiftes you keepe in stoare
> I doo no whit your likinge disavowe.

---

[78] Pigman, commenting on this passage, recalls the reports of the intensity of Princess Elizabeth's grief: she refused food for two days and wept incessantly (*Grief and English Renaissance Elegy*, 81, 152).

My high decree determyn'd it before.
 Whearat was heard a Clapp of wintrs thunder,
 Which old sawes saye turnes to a Summers woonder.

                                                      (1171–82)

The poet's address to his Muse stresses the poem's allegorical
sense. There is a profound contrast with the way Gorges had
dismissed his earlier works as 'vannetyes and toyes of yowth': here
he stresses the seriousness of his writing, and equates a capacity to
pierce through the external texture to the essence of an allegory
with moral insight:

But as for those, whom ignoranc so blinds,
 To count this Poeme Idle Ballatrye
 Because themselves with hood-winckt blunddringe mynds
 Cannot discearne a vailed misterye.
   Bid such dymme sighted Owles goe learne againe,
   What morales *Æsops* fables do containe.
                                                      (1189–94)

The recollection of Spenser (especially of the Proem to Book II
of *The Faerie Queene*) is maintained in the first of two concluding
sonnets: Henry's virtues, it states, will constitute a more lasting
monument than any physical memorial. The piece is a reworking of
a poem on Sidney. The second sonnet, with its reference to
Astraea, was probably originally composed on Queen Elizabeth's
death. And just as these short poems connect the three public
events that in some sense structure this study, so *The Olympian
Catastrophe* can stand as a compendium of styles and elegiac
strategies for the whole period it treats. The very obvious literary
influences—Spenser, Chaucer, Ralegh—and Gorges's humanist
relish for debate and personification are constantly manifest in the
allegory, sententiousness, nostalgic chivalry, and *contemptus mundi*.
The repetitions and compound epithets derive as much from
Sylvester as from Spenser. In all, the work is a remarkable blend of
ancient and modern, written by a man who, though born in the year
in which Tottel's *Miscellany* appeared, was closely connected with
the most advanced and forward-looking intellectuals of his day.
Gorges's longest and most ambitious original work is more than a
repository of elegiac commonplaces: it is a fitting culmination to his
eclectic and serious-minded career.
    Oxford University spawned three memorial volumes. *Iusta
Oxoniensium*, which, like *Lachrimae lachrimarum* declares itself to

consist of 'Lachrymae stillantes', distilled tears (and therefore, perhaps, epitaphs?), contains verse mainly in Latin, with a little Hebrew and Greek and one poem in French (F2ᵛ). Although the contributors included many who wrote English verses (such as Robert Burton, Brian Duppa, Henry King, and Richard Corbett), there is nothing in English. The verse is generally non-pastoral, with an apparent preference for locating Henry's life in the context of history, and there are many displays of learned wit. *Eidyllia in obitum* wears its learning less lightly, and displays a much greater range of languages, styles, and genres, though with a tendency to return to the Greek culture implied by the volume's title. *Luctus Posthumus* is an entirely Magdalen production, in which no fewer than 74 members of the College contribute to an anthology which testifies impressively to the College's sense of obligation to its patron.[79]

Epicedium cantabrigienses is in many ways similar to the Oxford collections, though rather more substantial and various in its range of languages and literary ambition.[80] What makes the text particularly significant in the present context is that in its second edition it includes, unprecedentedly for an official University funeral anthology, a collection of poems in English by a group of eleven writers (of whom Giles Fletcher, Thomas Scamp, Stephen Haxby, and Thomas Walkington had already contributed to the volume).[81] Giles Fletcher's Spenserian lament (N4ʳ-O1ʳ) is based on the separation of Henry from his bereaved nation: when animated by the Prince it had been 'The Garden of the World, whear nothing wanted, | Another Paradise, that God had planted' (N4ʳ), but now, thanks to its own pride, it is desolate. Britain is figured (echoing Lamentations) as a grieving widow:

---

[79] The full titles are as follows: *Iusta Oxoniensium* (1612), *Eidyllia in obitum fulgentissimi Henrici Walliae Principia* (Oxford, 1612), *Luctus posthumus sive erga defunctum Henricum Walliae Principem Magdalenensium officiosa pietas* (Oxford, 1612). Henry's visit to Magdalen is described in Birch, *Life*, 52–3; BL MS Royal 12 C VIII is a presentation volume to the Prince from the President of the College. See Wilson, *Prince Henry and English Literature*, 31–3.

[80] *Epicedium cantabrigiense in obitum Henrici principis Walliae* (Cambridge, 1612).

[81] See Ch. 6 below for an account of the increasing frequency with which vernacular verses appear in University anthologies in the years after 1612, and for a brief consideration of the commemorative volume for Sir Edward Lewkenor and his wife (1606), which may be a model for *Epicedium cantabrigiense*.

> Desolate house! what mantle now shall wrap
> Thy naked sides? poore widow, made to mourne
> To whom wilt thou thy sad addresses tourne?   (O1ʳ)

As the Spenserian mode might suggest, Fletcher, like Spenser in *Astrophel*, heads a procession. After him his colleagues rehearse most of the expected commonplaces—Henry as a plant (O1ᵛ), a comet (O2ʳ), a sun, a rose, a phoenix (O2ʳ⁻ᵛ). Thomas Walkington deploys a lofty poetic diction (birds are 'the' aeriall *choristers*' (O3ᵛ) and so forth); others are less artful. Thus an extract from Thomas Scamp's account of the impact of Henry's death on the five senses of London:

> Hearing   My Cryers crie all one, not sundrie ditties,
>   *Prince Henri's dead*: tenne thousand thousand pitties.
>
>   (P2ᵛ)

So there is no suggestion of a unified procession on the *Astrophel* model. What is important about the poems is above all that they exist at all, that they proclaim by their presence that the status of the vernacular now permitted its inclusion in works designed to achieve monumental permanence. In style and substance, of course, what appears in *Epicedium cantabrigiense* is markedly similar to dozens of other laments for the Prince.

Sir Thomas Erskine, a Scot who was a gentleman of Prince Henry's Privy Chamber, left little evidence of literary interests. But he did receive the dedications of Robert Allyne's only recorded publications.[82] In the dedication, Allyne claims to be able to speak for the Prince's closest friends, for whom 'Mourning's a naturall motion in the heart, | And scornes to be reform'd by rules of Art' (A2ʳ): he offers the volume both as comfort and as a token of future poetic achievement, 'some work more worthy of your Worship's sight' (A2ᵛ).[83] What follows is a miscellany of elegiac commonplace, disposed in seven unequal parts. The opening elegy, which consists of 30 six-line stanzas, features a speaker apparently exulting in the winds and rain, the swollen rivers that figure tears shed for the Prince. These natural forces, like the 'dirge specialist' to whose role Allyne aspires, articulate the sorrow that is locked up inside the

---

[82] Robert Allyne, *Funerall elegies* (1613) and *Teares of joy at the happy departure of Frederick and Elizabeth, prince and princesse Palatine* (1613).
[83] He was to proffer *Teares of joy*, as 'the interest of the rest to come' (A3ᵛ).

hearts of Henry's closest friends: inevitably, such a contrast conjures up the usual comparison:

> Ebbe channels roare, deepe streames in silence runne:
> Small woes haue words, but mightie cares be mute.
> Speach can express some shallow mourners mone,
> But dare not vndertake deepe sorrows sute. (A3^r)

After the elegy comes a poem of eleven stanzas addressed to the Prince's effigy, followed by an epitaph. The three pieces are generically distinct and correspond to distinct portions of the elegist's brief, as well as to different stages in the process of death and burial. They are followed by a sequence of pieces directed to Henry's family. In the first, the King is presented with the loss of a militant crusader son, whose 'glorious conquests in the continent' might have been controlled from London by James in order to precipitate 'the fall of Rome' (A3^r): 'Christendome hath lost her chiefest colume' (A4^r).[84] In a poem whose governing fiction is its performance over the effigy, Allyne deploys the normal tripartite division of body, soul, and fame in considering Henry's immortality, but protests his unworthiness and inadequacy to perform a task that would require 'some *Orpheus*' to create a literary monument to represent Henry's virtues as vividly as the effigy represents his body. His own verses are an extended version of the topos of inexpressibility—'mortall pennes vnworthy are to write | and too too base to treat a theme so great' (B2^r).

Consolation is discovered and proclaimed cheerfully enough in the survival of Charles ('Great *Brittaine*, and the world may vtter, | That *Henrie* dy'de but to admit his better' (A4^v)), a 'liuely mirror' of the dead prince and of his father. Allyne tangles himself in the coils of panegyric inflation when he likens Henry, Charles, and James to the Phoenix, 'whose onelie essence', he concedes, 'is to be but one' (B3^v), but for the most part he manages to deliver his sententious observations simply and clearly:

> The Ship sailes most that soonest gets her Port,
> He dies not soone that still on death is musing,
> Life's measur'd, not by time, but by times using. (B3^r)

---

[84] This passage abounds with commonplaces: Henry is likened to an actor and to Alexander (A3^v) and his death, as so often in the more militant Protestant works, is understood as divine punishment for the nation's sin (A4^r). Allyne's volume was quarried by other Scots poets, notably Andro Hart in his anthology *Mausoleum* and Sir Robert Ayton, who copied some of the verses into a manuscript (BL MS Add 10308, fo. 21^v).

Allyne's anthology is close in style and organization to some of the Tudor elegies on Queen Elizabeth, although its variousness and learning connect it with the stiff and formal modes practised by some of the Scots in exile, notably Sir William Alexander.

While Alexander's elegy on the Prince, in poulter's measure, is, like some of the pieces in *Aurora* (1604), in the public manner of Whetstone and Churchyard, its tone is close to the writings of Greville or to his own Senecan *Monarchick tragedies*.[85] The speaker adopts the stance of a nobleman praising his deceased lord to a wider public to whom each had been no more than a name:

> And heare me (happie Ghost) that Fame may spread them forth,
> I vow to reuerence and enroule the wonders of thy worth:
> That euen though chyldlesse dead, thou shalt not barren be,
> If Phoebus help to procreat posteritie for thee.
> Thus where that others did abandon thee with breath,
> As still aliue I trauell yet, to serue thee after death.   (A3ʳ)

The poem proceeds through the accumulation of aphoristic and sententious utterances, depicting its subject in an exclusively public, heroic light.[86] Henry's qualities, as one might expect, are enumerated: brave and wise, he had attained an age equal to the sum of the 'Sphaeres & muses joyn'd' (A2ᵛ), and had expired at the point of his greatest glory (like Attila and others): had he lived longer (echoing Donne's poem on Cecilia Bulstrode) he would have been worshipped as a god.[87] There are two supplementary pieces, one addressed to the King and the other a set of observations on mortality ('O, o I see that from the mothers wombe, | There's but a little step vnto the tombe' (A3ʳ)): neither departs from the stiffly formal manner of the elegy or modifies the volume's general character of decorous pithiness.

---

[85] Sir William Alexander, Laird of Menstrie, *An elegie on the death of Prince Henrie* (Edinburgh, 1612). For brief remarks on Alexander's close literary relationship with King James, see D. H. Willson, *King James VI and I* (1956), 67–8, 215–16. On the Senecanism of his plays, see J. Rees, *Fulke Greville, Lord Brooke, 1554–1628* (1971), 144, and D. Stone, *French Humanist Tragedy* (Manchester, 1974), 66–83. See also *The Works of Sir William Alexander*, ed. H. B. Charlton and L. E. Kastner (Edinburgh and London, 1921).

[86] R. Wallerstein dismissed the poem as 'imitation in the most superficial sense, a pastiche of familiar motives', in which medieval and Renaissance elements were rudely yoked together 'like a Norman cathedral . . . with new Gothic transepts'. (p. 60).

[87] 'For from lesse vertue, and less beautiousnesse, | The gentiles fram'd them Gods and Goddesses': Donne, 'Elegie upon the death of Mistress Boulstred', 54–5 (Milgate, *Anniversaries*, 63).

Great Brittaine, all in blacke was entered in the Stationers' Register on the day after Henry's death: such rapid response to public events was typical of the 'water-poet'.[88] Taylor had already developed a persona for his audience, the newly literate classes, and in the introductory sonnet he distinguishes himself from academic and courtly writers:[89]

> Oh that I could to *Virgills* vein aspire,
> Or *Homers* Verse, that golden languag'd Greeke,
> In polish'd Phrases I my lines would tire
> Into the depth of Art my Muse would seeke.
>   Meane time she mongst the linguist Poets throngs,
>   Although she want the help of Forraigne Tongs.   (A3ʳ)

As well as a variety of woodblock prints, the volume features an engraving of Henry (A1ʳ, based on Drayton's *Polyolbion*), whose martial presentation of the Prince as a British hero sets the tone for the verses that follow.[90] The major components are an attack on death, entitled the 'Equinoques on the deceased Prince HENRIE', and 'Great Britaines Greatest Woe . . . An Elegeicall Lamenting Poem'.[91] Taylor lives up to his nickname. Tears in floods, cascades, and torrents are summoned from the audience as they mourn 'the worlds admired Lampe' who 'Fell in his spring, and dide in golden prime' (B2ᵛ), as the Black Prince had before him. (B3ʳ). The speaker's need to blame someone for the death leads to an attack on medical incompetence which gives way to the unsurprising recognition that Henry died because God 'saw the sinne of man was so great'; all that remains is to await the inevitable 'awfull Rod', while Henry is installed in 'that blest Kingdom of eternall rest' (B3ᵛ) and the Stuart dynasty, which will 'Rule and raigne for euer, and for euer' (B4ʳ) offers some earthly consolation.

Structurally, as a series of related though generically distinct pieces, and in its commonplace content, Taylor's volume has much

---

[88] John Taylor, *Great Brittaine, all in blacke: For the incomparable losse of Henry, our late worthy Prince* (1612). A second issue (STC 23760.5) contains poems by Rowley. *Heavens blessing, and earths joy: Or a true relation, of the al-beloved mariage, of Fredericke & Elizabeth, . . . etc.* (1613) was entered two weeks before the wedding (30 Jan. 1613).

[89] See P. Sheavyn, *The Literary Profession in the Elizabethan Age* (2nd edn., rev. J. W. Saunders, Manchester, 1967), 86; L. B. Wright, *Middle-Class Culture in Elizabethan England* (repr. Washington, 1958), 98, 464, 498; Bergeron, *English Civic Pageantry*, 212–16.

[90] Williamson, *Myth of the Conqueror*, fig. 6; Wilson, *Prince Henry and English Literature*, frontispiece.   [91] The term 'Equinoques' appears to be a new usage.

in common with a number of other works. James Maxwell's *The laudable life, and deplorable death, of Prince Henry*, for instance, is even more of a hotch-potch.[92] The three major qualities of the work are its tone of apocalyptic prophecy, its ostentation of learning (displayed in marginal notes), and its distinctive language, peppered with aureate rhymes ('deuotious . . . reuerence . . . obsequious . . . diligence' (B2ᵛ)). The governing conceit of the entire miscellany is vegetable:

> MANS life full well is likened to a flower   *Man is like a*
> which growing vp goth grace a Gardens aire   *floure that either*
> with sweetest smell, but withreth in an houre: *withereth through*
> Or else is pluckt for sent, or colour faire: *age, or is pluckt*
> Looke on these lines: they shall vnto thy sence *in his prime.*
> Of this likenesse giue perfect euidence.[93]
>
>   (B1ʳ)

The *blason* of Henry's qualities begins internally, with the attributes of piety and quiet learning: but as well as hearing sermons 'with humble diligence' (B2ʳ), Henry had displayed 'mildnesse and affabilitie' to his peers (B3ʳ), and a 'magnificence' (B3ᵛ) which had spread his fame throughout Europe. His court had been decorous, building projects had been sensibly planned, and scholars and soldiers encouraged (to the former he had been 'As great *Maecenas* of the *Muses* nine'; to the latter, '*Albions* Ornament' (B4ʳ)): above all, he acted chastely amid the temptations of court life (B4ᵛ), and prepared himself for death in an exemplary fashion (C1ᵛ). The final part of the volume is stuffed with commonplaces: it is hard to think of any that is omitted. Stars, jewels, pearls, the Phoenix, flowers, and Alexander the Great are adduced for comparison, and confirm the volume's place in the Tudor tradition of 'remembrances'.

---

[92] Entered in the Stationers' Register 28 Nov. 1612. The work contains a praise of King James's 'Auspicious Entrie' (C4ʳ–D2ʳ), an account of his gift for curing scrofula (D2ᵛ–D4ᵛ), a 'Mysticall May-pole to the King' (E1ʳ–E2ᵛ), a poem on the auspiciousness of Prince Charles's birthday (E3ʳ–F2ʳ), and a similar piece on Princess Elizabeth (F2ᵛ–F4ᵛ). Later Maxwell was to publish the single sheet *The imperiall and princely pedigree* (1613), and *A monument of remembrance* (1613). Maxwell's career as a prophetic writer is discussed in M. Reeves, *The Influence of Prophecy in the Later Middle Ages* (Oxford, 1969), 391, 449 ff.; see also Thomas, *Religion and the Decline of Magic*, 461–514, esp. 465–6.

[93] Maxwell identifies Henry as a flower plucked by Jove because the Prince had appeared to be 'more meete | For to perfume the Paradise of Saints | Then for to spring among earths fading plants' (B1ʳ).

Thomas Rogers's *Gloucesters myte* is a more explicitly religious text.[94] Designed to provide 'Motiues to Repentance', it presents Henry's death in wholly conventional ways but adds a distinctive gloss, whereby the event is shown to instruct mankind about the 'inseparable perturbations annexed to this our mortall life' and the 'shortnesse of our earthly pilgrimage' (A2ʳ). He concludes, 'Our longest life, is as a minutes breath, | For in the mid'st of life, wee are in Death' (B2ʳ).

The title of the anonymous *Great Brittans mourning garment* recalls Henry Chettle's miscellany, *Englands mourning garment*, on Queen Elizabeth, and thereby locates itself within the Spenserian tradition. The work is a sequence of nineteen sonnets, conventionally constructed on the controlling conceits of human life as a day, a flower, and a comet, and invoking a political continuity as much as a poetic (so that Henry is proposed as the literal and metaphorical bearer of the Black Prince's standard (A3ʳ), and is 'linked with *Cordelion* in the Towre of Fame' (C3ʳ)). In addition, as the title implies, there is a Spenserian stress upon communal mourning: the book itself is physically part of that process, since it was dedicated to Sir David Murray and the Prince's household and then to have been '*Giuen* to all faithfull sorrowfull subiects at *the Funerall*' (A1ʳ) (with the suggestion that not all mourners might so qualify).

The first sonnet appears to hint at the opening of the revised *Arcadia*; the great grief of Henry's court is hidden from those who (like Strephon and Klaius) merely see the debris being washed up from the sea, and 'but as strangers on the shore lament . . . A common ship-wracke'. 'It is not meete', the poet announces, 'you should lament alone' (A2ʳ). He proposes himself as spokesman for 'So many friends so full of woe' (A3ʳ), and urges them to participate in mourning rituals of a decidedly Spenserian stamp:[95]

> Strow Cypresse, and pale Violets on his Tombe,
> And on his Faire Crest fixe a Crowne of Bayes
> Immortall . . .   (A2ᵛ)

---

[94] Thomas Rogers of Tewkesbury, *Gloucesters myte, delivered with the mournefull records of Great Brittaine, into the worlds register: For the remembrance of prince Henrie* (1612). The unique Bodleian copy is bound with an equally pious work, Sir William Leighton's *The tears or lamentations of a sorrowfull soule* (1613).

[95] The repeated rhyme, 'crown'd . . . ground . . . resound . . . found', imitates the way the assembly is meant to add its voice to the 'Funerall *Anthems*' (A2ᵛ).

The poet summons the Muses (II), rebukes Saturn and the Fates (III, V), and begs Melancholy to lead him to her cave:

> And let thy heauiest Musick softly sound
> Vnto the dolefull songs that I recite:
> And euer let this direfull voice rebound
> Through the vast den: Ah dead is *Britans* light.   (A4ᵛ)

The first half of the sequence, in which specific comparisons jostle with general reflections on the human condition, is unremarkable. But after eleven sonnets, the speaker begs Euterpe to 'poure new Fire into my frozen stile' (XII), and from that point the work is transformed. He appears deliberately to pass up the chance of a *blason* (XIII), for example, and, having associated Henry with others who died untimely (Hecuba, Dido, Mausolus, Pyrene, and Mark Antony (XVII)), he seems to renounce vain (and specifically Ovidian) works in favour of aspiring to an Orphic role (XVIII):[96]

> And of Prince *Henries* death now let vs sing,
> And teach the Rockes on *Monas* shore to weepe,
> And fright the sea with their vast bellowing:
>   That *Neptune* hearing of their pitteous cry
>   May thinke that all the Westerne world did die.   (C2ᵛ)

In characteristic sonneteering fashion, the speaker disclaims art: in the final sonnet, he postpones detailed consideration of Henry's qualities until his fame is fully established—in the meanwhile, his poems are merely 'simple tears' which can 'expresse | A sodaine sorrow' because he is possessed by 'rude grief which no adornment beares' (XIX). The speaker then steps outside the sequence, and concedes that his own unfamiliarity with the Prince has put him at a disadvantage:

> I doe but sound the Accents of Report
> And sure Report giues him a worthy name,
> That from his cradle liu'd in vertues Court . . . (C4ʳ)

Henry's courtiers would be more eloquent, since 'none so well, can sound his praise' as those who 'knew the vpright treadings of his ways' (C4ᵛ)), so the sequence ends with an admission of its own inadequacy and a decision to postpone both consolation and

---

[96] The renunciation of Ovidian writing recalls Sylvester's remark, in dedicating his translation of Du Bartas in 1598 to Essex, that Spenser, Drayton, and Daniel should 'weane our wanton Ile from *Ouids* heires' (cited in Norbrook, *Poetry and Politics*, 195).

treatment of the subject's fame. In a sense, then, the work employs two contradictory strategies; first, Henry is praised directly and implicitly as a subject capable of exhaustive and eloquent treatment; second, the poet's protestations of inadequacy elevate Henry as a figure whose loss is inexpressible. And exploration of the relationship between the private grief professed by the speaker and the act of writing differentiates this anonymous sequence, with its manifest self-consciousness, from the Tudor public elegy and its Jacobean successors.

A similar combination of public duty with private literary self-awareness is manifest in Henry Peacham's *The period of mourning*, a work whose title connects the wedding celebrations of February with December's funeral.[97] In his preface, Peacham learnedly justifies the hybrid, mixed-genre quality of his performance by recalling an Ethiopian custom, 'amid their feasts and Royall Banquets', of presenting the head of a corpse to the chief person present, 'in abundance of mirth to put them in minde of Mortalitie' (A3^r).[98] He then turns to his own predicament, and is unusually forthcoming, employing terms more normally associated with the conflicting emotions of erotic discourse:

My loue to his excellent vertues, and person to whom I was so many wayes engaged, drew, some while since these teares to their head, which encountring with a contrary passion of Ioy, for the happy *Marriage* of his Most-like *Sister* the *Princesse* my most gracious Lady; like fire and water (striuing for praedominancie) I was enforced to make both way euen to mine owne prejudice.   (A3^v)

It might be expected that Peacham's work would be highly visual, given the writer's skill as an emblematist and interest in the practice of painting: it might be expected that the author of conduct books who had already depicted the Prince as an armed knight in *Minerva Britanna* and contributed to the developing Henry cult would present the dead prince as an exemplary figure, and specifically as a Christian knight. But while these expectations are amply fulfilled,

---

[97] Henry Peacham, *The period of mourning: Disposed into sixe visions. Together with nuptiall hymnes* (1613); entered in the Stationers' Register 8 Feb. 1613. Another issue survives (STC 19513.5) with a cancel title-page which continues, 'Also the manner of the solemnization of the marriage at White-Hall' (presumably dating the issue later than the wedding on 14 Feb. 1613).

[98] Peacham is almost certainly drawing upon Montaigne's accounts of Egyptians (*Essays*, tr. Florio, D5^r, D6^r).

nothing in Peacham's other works prepares the reader for the extraordinarily allusive literary pastiche of the visions, where the main models are Spenser and Shakespeare.

The first vision, for example, is of a vessel sailing harmoniously to the sound of music. There is an obvious allusion to *Antony and Cleopatra* II. ii:

> And going out, she did beguile the way,
> With sound of trumpet, Shawmes and Cornet shrill,
> That fil'd the shore, and seem'd to charme the Sea:
> (For windes were ceas'd, and waves were calme and stil.)
>
> I saw (methought) from Cambers hilly shore
> A goodley Arke, as ever eye behold;
> Whose sayles were Silke, and Tackle twined Oare,
> That seem'd reflected, gloriously to guild
> The wave around, while thousand colours faire,
> Kept time aloft with every little ayre.   (B1ᵛ)

We learn that the ship 'Archon hight, for that she had no Peere', that she was 'from *Britaine* bound, | For new discoueries': in Spenserian vein, the progress of the ship, recalling Una and Redcrosse, is disturbed by an ominous storm.[99] The vessel founders (in a common metaphor for the dissolution of Henry's court), and the weeping speaker by the side of the water no less conventionally attributes blame to the iniquity of humanity (B1ᵛ).

The second vision is of a 'Palme, of body tall and straight' (a crown-bearing tree in which birds might nest and beneath which shepherds might shelter—clearly an allusion to Henry's role as a patron) undermined by a 'fearefull Serpent' and brought to earth (B2ʳ). In the third vision, Death, in his cave, declines responsibility and scorns those elegists who attack him (B2ᵛ).[100] The fourth shows Fame guiding a team of four lions drawing a 'Carre Triumphall, all of massie Gold', in which Una rides, accompanied by a 'warlick Impe . . . drad of all for awful Maiestie . . . *Hight Philocles*' (B3ʳ): Peacham invites the reader to identify these figures with Queen Elizabeth and Prince Henry, in the latter case reasserting, through allusion to Spenser's Arthur, the place of Henry within a specifically British chivalric tradition which had been central to the

---

[99] Spenser has 'Thus as thy past | The day with cloudes was suddeine ouercast' (*FQ* I. i. 6), Peacham has 'But suddeinly the Day was overcast' (B1ᵛ).
[100] See Williamson, *Myth of the Conqueror*, 184.

emblems he had presented to the Prince some years before.[101] He describes the destruction of the procession by a 'fiery wand' (B3^v) which scatters the banners and gives rise to contemplation of the brevity of mortal glory (B4^r). From such reflections, he proceeds to the longer fifth vision, in which the solitary poet, sleeping by the Thames, hears a voice like that of 'Thracian Orpheus'.[102] The voice summons the Muses to mourn Dion, since no fitter occasion could be imagined; and when the distraught harpist's 'voyce did fayle and hand began to slacke' (C1^r), he is joined by an assembly of birds and beasts (which Peacham helpfully glosses as 'Noble personages of the land whose crests these are'). The poet, like Spenser's Calidore on Mount Acidale (and to similar effect), rushes to join the mourners only to find 'The Man, the Musicke, Bird and Beast were gone, | I left to mourne disconsolate alone' (C1^v).

The sixth and final vision maintains the Spenserian manner as the poem moves from desolation to consolation. The dejected speaker is led by a 'louely childe' (C2^r) to a place from which he can see the heavenly dwelling of English monarchs and princes who had died young. Eventually they see Henry:

> By one degree rais'd higher than the rest:
> About whose brow an heauenly glory shone,
> And certaine beames appeared from his breast,
> > Which who so did with neerer eye admire
> > Were stricken blinde, or had their hearts on fire.
>
> > > > (C3^v) [103]

After this consoling apotheosis comes an 'Epicedium', which is directed specifically towards the unburied corpse, as Peacham himself makes clear: 'The difference between an *Epecede* and *Epitaph* is (as *Seruius* teacheth) that the *Epicedium* is propper to the body while it is vnburied the *Epitaph* otherwise; yet our Poets stick not to take one for the other' (C4^r). In keeping with such scrupulous antiquarianism Peacham provides an epicede in which the use of musical devices, most obviously repetition, acknowledges the concept that it is a 'sung' form, and this generic self-consciousness continues as the mourners are urged to resolve to

---

[101] See Sir Roy Strong's brief comments on Peacham in *Henry Prince of Wales*, 49–50; G. Parry, *The Golden Age Restor'd*, 75. [102] See Parry, *The Golden Age Restor'd*, 231–2.
[103] See *FQ* I. vii. 29–30; IV. x. 52; VI. ix. 8, etc.

honour the prince's tomb (D1ᵛ). As the location shifts to the grave, so the genre shifts from epicede to '*Elegiacke* EPITAPH' and the volume concludes with further oscillations between public and private registers: while 'even by Teares of yet vnborne | His marble wilbe wash'd and worne' (D3ʳ), the poet himself pledges the continuation of his devotion to the Prince's soul.[104]

It may well be that Peacham was a marginal figure at Henry's court, essentially a popularizer of the tastes associated with the Prince.[105] But whatever his status, his volume on the Prince is remarkable as a public elegy that is structured by Henry's cult, whose art is inseparable from the Prince's image: its variety and allusiveness give expression to the scope of Henry's influence and to the profound sense of historical continuity on which it drew, and in the relation of the solitary and grief-stricken speaker to the splendour of his court Peacham paints a picture that movingly connects the elegist's public function with personal loss.

Richard Niccols was a contributing editor of the 1610 *Mirror for Magistrates*. He was a professional writer whose range included elegiac writing (such as his *Expicedium* (1603) on Queen Elizabeth and his translation *Three precious tears of blood* (1611) on the death of Henri IV) as well as historical and occasional works. In a dedicatory sonnet in *A winter nights vision* (1610) he had praised Henry and other British princes above any Chapman's Homer might celebrate.[106] *The three sisters teares* is dedicated (in a sonnet punning predictably on her name) to Lady Honor Hay, wife of Lord Denny, Baron Waltham (A3ʳ); she appears, on the evidence of the surviving dedications, to have 'inherited' many of Henry's followers.[107]

The text is set up as an exchange between a grieving mourner

---

[104] The final portions of the volume—a series of poems and emblems on Henry's crown, the English rose, the Scots thistle, and so forth—are an earnest of such devotion: in *Prince Henrie revived* (1615), Peacham's promises were further fulfilled, as he celebrated the birth of a child to Henry's sister (see Williamson, *Myth of the Conqueror*, 192–3).

[105] See Strong, *Henry Prince of Wales*, 49–50 and 120, where he calls Peacham a 'hanger-on' and a 'popularizer'. For other comments on Peacham's relations with the Prince, see Wilson, *Prince Henry and English Literature*, 113–14.

[106] Sig. Oo4ʳ; see Wilson, *Prince Henry and English Literature*, 91. Perhaps the work by which Niccols is now best remembered is his Spenserian satire *The cuckow* (1607) (see Norbrook, *Poetry and Politics*, 252); but see also his *Sir Thomas Overburies vision* (1616).

[107] Apart from Niccols, Joseph Hall and Joshua Sylvester dedicated texts to Lady Hay (see Susan Snyder's introduction to her edn. of Sylvester's trans. of Du Bartas, *Divine weeks and works* (Oxford, 1978), 30). Niccols wrote an elegy on her death, *Monodia or Walthams complaint* (1615).

and a consoling, professional poet. The first, distraught, speaker
acknowledges the primacy of a 'dirge specialist':

> But giue I way to him, who knowes the way,
> And comes prepard to make the world to weepe,
> Since I want pow'r to thinke what I would say,
> Or say what I would thinke: (A3ᵛ)

The professional rapidly identifies himself as a Spenserian as he
describes the reckless vanities of an unsuspecting London prior to
the catastrophe of Henry's death:

> So many varying and so vaine delights
> Floating vpon that floud, I then did see,
> Such diuers showes and such fantastick sights,
> That *Thames* the Idle-lak then seem'd to be.   (B2ᵛ)

To the evident dismay of the merrymakers, the scene of revelry is
quickly extinguished by 'Angry Heauen', which disdains the 'vaine
puffe of Giant-Pride in men' (B2ᵛ). The poet, as distracted as the
rest, retraces some of Spenser's steps in *Prothalamion*, and
proceeds upstream to Westminster ('that great house of FAME'
(C1ʳ)), where kings lie among their trophies. Near Henry's hearse
are three women dressed in black:

> Their breasts they fiercely smot, where liu'd their woe
> And their sad eyes dispairing of releefe
> They vp did lift, whence streames of teares did flow,
> As heauen accusing guilty of their griefe.   (C2ʳ)

The first daughter identifies herself as Angela, one of Albion's
three daughters.[108] Her ancient name, Logis, has been changed by
the Saxons (C3ʳ). For her, Henry's death is like a flower withering
(C3ᵛ), and affects all who had been supported by him: she
addresses the Muses, 'Lament with vs, for you haue cause to mone,
| *Maecenas* now is dead, is dead and gone' (C4ᵛ). The Prince's
military accomplishments are recalled in conjunction with his
foreign policy objective of ridding Britain of '*Romes* Rats' (D2ʳ):
had he lived, he would have outshone Edward III and Henry V,
largely because his fierceness was grounded in moral superiority
and inner virtue—'A manly sternenesse sat vpon his brow; | Yet
mixed with an amiable grace'. The woman is led to reflect

---

[108] *The Faerie Queene*, II. X. 12–15.

consolingly that Henry had been so extraordinary that his assimilation by heaven had always been likely, and to move to an expression of hope in Charles in the space between stanzas:

> For though thy losse be now laid out on beere,
> Forget him not, thou canst not finde his peere.

> Except his royall Brother . . .   (D4ʳ)

The second daughter, Albana, professes a greater interest in literary decorum (in an echo of the opening lines of *The Testament of Cresseid* and of *Nouember*): 'A Mournfull subject should with mournfull skill | Be painted justly in letters fraught with teares' (D4ʳ). Her prolix account of Henry's life alludes via Astrophel to Adonis.[109] She, too, paints a picture of religious war, with King James ('Our Kingly shepheard') helping his son to protect their flock from the Roman wolves(E2ʳ). Henry's death is Fate's lesson to 'soothing Sycophants' and to the world at large, showing that all should 'turne from sinne, | That Heauen may turne her threatfull plagues from thee': then, like her sister, she finds consolation in the survival of Prince Charles and sinks silently to the floor before the hearse.

The third sister, Cambera, relates Henry, as might be expected, to other princes of Wales, noting the gap of time separating him from his predecessor.[110] The Prince's ostrich feathers are compared to a palm; the people are blamed for his death; hope for the future is identified in Charles; she falls to the ground next to her sisters and they all vanish.[111]

Attention then returns to the professional poet who has promised to articulate grief. He does so in an acrostic epitaph which the vision had prevented him from pinning to the hearse, and which briefly epitomizes the argument of the entire volume:

> Count this true Parradox, if treuly read,
> Euer Prince HENRY liues, and yet is dead.   (F2ᵛ)

Like Peacham's work, Niccols's poem contains much Spenserian material: yet neither can satisfactorily be assimilated to the

---

[109] 'Death, that wilde Boare entered in anon, | And now his liues leafe, bud, and flower are gone' (E1ʳ).

[110] The future Henry VIII (18 Feb. 1503 until his accession in April 1509): plans for the investiture of the future Edward VI were overtaken by Henry VIII's death.

[111] For another palm, see Peacham's account of a 'Palme, of body tall and straight' in *The period of mourning*, sig. B2ʳ.

Spenserian movement. Both focus strongly on the external trappings of chivalry and heroic romance, and depict the Prince in the tradition of the heroes of *The Faerie Queene*. In neither case is there the self-consciousness or radicalism of the other Spenserians: both writers show the way Spenserian fiction had become available for elegies in the public mode.[112]

More explicitly public, though equally self-conscious, are the elegies published by three of the age's dramatists.[113] Cyril Tourneur's prefatory remarks suggest both generic fastidiousness and concern at the 'stigma of print'.[114] He wrote: 'It was the season for Elegies of this kind, when I wrote this: before HIS Funeralls. I had no purpose (then) to haue it published. Importunity hath (since) drawn it from me' (A4^r). Further, in classing his poem as a 'broken Elegie' he imported from music (the 'broken' or mixed consort) a concept that prizes variety over homogeneity, while retaining a sense of the destruction of the court.

The poem is less novel than the preface. A variety of characterized speakers representing the Prince's interests (notably a soldier and a poet) deplore the shallowness of humanity in celebrating at a time of catastrophe (the volume was published at Christmas): humans 'knowe not what they doe' (B1^r). It is therefore important (the poet argues, following the *Anniversaries*, and referring to Henry as HEE and HIM throughout) to remember Henry, and to recognize that he will survive in every subsequent attempt to depict excellence, whether spiritual or physical (C1^r).[115] He had lived in an exemplary way in a degenerate world:

[112] But see also the lament for Henry as a patron of art, science, and scholarship: 'For few doe now the sacred Nine esteeme, | That haue the gift of *Mydas* golden touch, | Science diuine, a fruitlesse thing they deeme. | And count the learned base for being such. | O then let all that learned are lament | His losse, whose life was learnings ornament' (D1^r).

[113] *Three elegies on the most lamented death of prince Henrie, by C. Tourneur, J. Webster and T. Heywood* (1613). The title-page of the volume is black with white lettering. The three parts were issued separately; Tourneur, *A griefe on the death of prince Henrie* (1613); Heywood, *A funerall elegie upon the death of Henry, prince of Wales* (1613); Webster, *A monumental column, erected to the memory of Henry, late prince of Wales* (1613).

[114] G. E. Bentley, *The Profession of Dramatist in Shakespeare's Time* (Princeton, 1970), 11–37: Tourneur has been classed as 'a courtier and a soldier whose connection with the theatre was . . . brief and incidental' (*The Atheist's Tragedy*, ed. I. Ribner (1964), xxi). He had published in 1609 *A funerall poeme: Upon the death of Sir Francis Vere* (see Lewalski, *Donne's Anniversaries*, 34–5).

[115] 'When a Diuine, or Poet, sets downe right, | What other Princes should bee: Hee shall write | What THIS was' (C2^r). See Wallerstein, *Studies in Seventeenth Century Poetic*, 82–6.

> As Humanitie now goes;
> HEE liu'd a *Man* as long as any does.
> For (onelie) in those *Minutes* that wee giue
> To *Vertue*, wee are *Trulie* said to liue
> *Men*, and no longer.   (B4ʳ)

Thomas Heywood's elegy is dedicated (in language that owes something to Donne) to the recusant Earl of Worcester as the final instalment of grief, 'wishing all future occurrences, to be true, and essentiall causes of your ioyes: and this last, the last of your Teares' (A2ʳ).[116] It is aimed at the entire population, 'As well the learn'd clarke, as the ignorant Swaine', to those whose 'eyes droppe brine' in spite of their faith (A3ʳ):

> This Vniverse imagine a Theater,
> Nations spectators, and this land a stage,
> Was euer Actor, made by his Creator,
> That better scean'd his part vnto his Age?
> 'Mongst all compos'd of fire, aire, earth and water,
> So grauely yong, and so vnmellowed sage.[117]   (B1ʳ)

Heywood characteristically writes in a proverbial and sententious way, and the elegy features numerous pithy expressions of profoundly commonplace ideas (such as Henry's capacity to 'read' flatterers: 'As Mettals by the sound, so could he try | The flashy from the solid when they spake' (B4ʳ)) as well as italicized *sententiae* (*Pleasure and Sorrow still march hand in hand* (C2ʳ)) and homely saws ('Excesse of ioy begetts excesse of woe, | Oft generall weale precedes a generall wracke' (B4ʳ)).[118] But there is also a marked degree of self-consciousness, initiated by the observation that grief is 'Not for him . . . but for our selues' and the discovery that attempts to mourn Henry fail because the resources are not available: the world is 'a Theater too small' for the purpose' (C3ᵛ). In addition, Heywood, like many other elegists, adopts the sonneteers' pose of proposing the harshness and lack of formal elegance in his verses as the expression of his inner condition:

---

[116] Heywood had already dedicated *Troia Britanica* (1609) to Worcester, and was to dedicate to him *Gynaikeion* (1624) and an elegy on King James (1625).

[117] See the laments in two of Heywood's plays, *The brazen age* (1612), II. ii, and *The iron age* (1632), IV. ii.

[118] R. Wallerstein accordingly pronounced it 'uninspired' (*Studies in Seventeenth Century Poetic*, (91)).

> . . . all our Elegies begot from passion,
> Come from rent hearts, and those that giefe proclaime.
> Confused thoughts the best conceits destroy,
> And are more harsh then when we sing of ioy.   (C1ʳ)

John Webster's contribution to the volume, while more ambitious (not least in its dedication to the current royal favourite Sir Robert Carr), is also, to employ Heywood's terms, more 'confused' and 'harsh'. The poem aspires to literary and philosophical distinction, judging by the numerous borrowings from Sidney, Alexander, Donne, Montaigne, and Matthieu (whose life of Henri IV (translated by Grimestone, 1612) is the work's chief source); but nothing can hide the stodgy disjointedness of the jumble of commonplaces and digressions (such as one on the Black Prince (B1ʳ)).

Henry first appears as an Arcadian prince:

> His minde quite voyd of ostentation,
> His high-erected thoughts look'd downe vpon
> The smiling valley of his fruitfull heart.[119]   (A4)

He reconciled active and contemplative virtues (B1ʳ) and saw through flatterers ('none got his Countenance | But those whom actual merite did aduance' (B1ᵛ))—perhaps a sensitive point to make to the notoriously fawning and devious Carr, who found himself in 1613 faced with little opposition after the deaths of Henry and Salisbury.[120] After an apostrophe to Greatness (B2ʳ) and a passage on the distraught survivors (B2ᵛ), there is an allegory on Pleasure (B3ʳ), an apostrophe to Death (B3ᵛ), and a commendation of solitude (B4ʳ)—all drawn from Matthieu. References to crystal and to a broken watch (from Donne) and the picture of slander as a dog (Matthieu and Spenser) lead to an attack on other elegists for their technical and emotional unfitness. Webster accuses them of writing 'waste Elegies . . . more base | Then are the ragges they are writ on' (C1ʳ). In his most individual contribution, Webster suggests that the placing of Henry's corpse in Henry VII's chapel has restored the pomp of the building and shown that his body is more glorious than any bauble:

> Time was when Churches in the land were thought
> Rich Jewel-houses, and this Age hath brought

[119] Sidney, *Works*, i. 16 (*NA* I. ii. 9).   [120] Norbrook, *Poetry and Politics*, 205.

> That time againe, thinke not I faine, go view
> *Henry* the seuenths Chappell, and you'le find it true,
> The dust of a rich Diamond's there inshrin'd.   (C1ʳ)

He apologizes for his unwonted haste in composition ('let the
speede excuse, | The zealous error of my passionate *Muse*'), and sets
this worry about his unpreparedness in the context of an impulse to
erect a monument, to achieve permanence. Like *The Duchess of
Malfi*, whose composition appears to have been interrupted by that
of the elegy, the poem ends with the commonplace that 'The
evening crowns the day, and death crowns life' (C2ʳ).[121] Also like
the play is Webster's laureate ambition: the title-page had cited the
Aeneid and implied a correspondence between Virgil and Webster,
and the elegy contains praise of Henry as the 'graue Maecenas of
the Noble Arts' (C1ʳ).[122] Like the other dramatists in the volume,
Webster derives from the world/stage metaphor a terminology for
self-examination, and for judging aesthetically and morally: all
three of them show the shift of focus in public elegy from the
deceased to the mourner that parallels Bosola's words cited
earlier.[123]

The writings of the Spenserian poets, as David Norbrook has
eloquently shown, provide an index of the King's reputation almost
throughout his reign.[124] The advent of James had been eagerly
anticipated, not least because of his reputation as a poet, and
because he appeared to have endorsed Spenserian literary values in
a sonnet.[125] He also seemed to represent a means of reforming the
realities of political life to correspond to the ideal, of, so to speak,
making the court once again the fount of courtesy, a place where
poets could feel welcome. Prince Henry's court, as noted above,
served as a focus for their disillusion, which had much to feed on in

---

[121] M. C. Bradbrook, *John Webster: Citizen and Dramatist* (1980), 146–7, 163–4, 195.

[122] The Virgilian line is 'Ostendent terris hunc tantum fata' (*Aeneid*, 6. 869), 'Fame
shall give the world merely a glimpse of him'. Lucas records the tradition that the line
refers to Marcellus, and that the dead prince's mother swooned when she heard Virgil
read the line aloud at court (Webster, *Works*, ed. Lucas, iii. 285). Webster also borrows
(ll. 23–8) from Jonson (whose identification with Virgil had been announced in *Poetaster*),
especially the dedication to Prince Henry of *The masque of queenes* (1609). Camden, in
Remaines (1605), applied Virgil's line to Sidney (93ʳ).

[123] *The Duchess of Malfi*, IV. ii. 153–9 (*Works*, ed. Lucas, ii. 97).

[124] Norbrook, *Poetry and Politics*, 195–214.

[125] For the criticism of 'strong lines' and 'harshe verses after the Inglishe fasone', as
well as advocacy of poetry 'fil'd with smoothly flowing fire', see *The Poems of James VI of
Scotland*, ed. J. Craigie, 2 vols. (Edinburgh, 1955, 1958), ii. 114.

the years 1612–14. As far as the elegies on the Prince are concerned, certain common features can be noted at the outset.

The most obvious is the Spenserians' belief in poetry as a means of revealing transcendent truths.[126] Such a belief leads naturally to allegorical presentation: it is also intimately involved with the common compliment paid to Henry that he could pierce the veil of dissemblers, discern the true motives of flatterers. It is a mere step beyond these topics to the Spenserian community, those writers and readers who can read the allegory, see beneath the surface of the text, who are implicitly allied with the Prince and with the poet on the side of truth. Such writing about community normally coexists with the alienation of the individual poet, who is frequently located in some removed or enclosed or marginal position. Two other points should be made. First, most of the Spenserians who wrote on Prince Henry's death were extremely young: their aspirations are those of their age and class, but they are also those of the laureate poet, following the example of Spenser and Drayton (and providing a model for Milton), with all the artistic self-consciousness this implies. Second, Spenserianism in 1612–13 was a blend of nostalgia, satire and apocalyptic prophecy. As such, its surface simplicity is frequently charged with political and religious meaning.

William Basse was quite explicit in his claim to be Colin Clout's heir, his 'loued boy'.[127] His slim volume on Prince Henry, *Great Brittaines sunnes-set bewailed* (Oxford, 1613), contains 21 numbered eight-line stanzas, each on a separate page, each ending with an alexandrine couplet. The bulk of the work is the lament of a 'Soule ore-laden with a greater Summe | Of ponderous sorrow than she can sustaine', who 'bestowes | Vpon hir best friends eares, some children of her woes' (A2ʳ). And the volume is tied together by the reiterated image of tears as a stream, playing upon the tears/verses metaphor to impose order on the 'cease lesse currents of complaining verse' (B1ᵛ). The mournful soul, impressed by the 'true arguments of inward woe' displayed by the poet's face, finds in the poet an ideal audience. He extols those who display restraint in public, reserving extreme grief for their select friends: 'To you therefore I weepe: To you alone | I show the image of your teares,

---

[126] Norbrook, *Poetry and Politics*, 201.

[127] Basse, *Three pastoral elegies* (1602), E3ᵛ; repr. in *Spenser: The Critical Heritage*, ed. R. M. Cummings (1971), 111 (see also 190).

in mine, (A4ʳ) . . . 'I am turn'd woman: watrish feares benumbe |
My Heate: my Masculine existence thawes | To teares . . . ' (B1ʳ).
Basse recalls his own youthfulness, and glories in his tears 'while
older pens compose | More solemne Rites' (B1ʳ): he concentrates
on the sorrow occasioned by the fall of the 'high Pyramis'. Such
consolation as appears is located in the international community of
grief, as Florence mourns a duke, Spain a queen, and France a king
('she from *Henry* Great wee from Great *Henry* parted' (C2ᵛ)). In
the final stanza the flood of tears dries up as the speaker withdraws
silently:

> Downe to my silent breast my hidden face I bow:
> My *Phoebus* in his West, hath hid his heav'nly brow.   (C3ʳ)

After the decorous interval of a blank page comes something of a
shock: two further stanzas called 'A morning after mourning', in
which Basse moves from lament to joyful anticipation of Princess
Elizabeth's wedding, and the exhortation, 'all in mirth combine'
(C4ᵛ). So jarring a shift recalls some of the combinations of elegy
and panegyric in 1603: but the overall solemnity and gravity of the
piece make the volume the most secure prop of Basse's fragile
reputation as a minor Spenserian.[128]

One of the many volumes to give physical expression to the value
placed on community is the collaborative *Two elegies, consecrated to
the memorie of Henry, prince of Wales*, by Christopher Brooke and
William Browne of Tavistock, and dedicated to 'the Honourable
Gentlemen, and griefe-afflicted followers of our incomparable
Prince Henry, deceased' (A3ʳ). In addition, the work appears to
have a sharper political edge than many of the elegies so far
considered. There is, for example, an epigraph from Horace
(*Carm.* 3. 6. 17–20), whose application is that the dissolution of
Henry's court parallels the destruction of traditional Roman values
by accumulated private sinfulness.[129] In such a context, it is hardly

---

[128] See *DNB* and D. Bush, *English Literature in the Earlier Seventeenth Century* (2nd edn., Oxford, 1962), 83. Basse is not mentioned by Grundy, Wallerstein, Lewalski, or Norbrook.

[129] Horace's lines, 'Fecunda culpae saecula nuptias | primum inquinavere et genus et domus; | hoc fonte derivata clades | in patriam populumque fluxit', open the second section of the poem. Brooke uses the second pair of lines which read in isolation like an elegiac commonplace, 'ruin, channelled from this source, flowed out over country and people', leaving his readers to supply the context of the previous lines—'Generations prolific in sin polluted the marriage and the family and the home'. In the first portion of the Ode the poet urges Romans to renew worship of their gods let slip by their ancestors;

surprising that Brooke's speaker, addressing his fit audience of like-minded mourners ('of gentle SPIRIT, and softened Hart' (B1ᵛ)), professes indifference to

> Those baser mindes, vnknowing, sensuall, rude,
> That measure contraries indifferently;
> Whose *Summum bonum* is their sleepe and food,
> Preferring moments, to Eternitie;   (B1ʳ)

The objective of his elegy is simple enough: as well as consoling the elect, he seeks to ensure the preservation of Henry's reputation for the benefit of the world:

> Let this Fames Sunne through this round Transitory
> Shine, and ne're set; and fixed like the Poles,
> Whiles some stout *Atlas* props his heauenly frame,
> Let men (like Spheres) moue round about the same.   (B2ᵛ)

In keeping with such an impulse is the strongly biographical character of the work, and the space devoted to an inventory of the Prince's qualities and to an account of his pious death. Brooke employs the modesty topos, calling himself 'In will (tho not in skill) strong as the best' and allying himself to other, more distinguished writers ('I shall be proud yet to haue had a hand, | Vpon the bases, where their Columbs stand' (B2ᵛ)). Henry had been a compendium of excellences, a reconciliation of contraries whose soul had been 'a shrine | Burning in zeale of truth, and deeds Diuine' (B3ᵛ), whose actions had promised another Cyrus or Alexander ('A PRINCES Wisdome not in wrinckles lies: | God measures not his GIFTS by Age or years' (C1ᵛ)), and in whom had been 'drawne the Modell of a State' (C2ʳ).

When the household, 'Ruin'd in fortunes, and distrest in mind', gather about the hearse, they constitute 'A little *Iland* compast in with Teares', a spectacle that generates in the speaker a grief so intense that it overwhelms reason (C3ʳ⁻ᵛ). Only the final consignment of the corpse to the earth tempers the lament, as the speaker begins to contrast his own dejection both with the harmonious

---

Horace probably alludes to a programme of temple restoration instituted by Augustus in 28 BC. The contemporary application for Brooke may be twofold, implying on the one hand support for James's pacific neo-Augustan posture and religious reformation in line with Henry's puritanism. More generally, the remainder of the Horatian text dwells at length on the decline of familial values and political failure; its connection with the views of the Spenserians is thus strong. See *The Third Book of Horace's Odes*, ed. G. Williams (Oxford, 1969), 60–7 for text, transl. and commentary.

perfection of the dead prince and, eventually, with the unfathom-able symmetries of divine creation:

> Heau'ns Architector: Worlds Artificer;
> The Quintessence of all Perfection; . . .
> Let then no dusty Wormeling euer dare
> With his eternal Will to hold dispute,
> But wrapt in wonder, all be dumbe and mute.   (D1ᵛ)

It is a short step from such acceptance of divine will to the assertion that 'All things by prouidence begin, and end' (D1ʳ), and it is at that point that Brooke stops. He leaves the reader to hope in the ultimately beneficial operations of providence: he offers no guidance, and is scrupulously silent on the King and Prince Charles. Hope for the future is related exclusively to the faith of individuals, with God the 'Firme DIAMETER' who helps the faithful to order their emotions (D1ʳ).

While at one level Brooke's sturdily independent stance may be regarded as consistent with the Horatian epigraph of his elegy, at another it is more contemporary in its application, for his hostility to absolutism (expressed in *The ghost of Richard the third*, published anonymously in 1614) was already leading him to an oppositional, radical position.[130] Brooke was a securely established middle-aged man in 1612: his appearance in print in the guise of a Spenserian allied him not with his close friend Donne but with a younger generation of disenchanted radicals, with whom the rest of his brief literary career was to be intimately involved.

Two Latin phrases appear on the title-page of William Browne's elegy. The first, from Ovid's *Tristia*, is a straightforward comment on the ubiquity of grief, 'Wherever you had looked was the sound of mourning and lamentation' ('Quocumque adspiceres, luctus, gemistusque sonabant' (*Tristia*, 1. 3. 21)). The second is line 79 of Virgil's third Eclogue, 'Et longum formose vale, vale,inquit, Iolla', or 'And for a long time [*or* from afar] [Phyllis] said, "farewell, farewell, beautiful Iollas" ': the line comes from a verse competition between Menalcas and Dorcas. The application of the first passage appears obvious enough, though it is qualified in the course of the

---

[130] Such is the import of his writings: historians have pointed out the discrepancies between his rhetoric and his actions: see Norbrook, *Poetry and Politics*, 211 ('It is difficult to know just how seriously to take Brooke's political rhetoric') and M. Prestwich, *Cranfield: Politics and Profits under the Stuarts. The Career of Lionel Cranfield Earl of Middlesex* (Oxford, 1966), 141.

poem that follows. The second has the immediate effect of linking Browne's poem to its predecessor in the volume, and it further claims for the youthful Browne the status of a participant in the communal, competitive mourning of the Spenserians. After all, as Virgil's Palaemon puts it in the same eclogue, 'alternate song is what the Muses love'.[131]

Browne begins by likening November to a black-draped tragic stage: an apt setting for a prince's death (D3^r). He asserts the value of communal lamentation, and, like Brooke, rejoices that anyone can participate, can add 'one poore teare' to the store already shed. He is unusual in interpreting the silence of established poets panegyrically:

> Alas! I see each one, amazed stands.
> Shallow FOORDS mutter, silent are the DEEPE:
> Faine would they tell their griefs, but know not where,
> All are so full, naught can augment their store.   (D4^r)

Failures of eloquence on his own part are excused as evidence of his sincerity and as tokens of the general disruption caused by Henry's death. Throughout the poem Browne develops the metaphorical twinning of tears and elegies, and associates such concepts with tides of passions, springs of inspiration, and so forth, in a way that leads him to address fundamental problems of expression, and give vent to frustration at the inadequacy of his medium:

> Alas my plaint
> In such constraint
> Breakes forth in rage, that though my passions swimme,
> Yet are they drowned ere they landed be.
> Imperfect lines: oh happie were I, hurld,
> And cut from life, as England from the world.   (D4^v)

Browne rehearses possible precedents for the present sorrow (including a reference to 'our HEROE, honour'd ESSEX' (E1^r), who appears as Henry's predecessor as exemplar of Christian chivalry), and concludes that Henry's death is a unique event, which ought to be commemorated by other writers ('IMPES of MEMORIE' who must 'Erect a new *Parnassus* on his graue' (E1^v)), so that there will be a literary monument around which the distraught survivors may gather. He exhorts them to

[131] 'Amant alterna Camenae', Virgil, *Eclogues*, 3. 59.

> Keepe time vnto your songs with dropping teares
> Til droppes that fell
> Haue made a well.
> To swallow him which still vnmoued heares: (E1ᵛ)

Once more the emphasis is on the capacity of the like-minded mourners to be moved, and the consequence is that Henry's virtues will live on in 'the harts of MEN' (D3ᵛ), or at least those men who can participate in the Spenserian community, and who have been formed into a group by the experience of grief and by accepting some moral responsibility for Henry's death. Browne wittily describes how Henry's followers, on hearing that the Prince had sickened, entered the 'LABORINTH of *Woe*'; but for twine, they used Henry's vital thread. With the inevitable result:

> When we were almost come into the CENTER,
> Fate (cruelly) to barre our ioyes returning,
> Cut off our thread and left vs all in MOVRNING.   (E2ʳ)

There is no conventional consolation, beyond the confidence in the survival of Henry's qualities in the best of his followers, and that confidence is mimed by the poem's implicit accommodation to the diachronic community of shepherd-poets as well as to the synchronic group of Henry's supporters.

A writer anxious to join their number was George Wither, the most vigorous of the younger generation of Spenserians. *Prince Henries obsequies or mournefull elegies upon his death* (1612), dedicated to Sidney's brother Robert (and containing (A2ʳ) an elegy on Sir William Sidney), begins with a protestation of the writer's purpose that reveals a degree of self-regard and self-esteem typical of Wither's writings throughout his career:

> Then, though I haue not striued to seeme witty,
> Yet read, and reading note, and noting pitty.
> What though ther's others, use in this more *Art*?
> I haue as true; as sorrowful a hart
> What though *Opinion* giue me not a *Name*, . . .
> For here I mourne, for your—our publike losse;
> And doe my pennance; at the *Weeping Crosse*.   (A3ʳ)

After an epigram on Henry's triumph over death (A3ᵛ), the *Obsequies* begin. The work is a sequence of 45 sonnets. The implied generic equivalence of sonnet and elegy in Wither's title possesses significance, not least in hinting at a correspondence between the speaker in Wither's sequence and the lover-poet of a sonnet sequence, with all that is thereby suggested in terms of introspection, passion in conflict with reason and duty, and the rest. Like a melancholy lover, the speaker begins by withdrawing from company, seeking a 'dull Melancholy loneliness' to 'Fat my grief with solitarines' (A4ʳ): at this stage, he explicitly rejects the Spenserian faith in the value of community:

> For if it be a comfort in distresse,
> (As some thinke) to haue sharers in our woes,
> Then I desire to be comfortles.   (A4ʳ)

The justification presented by the speaker recalls Spenser's defence of Calidore's truancy, that, though 'out of course', it 'hath not been mis-sayd' (*FQ* VI. xii. 1): Wither's speaker protests that 'greefe, for such a losse, at such a season, | May be past measure, but not out of *Reason*' (A4ᵛ). Echoes of the pose of amatory sonneteers continue with an expression of scorn for the 'fained stuffe' of literary convention (A4ᵛ), and with attempts to establish the subject's uniqueness. Wither, like Niccols, collides with the difficulties of panegyric inflation in attempting to reconcile the essential uniqueness of the Phoenix with his wish to present Henry, his father, and brother simultaneously as the Arabian bird: he concedes the point that 'twas decreed when first the world begunne, | Earth should haue but one *Phoenix*' (B2ʳ).

The sequence falls naturally into two parts. In the first, explicitly laureate, section, poems are addressed severally to Britain, the King, and other members of Henry's family; both Prince Charles and the Elector Palatine are urged to continue Henry's work of striving against Rome (B1ᵛ, B2ᵛ), and Wither takes on the role of professional mourner who sheds his tears on behalf of the grieving relatives when he requests Princess Elizabeth, 'now leave off thy teares in vain to shed, | For why? To spare them I have powr'd out mine' (B3ʳ). The rest of the sequence is an anatomy of his own mourning, built on the assertion of its sincerity and passion: 'my griefe that Ceremonie lothes, | Had rather be in heart, then seeme in clothes' (B4ʳ).[132] While various conventions of the pastoral elegy are rehearsed (the summons to mourn, pathetic fallacy, and

---

[132] Wither referred to all his writings as the 'little *Index* of my minde' in the epigram to his father accompanying *Abuses stript and whipt* (1615); in *Withers motto* (1621) he

reversed nature—'Blacke was *White-hall*' (C4ᵛ)), the poet and his subject appear undisguised: 'I lou'd him as my *Prince*: as *Henry* more' (D1ʳ). And Wither's speaker looks back on the experience he has endured as another Fall:

> Thrise happy had I bene if I had kept
> Within the circuit of some little village,
> In ignorance of Courts and Princes slept,
> Manuring of an honest half-plough tillage:
> Or else I would as I were young agen,
> As when *Eliza* our last *Phoenix* dide:
> My childish yeares had not conceiu'd as then
> What t'was to loose a Prince so dignifide,
> But . . . now I know: and what now doth't availe?
> Alas, whilst others merry, feele no paine,
> I melancholy, sit alone and waile:
> Thus sweetest profit, yeelds the bitterst gaine.
> 　Why? *cause it came by the forbidden tree:*
> 　*And good things proue not, that ill gotten be.*[133]   (B4ʳ)

The operation of providence is identified in the coincidence of Henry's death with the anniversary of his deliverance from the Gunpowder Plot (D1ᵛ), and responsibility is unequivocally placed upon the foolish populace (D2ʳ). Henry himself had been able 'plainly' to 'prognosticate his end', with the result that his funeral procession was, to the eyes of the elect, a token of victory over death.[134] The sequence then concludes with a series of affirmations of trust in providence, referring specifically to Prince Charles—'So Iesses eldest *Sonnes* had most renowne, | But little *David* did obtaine the Crowne' (D3ʳ)—and the speaker turns to exhort to repentance the community he had earlier shunned. Then follows a dialogue, a 'Supposed interlocution betweene the Spirit of Prince *Henrie*, and great Brittaine', in which England recalls how 'All my sweet tunes and former signes of gladness | Are turn'd to *Elegies* and songs of sadness' (D4ᵛ). Henry's spirit appears as an echo, but after engaging in a lengthy series of questions and responses

remarks: 'My intent was, to draw the true Picture of mine own heart: that my friends, who knew me outwardly, might have some representation of my inside also' (A2ᵛ). See Grundy, *Spenserian Poets*, 167.

[133] Helgerson observes of the younger generation of Spenserians that, 'forced to choose, these men took the side of the country—a country they identified with the memory of the great queen'('The Land Speaks', in *Representing the English Renaissance*, 346).

[134] See Stannard, *Puritan Way of Death*, 72–95.

resolves to speak 'In plainer wise' (E1ʳ); he attacks the 'wicked whore of Rome' (E1ᵛ), and counsels his brother to shun flatterers and papists, cut out the tongues of blasphemers (E2ᵛ), and generally to be guided by a Puritan discipline in private life and public policy.

The use of the echo and the assertions of plainness are pastoral commonplaces.[135] But Wither strengthens the religious and political implications of such stock machinery that the other Spenserians had already begun to exploit. And in the *Obsequies* he represents his position through the medium of a sonnet sequence, achieving thereby a degree of subtlety and invention which he would later jettison from his poetic armoury in favour of more direct satire and polemic.[136]

John Davies's Spenserian credentials were strong. Even more than Brooke and Wither, he had close ties with the Pembrokes, and he participated in several collaborative literary ventures with the other Spenserians, as well as writing satirically about the Overbury scandal. His elegy on the Prince has a Spenserian title: *The Muses-teares for the losse of Henry Prince of Wales* (1613). And yet the poem's most obvious stylistic debt is to Donne's *Anniversaries*, echoed from the outset of Davies's poem.

After reproducing some of Donne's phrases, Davies delivers a series of commonplaces, whereby Henry is compared to a withered plant, a shooting star, an unprecedented combination of military and intellectual achievements, and a creature whose excellences were 'vnmatch'd by any of his yeares' (A2ʳ). The reader is presented with an ideal Christian prince, whose '*Spirit* and his *Body* were at endlesse strife | Which should be *Actiu'st* in all Princely *Parts*' (A2ᵛ). Davies's account of the ascent of Henry's soul, though couched in neoplatonic terms, is written in an approximation to Donne's manner in the *Anniversaries*:

> . . . Shee did flee
> The *World*, and such vaine *Pride*; yet fled more hie!
> She fled to Him whose *Center's* euery where,

---

[135] Rosenmeyer, *The Green Cabinet*, 49–52, 148–50, 185–6.

[136] See C. Hill, *Milton and the English Revolution* (1977), 59–64, and 'George Wither and John Milton', in *English Renaissance Studies*, 212–27; Grundy, *Spenserian Poets*, 161–76; Norbrook, *Poetry and Politics*, 209–13. Helgerson (ibid.) cites Wither's praise of Drayton prefaced to the 2nd vol. of *Poly-Olbion*: ' 'Tis well', wrote Wither, 'thy happy judgement could devise, | Which way a man this age might poetize, | And not write satires' (Drayton, *Works*, iv. 395).

> And *Circle* no where: for, true *Eaglet*, She
> On *Iustice* SONNE (her Eyes being *strong*, as *cleare*)
> Still lou'd to looke, to shew her *Dignity*!   (A3ʳ)

Davies concentrates on the way Henry's public personality (and his
'Princely lookes compos'd so rarely . . . Of venerable *grauity* and
grace' (A3ᵛ) represented his inner distinction, his status as a 'mortall
God', whose self-discipline turned his followers into righteous men
(A3ᵛ⁻A4ʳ). The concept of the interdependence of ruler and state
is developed into a discussion of ideal governorship (contrasted
with despotism), which Henry had exemplified:

> He was the richest *Trophey* FORTVNES Pow'r
> Could reare in HONORS *Theater*; for, stil
> NATVRE did doate on *Him* (her *Bellamoure*,
> Or *Master-peece*) the Wonder of her skil!   (B1ʳ)

As so often in Spenserian texts, Henry's penetrating glance is
stressed, and linked to an ability to see through the trivial dross of
quotidian existence to another, superior reality:[137]

> . . . He most strictly ey'de his better *Part*;
> And in the *Glasse* of Heau'ns eternall LAW
> Righted th'Apparell of his royall Heart
> As best became his FORME, which there he saw: (B1ᵛ)

There is a passage full of generalities on the human condition
('*Man's* a *Maze* of *Mutability*' (B1ᵛ)), after which Davies describes
the ubiquity and magnitude of the tidal flood of grief at Henry's fall
(B2ᵛ). A conventional analogy is made with the human body. Henry
(the heart) had, by dying, slain both the head (the King) and the
limbs and organs (society):

> So, HEAD and *Members* die with this our HEART!
> We die, though yet we moue, with *griefe* conceau'd
> For this his death; whose Life gaue all our Parts
> Their liuely motion; which they had receau'd
> From his rare vertue, *Life* of all our *Hearts*.[138]   (B3ᵛ)

No less typical is Davies's double assertion that, while the mass
of mankind is responsible for Henry's death, the Prince's followers

---

[137] See Donne, *Sermons*, vi. 285–6; Lewalski, *Donne's Anniversaries*, 212–15.
[138] Donne had adventurously applied this conceit to a commoner, Elizabeth Drury:
Browne used the example of Caligula's reported wish to decapitate the populace in the
person of a single individual (*Two elegies*, E1ᵛ).

may constitute themselves into a consoling, self-supporting community ('It is a kind of Ioy in case of *moane* | Not to be single' (B3ᵛ), where it is possible to achieve a sense of perspective—'*Our* ALL's but *Nothing* than: For, that which IS | Must be eternall' (B4ʳ). The speaker expresses the value of grief by analogy with a smithy:

> Men must be wrought like Ir'ne; that's first made soft
> With *fire*, yer *water* cooles it: *fires* of *Wit*
> Must make them more then supple (sure, and oft)
> Y'er Teares can coole strong *passions* burning-fit.　　(C2ʳ)

And he classes his writings as 'blubbred lines', as unvarnished outpourings of passionate grief, in dedicating them to the Elector Palatine, whose good fortune it will shortly be to marry '*Good* in the *Abstract*' (Princess Elizabeth). The poet notes that Henry's bones will be laid to rest next to those of his grandmother in Henry VII's chapel, but locates consolation in the continued existence of goodness in the world ('die he neuer can while *Vertue* liues, | For, He, and SHE are still Corelatiues!' (C3ᵛ)).[139] He also, like most Spenserians, anticipates the preservation of Henry's values in his followers, a topic that informs the ensuing 'Sobs for the losse of the Prince', where the company of mourners pray for strength 't'vpholde the *Common-wealth* | Of our owne *Stocke*' (C4ᵛ). Davies addresses words of advice to the members of Henry's family in turn, advocating a scorn of earthly glory for its own sake ('nought is Great on *Earth* but that Greate *Minde* | That's moou'd with nothing great produc'd by KIND' (E1ᵛ)), while prudently asking for protection from the Queen—'Blesse, with your *Beames* of grace, these graceless *Lines*' (E3ᵛ).

Davies's volume conforms loosely to classical practice in its tripartite structure (narrative, 'sobs', consolation); in its title and matter it is explicitly Spenserian; in its style it mimics Donne's recent innovations in the *Anniversaries*. Obviously, its various, miscellaneous character eloquently indicates the range of elegiac possibilities that had become available by 1612. In addition, the panegyric implications of such variety are apparent, both in terms of imitating Henry's comprehensiveness and magnanimity and because they embody both the poet's professedly uncontrollable passion and his (implicitly complimentary) struggle with the problems of writing.

---

[139] See Parry, *Golden Age*, 254–5.

William Drummond's *Teares on the death of Moeliades* has generally been admired by critics: to E. C. Wilson it was a work of 'distinction'.[140] It has been common to consider Drummond's poem exclusively in terms of the tradition of pastoral elegy, and more particularly as a link in the chain that leads from Theocritus and Bion to *Lycidas*.[141] There has been a tendency to underplay Drummond's inventiveness and eclecticism, qualities that were especially apparent at the outset of his career, and in a text with which he made his poetic debut.[142] Thus, although Drummond's most celebrated personal contacts with English writers were with Jonson and with Donne and his circle, Sidney and Spenser are the major British influences on the *Teares*. A recent editor referred to Drummond as 'a kind of literary squirrel who saved anything that came his way', and the allusiveness of *Teares* supports its status as a declaration of impending greatness.[143] For a poet who privately compared himself to Orpheus, Henry's death was a heaven-sent opportunity to match his talent to a challenging occasion.[144]

Perhaps in recollection of Donne's practice in the *Anniversaries*, the poem is divided into five sections by a refrain whose lofty diction and exotic proper names claim kinship with laments in the pastoral high style: 'Moeliades *sweet courtly* Nymphes deplore | From Thuly *to* Hydaspes *pearlie* Shore'. The speaker begins by questioning the fact of Henry's death:

> *O Heauens!* then is it true that thou art gone,
> And left this woefull *Ile* her Losse to mone,

---

[140] Drummond, *Teares on the death of Meliades* (Edinburgh, 1613); my text is from Drummond, *Poems*, ed. Kastner. See Wilson, *Prince Henry and English Literature*, 149.

[141] See Harrison and Leon, *The Pastoral Elegy*, 193–8, 287–8, and W. Kirkconnell, *Awake the Courteous Echo* (Toronto, 1973), 239–40.

[142] I would thus place Drummond firmly in the context of the elegiac cultivation of generic variety as surveyed by R. Colie in *The Resources of Kind* and by J. Wittreich in 'From Pastoral to Prophecy: The Genres of *Lycidas*', *Milton Studies* 13 (1979), 59–80; see below, ch. 6; see also R. D. S. Jack, *The Italian Influence on Scottish Literature* (Edinburgh, 1972), 75–6, 113–43, 156.

[143] R. M. Macdonald, ed., *William Drummond of Hawthornden: Poems and Prose* (Edinburgh, 1976), xiii; for an account of Drummond's reading of Sidney and others, see Macdonald's *The Library of Drummond of Hawthornden* (Edinburgh, 1971), 131–40. Insularity, not to say parochialism, underlies Ben Jonson's criticism that Drummond's verses were 'all good . . . saue that they smelled too much of the schooles and were not after the Fancie of the tyme' (Jonson, *Works*, i. 135).

[144] *Poems and Prose*, ed. Macdonald, xi, citing Hawthornden MSS, NLS MS 2061, fo. 146[r].

Moeliades? bright *Day-Starre* of the *West*,
A *Comet*, blazing Terrour to the *East*:   (1–4)

The event is interpreted as a token of fortune's instability and of death's power: now that the 'Northerne Blast' has destroyed the 'virgine *Rose*', mankind recognizes its vulnerability in a malevolent universe: '*Heuens* neglect our *Cryes*, | *Starres* seeme set only to act *Tragoedies*' (13–14). The speaker deviates from conventional *puer senex* strategies, by complaining that Henry had died before he had had a chance to deal with the Turk and the Pope, or to develop—as he surely would have, since '*It was* not want of worth, o no, but *Yeares*'—into the proper subject of a new national epic (52–8): but the heavenly powers, as so frequently in these elegies, were impatient to welcome 'that which is braue | On *Earth*'. The first occurrence of the refrain urges universal lament for the Prince, thereby continuing and in a sense confirming the elevated mode of the opening section.

The second part features the mourning of the rivers of Scotland, which join their tears to the sorrows of seas, oceans, and lesser rivers to make 'Hudge Streames of Teares, that changed were in Floods'.[145] Drummond pictures the demoralization of the race of shepherd-poets, noting especially Sir William Alexander:

The Shepheards left their Flockes with downe-cast Eyes,
Disdaining to looke up to angrie *Skies*:
Some broke their Pipes, and some in sweet-sad Layes,
Made senselesse things amazed at thy Praise.
His Reed *Alexis* hung upon a *Tree*,
And with his Teares made *Doven* great to bee.[146]   (89–94)

Drummond opens the third section, in which other writers are summoned to mourn the Prince, with an explicit echo of Sidney. He urges them to set aside other kinds of writing—especially erotic verse—in order to grapple with this new subject:

---

[145] Such fulsome accounts of floodgate grief are remarked on by Pigman as part of the 'shift from anxious elegy' to a form which gives full weight to the emotion of lament (*Grief and English Renaissance Elegy*, 59–62). More specifically, Drummond's phrasing, both in his presentation of the 'floods of tears' and the *puer senex* topoi, appears close to similar passages in Holland's contribution to Sylvester's *Lachrimae lachrimarum* (1613), D3. See below, p. 186.

[146] For the antiquity of such introduction of friends under pastoral disguise, see Rosenmeyer, *The Green Cabinet*, 105–7.

> Chaste *Maides* which haunt fair *Aganippe Well*,
> And you in *Tempes* sacred *Shade* who dwell,
> Let fall your Harpes, cease Tunes of Ioy to sing,
> Discheueled make all *Parnassus* ring
> With *Antheames* sad, thy Musicke *Phoebus* turne
> In dolefull Plaints, whilst *Ioy* it selfe doth mourne:
> Dead is thy *Darling*, who decor'd thy Bayes,
> Who oft was wont to cherish thy sweet Layes,
> And to a *Trumpet* raise thy amorous *Stile*,
> That floting *Delos* enuie might this *Ile*.[147]   (97–106)

As is the case with many elegists of Drummond's generation, there is an evident criticism of the reticence of older poets whose understanding has been blunted, whose capacity to recognize greatness has been dulled by the conditions under which they have opted to write. After all, he argues, Henry had been a second Adonis, or a second Mars: as such he demands to be mourned, and the image of floods of tears resurfaces in the account of the rivers of Europe: once they competed for Henry's hand; now they vie with each other in the intensity of their grief. And Drummond provides his own assertion of poetic tradition in the fourth section, which is closely based on Sidney's pastoral dirge from *Arcadia*, itself connected with the most ancient Greek laments. The most obvious echo is the address to the Hyacinths, with its allusion further back to Moschus ('O *Hyacinths*, for ay your *AI* keepe still'), but Drummond makes the point at greater length than Sidney by adding an explanatory line in urging the flowers to fill their leaves with 'more Markes *of Woe*'. Sidney's speaker had wrestled with problems of meaning and expression, and with his source in Sannazaro. But Drummond's borrowing has a different effect: it is as if everything included in the poem requires elucidation, reinterpretation, translation. And while such explicit eclecticism says something about Henry's international standing, and about the concept of poetic tradition, its most evident consequence is to thrust the speaker into the foreground. Not for him the diffidence and hesitancy of Sidney's poet, who qualifies his perceptions with phrases such as 'me thinks', and appears to seek rational explanations for phenomena that other elegists have traditionally taken as tokens of reversed nature. Drummond's voice is public, certain, and imperative. Thus Sidney's

---

[147] The echo is of *Astrophil and Stella*, Sonnet 74.

> And well (mee thinks), becomes this vaultie skie
> A statelie tombe to cover him deceased   (58–9)

is transformed into

> Stay *Skie* thy turning Course, and now become
> *A* stately *Arche*, vnto the *Earth* his Tombe   (137–8)

Grief, whose ubiquity had been established in the first half of the poem, is now claimed to be permanent: Henry's death, the implication seems to be, is a 'real' subject that swallows up fictional exemplars. The speaker acknowledges that loss is a mortal sensation, and that Henry has been placed out of the reach of such pains:

> Beyond the *Planets* Wheeles, aboue that Source
> Of *Sphaeres*, that turnes the lower in its Course,
> Where *Sunne* doth neuer set, nor vgly *Night*
> Euer appeares in mourning Garments dight; . . .
> From *Cares* cold Climates farre, and hote *Desire*,
> Where *Time* is banish'd, *Ages* ne're expire . . .   (147–54)

From such a vantage-point, Henry may perceive the triviality of human endeavours (163–4, 169–70), and the speaker acknowledges as much in a valediction to his subject (in which he perhaps alludes to the *Cantoes of Mutabilitie* (1609)):[148]

> Rest blessed *Spright*, rest saciate with the Sight
> Of him, whose Beames both dazell and delight,
> *Life* of all Liues, *Cause* of each other Cause,
> The *Sphaere*, and *Center*, where the *Minde* doth pause:
> *Narcissus* of himself, himselfe the *Well*,
> *Louer*, and *Beautie*, that doth all excell.   (179–84)

The final lines of the poem analyse Henry's immortality in wholly familiar terms. His ghost is lodged safely in heaven, his reputation enrolled by Fame 'In golden Annales', and his body laid to rest in a tomb which is decorated with flowers and honoured by weeping virgins. This commonplace tripartite division (see Donne's *First Anniversary*, 473–4) connects with the final occurrence of the refrain, where the speaker effectively epitomizes and confirms the poem's relation to spiritual and material lamentations; the conjunction

---

[148] Drummond possessed a copy of the 1609 Spenser folio, STC 23083, according to the catalogue of his library. See R. M. Macdonald, *The Library of Drummond of Hawthornden*, Item 922.

of tears and garlands reactivates an ancient and potent metaphor for verses, and is connected with hints at repetition, re-enactment, and, by implication, resurrection and consolation.

Drummond's first published poem is accomplished and ambitious. It shows, just as much as *Lycidas* would, a poet anxious to join the most eminent of modern writers and to give notice of an epic project. It features a cosmopolitan range of allusion, as well as a marked self-consciousness, and can be seen as a remarkable coincidence of the elegiac strategies of Sidney, Spenser, and Donne, transformed in the hands of a writer who was less concerned with the difficulties of writing than with its meaning and implications.

Many of the commemorative volumes are decorated in appropriately gloomy fashion: Joshua Sylvester's *Lachrimae lachrimarum* (1613) is one of the finest examples, with its black pages, margins adorned with skeletons, and so forth.[149] Sylvester seems to have taken on the responsibility of organizing an anthology of poems from the Prince's followers (as is suggested by the title under which the volume first appears in the Stationers' Register: 'Lachrimae Domesticae . . . by his highness fyrst worst Poett and Pencioner IOSUA SYLVESTER').[150] There are three early editions, dated 1612 (two) and 1613. They contain, alongside pieces by Sylvester, contributions in four languages by Walter Quin, the Dubliner who had been one of the Prince's tutors.[151] The third edition represents a major expansion: after poems by Sylvester, Quin, and Joseph Hall, a separate title-page introduced elegies and epitaphs by Sir Peter Osborne, George Garrard, Hugh Holland, John Donne, Sir William Cornwallis, Edward Herbert, Sir Henry Goodyer, and Henry Burton: in Bald's words, 'Donne's circle made a concerted effort to celebrate the Prince's memory'; Sylvester's standing made him the natural leader of such an enterprise.[152]

---

[149] See J. P. Edmonds, 'Elegies and other Tracts on the Death of Prince Henry', *Publications of the Edinburgh Bibliographical Society*, 6 (1906), 141–58: Sylvester's printer, Humfrey Lownes, employed the same skeletons in the 1608 (4th) edn. of the so-called 'Queen Elizabeth's Prayerbook', Richard Day's *A booke of christian prayer*.

[150] For accounts of Sylvester's association with Prince Henry, see L. Parsons, 'Prince Henry (1594–1612) as a Patron of Literature', *MLR* 47 (1952), 503–7: Wilson, *Prince Henry and English Literature*, 105–6; Snyder, *Du Bartas*, i. 18–25; Strong, *Prince Henry*, 54.

[151] In *Sertum poeticum, in honorem Jacobi sexti* (Edinburgh, 1600), Quin had predicted Henry would become another Arthur (B4ᵛ). After 1612, he transferred his praises to Prince Charles.

[152] See Bald, *John Donne*, 268–9. The volume also includes Sylvester's elegy on Sir William Sidney, dedicated to Sir William's father, Viscount Lisle, doubtless with a view to attracting patronage of some kind. See Brennan, *English Literary Patronage*, 133–4.

Sylvester's elegy is preceded by an 'Argument, in an EPITAPH', for *'Heroik* Henry', who had been the *'Terror of the Pope'* (A2ʳ).[153] Sylvester adopts a modest pose, acknowledging both his own unfitness and (punningly) his inferiority to at least one of the contributors:

> HOW-euer, short of Others *Art* and *Wit*,
> I know my powers for such a Part vnfit;
> And shall but light my Candle in the *Sunn*,
> To doe a work shall be so better Donne: (A2ʳ)

His assertion of the inexpressibility of his loss is twinned with a further recognition that the formal disciplines of art constitute a misleading representation of his inner state:

> Could *Teares* and *Feares* giue my Distractions leaue,
> Of sobbing words a *sable Webbe* to weaue;
> Could *Sorrowe's Fulnes* giue my voice a vent;
> How would! how should my saddest *Verse* lament,
> In deepest Sighes (in stead of sweetest Songs) . . .   (A3ʳ)

And he proceeds, with his usual rhetorical strategies, to mourn his 'Cedar'; as a poet, he had had 'no *Prop* But HENRY's *Hand*: and, but in *Him*, no *Hope*' (A3ʳ).[154] The elegy is stuffed, like the volume it inaugurates, with elegiac commonplaces: Sylvester's talent for anthologizing starts close to home.[155] Thus Henry is a cedar and a jewel; his death prompts reflections on mortal transience ('Swift, as the Current of the quickest Stream; | Vain, as a Thought; forgotten, as a Dream' (A4ʳ)), and is attributed (along with similar instances of young princes doomed by the faithlessness of their future subjects) to the sin of all classes of society:

> All, briefly All, all Ages, Sexes, Sorts,
> In *Countries, Citties, Benches, Churches, Courts*
> (all *Epicures, Witt-Wantons, Atheists,*
> *Mach'-aretines, Mimes, Tap-To-Bacchonists,*
> *Batts, Har Pies, Sires, Centaures, Bib-al-nights.*
> Sice-sink-ap-Asses, Hags, Hermaphrodites)   (B3ʳ)

---

[153] Unless otherwise stated, all subsequent refs. are to the Bodleian copy of the revised 3rd edn. STC 23578.

[154] A succinct consideration of Sylvester's style is provided by Susan Snyder in her edn. of Sylvester's *Du Bartas*, 48 ff. She remarks of both Sylvester and his source that 'their ideal is Urania dressed in *Copia* and elaborate wit. Sylvester's elaboration is essentially verbal, Du Bartas's conceptual' (48–9).

[155] See Lewalski, *Donne's Anniversaries*, 15–41.

In this role as social critic, Sylvester takes on the Spenserian mantle as spokesman, directing his readers to consolation by announcing that Henry's '*Vertues* cannot *Dye*' (C1ʳ), and advising that the proper subject for tears is each mourner's sin:

> . . . day by day, vntill our last expire,
> With bended Knees, but more with broken Harts,
> and th' *inward* rest of high *Repentant* Parts,
> Prostrate our Soules in *Fasting* and in *Prayer*,
> Before the Foot-stool of th' *Empyreal* CHAIRE . . .   (C2ᵛ)

Such tears would be an abiding badge of fallen mortality, but they would also ensure that the last day would find the Prince's followers 'Heav'nly *Markt*' (C2ᵛ), so that tears themselves may be interpreted as tokens of consolation, self-criticism, and faith. Such reflections are, at a crude level, a justification of the anthology as a whole, and a gloss on its title and subtitle—the spirit of tears distilled.

After a separate title-page comes an apology to the various authors of the '*surrepted Elegies*' which make up the rest of the volume; inaccurate texts surreptitiously printed are justified by the publishers' affection for the Prince '*Whose* Honor *is our only Aime and Scope*; | Without Impeachment vnto Yours, we hope' (C–D3ᵛ).[156]

The first of the elegies, by Donne's close friend George Garrard, trades on the notion of amateur, coterie art.[157] The speaker proclaims his inability to match his subject. But he does not claim any special intimacy: rather he attacks those mercenary mourners 'hir'd to crie | And howle at euery Great-mans Obsequie', and opposes to them his own sincerity:

> (For, This Man's Eye was neuer cast on Mee;
> Nor could I dreame that euer it should bee):
> Nor do I, with the fashion, *Mourne* in *Black*:
> My *Sorrow's* in my Heart, not on my Back: (C–D4ʳ)

---

[156] The tone of these remarks cannot be determined. Perhaps they were, as Milgate has suggested, 'designed to protect the reputation of the authors as gentlemen amateurs' (Milgate, *Anniversaries*, 190). I have shown elsewhere that at least one poem from this circle, probably by Sir Walter Aston, was not published by Sylvester, although it circulated in MS with the elegies by Holland and Goodyer: see my article, 'Poems by Sir Walter Aston, and a Date for the Donne/Goodyer Verse Epistle *"Alternis Vicibus"* ', *RES*, NS, 37 (1986), 198–210.

[157] Bald, *Donne*, 159; Marotti, *John Donne, Coterie Poet*, 178, 193, 244–5, etc.

Garrard is particularly scornful of those writers who seek to exploit Prince Henry's death for their personal advancement, those Wits 'that closely wooe Applause | By curious handling This sad common Cause', and those who blot paper with 'idle Rimes', while 'Foolishly thinking, in a *measur'd* Verse | A *Losse* beyond *Dimension* to rehearse'. The familiar argument, that the grief that can be expressed in structured utterance is less profound than unfettered lament, is somewhat incongruously allied to scorn of the very poetic competitiveness that the volume itself seems to enshrine, full as it is of poems which indicate that their authors have been 'striuing to out-strip each others braine'. Garrard's advice to other poets is no less familiar, and appears to be an implicit distinction between erotic and plaintive elegiac modes:

> When yee do write of *Loue* and *pleasant* things,
> Then smooth your Lines: but in the *Losse of Kings*,
> When all Eyes *weep*, and all true Hearts do *bleed*,
> *Please* no-man with a Line that he shall read.   (C–D4^r)

The truest eloquence, the most copious utterance, the speaker goes on, is merely to articulate the fact of Henry's death. The world ought to be stupefied to hear a poet 'pronounce . . . with a voyce of Thunder, | Prince HENRY's gon': but all the elegies appear to prove is the uselessness of words, which come to stand as emblems of futility, since they 'neither may | Reach to *His Vertues*, nor Our *Losse* regain'. No consolation is offered in the midst of these gloomy reflections, other than the assurance that Henry is safely installed in heaven. What remains is summed up in a tersely melancholy conclusion:

> HEE hath *His Peace*; Wee, Grief; all Times, His Glorie;
> So yong so *good* was neuer found in Storie.   (C–D4^v)

After an epitaph, which was to enjoy great popularity with the compilers of manuscript miscellanies, the title-page is repeated: then follow six numbered elegies. There is no obvious ordering principle in their disposition; their model is not Spenser but Donne's *Anniversaries*. What is more, it is likely that at least three of the poets (Donne, Goodyer, and Herbert) wrote in emulation of each other.[158]

---

[158] See T. G. Sherwood, 'Reason, Faith and Just Augustinian Lamentation in Donne's Elegy on Prince Henry', *SEL* 13 (1973), 53–63: also his *Fulfilling the Circle: A Study of John Donne's Thought* (Toronto, 1984), 30–4, 112–13.

The other three poems appear to have more modest literary ambitions. Hugh Holland's speaker announces his shock at 'This'—an event which cannot be named and which could not have been imagined (until it happened) save by a madman, blasphemer, or traitor. He quickly reassures his reader that Henry is safely installed ('*Cround* and *Sainted*') among the heavenly 'Angells Crowd' (D2ʳ). He is then free to elaborate on the contrast between former glory and present grief with a degree of unrestraint that is presumably meant to mime uncontrollable sorrow.

The speaker apostrophizes the body as a rose which displayed in death the dynasties it had united—'The *Rose* of LANCASTER, that fairely burned | In his fresh Cheeks, to that of YORK is turned'— and his revery of Henry's appearance on horseback is shaken by the recollection of his death:

> Then brake He staues: But now Our Staffe is broken,
> So are our hearts, although our hearts were Oaken:
> For now, in stead of Steed, the Beer him beareth,
> No more his Steed the flying Center teareth,
> But sadly walks before; and will no faster
> For hurting her that must imbrace his Master.[159]   (D3ʳ)

The sorrow is proportionate to the expectation reposed in the Prince ('nor less then our Desire is our disaster'), and the speaker proposes that the mourners give themselves up to the immensity of their grief ('His braine is idle | Who giues not vnto his Teares the bridle' (D3ʳ)), weeping until 'in the South they make a second *Humber*'. He urges the Universities to initiate national mourning and then embarks on a summons to mourn that fills the rest of the poem, and is based on the commonplace notion that 'True grief indeed, that cannot well be choaked | Will find a vent and needs not to be cloaked' (D3ᵛ). The elegy concludes with a vision of Henry's body steeped in his mother's tears:

> His Bodie with those Teares let be embalmed,
> And to sweet Odours those sad Sighes be calmed:
> For, lo, the Spirit is Flowen to God immortall,
> Whose House high *Heauen* is, and death the Portall.
> So, We perhaps may giue Him worthy Buriall,
> Whose Tomb shall be another new *Escurial*.   (D4ʳ)

[159] Holland proposes the appearance of black-draped official buildings as a permanent embodiment of 'nature reversed': 'all with *black* is walled, | Nor shall again in haste *White-Hall* be called' (D3ʳ).

Holland's performance is based on a conception of elegy as a sung genre, associated with howling laments at the moment of burial. Holland's own Latin epitaph was affixed to Prince Henry's catafalque, and represented a generically distinct contribution, whose connection with a physical memorial is stressed by the choice of language. While the elegy deploys many highly traditional topics, it contains much particularity of personal reference and a good deal of verbal wit (as when Henry's charger 'snowed' with his mouth along the ground, or in such lines as 'Lo, with the ground where lowe he lies' (D2^v). Its use of feminine rhyme (itself a genuflection to both Spenser and Sidney) indicates a disdain for what Campion called the 'vulgar and easie kind of Poesie'; such fastidiousness operates in counterpoint to the constant assertions of a grief so overwhelming that it sweeps art and invention away.[160]

William Cornwallis was a friend and correspondent of Donne's. Many of his writings display an apparent relish for arguing for deliberately perverse propositions.[161] But his elegy on Prince Henry is an elegant and sombre exemplary biography which (like the works of Alexander and Chapman) advocates stoicism in the face of the vicissitudes of fortune, and holds up for admiration Henry's 'integrity of life': the phrase, eagerly seized upon by Webster for *The Duchess of Malfi*, might serve as the subtitle of Cornwallis's poem.

The style is sententious and grave ('It is not Night; yet all the World is black: | The *Fiat's* past, and yet *Our Sunne* wee lacke'): the speaker urges his readers to 'binde . . . Posteritie to plain', to pay yearly 'Tribute' to the '*Reuolution* of This Day of *Lamentations*' (E3^r). The catalogue of Henry's excellences proceeds rapidly from external attributes to the Prince's filial piety and to his capacity to remain unsullied by the temptations of court life. No longer, Cornwallis argues, need we 'admire . . . PHILIP's Sonne: Neuer was life in little better donne'; for evidence, the direction of Henry's court to 'some more serious course' is cited, along with his delight in exercise, designed as it was 'To make a well-breath'd Bodie fitt

---

[160] A later scribe became confused in making attempts to 'regularize' the metre in Bodley MS Eng. Poet. e 37, p. 52.

[161] Grierson printed a verse epistle from him to Donne (*Donne*, ed. Grierson, ii. 171–2): the poem survives in Bodley MS Tanner 306 (fo. 237). On his literary output, see *John Donne: Paradoxes and Problems*, ed. H. Peters (Oxford, 1980), xxi–xxii; also Bald, *Donne*, 117–8, etc. Cornwallis was the son of Prince Henry's Treasurer and biographer, Sir Charles Cornwallis.

for Toiles . . . To be prepar'd against his Country's harmes'. Although an excellent dancer, Henry, we read, preferred the 'much more masculine' pursuits of running and (perhaps fatally) swimming (E3ᵛ).

Cornwallis's assessment of Henry's intellectual capacity is similar to Bacon's:[162]

> . . . For, though in pedant Arts
> Hee were not lip-learnd: yet his Iudgment knew
> The Latitude of things: and how to view
> The court and her Invisibilities.
> Which, seen, are not seen, often, by the Wise.   (E4ʳ)

The Prince's silence had been as profound as the sea's, and showed a gift to 'read Men, in stead of Books' (E4ᵛ): the condition is one to which the elegist aspires, as he leaves off mourning the 'Miracle of Nature' in favour of lamenting the loss of 'The Ioye and Beautie of the World' in a 'silent *Doue-like* Dirge' (E4ᵛ). With grief thus transformed to an inner chant, the poet figures consolation in the phoenix, with Charles advised to follow the 'Print of these faire stepps', and warned that '*Greatness* is mistaken, if not grac't | With *Iustice*, Goodnes and *Integritie*' (F1ʳ). The poet concludes by turning his attention to the King ('our Assurance known'), urging him to perform in an exemplary stoic manner:

> Should Clowdes for-ever shade the fruitful Sun,
> The Earth and all her Of-spring were undon.
> You are our Sunn: and from your glorious Beams,
> The Happiness of all your subiects streames:
> For *Iustice* sake, your Owne, and all this Land,
> O're-come this great Eclipse; your Selfe command. (F1ᵛ)

A similar stoicism is advocated by Henry Burton, whose allegory 'A Pilgrim's sad Obseruation vpon *a distastrous Accident*, in his Trauaile towards the HOLY-LAND' (G1ʳ) is placed at the end of the anthology. Burton's Pilgrim, on his allegorical journey, comes upon a company of mourners, a 'sable world', whose eleven members utter individual laments which the Pilgrim records before adding his own.[163] Although the speakers are differentiated, each is at the

---

[162] See Bacon, *Works*, vi. 327: Birch, *Life*, 402–4.

[163] Eleven is traditionally associated with mourning: more specifically, with the decorous observance of funeral rites. For an account of lore on this point, see above, Ch. 2 n. 15. It should also be noted that there are 11 contributors to *Lachrimae lachrimarum*.

same stage of mourning, and it is for the Pilgrim to draw their griefs together and abstract a moral. The King, the Queen, Prince Charles, and the Palsgrave are the first to speak, followed by Henry's household, who thank the Prince for the generosity of his provision for them and rejoice above all that they may for ever declare 'We were Prince HENRY's Followers' (G2ʳ).[164] The Church interprets Henry's death as the consequence of sin, lamenting the sacrifice of 'This Innocent'; the Nobility prize Henry as the sum of those excellences displayed by foreign princes (G3ʳ). The clergy interpret the 'present Cause of dolefull Dreriment' as a sign of the impending destruction of this 'sinfull land', proving that 'No worldly Happines can long time last' (G3ᵛ). The 'astonisht' gentry mourn their 'Heroick *Chiefetain*', while the poets are similarly dumbstruck—Henry, whose virtues deserved Homer or Virgil, had the misfortune to be born into a lesser age: 'where's the *Muse* so rich, as can set forth | The halfe of short-lyu'd HENRY's long-lyu'd *Worth*?' (G3ᵛ).

The weeping Pilgrim, having recorded these complaints, turns back to his journey to Jerusalem, a physical and spiritual quest which expresses his trust in providence:

> Patience, the Champion, conquers all distress:
> Heav'n is the Hauen of all my Happinesse,   (G4ʳ)

Burton preaches acceptance of death and the need to continue with the journey of life, portraying allegorically the transformation from lament to consolation:

> . . . for, my Teares
> Must be the Sea my brittle Vessell beares;
> My Sighes, the Windes: my Faith the Sterne and guide:
> My Fraight is Charity; Hope, Anchor try'd:
> GOD's *Word*, my Carde; his SON, my Light, his SPIRIT
> The Earnest, that assures me to inherit.[165]   (G3ᵛ)

This work of Puritan piety from the centre of Henry's court describes the Christian's struggle to comprehend death: comfort

---

[164] Burton himself was Keeper of the Closet to the Prince, and perhaps derived from the role a sense of himself as a spokesman for the court to the Prince.

[165] The images are iconographical commonplaces, but it is possible that Burton was recalling Donne's *First Anniversary*, 317–22. He may also have come across Edward Herbert's 'The State Progress of Ill', or Donne's reply, the verse epistle ('To Sir Edward Herbert, at Julyers') beginning 'MAN is a lumpe, where all beasts kneaded bee, | Wisdome makes him an Arke where all agree'.

derives from the framing allegory and from the hints of a diversity
of consolatory strategies—praising God (the King), resignation and
prayer (the royal family), praising the Prince (the household),
repenting and rejecting earthly vanity (the Church and clergy).
Poets, gentry, and nobility are excluded from the consolatory
movement by their worldliness. The governing metaphor of the
pilgrimage 'explains' bereavement as an episode on our soul's 'long
journey of considering God'.[166]

The sophistication of Burton's poem is matched and surpassed
by those of Donne, Herbert, and Goodyer. Goodyer explores the
reasons for writing an elegy at all, speculating on the value of such
an enterprise for subject, audience, and poet. It has been remarked
that the focus of the poem is 'the nature of grief and poetic lament,
not human knowing and death'.[167] Goodyer appears to use death as
a device for exploring the relation between human understanding
and divine providence.[168] And his speaker opens by questioning the
value of attempting to bind 'Vnmeasur'd Griefs, in measure'd lines'
by the power of 'poetik Magick' (F2ʳ).[169] He recognizes that any
elegy inevitably diminishes Henry and implicitly glorifies death,
and concedes that he cannot treat both earthly grief and celestial
rejoicing in the same text. But he cannot help himself:

> . . . I neither aske relief
> Nor counsell now of anie, but my Grief.
> Self-preseruation moues me: I shall break
> If I stay, thinking still, and doo not speak.   (F3ʳ)

He imagines his detractors claiming he has sketched an inaccurate
miniáture, like '*Artists* which pretend to take | Great Heights with
little Instruments': but he retorts (in a passage that owes much to

---

[166] The standard account of the metaphor is R. Tuve, *Allegorical Imagery* (Princeton, 1966), esp. ch. III; see also Stannard, *The Puritan Way of Death*, 74–6.

[167] Sherwood, 'Reason, Faith', 53–6. Goodyer (1571–1628) was one of Donne's closest friends and was his chief correspondent for most of his life. He witnessed Sidney's will, was knighted by Essex in 1599 and became a Gentleman of the Privy Chamber in 1605. See the many refs. to his career and association with Donne in Bald, *Donne*, and in Marotti, *John Donne, Coterie Poet*.

[168] Sherwood maintains that Goodyer's 'theory of elegy' assumes that 'suffering is the legacy of fallen man' ('Reason, Faith', 58); I would argue that Goodyer presents suffering (rightly understood) as a positive and instructive benefit for fallen mankind rather than a badge of the fall. See also Wallerstein, *Studies in Seventeenth-Century Poetic*, 82–5.

[169] In addition to the version in *Lachrimae lachrimarum*, a copy survives in Bodley MS Eng. Poet. e 37, p. 49.

Donne) that the 'Vnpardonable errors' arising from such processes are impossible, given the qualities of his subject.[170] Would his detractors wish to eradicate all traces of Henry's existence? Such annihilation would be 'an vniust Impiety': and it is better for posterity to suffer through recollection of Henry's loss than that 'His Worth should die' (F3ᵛ). A further argument for embracing grief is that Henry's death prefigures the world's fate, destroyed once by flood and destined to be consumed by fire. And, just as Seth had had the foresight to erect pillars of brick and stone 't'out liue the Worlds death', on which were engraved 'All Sciences' to provide a basis for the rebirth of civilization, so Henry has left his father and brother to represent 'what so-e're wee priz'd | In Our lost World' (F4ʳ). The speaker is consoled by the 'Soueraine Harmonie' of this truth, which 'tames . . . Grief's rate', transforming his dirge into a token of hope:

> . . . now, as ELEGIE
> Made at the first for *Mourning*, hath bin since
> Imploy'd on *Loue*, *Ioy*, and *Magnificence*.
> So this particular *Elegie* shall enclose
> (Meant for my Grief for HIM) with ioy for THOSE   (F4ʳ)

The poem's style and its argumentative sophistication recall Donne—who had used Seth's pillars himself in *The Progresse of the Soule*.[171] Goodyer's serious and articulate examination of bereavement dextrously introduces and justifies both lament and consolation, while praising Prince Henry as God's sign of providence.

The philosophical terminology of Herbert's poem cloaks an argument that is both simple and an elegiac commonplace.[172] The speaker, representing a grieving community, initially questions the fact of death: how, he asks, might such a thing happen when his followers loved him so much (and 'what are *Soules*, but loue?' (F2ʳ)). The

---

[170] e.g. 'This grief, that vniversally so infects, | That each Face is a Glasse whence it reflects, | For, as who doth ten thousand Glasses try, | Receiues his owne Face back into his eye: | So, if on twenty millions you light, | Each face reflects your owne Grief in your sight: | Grief, which from vs must be deriued so, | As many Learned thought our Soules to goe, | By *Propagation*; and must reach to all | The After-born, like *Sinn Originall*' (F3ᵛ).

[171] For an account of the pillars (which have in addition a strong association with Imperial iconography), see my article, 'Gonzalo's "Lasting Pillars": *The Tempest*, V. i. 208', *Shakespeare Quarterly*, 35 (1984), 322–4.

[172] It will be evident that I regard Sherwood's view that the poem attempts to prove that 'Mortal life is the struggle for the recovery of value' ('Reason, Faith', 57) as something of an over-reaction to the piece, which I take to be a much more commonplace exercise than he does. See Wallerstein, *Studies in Seventeenth-Century Poetic*, 82–4.

solution that first occurs to him is highly traditional—it is the
survivors who are dead, while Henry lives eternally: and 'though Wee
dy'd with HIM, wee doo appear | To liue and stirre awhile; as if *HEE*
were | Still quickning vs' (F2ʳ). He then changes his mind, and
suggests that, through the animating power of Henry's memory
(since he had been 'our World's *Soule*' (F2ᵛ)), men are actually
justified in deeming themselves to be alive.[173] He briefly surveys
the shortcomings of mortal attempts to understand mortality—
exemplified in such instances as the seed which appears dead but
contains new life—and concludes that, although men are indis-
tinguishable from corpses in their indifference to joy and pain, they
are kept alive by Henry's influence: 'in that Power Wee may seem
yet to liue | Because *Hee* liued once'.

In this context the only purpose of preserving the human race is
to perpetuate Henry's memory:

> should wee proceed
> To such a wonder, that the *dead* should breed;
> It shall be wrought, to *keep* that Memorie,
> Which being HIS, can therfore *neuer dye*.[174]

Though undoubtedly tortuous and self-consciously 'difficult',
written in the clotted, argumentative mode characterized by
metrical irregularity, run-on lines, questions, ejaculations, and
apostrophes, Herbert's poem has much in common with many
other elegies. Indeed the central ideas—Henry's death as a
punishment and the reversal of roles—are markedly commonplace.
More distinctive is Herbert's exploration of the implications of
these topoi for the individual mourner. He touches on the nature of
the soul, the qualities of death and life, the circumscription of
mortal intelligence, and contrives to present these familiar reflec-
tions on death as both intellectually challenging and implicitly
panegyric. Further, it might be argued, the mental effort required
to follow the twists of the argument proves its own point, that the
immortal, rational soul 'swallows up the other soules of vegetation,
and of sense, which were in us before'.[175]

---

[173] Lewalski judiciously observes of these turns in the argument that 'the tone is
analytical and catechetical, a series of rhetorical questions . . . addressed to a public
audience' (*Donne's Anniversaries*, 325).
[174] As Donne had used alchemical metaphors, Herbert employs specifically biblical
language (notably from 1 Cor. 15) to express the transformations effected by death.
[175] Donne, *Sermons*, ii. 358 (also viii. 221 and iii. 85). For a note on Donne's use of

As with Herbert's elegy, it would be a mistake to read too much into Donne's poem on the Prince, to assume an 'originality' in theme, structure, and manner. Of course, modern readings of the text start from Jonson's reported observation to Drummond that Donne had said 'he wrott that Epitaph on Prince Henry Look to me Fath to match Sir Ed: Herbert in obscureness'; they have gone on to show how the elegy was witty but sincere, conventional yet novel, of an age but for all time, and so forth.[176] It should, I hope, have become clear in an earlier chapter that ingenuity and intellectual complexity were central to Donne's conception of panegyric: 'obscurenesse' in one of its senses approximates to this notion.[177] Of equal importance generically, however, is the way the flexible, musical, compendious form of Donne's commemorative writings increasingly resembles the form of the sermons he was soon to write: thus, it is not merely a question of the matter of his poems reflecting Donne's apparent preoccupation with moral, spiritual, and theological issues at this stage in his career: the form likewise, with its statement, division, proof, and application, represents a movement from the syllogistic organization of the poet's most typically conceited and metaphorical texts.

Two themes—the gulf separating earthly from heavenly understanding, and the relationship of reason to faith—dominate the poem: both are familiar topics in Donne's work.[178] The speaker proposes Henry as a figure who had given promise of resolving these oppositions (15–20):

> For, *Reason*, put t'her best *Extension*,
> Almost meetes *Faith*, and makes both *Centres* one:
> And nothing euer came so neer to This,
> As *Contemplation* of that PRINCE wee misse.

Aristotle's theory of the threefold soul (memory, will, understanding), see Milgate's edn. of the *Anniversaries*, 160. See also Herbert's *Poems, English and Latin*, ed. G. C. Moore Smith (Oxford, 1923), 149–51.

[176] Jonson, *Works*, i. 136: see L. D. Tourney, 'Convention and Wit in Donne's *Elegie on Prince Henry*', *SP* 71 (1974), 473–83.

[177] In Lewalski's words, 'witty praise is of the essence of Donne's poetry of compliment' (*Donne's Anniversaries*, 69); in the poet's own words, 'Nor must wit | Be colleague to religion, but be it' ('Honour is so sublime perfection', 44–5: Milgate, *Satires*, 102).

[178] A notable instance is the verse epistle to Lady Bedford, 'Reason is our Soules left hand, Faith her right' (Milgate, *Satires*, 90). See also T. G. Sherwood, 'Reason in Donne's Sermons', *ELH* 39 (1972), 353–74, and his *Fulfilling the Circle*, 15, 55–6, etc.

> For, All that *Faith* could credit Mankinde *could*,
> *Reason* still seconded that this PRINCE *would*.   (E1ʳ)

Henry's qualities had inspired apocalyptic hopes (E1ᵛ; 35–8):

> Was it not well believ'd, that *Hee* would make
> This *general Peace* th'eternall ouertake?
> And that *His* Times might haue stretcht out so far
> As to touch Those of which they *Emblems* are?

The recent shock has jarred the two centres (Reason and Faith) of
the elliptical orbit of man's mind: as the speaker remarks (2), 'both
my *Centres* feel This *Period*' (E1ʳ)).[179] The first section of the poem
defines the influence of each. Reason's orbit is 'All that this naturall
world doth comprehend . . . Shut-in for men in one circumference'
(6–8), while Faith's realm embraces that which defies such
circumscription, the 'disproportion'd . . . angulare . . . enormous
greatnesses', questions relating to God and eternity.[180] His text
thus 'divided', Donne proceeds to its 'proof'.

He deals first with Faith. Now Henry is dead, hopes once
reposed in him are redefined as 'heresie', the relation of *res* to *verba*,
of emblem to substance, remains in its former state, and humans
live only to mourn ('such a life wee haue | As but so manie
mandrakes on his graue' (54)). Then Reason is shown to be
unreliable, in the absence of 'the only subject Reason wrought
upon' (70), and Donne combines the topoi of reversal and
inexpressibility:

> But, now, for us with busie proofs to come
> That w'have no Reason, would prove we had some:
> So would just lamentations. Therefore wee
> May safelier say, that wee are dead, then hee.
> So, if our griefs wee doo not well declare,
> W'have double 'excuse; hee is not dead, wee are.   (77–82)

The 'application' begins when the speaker recognizes that after all
he is not actually dead. What is more, by sharing Henry's humanity
he is able to glimpse the Prince's real nature as 'Our soule's best
bayting and mid-period | In her long journey of considering God'

---

[179] Having provided in these few citations a sample of Sylvester's typography, I revert
to Milgate's edn. of the poem in the *Anniversaries* vol., pp. 63–6, to which all subsequent
refs. are made.

[180] Milgate, *Anniversaries*, 191–2, provides an extremely lucid account of the opening
of the poem.

(85–6). He proposes that his own life would be more tolerable if, in the absence of Henry, he could contemplate 'That shee-intelligence which mov'd this sphaer' (90).[181]

The identity of this figure has provoked predictable speculation. While it seems most implausible, given Henry's apparently rampant misogyny, that Donne is, in Milgate's words, 'imagining a lady whom the Prince might have loved', none the less the suggestion in the poem that the 'shee-intelligence' might be seen by the readers indicates that she took corporeal form.[182] The obvious candidates are the Prince's mother and sister, with the latter the more likely.[183] As in some of his other elegies, then, Donne 'discovers' his subject in the surviving relatives. It is presumably proposed that through contemplation of this person the speaker has recovered some elements of the dead Prince.[184]

The poem concludes with a request to this female. Reading these lines, Donne promises, she will wish to enlighten the poet by telling the 'historie' of Henry and herself: the acquisition of this knowledge, and the consequent responsibility to publish it would transform him (in a recollection of the *Anniversaries*) into an angel. Thus the final lines suggest an elevation, almost an apotheosis, rather than a more conventional consolation. But they are also a thinly veiled appeal for patronage. The speaker addresses the lady:

> I conjure thee by all the charmes hee spoke,
> By th'oathes which only you two neuer broke,
> By all the soules you sigh'd: that if you see
> These lines, you wish I knew your historie:
> So, much as you two mutual Heav'ns were here,
> I were an angel singing what you were.   (93–8)

---

[181] See W. M. Lebans, 'A Critical Edition of the "Epicedes and Obsequies" of John Donne', B.Litt. thesis (Oxford, 1964), 95; also I. Macfarlane, *Buchanan* (1981), 355–78, on the *Sphaera* of George Buchanan (who had been tutor to King James).

[182] Milgate, *Anniversaries*, 195.

[183] Elizabeth is known to have paid Sylvester for *Lachrimae lachrimarum*: Donne composed her epithalamion (as did Goodyer). Visiting Heidelberg in 1619, he preached before her and later sent copies of his *Devotions* (1624) and of *The first Sermon preached to King Charles* (1625). See Milgate, *Anniversaries*, 114, and Donne, *Sermons*, ii, no. 12 (but also note the cautionary remarks (ii. 36–7) in which Potter and Simpson cast doubts on the authenticity of the caption); also Bald, *Life*, 351–2. Bald (171) suggests that it may have been through Lady Bedford, whose parents had taken care of the Princess, that Donne made her acquaintance.

[184] An alternative reading would be that the 'shee-intelligence' might be perceived in Henry's truest followers; that the intelligence, however singular and unique, may be glimpsed in many places.

The elegy is recognizably part of Donne's development as an elegist in the years after 1609, although its self-advertising philosophical seriousness ('obscurenesse') perhaps locates it in the earnest and competitive milieu of Henry's circle.[185] As a subject, Henry required none of the defences or self-justifications that had attended the *Anniversaries*, and Donne seems to have used the elegy as an opportunity to particularize the general considerations of the earlier pieces. He dramatized a process of consolation that was both an education in individual meditation and understanding, and also a panegyric inseparable from a particular event. The 'Obsequies of the Lord Harrington' of the following year would display a similar intensity of particular application.

Lachrimae lachrimarum, despite the foregrounding of Sylvester's role, and the self-referential allegory by Burton with which it concludes, is not a funeral anthology in the mode of Spenser's *Astrophel* collection. That its real counterparts should be the University miscellanies eloquently confirms the status of Henry's household as 'intended by the King for a courtly college or a collegiate court'.[186]

A more obviously unified volume is Thomas Campion's *Songs of Mourning*.[187] The collection of seven songs is prefaced by an elegy in thirty-six heroic couplets.[188] In the first of five unequal sections, the speaker presents himself as the 'humble priest' of the 'sanctuary of all heauinesse | Where men their fill may mourne, and neuer sinne'. Perhaps glancing at the 'metaphysical' elegies of Donne and

[185] Jonson's remark to Drummond is given some support by the survival of a single folio sheet inserted into Bodleian MS Rawl. Poet. 26 (fo. 91), which consists of copies of Donne's and Herbert's elegies, evidently folded and sent as a letter. See also the 'Prince Henry Group' of elegies by Holland, Goodyer, and Aston, in Bodley MS Eng. Poet. e. 37 (Kay, 'A Poem by Sir Walter Aston', 200–6).

[186] The phrase is that of the Governor of the court, Sir Thomas Challoner, cited in Thomas Birch, *The Life of Henry, Prince of Wales* (1760), 97.

[187] Campion's political position makes him a slightly surprising elegist for the Prince, although he did collaborate on masques with Constantino de'Servi, who was the Prince's architect (see Strong, *Prince Henry*, 88–105, etc.). On his association with the Howard faction, see D. Lindley's *Thomas Campion* (Leiden, 1986); also L. L. Peck, *Northampton: Patronage and Policy at the Court of James I*(1982); Brennan, *Literary Patronage*, 127–30; for a brief appreciation of the sequence, see Parry, *Golden Age*, 89–91. Campion's collaborator, Giovanni Coprario, had (as plain John Cooper) composed a sequence of funeral songs on the death of the Earl of Devonshire (*Funeral teares for the death of the Earle of Devonshire: Figured in seaven songs* (1606)).

[188] Leaving to one side the possibility of an allusion to the 18-year span of Henry's life, the poem indicates that Campion had moved from his well-known condemnation of 'the vulgar and vnarteficiall custome of riming' (*Works*, ed. P. Vivian (Oxford, 1909), 33).

others, the speaker observes that 'Law-Eloquence' will not be necessary to convict Fate of Henry's murder. He employs a disjointed style to express chaos, grief, and dissolution, and a more regular mode to praise the Prince's harmony:[189]

> In harmony hee spake, and trod the ground
> In more proportion then the measur'd sound.
> How fit for peace was hee, and rosie beds!
> How fit to stand in troopes of iron heads,
> When time had with his circles made complete
> His charmed rounds! All things in time grow great. (29–34)

In the third section, Henry is figured as a comet; then the speaker proceeds to general observations about the veiled operations of providence—the death of Henry, like that of Henri IV, prompts the apostrophe, 'O earthly state | How doth thy greatnesse in a moment fall | And feastes in highest pompe turn funerall' (42–4). The uniqueness of Henry, it is suggested, had resided in the scale and variety of his accomplishments: he had been like Alexander, but with an added religious purpose:

> . . . though his yeares were greene
> Their fruit was yet mature: his care had beene
> Suruaying India, and implanting there
> The knowledge of that God which hee did feare:[190] (49–52)

In death, the Prince is pictured as embarking on an heroic journey, 'strugling with the windes, for our auayles | T'explore a passage hid from human tract' (54–5). The speaker concludes with assertions of confidence in 'all-seeing providence', founded on admiration of Henry's family, of those left behind: and he claims that the songs which follow are fitting tributes because they reflect their subject's taste:

> . . . wee offer now
> Guifts which hee lou'd, and fed: Musicks that flow
> Out of a sowre and melancholike vayne,
> Which best sort with the sorrowes wee sustaine. (69–72)

[189] Refs. to peace are politically loaded, and show Campion's advocacy of a Howard foreign policy; see K. Sharpe, *Sir Robert Cotton, 1586–1631: History and Politics in Early Modern England* (Oxford, 1979), 113–50; L. Peck, *Northampton*, 89, 187–90, 194.

[190] James Maxwell, another Howard poet, had employed the same idea. Campion, like many of Henry's associates, admirers, and elegists (Brooke, Donne, Goodyer, Inigo Jones, Holland) dedicated verses to Thomas Coryate, who was actually in India at the time of Henry's death. See also Pitcher, *Brotherton MS*, 24–6.

It is hardly possible to discuss the songs away from their musical context, although, from an elegiac perspective, the competing tendencies towards disjointed, declamatory modes on the one hand, and resolved, harmonious modes on the other, may be seen to complement the expression of variety and inclusiveness both in the sequence and, by statement and implication, in the subject. The songs are addressed to the members of Henry's family in turn, and then to Great Britain and to the world. Each is fitted stylistically to its addressee, and Coprario's settings place the pieces in various kinds of public and private, intimate registers.[191]

Chapman's career never recovered from Henry's death. Unlike Drayton, who could turn to Sir Walter Aston, but like Ralegh, Chapman had no alternative source of security. His *Epicede* is dedicated to 'his best deserving friend', Henry Jones, with a promise of 'future labours': but the phrasing of the dedication is literally dejected, as Chapman (echoing perhaps his own Bussy d'Ambois) claims that Henry's death 'hath so stricken all my spirits to the earth, that I will neuer more dare, to looke vp to any greatnesse; but resoluing the little rest of my poore life to obscuritie, and the shadow of his death; prepare euer hereafter, for the light of heauen' (A2ʳ).[192] Henry was buried on 7 December. Chapman's volume, including a description of *The Funeralls of the High and Mighty Prince Henry*, was entered in the Stationers' Register four days later. The *Epicede* thus constitutes part of the immediate reaction to the funeral and, like Sylvester's anthology, springs from the literary culture of Henry's court.

The opening lines of the poem are in many ways conventional; yet, while they baldly affirm the uniqueness of the present occasion, and deploy the topics of reversed nature and the glimpsed jewel, they also give prominence to the author's personal circumstances.

---

[191] There is a modern recording by Martyn Hill and the Consort of Musicke on Decca D3LO (1977).

[192] In 1615 Henry (to whom the transls. of the *Iliad* (1610 and 1611) had been dedicated) was the posthumous dedicatee of Chapman's *Whole works of Homer*, in which Chapman complained that the generous provisions of the Prince's will had been neglected: 'Not thy thrice sacred will | Sign'd with thy Deathe: moues any to fullfill | Thy just bequests to me: Thow, dead, then; I | Liue deade, for giuing thee Eternitie: | Ad Famam | To all Tymes futures This Tymes Marck extend: | Homer, no Patrone found: nor Chapman friend': *The Poems of George Chapman*, ed. P. B. Bartlett (New York, 1941), 388–9. See Norbrook, *Poetry and Politics*, 205–6; Brennan, *Literary Patronage*, 120–1, 125, 131.

In addition, the musical connotations of the term 'epicede' are given expression through the use of repetition:

> If euer aduerse Influence enui'd
> The glory of our Lands, or tooke a pride
> To trample on our height; or in the Eye
> Strooke all the pomp of Principalitie,
> Now it hath done so; Oh, if euer Heauen
> Made with the earth his angry reckening euen,
> Now it hath done so; Euer, euer be
> Admir'd, and fear'd, that Triple Maiestie
> Whose finger could so easily strike a Fate,
> Twixt least Felicity, and greatest state:
> Such, as should melt our shore into a sea,
> And dry our Ocean with Calamitie.
> Heauen open'd, and but show'd him to our eies,
> Then shut againe, and show'd our Miseries.[193]   (B1)

The patterned syntax and repeated emphases are characteristic of Chapman's most grandiloquent manner; the rest of the poem operates at a less majestic level. Henry is presented as a 'Masterpeece' whose 'Patterne' will direct the 'erring faculties' of the survivors (B1ᵛ). Despite being 'One that in hope, tooke vp to toplesse height | All his great Ancestors', Henry had succumbed to death, and vanished as if he had been 'one of no importance' (B2ʳ). Then follows a lengthy apostrophe to death (B2ᵛ), after which the speaker turns to the dissolution of the Prince's household: 'Now, as inuerted, like the'Antipodes, | The world . . . Is falne on vs . . . thy ruines lye | On our burst bosomes' (B3ᵛ).

Henry's court is figured as an academy, led in its speculations by the Prince himself, who 'his diuine Ideas ideas did propose, | First to himselfe, & then would forme in them' (B4ʳ). Indeed, neoplatonic terms such as these occur throughout; Henry's life, the speaker claims, gave 'faire act to . . . Heroic formes' (C3ʳ). After a list of the locations prominent in Henry's life, Chapman turns to bewail the fall of the court at Troynovant:

> O what a frame of Good, in all hopes rais'd
> Came tumbling downe with him: as when was seisde

---

[193] *An epicede or funerall song; on the death of Henry Prince of Wales* (1612): I cite the Bodleian copy of the *Epicede*, which is the corrected state: for bibliographical information, see Bartlett's edn., 451–2.

> By Grecian furie, famous *Ilion*,
> Whose fall, still rings out his Confusion.   (B4ᵛ)

The speaker rehearses the usual litany of his subject's qualities: he
praises Henry's resistance to flattery, his determination to learn
'The grounds of what he built on' (C1ᵛ). The passage employs
conventional topics, such as the *puer senex* and the reconciliation of
opposites, and ends pithily:

> In summe, (knot-like) hee was together put
> That no man could dissolue and so was cut.[194]   (C2ᵛ)

Henry's integrity is exalted in the extended simile of the temple
(C3ʳ⁻ᵛ): just as the remains of a great city or monument may inspire
later generations, so Chapman hopes that his poem will 'show
[Henry's] ruines, bleeding in my verse' (C4ʳ). But all of this praise
is set aside as mere prologue, as the speaker turns to beg his muse's
assistance in attempting the supreme funeral song, a task for which
he must be filled with 'sacred rage' so that he can outshine
inferior mourners:

> That all the wits prophane, of these bold times
> May feare to spend the spawne of their rancke rymes
> On any touch of him, that shold be sung
> To eares diuine, and aske an Angels tongue.   (C4ʳ)

What follows represents a shift in style and tone. In the first part of
the poem, the speaker had adopted a dense, epigrammatic manner
suggestive of the biographical panegyric narrative and the epitomiz-
ing terseness of epitaph.[195] And the muse who succeeds him writes
with 'A Penne so hard and sharpe . . . It bit through Flint, and did
in Diamant write': yet she also sings in the musical, repetitive,
lachrymose mode appropriate to a funeral song or elegy: 'Her
words, she sung, and laid out such a brest, | As melted Heauen, and
vext the very blest' (C4ʳ). In keeping with ancient precedent, then,
praise gives way to lament.

---

[194] Chapman thus adroitly joins an allusion to Alexander and the Gordian knot to the
image of the Parcae.

[195] An example is the blending of the topics of compendiousness and the *puer senex*:
'His Good he ioyn'd with Equitie and Truth; | Wisedome in yeeres, crown'd his ripe
head in youth; | His heart wore all the folds of Policie, | Yet went as naked as Simplicitie.
| Knew good and ill: but onely good did loue; | In him the Serpent did embrace the
Doue' (C2ʳ⁻ᵛ).

Chapman's speaker had said an 'Angels tongue' was needed to articulate the lament. And that is precisely what appears. The bulk of the remainder of the *Epicede* is closely based on a Latin elegy by Angelo Poliziano.[196] At the same time, it is clearly a response, evidently intended as a corrective, to Donne. On the simple level of Poliziano's Christian name, there is presumably a glance at the way Donne's elegy on Henry had concluded with the line, 'I were an angel singing what you were' (98). Donne's *Anniversaries*, however, are the more significant target. Chapman chose for his model Poliziano's elegy on Albeira di Tomasso degli Albizzi, who died in July 1473 in her sixteenth year.[197] Where Donne had praised a child he had never met by employing a panegyric mode proper to princes, Chapman appears to have attempted to reverse this panegyric inflation by adapting a Latin elegy on a young girl for application to a prince.

Chapman's version of his source is modified only in a few particulars. There are some digressions which incorporate circumstantial details of Henry's last illness and a reference to the storm off the Bermudas. Perhaps more telling are some other injections of particularity: thus the singling out of Archbishop Abbot and Sir Edward Philips ('Whose worth in all workes should a *Place* enioie | Where his fit Fame her Trumpet shall imploie' (D4')) as visitors to the dying prince locates the matter of Poliziano's elegy squarely in the midst of Jacobean religious and political affairs.[198] Abbot's appearance, for example, emphasizes Henry's inheritance of the leadership of the Leicester/Sidney group, and occasional verbal allusions to Spenser are consistent with these other details.[199]

[196] *Angeli Politiani Operum* (Lyons, 1546), ii. 556–66. For a newly-edited text with a brief but informative introduction see A. Perosa and J. Sparrow, eds. *Renaissance Latin Verse: An Anthology* (1979), 126–32.

[197] For accounts of Chapman's use of his source, see S. Lee, *The French Renaissance in England* (1910), 466; F. L. Schoell, 'Chapman and the neo-Latinists of the Quattrocento', *MP* 13 (1915), 215–38; *Poems*, ed. Bartlett, 453–5.

[198] Abbot had been a Leicester supporter: see E. Rosenberg, *Leicester, Patron of Letters* (New York, 1955), 185–229, 278–322; P. A. Welsby, *George Abbott: The Unwanted Archbishop* (1962), 7–9. Phillips was Chancellor of Henry's household and later Master of the Rolls. On his literary patronage, see Bald, *Donne*, 285–6, and Sharpe, *Cotton*, 206. Chapman wrote dedicatory verses to Phillips in *Petrarchs seven penitentiall psalmes* (1613) and in his transl. of Homer (*Poems*, ed. Bartlett, 203, 404, 445, 484). Chapman's masque for Princess Elizabeth's wedding, *The memorable mask of the Middle Temple and Lyncolns Inne* (1613), began with a procession from Phillips's house to Whitehall; on its relation to colonial expansion, see D. J. Gordon, 'Chapman's *Memorable Masque*', in his *The Renaissance Imagination*, ed. S. Orgel (Berkeley, 1975), 194–202.

[199] In an interpolation based on Bion is an allusion to Spenser's *Astrophel* (and thereby

And in the final section of the poem (identified by Wallerstein as the 'dirge'), where the obsessional state of the speaker is mimed by the insistent repetition, there appears to be an approximation of Spenser's manner in *Astrophel*:[200]

> On on sad Traine, as from a crannid rocke
> Bee-swarmes rob'd of their honey, ceasles flock.
> Mourne, mourne, dissected now his cold lims lie
> Ah, knit so late with flame, and Maiestie.   (E1ᵛ)

The evocation of Spenser matches the earlier passages where Donne had been invoked. Chapman had deployed Donneian repetitions ('all, all' (B2ʳ), 'All, All' (D3ᵛ), for example), learned and scientific vocabulary (Chapman's frame of reference includes natural philosophy (as in the magnets at B3ᵛ) as well as technical terms from philosophical discourse, such as 'idea', 'form', and so forth): also reminiscent of Donne is the satirical attack upon flatterers (C1ᵛ) and the frequent tactical modulation from metrical regularity to a knotty, argumentative style. And, though Chapman's view of the value of intellectual enquiry seems less contemptuous than Donne's, both poets proclaim the boundaries and failings of human understanding.

Chapman locates his work in various traditions. The variety of his poem imitates a series of relationships with his predecessors, from Bion through Poliziano through Spenser to Donne. The great similes and the marginal notes underpin an aspiration towards epic loftiness, and the self-conscious reinvention of the epicede as the solution to the generic problems faced and often acknowledged by the writers of his time constitutes a scarcely veiled claim to laureateship, and to poetic primacy. Nothing can obscure the profound and moving sense of loss this weighty and brooding piece still conveys; but no less striking is the poet's magisterial recovery of the epicede as a mixed form partaking both of the musicality of the elegy and the monumental character of the epitaph. Like all great elegies, it is an essay in poetic tradition.

The final words of Shakespeare's last play, *The Two Noble Kinsmen*, are spoken by Duke Theseus. Faced with a death to lament and a marriage to celebrate, he tells the assembly on stage,

---

to Sidney): 'as when the Calidon Bore | The thigh of her diuine Adonis tore' (E2ᵛ); see also Niccols, *The three sisters teares* (1613), E1ᵛ.

[200] Wallerstein, *Studies in Seventeenth-Century Poetic*, 90.

'Let's go off, and bear us like the time'. His words epitomize the challenge elegists faced in the winter of 1612–13, and this chapter has presented many of the attempts by writers to make their voices sound to present occasions, to bear themselves according to the requirements of the time. And while it may be that many of the laments discussed in this chapter are works of considerable distinction, it is perhaps the very scale of the lamentation that is initially most remarkable. From the point of view of the history of the English funeral elegy, Henry's death provides an extraordinarily various and vivid picture of literary culture, frozen, so to speak, at a particular moment—I include in this remark, although they fall outside the scope of the present study, more oblique treatments, such as Webster's *The Duchess of Malfi* and *The Two Noble Kinsmen* itself. Ralegh, in prison, clearly recognized the sudden transformation of his fortunes, and faced the impracticability of his projected *History of the World*. That Henry's death would ensure a future of silence, impotence, and indefinite incarceration loads with bitter irony Ralegh's celebrated peroration, in which his patron's death is seen as a rhetorical act, a demonstration of power through words:

O eloquent, just, and mighty Death! whom none could advise thou hast per-suaded: what none hath dared, thou hast done: and whom all the world hath flattered, thou only hast cast out of the world and despised: thou hast drawn together all the far-stretched greatness, all the pride, cruelty, and ambition of man, and covered it all over with these two narrow words, *Hic Jacet!*[201]

More than any previous event Henry's death constituted a challenge to almost all writers, from the most established to the neophyte, from most political and religious groupings. And even if no subsequent occasion would attract the same range of poets, a major consequence of the mourning for Prince Henry was that the vernacular funeral elegy had become established almost overnight as a form (or series of forms and strategies) which every educated person would be expected at some stage to practice. From 1613 the elegy was a canonically laureate form: but it was also established as poetry of social gesture, as a medium for self-examination, and as a form in which writers could learn to imitate, recognize, and investigate the elements of their art.

[201] Ralegh, *Works*, vii. 901; *The history of the world* (1614), 776; See L. Tennenhouse, 'Sir Walter Ralegh and the Literature of Patronage', in Lytle and Orgel, eds., *Patronage in the Renaissance*, 235–58, esp. 252–8. See also the poem, 'What teares, (Deare Prince)', attributed to Ralegh in BL MA Add. 22118; Ralegh, *Poems*, ed. Latham, 52.

6. FROM JONSON TO MILTON: ELEGIES 1603–1638

Henry's court had attracted men of diverse ages and interests. With its dissolution, those elements, once held together by the hopes reposed in the Prince, were scattered forever. Henry's death provided new—and to many conclusive—evidence that the world was speeding to its end, and fragmenting as it did so. After that event, there would never again be an occasion when so many writers addressed their minds and wits to a common subject: nor indeed would there be again such a wide range of options for the elegist to choose from. The increasingly self-conscious politicization of literary discourse during the reigns of James I and Charles I had as an incidental consequence the effect of turning the elegy into a highly political genre, one where the poet's choice of mode was an expression of political view, and where, under the veil of literary commentary, political and religious points might be made more or less obliquely. Thus, as Kevin Sharpe has suggested, there is surely an ironic character to Thomas Carew's protestation that he is a peripheral, trivial figure, whose art cannot aspire to handle heroic subjects: in his celebrated reply to Aurelian Townshend's request for an elegy on Gustavus Adolphus, he disingenuously wrote:

> Alas!, how may
> My Lyrique feet, that of the smooth soft way
> · Of love, and Beautie, onely know the tread,
> In dancing paces celebrate the dead
> Victorious King, or his Majesticke Hearse
> Prophane with th'humble touch of their low verse?[1]

Yet it is nevertheless the case that major issues and events tended to be accorded less direct treatment—Carew is after all explaining why he will not be writing an elegy. The languages of love, romance, and death, of art and imitation, were assimilated into the languages of politics and religion. The mutual interpenetration of the intimate, the personal, and the realm of public affairs that had been embodied, to cite the most striking instances, in the

---

[1] Carew, *Poems*, ed. Rhodes Dunlap (Oxford, 1949), 74; Sharpe, *Criticism and Compliment*, 145–7, 174–6.

behaviours and speeches of Queen Elizabeth and in the later writings of Spenser, had important consequences for the writers of elegy.[2] The tendency to self-examination that was remarked on many occasions in the previous chapter developed into a propensity for something like self-obsession, and that self-obsession became increasingly a vehicle for writing not just about writing or the state of humanity but more specifically about the nation—and the writer's situation within it—as it proceeded towards civil war. Such reflections underpin the account of the history of the elegy up to and including *Lycidas* with which this study concludes.

There are no great Jacobean public elegies, no successors even to the heraldic roles of Churchyard and Whetstone. If there had been, they would have been written by the poets who manifested laureate ambitions—notably Jonson, Daniel, and Chapman. But there were none. It would in any case be naïve to suppose that great political events or issues, even in Elizabeth's day, had been treated unequivocally—Annabel Patterson has usefully established the 'functional ambiguity' inherent in much courtly and political literature.[3] Yet whereas poets did write on the Queen's death or on the death of Prince Henry in large numbers, there was reticence amounting almost to silence on the death of King James, and a general tendency for poets to create a distance between themselves and great public and political events. Such a process could lead to parabolic or allegorical treatment, culminating in the way the young Lord Hastings was mourned as a surrogate for Charles I in *Lachrymae Musarum* (1649).

But even if the most celebrated writers were shy of major public subjects, they still, like everybody else, wrote elegies. Ben Jonson's career as a commemorative poet, for example, may be crudely

---

[2] See M. W. Bloomfield, 'The Elegy and the Elegiac Mode: Praise and Alienation', in Lewalski, ed., *Renaissance Genres*, 147–57.

[3] A. Patterson, *Censorship and Interpretation*, 18: she describes how in 16th-cent. England there arose 'a system of communication in which ambiguity becomes a creative and necessary instrument, a social and cultural force of considerable consequence' (p. 11). A similar conclusion was trenchantly articulated by Cedric Brown, 'Any poet writing for patronage or occasional celebration who was worth his salt . . . understood that the decorousness of the social gesture and the self-evident integrity of the poet were considerations which went hand in hand. Servility in compliment failed to protect the dignity both of patron and writer', in *John Milton's Aristocratic Entertainments* (Cambridge, 1985), 154–5. See also L. L. Peck, ' "For a King not to be Bountiful were a Fault": Perspectives on Court Patronage in Early Stuart England', *Journal of British Studies*, 25 (1986), 31–61.

characterized as a journey from epitaph to apotheosis by way of
elegy. His earliest pieces are essentially epigrammatic, combining
restrained lapidary terseness with personal and individual local
details, with the expressed objective of effecting a reconciliation
between ephemerality and enduring art.[4] Employing the epideictic
strategies and objectives of the epigram, Jonson established in his
epitaphs the initial boundaries of the neoclassical English literary
epitaph, the genre brought to fruition by his disciple Herrick.
Jonson's subjects were for the most part praised for qualities (male
heroism, female chastity) that had been exalted by his ancient
models, or were likened to the subjects of classical epitaph; the
consequence was that they could be presented, like Shakespeare, as
being 'not of an age but for all time'. In addition, however, Jonson
deviated from his models, most notably in his regular departure
from the formal and structural limits of the epigram and in his
choice of subjects who were not in any conventional sense 'persons
of eminent place of government in the weal publicke'.[5] Jonson
claimed licence both because he was exalting Jacobean England
above ancient Rome and because he conceived of his own artistic
achievement, however superficially aberrant, indecorous, or merely
fanciful, as its own triumphant justification—'they are no ill pieces,
though they be not like the persons'; his method is the antithesis of
the mock heroic.[6]

As in the epigrams, the subjects of Jonson's epitaphs are treated
both generally and specifically: the most common particularizing
device is the use of the name as the epitome of the individual's
qualities ('I do but name thee, Pembroke, and I find | It is an
epigram on all mankind' (57)).[7] But it still seems to require a major

[4] H. MacLean, 'Ben Jonson's Poems: Notes on the Ordered Society', in *Essays in English Literature from the Renaissance to the Victorian Age*, ed. M. MacLure and F. W. Watt (Toronto, 1964), 43–68; B. R. Smith, 'Ben Jonson's *Epigrammes*: Portrait-Gallery, Theater, Commonwealth', *SEL* 14 (1974), 91–109.

[5] Weever, *Ancient funerall monuments*, 10; Camden, *Remaines*, 28; Puttenham, *Arte*, 39–44; D. H. Parker, 'The English Literary Epitaph in the Seventeenth Century', B.Litt. thesis (Oxford, 1970), 36 ff. On the question of the ideal dimensions of the epitaph, see Parker, pp. 12–57; also *The Poems of Sir John Davies*, ed. R. Krueger (Oxford, 1975), xliii, and Puttenham, *Arte*, 55–6.

[6] Jonson, *Poems*, ed. I. Donaldson (Oxford, 1975), 6 (all subsequent refs., unless otherwise indicated, are to Donaldson's edn); E. Partridge, 'Jonson's *Epigrammes*: The Named and the Nameless', *SLI* 6 (1973), 153–98.

[7] See also the discussion of Epigram 76 (which ends, 'My Muse bade, *Bedford* write, and that was she' (*Poems*, ed. Donaldson, 40–1)) in Barbara Lewalski's article, 'Lucy, Countess of Bedford: Images of a Jacobean Courtier and Patroness', in Sharpe and

effort for a modern reader to cultivate sensitivity to the 'finesses whereby . . . generic features are edged into sharpness' in poems crafted by a writer who professes that it is his 'onely Art, so to carry it, as none but Artificers perceive it'.[8]

The tendency to observe decorum by means of breaching it is apparent also in the *Underwoods* collection, which features several lengthy 'epitaphs'. The poem on Vincent Corbett, for example, is intensely particular. Its manner approximates to that of Jonson's verse epistles, and the speaker presents the subject as fully worthy of elevated celebration as a latter-day Kalender:

> His mind as pure, and neatly kept,
> As were his nurseries, and swept
> So of uncleanness or offence,
> That never came ill odour thence:
> And add his actions unto these,
> They were as specious as his trees.[9]   (15–20)

Jonson's praise of his subject's conduct as 'even, grave, and holy' (23), leads to another assertion of his right to epitaph and tomb, which is itself cast in the form of an epitaph:

> Reader, whose life and name did e'er become
>   An epitaph, deserved a tomb;
> Nor wants it here, through penury or sloth;
>   Who makes the one, so it be first, makes both.   (37–40)

Like most of the other early commemorative pieces, the Corbett poem derives from a markedly private and social context: like them, too, it is somewhat unexpectedly personal. It may be that such characteristics can help to account for Jonson's gradual abandonment of neoclassical generic regularity in favour of the more diffuse form of elegy, with its focus on the speaker and his reactions; it would certainly appear that the separation of the epitaph from the rest of the poem indicates a consciousness of departure from ancient precedent.[10]

Zwicker, *Politics of Discourse*, 52–77, esp. pp. 65–7; more generally, see M. Maurer, 'The Real Presence of Lucy Russell, Countess of Bedford . . . etc.', *ELH* 47 (1980), 205–34.

   [8] Fowler, *Conceitful Thought*, 134; Jonson, *Works*, viii. 587 (ll. 780–1). See also S. Fish, 'Author-Readers: Jonson's Community of the Same', *Representations*, 7 (1984), 26–58.   [9] Jonson, *Poems*, 146–7.

   [10] See the thoughtful account of the conflict of reason and emotion in Jonson's commemorative poems in Pigman, *Grief and English Renaissance Elegy*, 85–95. I take one

The poems Jonson called elegies are the products of his later years, from long after the *Anniversaries* and the death of Prince Henry. The lament for the Marchioness of Winchester, who died during pregnancy at the age of 24 in 1631, disclaims ingenuity and novelty, since 'who doth praise a person by a new | But a feigned way, doth rob it of the true' (37–8).[11] The speaker, led by the 'gentle ghost' of his subject, undergoes a metamorphosis into marble:

> Alas, I am all marble! Write the rest
>   Thou wouldst have written, fame, upon my breast:
> It is a large fair table, and a true,
>   And the disposure will be something new,
> When I, who would her poet have become,
>   At least may bear the inscription to her tomb.   (13–18)

In an apparently self-conscious allusion to the mode of Churchyard and Whetstone, Jonson's speaker then begins to list the details of names and places and family (matters which 'the heralds can tell' (20)), only to set them aside; he asks fame itself not merely to 'serve . . . forms', but to 'give her soul a name'—a task for which he declares himself unfitted ('It is too near the kin of heaven, the soul, | To be described' (29–30)). Such protestations underpin the terse version of the catalogue of Lady Paulet's qualities, which derives much of its force from its allusion to Spenser's Amoret (*The Faerie Queene*, IV. xi. 48–52):

> Her sweetness, softness, her fair courtesy,
>   Her wary guards, her wise simplicity,
> Were like a ring of virutes 'bout her set,
>   And piety the centre, where all met . . .
> What nature, fortune, institution, fact
>   Could sum to a perfection, was her act!
>
>   (39–42, 45–6)

implication of Pigman's argument to be that the very choice of the form of epitaph (rather than elegy) is part of a strategy to subdue and discipline grief, and another that anxiety about expressing grief informs the elegies, with their lengthy explanations of what they *might* be about which precede their arguments. It ought also to be noted, however, that (as will become apparent in the consideration of *Jonsonus virbius*) demonstrations of grief were coming to be associated with Puritanism—a process accelerated (if not inaugurated) by the hyperbolic zeal with which Prince Henry had been lamented. See also Lewalski's remarks on Jonson's elegies in *Donne's Anniversaries*. 337–42.

11 *Underwood*, 83; *Poems*, ed. Donaldson, 256–9.

More substantial is the account of the subject's death. Jonson presents a series of dramatic illustrations of how Lady Paulet 'in her last act, taught the standers-by | With admiration and applause to die' (61–2). Her contempt for the world arouses wonder, and she performs a death in accordance with the loftiest ideals of Christian stoicism (47–60). Drawing both on biblical and Senecan commonplace, Jonson then describes his subject's heavenly apotheosis, where she recognizes her maker, 'the beginnings of all beauties' (74), in contrast with which (in an echo of Donne), everything on earth is either 'dead . . . or about to die' (86).[12] The elegy concludes with a statement of the capacity of the Christian soul to defeat mortality, crush the serpent's head, and make a triumphant entry to its celestial inheritance (95–100).

The poem is erudite in the extreme, but its overall design is extremely simple, and proceeds with every appearance of confidence towards a consolatory resolution.[13] Jonson dramatizes inexpressibility by creating an impatient speaker who dismisses the various possible commemorative strategies: an important effect is the creation of a mixed kind, an implicitly panegyric compendium which acknowledges (and imitates) the subject's virtues. The mixture, significantly, includes both modern vernacular and more venerable components, so that, while Jonson may in some sense be writing an elegy against elegy—or at least an elegy designed to minimize rather than indulge or portray grief and mourning—he does so in the aggregative mode associated with the form as practised by most writers of his time, and, further, by creating a distinctive dramatic voice, and an image of a speaker whose responses to the death are kept emphatically in the foreground.[14]

Similar reflections may be prompted by the *Apotheosis, or Relation to the Saints*, of Lady Venetia Digby, the ninth of a ten-poem cycle *Eupheme* which Jonson composed in her honour.[15] And the sequence's Statian epigraph ('Vivam amare voluptas, defunctam

---

[12] See Seneca, *Consolatio ad Marciam*, 25. 2; Jas. 1: 12, Rev. 2: 10, 1 Cor. 15: 19.

[13] See O. B. Hardison's account in *The Enduring Monument*, 142–4.

[14] Pigman, noting that neither the subject's youth nor her pregnancy is mentioned in the poem, argues that Jonson 'deliberately avoids stirring the reader's compassion' (*Grief and English Renaissance Elegy*, 93).

[15] *Poems*, ed. Donaldson, 268–74; Jonson, *Works*, xi. 103–5. Her monument was described by Aubrey (Bodley MS Aubrey 6, fo. 101ʳ). Other elegies were composed by Felltham, Habington, Randolph, Rutter, and Townshend (on which last poem, see Sharpe, *Criticism and Compliment*, 155, 159–61); see Beal, *Index*, 249–55.

religio') indicates both a modification of Jonson's scorn of hyperbolic celebration, and a justification for lament.[16]

Again, we first encounter the speaker's reactions: he begins in distracted despair—'what's left a poet when his muse is gone?' (28)—as the image of thoughtless and destructive grief:

> My wounded mind cannot sustain this stroke:
> It rages, runs, flies, stands, and would provoke
> The world to run with it: in her fall,
> I sum up mine own breaking, and wish all.   (23–6)

This figure, forced by sorrow to 'murmur against God' (33), proceeds from envy of his subject's happiness to admit its consoling implication and to reflect on the immortality of the soul and the theology of resurrection. He concedes the futility of praising heavenly joys ('Better be dumb, than superstitious' (73)) and the folly of making 'busy search into Divine mysteries' which were better 'wondered at . . . with silence and amazement' (77–80).

What follows reads rather like a version of, or a belated riposte to, the *Anniversaries*, as the speaker dismisses mourning as inconsistent with faith, and creates a lengthy account of Lady Digby's apotheosis. The physical centre of the poem prefigures the ultimate reunion of body and soul (113–16), and leads to praise of God's inclusiveness as 'all in all' (120).[17] God, whose mysteries are ultimately to be revealed, is presented as the supreme anatomist, able to 'dissect | The smallest fibre of our flesh' (150–1), and thereby discover the excellences of Lady Digby (which the speaker himself then lists (159 ff.)), who had been 'in one, a many parts of life' (173). The speaker narrates his subject's charitable deeds, claiming that they had been informed by such intense meditation on their removed meaning that death was experienced as a 'sweet

---

[16] 'While she is alive to love [a wife] is a delight; when she is dead, it is a religion', Statius, *Silvae*, 5, Preface. The same line appears in the dedication of Joseph Rutter's *The shepheards holy-day* (1635), which includes (H1ʳ–H3ʳ) an elegy on Lady Digby, headed 'Thyrsis: A Pastorall Elegie in the person of Sir *Kenelme Digby*, on the Death of his Noble Lady, the Lady *Venetia Digby*'. Digby composed a fictionalized autobiographical romance in which he (Theagenes) woos his wife (Stelliana): the text, from BL MS Harley 6758, has been published in a modernized edn., *Loose Fantasies*, ed. V. Gabrieli (Rome, 1968).

[17] On the significance of the centre, see Fowler, *Triumphal Forms*, 62–88: Lady Digby's harmony is imaged musically: 'her whole life was now become one note | Of piety and private holiness' (178–9).

ecstasy' (225).[18] The baroque rapture contrasts sharply with the
stark expression of the earth-bound poet's loss which concludes the
elegy: 'My muse is gone' (228).[19]

It is likely that the missing tenth poem of the sequence ('being
her Inscription, or Crown') would have been an epitaph. And even
in its incomplete state, *Eupheme*, with its elaborate artifice and
obvious generic variousness, is a collection which employs the idea
of the anthology or compendium panegyrically. The elegy itself,
even more than the poem on the Marchioness of Winchester, is
sharply distinct from the epitaphs and represents a particular and
defined element of the response to death. Consolation is the
province of the epitaph and of the overall fiction of the funeral
anthology (whose purpose here is announced in its title, the 'fair
fame' of its subject); the elegy can deal with—even if it ultimately
dismisses them—the reactions of the speaker to bereavement,
alongside a panegyric narrative. It treats of sorrow in the immediate
way alluded to in its own epigraph from Statius: 'Sera quidem tanto
stuitur medicina dolori': 'Indeed the medicine made for such a
great grief comes late' (*Silvae*, 5. 1. 16). Jonson's turning to elegy so
late in his career may be attributed to his apparent nostalgia at that
time for earlier forms, or to the ubiquity of elegy, in the 1630s. But
like all of his contemporaries, he found himself writing within the
traditions founded by Spenser and Donne.

Drayton's slowness in coming to the form has already been
noted; he expressed puzzlement himself that he had not written on
the death of either Henri IV or of Prince Henry, and could offer in
explanation only the conventional protestation of sincerity, 'To
observe custom I use not to praise'.[20] The form, as it developed in
the years after 1612, sorted well with the poet's preoccupation with
the 'evill time', and Drayton's plaintive elegies all relate particular
occasions to the general decline of the world for which they are

---

[18] 'In frequent speaking of the pious psalms | Her solemn hours she spent, or giving
alms, | Or doing other deeds of charity, | To clothe the naked, feed the hungry. She |
Would sit in an infirmary whole days | Poring, as on a map, to find the ways | To that
eternal rest, where now she hath place | By sure election, and predestined grace' (191–8).

[19] On baroque presentations of death, see R. Huebert, *John Ford, Baroque English
Dramatist* (Montreal, 1977), 55–8. E. Mercer observed that English funeral art after
1625 was characterized by 'religious emotionalism' (*English Art, 1553–1625*, Oxford
History of English Art, 7 (Oxford 1962), 241–6). See also J. L. Klause, 'Donne and the
Wonderful', *ELR* 17 (1987), 41–66.

[20] Drayton, *Works*, iii. 219. See above, Ch. 5.

held to provide evidence.[21] Like the verse epistles, the elegies are markedly dramatic. The vivid account (17–33) of the shock caused by Lady Clifton's death, for example, has been characterized as 'at home in a Jacobean tragedy'.[22] Also like the epistles is the particularity, the intimacy, of the poems. Thus Lady Clifton is remembered in the grove at Clifton where the poet had met her in happier times.[23] The speaker acknowledges the impossibility of describing the 'wondrous Master peece' (50) in whose features nature had drawn a 'Map of heaven' (73); instead of offering straightforward consolation, he advises his readers, 'no harsh, or shallow rimes decline | Upon that day wherein you shall read mine' (115–16). He asserts the conventional Spenserian distinction between mere verse and true poetry, and claims that his own lines derive their authenticity from the subject herself. Thus, where other laments will be insubstantial and transitory, sitting 'like mothes upon her herse' (118), each performance of the fruits of his own 'sacred rage' (120) will recreate the funeral, and conjure, for the alert and well-disposed reader, the sensation of bereavement.

The elegy for the three sons of Lord Sheffield is in effect an extended protestation of the pointlessness of writing elegies, coupled with the claim that the subject 'doth farre exceed | All forc'd expression' (44–5)—in other words that it is in itself unprecedented and beyond the capacity of trivial rhymers. Yet despite this Spenserian contrast between the servile jingles of poetasters and the inspired measures of true poets, Drayton's speaker returns to his own uselessness in the face of providence:

> . . . wherefore paper, doe I idly spend,
> On these deafe waters to so little end,
> And up to starry heaven doe I not looke,
> In which, as in an everlasting booke,
> Our ends are written . . .[24]   (81–5)

The poet was not always quite so tentative and apologetic. The elegy on Mistress Fallowfield is couched in a vigorous, more

[21] Drayton, *Works*, v. 213–18; R. F. Hardin, *Michael Drayton and the Passing of Elizabethan England* (Lawrence, 1973), 72–105, esp. 88–95; Norbrook, *Poetry and Politics*, 195–235; also G. Williamson, 'Mutability, Decay, and Seventeenth Century Melancholy', *ELH* 2 (1935), 121–50.

[22] Drayton, *Works*, v. 213.

[23] B. H. Newdigate, *Michael Drayton and his Circle* (1941), 208.

[24] Drayton, *Works*, iii. 213–15; v. 215.

recongnizably public style, and the subject is praised for the virtues habitually associated with her age, class, and sex. In keeping with the external focus of the piece, Drayton includes no personal details or particularities and contents himself with bland assurances that good report and fame will serve the bereaved well.[25] Similarly confident is the elegy on Lady Olive Stanhope, a poem that is typical of its period.[26] The speaker, faced with the task of celebrating someone he did not know (18), argues that their spirits had been acquainted (19 ff.) and that his soul had sensed the moment of her death (39 ff.). His spirit offers the elegy as a trophy designed to outlast the present age of iron (28), and he praises Lady Stanhope both through a version of the *puer senex* and through a characteristic topographical compliment, when he argues that the Peak District is glorified by her having lived there (65–72). The poem is a curious mixture of the intimate and the perfunctory.

The poet's most intimate lament is on the death of Henry Rainsford, who married Anne Goodyer, the 'Idea' of Drayton's sonnet sequence.[27] The poem is self-conscious, self-questioning, and expresses the speaker's waning confidence in the value and durability of art. Drayton evokes an ironic picture of his predicament that anticipates in substance Donne's letter on Lord Hamilton's death and recalls in manner the protestations of innumerable sonneteers; his own abundant habitual eloquence has dried up when faced with a uniquely biting personal sorrow:

> 'Tis strange that I from my abundant breast,
> Who others sorrowes have so well exprest;
> Yet I by this in little time am growne
> So poore, that I want to expresse mine owne.   (15–18)

The speaker acknowledges that the conspiracy of the malignant fates ought to be endured with Christ-like patience (14–70), but finds himself drawn more powerfully by the temptation to yield to violent grief, to follow the example of melancholics and misanthropes such as Timon (77 ff.). Like Wither in his elegy on Prince Henry, Drayton appears to repudiate the normal Spenserian invocation of

[25] Drayton, *Works*, iii. 242–3; v. 218.

[26] Drayton, *Works*, iii. 236–7; v. 215: Newdigate, *Drayton and his Circle*, 204. See also the four elegies by Edward Radcliffe reproduced in app. B below.

[27] Drayton, *Works*, iii. 232–5; v. 217; Newdigate, *Drayton and his Circle*, 51–3; see also John Buxton's edn. of *The Poems of Michael Drayton* in The Muses' Library, 2 vols. (1953), I. xvi.

poetic community. Rainsford's death is adduced as evidence of the sickness of the world and the vanity of mortal endeavour; it also eloquently proves the impermanence of human relationships, since he had been 'a thousand friends' (128). The tone throughout is bitter, regretful, and the poem is less an anatomy of the subject than an exploration of the meaning of his death for the speaker. Drayton dramatizes the plight of the accomplished professional writer brought face to face with his inability to find words to write of something close to his heart, and he shows himself led to sombre conclusions as to the essential triviality and meaninglessness of all utterance. Even Spenser's disciple did not now write pastoral elegy; nor did he tackle great public subjects. For him the elegy was pre-eminently a medium for self-exploration and self-discovery, a private and reserved form.

Daniel's Jacobean career tells a similar—perhaps even more gloomy—story. The poet welcomed King James on his accession and, as one of the seven grooms of Queen Anne's Privy Chamber, participated in Prince Henry's funeral. He had dedicated *Philotas* to the Prince and contributed substantially to the creation of his myth by composing *Tethys festival* for him.[28] Daniel's silence at Henry's death may therefore seem somewhat puzzling; but he had, by 1612, become increasingly reserved and austere, much preoccupied with 'the distemperature of the times', and conscious of a decline in the status and achievement of poetry in the context of the new age. His developing concern was with history rather than celebration, with analysis rather than propaganda, and, flexible as the elegy had become, it can hardly have seemed a congenial form to him.[29]

His most significant commemorative work is the *Funerall poeme* on the Earl of Devonshire.[30] Mountjoy had been a sensitive and intelligent patron, 'the fosterer of mee and my *Muse*'; like Greville, he had been able to quell Daniel's intermittent self-doubt and to

---

[28] J. Pitcher, ' "In those figures which they seeme": Samuel Daniel's *Tethys' Festival*', in D. Lindley, ed., *The Court Masque* (Manchester, 1984), 33–46.

[29] The best accounts of Daniel's Jacobean career are J. Rees, *Samuel Daniel: A Critical and Biographical Study* (Liverpool, 1964), ch. VII: Norbrook, *Poetry and Politics*, 178–9, 198–9, 201; J. Pitcher, ed., *Samuel Daniel: The Brotherton Manuscript*, Leeds Texts and Monographs, NS, 7 (Leeds, 1981), 93–100, 189–93.

[30] *A funerall poeme uppon the death of the late noble Earle of Deuonshire* (1606); a revised text appears in Daniel's *Whole workes* (1623), pt. 2, 15–26. See J. Pitcher, 'Samuel Daniel's Occasional and Dedicatory Verse: A Critical Edition', D.Phil. thesis, 2 vols. (Oxford, 1978), i. 153–68, ii. 303–29.

point him in challenging directions.[31] Daniel's poem concentrates as much on his subject's inner qualities of integrity and self-knowledge as on his more visible attributes as politician and general. He also takes pains to create for the speaker the persona of a plain-speaking and objective person, under no obligation to distort truth or suppress unpalatable details; as such he (wholly conventionally) claims that he is utterly different from the common run of elegists: 'it is the property | For free men to speake truth, for slaues to lye'. The earlier, less public, version (1606, close to the event it commemorates) may well express its private, intimate nature through an additional, numerical, compliment, as John Pitcher has suggested: the line total (388) may allude to Mountjoy's being the 388th election as a Knight of the Garter, and thereby silently defend him against slurs on his achievement and character, not least by allusion to the Garter motto, 'Honi soit qui mal y pense'. The speaker pleads that the notorious liaison with Penelope Rich (Mountjoy's 'weaknesses') should not be allowed to obscure his many noble qualities, most notably his 'quiet calme sincerity' maintained in the face of a world increasingly less hospitable to such distinction.[32] The lines added in the revision (1623) transform the character of the poem, and amplify the public aspects of Mountjoy's life; he is furnished with appropriately heroic speeches at moments of crisis in battles, and is displayed performing his official duties with becoming dignity and gravity.[33] Daniel pruned passages which dealt with Mountjoy's private life, and presented his own relationship with the subject in a more muted, dispassionate way.[34] Yet the picture that emerges even from the revision is of a compendium of virtues, an ideal Renaissance governor who perfectly combines martial, scholarly, and human virtues, who embodies the harmonious conjunction of action and contemplation. He is praised for Danielesque gifts of plainness, truthfulness, and integrity:

> His tongue and heart did not turne-backes, but went
> One way, and kept one course with what he ment

[31] See Rees, *Samuel Daniel*, 62–74, and her *Fulke Greville, Lord Brooke, 1554–1628: A Critical Biography* (1971), 30–1.   [32] See Pitcher, *Brotherton MS*, 102, 209.

[33] Daniel, *Whole workes*, 21–2; Pitcher, 'Daniel's Occasional Verse', ii. 303–6.

[34] See also Ford's elegy, *Fames memoriall* (1606), of which a presentation MS copy (Bodley MS Malone 238) was made to be given to the Earl's widow: see K. Duncan-Jones, 'Ford and the Earl of Devonshire', *RES*, NS, 39 (1978), 447–52, and her 'Sidney, Stella and Lady Rich', in *Sir Philip Sidney: 1586 and the Creation of a Legend*, 170–92.

He vs'd no maske at all, but euer ware
His honest inclination open-faced . . . [35]

Daniel's elegy is historical in the spirit of the new critical history of his day. At the same time, it is also an essay (owing much to Montaigne) on quiet and tranquillity of mind. While it professes itself to be scrupulous in the accuracy of its historical detail, it is none the less a polemical and pedagogic piece, and includes a defence of Mountjoy against envy and slander and an attack upon flattery and court vice, within the framework of the expressed aim to create a lasting memorial. Daniel's method illuminates the connection between panegyric and history; and his style, which is notable for the flexibility which Lipsius exalted as an adjunct to terse brevity, is itself a means of tacitly advocating the values of scepticism, enquiry, learning, and integrity.[36]

Such elements are even more apparent in the Brotherton Manuscript, whose verse epistles appear to have been arranged, as John Pitcher has suggested, in order to measure the greatness of Prince Henry against a 'wild age confounded with excess'.[37] Of course, Henry's death effected a generic transformation in the verse epistle addressed to him. The poem could no longer be a work of advice to a Prince, or even a conventional verse epistle/ essay; it was modified into a celebration of Henry's qualities and a demonstration of the fragmentation and decline of the world exemplified and accelerated by his death. There is an obvious parallel with the effect of Henry's death on the composition of Ralegh's *History of the World* (see above, p. 203), and perhaps the act of shaping the collection of epistles into something resembling a sequence recalls Spenser's creation of an overarching fiction in the *Astrophel* anthology. Daniel's apparent attitudes to history and to human values are trenchantly expressed both in the substance of his argument and in the stylistic variety of the pieces. As with the

---

[35] Daniel, *Whole workes*, 23.

[36] The relationships between epideisis and epic, between panegyric and history, are fluid and complex in this period. See Bacon, *Works*, iv. 219; B. Vickers, *In Defence of Rhetoric*, 52–64; Justus Lipsius, *Sixe bookes of politickes or civil doctrine*, tr. W. Jones (1594), 55 ('flatterie being couered with plainnesse, is best pleasing to Princes'); T. H. Cain, *Praise in 'The Faerie Queene'* (Lincoln, 1978); Norbrook's excellent study of Greville in *Poetry and Politics*, ch. 6; on Daniel and Montaigne, see R. Himelick, 'Samuel Daniel, Montaigne and Seneca', *N&Q*, NS, 3 (1956), 61–4. I am indebted to Norbrook's D.Phil. thesis, 'Panegyric of the Monarch, and its Social Context under Elizabeth I and James I' (Oxford, 1978), esp. 145–80.   [37] Pitcher, *Brotherton MS*, 93–100.

Devonshire poem, Daniel moves outwards from his present occasion not to satire or self-questioning but rather to analysis of the human condition, to an examination of ways of understanding and interpreting the individual human being, of what might be held to be general characteristics of human nature, and of the means to acquire true knowledge. Daniel's poems are couched in a style that seems designed to inculcate the very processes of thought and apprehension whose cultivation they advocate.[38]

In contrast with Daniel, Chapman's need for patronage was more urgent, his ambition necessarily more obvious. It has already been suggested that his *Epicede* was a poem written against or in emulation of Donne. Chapman's effort to overgo the *Anniversaries* was resumed in his vastly ambitious and grandiloquent *Eugenia* (a forerunner of Jonson's *Eupheme*).[39] The work is structured into four 'vigiliae', each of which has a separate 'Inductio', and Chapman's reworking of Donne's style is placed in the realm of a Spenserian allegory, where the House of Fame becomes a retreat in which Eugenia (true nobility) and Religion hear of Russell's death, are in turn devastated at the news and then revived by Fame's consoling report of his good life and blissful sojourn in heaven, and then by the news that Russell's son, the image of his father, has survived to perpetuate his qualities. The reminiscences of *The Olympian Catastrophe* in the organization and fiction of the piece are powerful, but the individual speeches, especially those of Eugenia herself, abound, as Barbara Lewalski has demonstrated, with echoes of the *Anniversaries*.[40] In addition, a speaker called Poesie promises annual reiteration: 'O heare | These Rites of ours, that every yeare | We vow thy Herse' (1065–7). Like the earlier *Epicede*, Chapman's *Eugenia* shows in its range, scope, and ambition some of the consequences of panegyric inflation; it is also, as an anthology of related pieces written in a variety of styles, related to the numerous elegiac sequences of its time: Chapman's attempt to recover an ancient genre in the *Epicede* was not pursued further.

---

[38] See Chaudhuri, *Infirm Glory*, chs. I and III for other instances.

[39] *Eugenia: or true nobilities trance, for death of William Lord Russell* (1614); text from Chapman, *Poems*, ed. Bartlett, 269–300. Sidney bequeathed his 'best gilted armour' to Russell ('Sidney's Will', in *Miscellaneous Prose*, ed. Duncan-Jones and Van Dorsten, 149): Russell succeeded Sidney as Governor of Flushing and later (1594) became Lord Deputy of Ireland (ibid., 217–18).

[40] Lewalski, *Donne's Anniversaries*, 329–31.

For many poets, as will have become apparent in the previous chapter, Donne's *Anniversaries* acted as a stimulus, promising a new mode of expression, even for poets from very different traditions.[41] The Spenserian John Davies of Hereford, for example, mourned Elizabeth Dutton in a series of explicit echoes of Donne's poems.[42] Yet he tempers what he borrows; his subject is praised in more conventionally Petrarchan terms than Elizabeth Drury had been, and Donne's more extreme hyperboles are moderated: indeed, Davies seems to make a point of fastidious qualification:[43]

> *Poets* (I grant) have libertie to give
> More *height* to *Grace*, then the *Superlative*:
> So hath a *Painter* licence too, to paint
> A Saint-like *face*, till it the *Saint* out *saint*.
> But *Truth* (which now mine *Art* to shaddow strives)
> Makes *licence* larger by the *grace* she gives.
>   But yet,
> To say thou wast the *Forme* (that is the *soule*)
> Of all this *All*; I should thee misenroule
> In *Booke* of *Life*; which (on the Earth) they keepe
> That of *Arts fountaines* have carowsed deepe.   (113ᵛ–114)

I have cited the example of Davies in order to illustrate a significant development whereby the self-referential, aggregative method of elegy was acquiring an explicitly literary-critical component. As well as writing about their own predicament, and about writing (and its problems), elegists like Davies engaged in debate with other writers, and exploited the improvised nature of the form to include parody and imitation. And inevitably, as the exchange of insults between the Puritan Price and his conservative opponents Corbett

---

[41] Nevertheless, the case of the reactions to Daniel Price's sermons on Prince Henry is instructive. Price, one of Henry's chaplains, published *Lamentations for the death of prince Henrie* (1613), *Prince Henry his first anniversary* (1613), and *Prince Henry his second anniversary* (1614); all are heavily indebted to Donne's poems (see Lewalski, *Donne's Anniversaries*, 312–16, and Smith, *Donne: The Critical Heritage*, 37–8). He was scorned by Richard Corbett and by Brian Duppa (later respectively contributor to and editor of *Jonsonus virbius*), with whom he engaged in an exchange of verses to defend himself against the charge of excessive, absurd (and low-born) zeal in mourning the Prince (Corbett, *Poems*, ed. Bennet and Trevor Roper, 8–11, 107–9); see Norbrook, *Poetry and Politics*, 206.

[42] In *The muses sacrifice* (1612); see A. J. Smith, ed., *Donne: The Critical Heritage*, 70–1; Lewalski, *Donne's Anniversaries*, 309–10, 326–9.

[43] Lewalski, *Donne's Anniversaries*, 328.

and Duppa demonstrates, such concerns were inseparable from religious and political considerations.[44]

The fashion for funeral anthologies, effectively inaugurated at the time of Sidney's death, continued thereafter, both inside and outside the Universities. Oxford, for example, produced volumes on Sir Christopher Hatton (1592), Sir Henry Unton (1596), and on Ferdinando Strange (1596); Sir Horatio Pallavicino was mourned with the aggressively Protestant *An Italians dead bodie, stucke with English flowers: Elegies on the death of Sir Oratio Pallavicino* (1600), edited by Theophilus Field, Fellow of Pembroke, Cambridge.[45] Common to these volumes are the assertion of communal grief and the implication that the number and variety of the contributors represent the abundant, copious virtue of the subject. One of the most remarkable collections of this type is, like the Pallavicino anthology, while not an official product of Cambridge, strongly connected with the academic community there. The work is a memorial volume for Sir Edward Lewkenor and his wife, probably compiled and ordered by Joseph Hall's friend William Bedell.[46] The core of the book (B4^r–F1^r) is a set of academic laments mainly in Greek, Latin, and Hebrew, culminating in a vision of the couple's apotheosis (E4^v–F1^r); but its most striking feature is the Spenserian framing verses (in English) which provide a context (both narrowly artistic and, more obviously, political and religious) for the corporate lament; indeed, they could be said to create both the fiction and the reality of a community. The poet (perhaps Bedell himself) summons the Muses to assist the shepherds' grieving:

> Help vs to dight
> Their herses with your plaints, and if no more
> Help with your teares our common losse bewaile.
> Your teares are left if other power do faile:
> And fellowship is ease though griefe do nought availe.   (B1^v)

Before the Muses come to his aid, the speaker rehearses, in solemn neo-Spenserian stanzas with a concluding alexandrine, a narrative

---

[44] For another instance of Donne's influence, see M. R. Parker, 'Diamond's Dust: Carew, King and the Legacy of Donne', in C. J. Summers and T.-L. Pebworth, eds., *The Eagle and the Dove: Reassessing John Donne* (Columbia, 1986), 191–200.

[45] See L. Stone, *An Elizabethan: Sir Horatio Pallavicino* (Oxford, 1956), 13–14, 37–8, 190.

[46] *Threnodia in obitum D. Edouardi Lewkenor equitis: Funerall verses* (1606). See Hall, *Poems*, ed. Davenport, 269–70; Norbrook, *Poetry and Politics*, 274.

of the Lewkenors' lives, full of dramatic touches (at the moment of his wife's death, Sir Edward cries out, '*Dearest I come*; what boots me longer life?' (B3^r)) and sententious observations on death and providence. The Muses are invited, in a passage dense with recollections of Spenser ('Two sonnes they had (Ah now no longer they)', etc.) to create a company to join with the earthly mourners:

> The power of words is subject to your skill:
>   And words well plac'd can charme the wounded hart,
>   Vp then ye Muses. And if so ye will,
>   We sheepheards swaines will helpe to beare a part.
>   Vp then thou first mournfullst Melpomene,
>   And Erato with thee: Terpsichore
> Shall with Thaleia sing, when PHOEBVS shall you see.   (B3^v)

The 'link-poet' then reappears to introduce a group of vernacular elegies ('The ruder song of simple countrey swains'—i.e. Cambridge dons) later in the volume (F1^r), and the poems are indeed appropriately domestic and simple, though dignified by the implied connection with ancient pastoral which emerges from the framing verses. Contributors frequently justify stylistic *naïveté* as the expression of spontaneity and sincerity. W. Firmage, for example, claims liberation from the stifling tutelage of the Muses—'Suffice me that my sorrowes selfe may be | Both Muse and matter to mine Eligee'—and distinguishes himself from those 'howling hirelings . . . | That helpe affection with their mourning art' (F3^r). His concluding address to the Lewkenors in heaven—'Liue long in blisse you heauen-beloued soules | For vs' (F4^r)—typifies the repeated stress on community, on the shared beliefs and values which, it is argued, persist beyond the deaths of individuals. The volume as a whole ends with a remarkable piece entitled 'DEATHS APOLOGIE, and a Reioynder to the same' (F4^r), whose model is Chaucer rather than Spenser. Personified Death is closer to Chaucer's Pardoner than to Spenser's Despaire (both of whom are echoed); he advises his audience 'Let no man trust me' (F4^v), but then ingratiatingly invites them to seek revenge by attempting to slay death (G3^r). The 'rejoinder', in the persona of the 'link-poet', has none of Harry Bailey's intemperance. He sees through the webs of deceit woven by Death's seductive eloquence—'I will despise and scorne thy hurtlesse hisse'—and briefly states his personal resolve and Christian contempt for the world: 'Christ is my boot that neuer made offence. | His death or rather life shall enterance winne | For me to Heauen . . . Go now and vaunt to giue the thing thou neuer hast!' (G4'). The effect of this Christian dialogue is to generalize the earlier laments; the Spenserian fiction is furnished with a further dimension, with the consequence that the whole volume grows into a more wide-ranging image of grief and consolation, proceeding from the formal epitaph on its title-page through a rich variety of languages, styles, and literary forms to a pious and spiritual conclusion. At the simplest level, *Threnodia in obitum* is a vivid illustration of the move towards anthologies and mixed genres, of the combination of learned and vernacular composition, of the coincidence of Protestantism and literary community and artistic invention. In all of these respects, and in the way the role played by Bedell develops Spenser's performance in the *Astrophel* anthology, it is an important analogue and model for Milton's debut as elegist in the later Cambridge anthology *Iusta Edouardo King*.

Of course there were contrasting, that is to say non-Spenserian, means of ordering anthologies and sequences. Works by individuals, such as Jonson's *Eupheme* and Chapman's *Eugenia*, as well as the sequences of funeral songs (by Campion, Coprario, and others) noted in Chapter 5, are obvious examples.[47] And neither of the funeral anthologies occasioned by the deaths of Donne and Jonson is a sequence in the *Astrophel* tradition.[48] Each is, as an anthology, inevitably wedded to the panegyric topos of inclusiveness, and each, no less conventionally, presents an image of a world diminished and impoverished by its loss. In addition, the collections develop this theme of decline and bereavement in specifically literary senses.[49] Hasty production is common to many volumes of this kind, and there are numerous instances of contributions arriving

[47] See also William Habington's sequence of eight poems on the death of George Talbot in *Castara* (1635), 151–67; for a modern text, see *The Poems of William Habington*, ed. K. Allott (Liverpool, 1948), 101–11, 193–5. Lewalski discusses the sequence briefly in *Donne's Anniversaries*, 331–5. Carew is the focus of much recent attention; see J. Fitzmaurice, 'Carew's Funerary Poetry and the Paradox of Sincerity', *SEL* 25 (1985), 127–44.

[48] Donne, *Poems: With elegies on the author's death* (1633); *Jonsonus virbius: or, the memorie of Ben: Jonson revived* (1638); for modern texts, see Milgate, *Anniversaries*, 81–107, 220–31, and Jonson, *Works*, xi. 428–81.

[49] See A. J. Murphy, 'The Critical Elegy of Earlier Seventeenth Century England', *Genre*, 5 (1972), 75–105; S. Gottlieb, 'Elegies Upon the Author: Defining, Defending, and Surviving Donne', *John Donne Journal*, 2 (1982), 23–38; R. Hannaford, ' "Express'd by mee": Carew on Donne and Jonson', *SP* 84 (1987), 61–79; A. Van Velzen, 'Two Versions of the Funeral Elegy: Henry King's "The Exequy" and Thomas Carew's " . . . Elegies Upon . . . Donne" ', *Comitatus*, 15 (1984), 45–57.

too late for inclusion; such occurrences further distinguish these later anthologies from the more carefully planned and structured products of the Spenserian tradition.[50]

Also exceptional, though for somewhat different reasons, is *Lachrymae Musarum* (1649), the volume of laments for the young Lord Hastings, mourned less for himself than as a surrogate for the freshly executed Charles I. Yet though in some respects a self-consciously defiant sequence, it is also a manifestation of defeat: Marvell is by no means the only contributor who questions as much as he asserts.[51]

To a far greater extent than *Lachrimae lachrimarum*, for example, *Iusta Edouardo King* shows clear signs of conscious organization—perhaps even a degree of competitiveness—among the contributors; each section of the volume concludes with a pastoral elegy that seems to have been placed in order to mark the transition between distinct stages of mourning.[52] Some contributors to the memorial volume for Edward King apologize for their lateness while rejoicing that they had had time to write in a considered way.[53] The volume is, at least superficially, less pessimistic than most of the other works mentioned in this chapter, and several texts (most obviously—in the view of some commentators—Milton's *Lycidas*) have been held to display a certain confidence in the power of art, and the related vocations of poet, priest, and prophet, to uncover some meaning and purpose in early death.[54] Milton's 'monody' represents the next great innovation in the history of the English elegy, and has traditionally constituted both the starting-point for historians of the genre and a standard against which later specimens are judged. But

---

[50] For an example from *Jonsonus virbius*, see Jonson, *Works*, xi. 485–6. Richard Lovelace's poem on the death of Princess Katherine was a late addition to *Musarum Oxoniensium Charisteria* (1638); see *The Poems of Richard Lovelace*, ed. C. H. Wilkinson (Oxford, 1930), 260–1.

[51] See M. Gearin-Tosh, 'Marvell's "Uppon the Death of the Lord Hastings" ', *Essays and Studies*, 34 (1981), 105–22.

[52] M. Lloyd, 'Justa Edouardo King', *N&Q*, NS, 5 (1958), 432–4; J. A. Wittreich, *Visionary Poetics: Milton's Tradition and his Legacy* (San Marino, 1979), 89–98, 248–50.

[53] *Iusta Edouardo King Naufrago* (Cambridge, 1638), sigs. G2ᵛ, G3ᵛ.

[54] See J. Creaser, '*Lycidas*: The Power of Art', *Essays and Studies*, 34 (1981), 123–47; A. T. Turner, 'Milton and the Convention of the Academic Miscellanies', *YES* 5 (1975), 86–93; Wittreich, *Visionary Poetics*, 98–117, 250–4, argues that Milton's poem draws upon the 'master-theme', the Order for the Burial of the Dead, to interpret the meaning and purpose of bereavement. See Sacks, *The English Elegy*, 90–117; R. Mallette, *Spenser, Milton and Renaissance Pastoral* (Lewisburg, 1981), ch. IV; and P. Alpers. '*Lycidas* and Modern Criticism', *ELH* 49 (1982), 468–96.

its achievement, remarkable though it is, confirms the traditions to which it belongs rather than making them obsolete.[55] It is therefore a highly appropriate text with which to conclude the account of the traditions of elegy sketched in these pages.

There are parallels between the critical reactions to the *Anniversaries* and to *Lycidas*. In each case, prompted by an uneasy recognition that these unarguably canonical texts were generically hybrid, irregular, and, at first sight, unassimilable to neoclassical norms, commentators have for many years made an immense effort to uncover the subject and, even more, the 'unity' in these poems.[56] More recently, greater sophistication in understanding the principles underlying imitation and composition seems to have resulted in a widespread acceptance of the vigour and inventiveness of mixed-genre compositions, and, as I suggested tentatively when considering Donne's poems, a concept such as 'coherence' might be considered more helpful than the loaded term 'unity'.[57] Of this more later; but with *Lycidas* in any event we are dealing with a pastoral, and, as Earl Miner pithily put it, 'the pastoral is no single thing'. *Lycidas*, in its variety, density, and comprehensiveness, is in some respects more of an anthology than the volume it concludes: it collects, assimilates, orders, translates, modifies, subverts, transcends the traditions from and against which it emerges.[58] The poem is massively resistant to over-simplification, and seems to derive much of its vitality from opposition, contradiction, paradox, multivalency, and a combination of obliquity and plainness.[59] It is worth remembering, for example, that the most obvious formal

---

[55] See the analogues cited in the *Variorum Commentary* or in C. Hunt, *Lycidas and the Italian Critics*, ed. I. Samuel (New Haven, 1979): see also W. Kirkconnell, *Awake the Courteous Echo* (Toronto, 1973), 79–245, and E. Z. Lambert, *Placing Sorrow: A Study of the Pastoral Elegy Convention from Theocritus to Milton* (Chapel Hill, 1976), *passim*.

[56] For a dense account, see Pigman, *Grief and English Renaissance Elegy*, 110–11. For a comparison of Donne and Milton, see Z. Pollock, ' "The Object, and the Wit": The Smell of Donne's *First Anniversary*', *ELR* 13 (1983), 301–18.

[57] See above, Ch. 4.

[58] Earl Miner, 'Milton and the Histories', in Sharpe and Zwicker, *The Politics of Discourse*, 181–203, esp. 192: Miner refers to the 'ordonnance of multiple schemes' in Milton's text (191), and employs the concept of coherence (192). See also W. Iser, 'Spenser's Arcadia', in P. Steiner *et al.*, eds., *The Structure of the Literary Process*, (Amsterdam and Philadelphia, 1982), 211–41.

[59] For a succinct account of pastoral assimilation and comprehensiveness, with particular reference to the pastoral elegy, see Wittreich, *Visionary Poetics*, 120–1. See also Hunt's remarks on the history of ancient and Renaissance literary theory on the subject, which reinforces the notion that the pastoral resists narrow definition (*Lycidas and the Italian Critics*, 32–4), also J. Hollander, *The Figure of Echo*, esp. 127–8.

deviations, such as the self-proclaimed digression (113–31, which itself echoes Spenser's *Maye* Eclogue), are the moments of most undisguised directness, the points of most unambiguous contact with the world from which the text sprang and which it trenchantly addresses.

Milton's decision to compose and publish a pastoral elegy represented a manifest and public repudiation of metaphysical tradition. He distanced himself aesthetically, and therefore politically and theologically, from the wit and confidence of the followers of Donne and Jonson, whose elegies tend to focus on the discovery by the speaker of the point or meaning of an individual death through a turn of wit, the display of ingenuity.[60] It is, however, worth noting that the pastoral elegy was, though admittedly rare, not quite extinct in the 1630s, as many commentators seem anxious to imply.[61] It is clear that Milton looked beyond the Arcadian court pastoral of his own day to the Spenserians, making what Norbrook calls 'a decisive and unambiguous commitment to the Spenserian tradition'.[62] He also looked further, to the great model of Spenser, and beyond him to the ancient writers of pastoral: in doing so, he invoked, as Spenser had before him, the Virgilian precedent of the epic poet's career founded on a pastoral début.[63]

It has become commonplace in recent years to dwell on Milton's indebtedness to Virgil's Tenth Eclogue, a text whose amatory subject was normally glossed by Renaissance commentators as having an important political component.[64] Like Edward King,

[60] One example (exactly contemporary with *Lycidas*) must stand for many. Lovelace's poem in the Oxford anthology mourning Princess Katherine (1638), writes of an early Christian martyr thus: 'Oh how he hast'ned death, burn't to be fryed, | Kill'd twice with each delay, 'till deified' ('An Elegie: *Princesse* KATHERINE *borne, christened, buried in one day*', *The Poems of Richard Lovelace*, ed. C. H. Wilkinson (Oxford, 1930), 30). See also G. T. Dime, 'The Difference Between "Strong Lines" and "Metaphysical Poetry"', *SEL* 26 (1986), 47–57.

[61] There is even a pastoral lament for Jonson, by Falkland, in *Jonsonus virbius* (Jonson, *Works*, xi. 430–7); for a useful list of pastoral elegies in this period, which supplements those habitually cited in studies of the genre, see Pigman, *Grief and English Renaissance Elegy*, 159–60.

[62] Norbrook, *Poetry and Politics*, 269.

[63] Helgerson, *Self-Crowned Laureates*, passim; J. Loewenstein, *Responsive Readings: Versions of Echo in Pastoral, Epic, and the Jonsonian Masque* (New Haven, 1984), 83.

[64] See J. M. Evans, 'Lycidas, Daphnis, and Gallus', in Carey, ed., *English Renaissance Studies*, 228–44; Norbrook, *Poetry and Politics*, 273 and Pigman, *Grief and English Renaissance Elegy*, 111–16. An important recent study of the tradition of Virgil criticism is A. Patterson, *Pastoral and Ideology* (Oxford, 1988); especially germane to the present study are the first two chapters on Petrarch and on Renaissance humanism (19–132); of

Virgil's Gallus was a real individual; both men were admired as poets.[65] Unlike Gallus (at the time Virgil wrote about him), Lycidas is dead; what is more, he is figured as having spurned the temptations held out by the promise of political and sexual favour.[66] As such, like the Lady in *Comus*, he stands opposed to the values of the court, and his choice of an academic life is by implication exalted as an example. The death of Edward King was not in itself a public subject; it was Milton's treatment that made it so, most directly in the 1645 text with its headnote, which informs the reader that 'In this monody the author bewails a learned friend, unfortunately drowned in his passage from Chester on the Irish Seas, 1637. And by occasion foretells the ruin of our corrupted clergy then in their height.'[67] The poem had originally been composed at what seems to have been a personal time of crisis for Milton, when the choice of career was far from obvious, and when the working out of what it might mean to be a 'pastor'—a shepherd-poet, a priest, a prophet—was unclear. Just as King himself had been a poet as well as a priest, and Milton's voices and surrogates in the poem are numerous, so the text's audience was

particular relevance at this point is her observation about the 'leap in "translation" accomplished by Petrarch—the recognition that the theme of love in Virgil, which Virgil himself had represented, through Corydon and Gallus, as at best solipsistic and at worst self-destructive, could itself be redeemed by *translatio*, . . . by transforming sexual love into a metaphor for something beyond itself without abandoning the literal fact' (49). An important study of Petrarch's reading of Virgil, and its wide-ranging implications, is Greene's *The Light in Troy*, 85–90, 112–23.

[65] In his treatment of the sorrows of a fellow poet who was prominent in war and politics, Virgil deliberately echoes Theocritus's *Idyll*, 1, in which the poet laments the mythical Daphnis; he also makes use (*Eclogues*, 10. 31–6) of a contrast between actual sorrows and Arcadian happiness which Milton accommodates to the interactions between the real and the fictitious in *Lycidas* (see *Variorum Commentary*, 554, and A. S. P. Woodhouse, 'Milton's Pastoral Monodies', in M. E. White, ed., *Studies in Honour of Gilbert Norwood* (Toronto, 1952), 264, 274). Gallus is praised as a poet in Virgil's *Eclogues*, 6. 64–73, and cited as a distinguished elegist by Quintilian (10. 1. 93) and by Ovid (*Tristia*, 4. 10. 53). His prominent political career ended in disgrace and suicide in Egypt. See Rosenmeyer, *The Green Cabinet*, 116–17.

[66] Evans, 'Lycidas, Daphnis, and Gallus', 242–4.

[67] J. Carey, ed., *Milton: Complete Shorter Poems* (1968), 239: all refs. will be to his text. The relation of Milton's poem to the general political circumstances, and to the particular constraints of censorship and suppression, have been well documented in recent years; see e.g. Brown's account of Milton and the 'problems of address' (*Milton's Aristocratic Entertainments*, 156–8), and Norbrook's fuller study of the way 'Ecclesiastical reaction seemed to be in danger of stifling Protestant prophecy' (*Poetry and Politics*, 275–7). For a stimulating and wide-ranging account, see the chapter 'Prynne's Ears; or, The Hermeneutics of Censorship', in Patterson's *Censorship and Interpretation*, 44–119.

correspondingly diverse, ranging from the company of fellow poets in the volume through the reform-minded scholars of Cambridge to the nation in general. Cedric Brown observed that in *Lycidas* Milton 'reminded his audience of the best role of a godly educational community, training shepherds for Britain . . . '.[68]

And the occasion is explicitly related to a general crisis in the state in the central episode, St Peter's speech:

> How well could I have spared for thee, young swain,
> Enow of such as for their bellies' sake,
> Creep and intrude, and climb into the fold?
> Of other care they little reckoning make,
> Than how to scramble at the shearer's feast,
> And shove away the worthy bidden guest;
> Blind mouths! that scarce themselves know how to hold
> A sheep-hook, or have learned aught else the least
> That to the faithful herdman's art belongs!
> What recks it them? What need they? They are sped;
> And when they list, their lean and flashy songs
> Grate on their scrannel pipes of wretched straw,
> Their hungry sheep look up, and are not fed,
> But swol'n with wind, and the rank mist they draw,
> Rot inwardly, and foul contagion spread;
> Besides what the grim wolf with privy paw
> Daily devours apace, and nothing said,
> But that two-handed engine at the door,
> Stands ready to smite once, and smite no more.   (113–31)

The contrast between the teaching of pastors like Lycidas, who nourish and feed their flocks, and the 'lean and flashy songs' of the ignorant and greedy time-servers who have outlived him, is couched in familiar Spenserian terms, and recalls the language of several of the Prince Henry elegies.[69] The digression is, from one perspective, the heart of the poem, addressing as it does a spiritual crisis in the nation; King's death becomes an omen, an event whose meaning is much larger than the exemplary demise of a virtuous individual.[70] Many commentators have seen the 'two-handed engine' (130–1) as the double-edged sword (from Revelation 1.

---

[68] *Milton's Aristocratic Entertainments*, 157; Brown writes movingly (168) of the 'anguish' that informs the piece.

[69] See above, pp. 135–7, and Norbrook, *Poetry and Politics*, 278.

[70] See C. Brown, 'The Death of Righteous Men: Prophetic Gesture in Vaughan's Daphnis and Milton's Lycidas', *George Herbert Journal*, 7 (1983–4), 1–24.

16; 19. 15), which was an image of the word of Christ in terms of retribution and reform.[71] The mass of commentary on the passage over the centuries demonstrates the image's indeterminacy, which made it in some sense especially truthful or prophetic, and in addition rendered it finally invulnerable to censorship, a subject much on Milton's mind. Norbrook notes that 'At the time he wrote *Lycidas* Milton had been doing some research into Papal censorship of [Dante's] *De Monarchia* . . . such censorship, he believed, was ineffectual . . . the prophetic voices of preaching and poetry could never be completely silenced. Retribution, says St Peter, stands "at the door" '.[72] The fulfilment of the prophecy was taken out of the poet's hands and placed in the hand of God. The working out of providence would ultimately resolve the ambiguities in the text; history would gloss the passage, would show where righteousness lay. And political developments in the years between 1637 and 1645 could have given Milton the confidence to make his assault on the episcopacy less indirect (as he did by providing the headnote), to argue that the tide of events was moving in a divinely ordained direction towards a victory for reform, and to assume a more unequivocally prophetic role.[73]

The evident and self-proclaimed musicality of *Lycidas* ('Begin, and somewhat loudly sweep the string' (17) . . . 'Thus sang the uncouth swain' (186)) is, like so much else in the piece, a mixture of the backward-looking and the contemporary. At the simplest level, the deployment of obviously musical devices such as repetition, echo, and imitation recall in general terms the 'sung' quality of the ancient pastoral elegy or dirge, and hint at the use by ancient authors of the refrain. They also, naturally, recall the native pastoral tradition deriving from Spenser and Sidney. In addition Donne's use of musical devices to structure the *Anniversaries*

---

[71] For a lengthy summary of glosses of this passage, see the *Variorum Commentary*, 686–706.

[72] *Poetry and Politics*, 279. Norbrook cites Milton's 'Commonplace Book' (*Prose Works*, i. 438). Three or four years later, Milton quoted approvingly an important passage from Bacon's *A Wise and Moderate Discourse* (1641). The entry reads: 'prohibition of books not the wisest cours. "When ideas are punished, power blazes forth." and indeed wee ever see that the forbidden writing is thought to be a certain spark of truth that flyeth up in the faces of them that seek to chok and tread it out, whereas a book authorized is thought to be but the language of the time.' (*Prose Works*, i. 450–1).

[73] See Brown, *Milton's Aristocratic Entertainments*, 168.

should be borne in mind.[74] Traditionally, elegists have, as we have seen, investigated the idea of harmony (with its implications for identifying purpose or meaning in the death of the subject) through these musical devices, and many poets have represented consolation through a formal, musical resolution of the speaker's grief: the altered refrain in the *consolatio* of Spenser's *Nouember* is an obvious example.[75] It has been argued that in *Lycidas*, for instance, the opening sequence constitutes an 'eroded sonnet' in contrast with the final eight lines, 'a perfect concluding stanza of *ottava rima*, a stanza that accepts the daily movements of time and reaches out with hope toward another day'.[76] Thus the opening sequence, with its suggestions of disruption and precipitateness ('I come to pluck your berries harsh and crude, | And with forced fingers rude, | Shatter your leaves before the mellowing year' (3–5)) concludes with a self-referential call for a smoother, more consolatory elegy— (a call finally to be answered by lines 186–93):

> Who would not sing for Lycidas? he knew
> Himself to sing, and build the lofty rhyme.
> He must not float upon his watery bier
> Unwept, and welter to the parching wind,
> Without the meed of some melodious tear.   (10–14)

And however clear Milton's indebtedness to English and classical traditions, the art of his 'polemically intended reformist poem' is closest to that of Italian forms such as the *canzone*.[77] Students of the rhyme scheme and structure of *Lycidas* have generally been drawn to music, particularly the music of the early baroque period, to provide an aesthetic context for Milton's experiment and variety, seeing Milton as constantly creating formal expectations in the reader, only to frustrate them—until the last moments of the poem, where the swain 'touched the tender stops of various quills' (188).[78]

[74] Not only in the suggestions of repetition in the opening of the piece ('Yet once more' (1)), but also in the use of the speaker's cries to mark off portions of the text, as e.g. 'Ay me', at ll. 56 and 154, 'Ah' at 107, 'O' at 37, 'Alas' at 64.

[75] See above, p. 36.

[76] L. L. Martz, *Poet of Exile* (New Haven, 1980), 74.

[77] The phrase is that of Brown, *Milton's Aristocratic Entertainments*, 158. As John Carey observes, 'Though the structure of *Lycidas* cannot be exactly paralleled in Italian Literature, it is clearly an extension of M's experimentation with Italian verse forms in *Time* and *Solemn Music*' (*Complete Shorter Poems*, 233–4). See also Hunt, *Lycidas and the Italian Critics*, 19–20, 63–87.

[78] See F. T. Prince, *The Italian Element in Milton's Verse* (Oxford, 1954), 71–88;

Mannerist and baroque aesthetics are invoked in many attempts, most obviously those based on numerological principles, to come to terms with the structure, form, and meaning of the text.[79]

What is perfectly evident is that, in the most narrowly formal sense, Milton spurned the dominant verse form, the decasyllabic couplet, which had been rapidly developing into an explicitly political device, whose self-advertising balance, proportion, harmony, and inevitability made it the ideal medium of Augustan certainties. Suckling, for example, prescribed that a laureate muse should be easy and free.[80] Milton is neither in *Lycidas*. The poem, written under political constraints, is also deliberately difficult. Many pastoral writers have expressed concern that their writings should not be regarded as trivial and purely recreational; in the Proem to Book II of *The Faerie Queene* Spenser distinguishes his own writing ('matter of just memorie') from trivial works, 'th' aboundance of an idle braine . . . painted forgerie'. Milton takes pains to load his text with material that stretches its implications beyond the immediate. At the most detailed level, Milton frequently plays with the latent etymological sense of words (thus, as many commentators have noted, the Laudian 'blind mouths' (119) are perversions of the role of pastor (one who feeds) and bishop (one who sees)); and he loads his text with puns, as when Camus 'footing slow' plays on the literal sense of 'pedantic'. Similarly, the text frequently glances at itself, using conventional terms for poems (tears, leaves, flowers) and referring to its own structure (as at line 21, where 'And as he passes turn', invokes the etymology of 'verse', or at lines 87, 188, etc.); there are in addition dense layers of allusion, often illuminated by

Wittreich's important chapter on 'The Art of Lycidas' in *Visionary Poetics*, 153–84 (esp. pp. 167–84); Norbrook, *Poetry and Politics*, 270–1, 283. For general accounts of Milton and music, see M. H. Frank, 'Milton's Knowledge of Music: Some Speculation', in *Milton and the Art of Sacred Song*, ed. J. M. Patrick and R. H. Sundell (Madison, 1979), 83–98; P. le Huray, 'The fair musick that all creatures made', in C. A. Patrides and R. B. Waddington, eds., *The Age of Milton: Backgrounds to Seventeenth-Century Literature* (Manchester, 1980), 241–72. For an account of the implications of Milton's defining the poem as a monody, see C. Hunt, *Lycidas and the Italian Critics*, 159–70, 191–2.

[79] Fowler, '"To shepherd's ear": The form of Milton's *Lycidas*', in his *Silent Poetry*, 170–84; Fowler also argues that a numerical scheme may be perceived in the overall design of the *Iusta Edouardo King* volume as a whole (nn. 6, 22, pp. 181, 183).

[80] From Suckling's remarks about Carew in his 'The Wits' (or 'A Sessions of the Poets'): 'His Muse was hard bound, and th'issue of's brain | Was seldom brought forth but with trouble and pain. | And | All that were present there did agree. | A Laureats Muse should be easie and free (35–9): (*The Works of Sir John Suckling: The Non-Dramatic Works*, ed. T. Clayton (Oxford, 1971), 73).

a single word (such as the Spenserian 'daffadillies' (150)) or phrase (such as 'Who would not sing for Lycidas' (10), which recalls 'neget quis carmina Gallo?' of Virgil's *Eclogues* 10. 3). The sheer variety of verse in *Lycidas* may at one level be designed to show, in David Norbrook's words, that 'life and death constantly evade harmonious patterns'.[81] But in addition, the stress on variety and diversity in the text, and its own encyclopaedic nature, suggest that there exist harmonies and patterns which are not discernible by everyone. Therein exists one of the chief consolatory strategies of the text. The pain and grief of death are not argued away; they are allowed to remain alongside confident faith in the order and symmetry of God's purpose.[82] Those whose discourse is 'lean and flashy' could hardly be expected to apprehend the fullness of *Lycidas*. Milton creates his reader, his fit audience, by posing challenges. Compendiousness was, to some Renaissance theorists, axiomatically more worthy than simplicity or singleness: Tasso, for instance, remarked that 'as among composite bodies the perfect are those that intermingle and temper all qualities, so among fables the most composite are best'.[83] And in such texts, the act of reading what Spenser calls 'signes . . . set in sundry place' is both morally beneficial and implicitly heroic.[84] As Brown observed of Milton's creation of an ideal readership, *Lycidas* 'seems to ask the reader to become partisan'.[85]

---

[81] *Poetry and Politics*, 272.

[82] Pigman, writing generally about Milton's elegies, both Latin and English, remarks that 'Feelings of loss are allowed to coexist with confidence that the dead are in heaven . . . for Milton, there is no conflict between mourning and faith; his elegies show almost no struggle to overcome grief' (*Grief and English Renaissance Elegy*, 109).

[83] Tasso, *Discourses on the Heroic Poem*, tr. by M. Cavalchini and I. Samuel (Oxford, 1973), 205.

[84] Belphoebe makes explicit an equivalence between the conventionally heroic career of the knight errant and the labours of a serious and diligent reader: 'Abroad in armes, at home in studious kinde, | Who seekes with painefull toile, shall honor soonest finde' (*FQ* II. iii. 40). Tasso, at the opening of Book II of his *Discourses*, makes a similar point: 'Of all the activities of human reason, . . . none is harder, none more praiseworthy than intellectual choice . . . choosing is proper to man, who takes counsel with himself, and choosing well is most proper to the prudent man. Still, the less certainty in the things chosen, the greater the prudence shown in making choices. But what is more uncertain, what more variable, what more inconstant than the material [of poetry]? Supremely prudent he must therefore be who would not go wrong in choosing where there is so much variability and uncertainty in the things involved' (ed. cit. 21).

[85] *Milton's Aristocratic Entertainments*, 164. See also M. A. Caws, *The Eye in the Text: Essays in Perception, Mannerist to Modern* (Princeton, 1981), and, for a consideration of similar ideas in a dramatic context, D. Kay, ' "To hear the rest untold": Shakespeare's Postponed Endings', *RQ* 37 (1984), 207–27.

The self-consciousness of the poem permits the poet to place himself and his readers in a superior position in relation to the tradition. There are points, for instance, at which he appears to draw attention to the artificiality of its conventions: thus the 'pathetic fallacy' section ('But O the heavy change, now thou art gone . . . ' (37–48)) is capped with a distancing summary, 'Such, Lycidas, thy loss to shepherd's ear' (49). Pigman observes that the speaker 'is not so naïve as not to see through the pathetic fallacy'.[86] Questioning of 'pastoral efficacy' was itself part of the tradition Milton took from Virgil.[87] His performance also owes something to that of Sidney's Agelastus, who constantly 'explains' the natural phenomena which give rise to assertions that nature is reversed, showing, for example, that the earth is black not because it has been transformed out of respect for Basilius but because great flights of ravens swarm upon it.[88] Such strategies do not lead, however, to a rejection of the tradition: even from the simply consolatory point of view, the fiction of scattering flowers or elegies or tears on the grave of someone who died at sea and had no bier or tomb, may be thought to 'interpose a little ease' (152).

Of course Milton's great prophetic elegy has, as will have been apparent from its first publication, much wider implications than its immediate occasion. I hope it will be evident even from these brief observations that *Lycidas* draws much of its remarkable force from the native elegiac traditions, deriving in different measure from Spenser, Sidney, and Donne, in which it triumphantly participates. Yet Milton's performance was the reverse of nostalgic. The 'fresh woods, and pastures new' of the final line proclaim the forward-looking radicalism of the still obscure poet, the 'uncouth swain', who has claimed for himself the roles of poet and prophet, pedagogue and epic poet, to a nation in urgent need of his guidance.

When Wordsworth was an undergraduate at Cambridge, the Master of St John's died, and the coffin was brought into Hall to be decorated, according to custom, with 'copies of verses English or Latin'. The poet later recalled that his uncle (visiting Cambridge at the time):

---

[86] *Grief and English Renaissance Elegy*, 112.
[87] See S. Fish, '*Lycidas*: A Poem Finally Anonymous', *Glyph*, 8 (1981), 1–18, esp. p. 7.
[88] See above, p. 42.

seemed mortified when upon enquiring he learnt that none of these verses were from my pen, 'because', said he, 'it would have been a fair opportunity for distinguishing yourself'. I did not, however, regret that I had been silent on this occasion, as I felt no interest in the deceased person, with whom I had had no intercourse and whom I had never seen but during his walks in the College grounds.[89]

This anecdote shows Wordsworth and his uncle standing on opposite sides of the chasm that separates us from the culture of Spenser, Donne, and Milton. And the double sense latent in Wordsworth's uncle's words—a fair opportunity for distinguishing yourself—make them a fitting summary of what the elegy had come to mean not merely for Milton in *Lycidas* but also for countless writers in the period covered by this book, a combination of display and introspection, of public statement and self-examination. As Coleridge put in his *Table Talk*: 'Elegy is the form of poetry natural to the reflective mind. It *may* treat of any subject, but it must treat of no subject *for itself*; but always and exclusively with reference to the poet himself'.[90]

[89] Christopher Wordsworth, *Memoirs of William Wordsworth, Poet-Laureate, DCL*, 2 vols. (1851), i. 13–14; see John Buxton, *Sir Philip Sidney and the English Renaissance*, 25–6.

[90] *Specimens of the Table Talk of Samuel Taylor Coleridge*, ed. H. N. Coleridge, 2 vols. (1835), entry for 23 Oct. 1833.

APPENDIX A

'Cestria Lugens': A Collection of epitaphs and elegies on Prince Henry by one 'G. B.', (from Bodley MS Rawl. Poet. 116, fos. 1–16)

[fo. 1]

Cestria Lugens

Mira cano Sol occubuit, Nox nulla secuta est

[*in a different hand*]

Verses & Epitaphes on ye death of prince Henry

[fo. 1^v *blank*]

[fo. 2^r]

Thinke it not strange y^t here Prince Henry ded
Breaths out his seconde life though Spoyled of breath
Dead things have life; to him Imortall bred
Death bringeth life, whose life was lingering death.

Alias.

I cannot saie that here Prince Henry Sleepes
Whom great Eternity hath from vs reft
or figure out the Region where he keepes
But sure his harte behinde him he hath left
as sacred pledge of his eternall loue
To parents Kingdoms signed from aboue

Alias,

Conuert to teares thy Ink, to Sighes thy Pen,
Striue not in wordes to wayle this Prince of men
Thy Muse could play her prize could verses rayse him
Oh therefore feede on Sorrowes, cease to prayse him

ffathers Comforte Mothers bliss
Brothers findinge, Sisters miss
Brittayns loss here buri'de is

Alias

The map of Empire & the Tipe of woe
Belou'd of God, & all men but gods foe

Prince Henry here lies under grounde full lowe
Mirror wherein kings may theire glories knowe.

Alias,
Foe vnto none, but to the foes of god
Beloud of god, and all men, but gods foes
Loe vnder couert of this withered clod
this *Prince of Brittaine* god doth here dyspose.

[fo. 2ᵛ]

Alias.
Of Henryes death I knowe not which may boste
For though that heauen have gaind what earth hath not
the earth againe enioyes what heau'n hath not
But wheather heau'n or earth have gotten most
Brittaine I know a Peerles Prince hath lost
of cruell death the spoile, & natures upshot

Alias,
Great Prince if worde a Tombe to thee could frame
perhaps with others I could make thee one
But loe I buyld it to thy Sacred name
In thy eternall Soule in steed of stone
which still shall waile & neuer thinke of mirth
till it have left her dwellinge base on earth.

His Countrys Atlas, Terror to his foes
Pieties shielde, Ascanius of estate
Creations Sphery globe; his Brittaines Rose
The Conqueror of death, & niggard Fate
his Spirit imortall entred heauens Gate
here for a tyme his Body doth repose.

Alias.
If you demaunde whose is this monument
Tis vertues Tombe, boute which yᵉ graces daunce
with warlike Brittaines damaske Roses sprent
and with the goulden lillies, crownde of fraunce

[fo. 3ʳ]

Alias
Here lies within this maestfull Monument
of present age, the pretious ornament

To futur Princes, Tymes a mirror bright
Henry saunce Peere, great Brittaines lost delight

Alias

There is a Lymit Periodicall
of life fordoomd by God to Creatures all
which none can shun else had this Princele Gemͤe
Liv'd t'haue enricht the Brittish diadem
Since nothinge therefore is more sure then death
who wold relye his hopes on smoaky breath.

Alias

If thou aske who lyeth here
it is neither Monke nor freere
knight nor Baron, Prince or earle
but the worlds unualu'de Pearle
which could not be bought for gould
yet dissolued in this moulde

Alias

Muses wonder
Battayles Thunder
Rent in Sunder
Heere lyes under

[fo. 3ᵛ *blank*]

[fo. 4ʳ]

Cestria Lugens

or

Epitaphs Elegiacal Sacred
to the lyuinge memory of her
deceased Earle, the late
High, & mightie,
Henry Prince of wales, Duke
of Cornwale, & Earle
of Chester &c.

Written by G.B. an vnworthie
apprentice in the profounde
misteries of Sprightly
Poesy

Whoe in generous sorowe, to the
noble eies of learninge,
& honor, & to no other,
presenteth this his
  weeping Reme =
mbrances.

[fo. 4^v]

  To the everlasting memory of Prince Henry &c.

Though not a Maro, yet as somtyme hee
of dead Marcellus youthfull hope did singe
Soe I of thine, Sonne to the greatest kinge
that euer yet swayde warlike Brittañnye

And for my plaints on broken numbers run
Such as ill seeme the Helicon of Arte
yet since they springe from a distracted harte
bred in the north, far from ye Southern Suñ

Admitt them enteruene amongst those many
which geue thee life in their immortal layes
They are as full of louing greefe as any
though not so powrefull bodies dead to rayse
The kyte noe falcon is, yet towres the skye
Maro marcellus wayles, Prince Henry I.

  To the honorable Sonnes of Appollo
  & Pallas & to no other.

I dare not pass these sorrowes to the press
for feare the inquisition merciless
of Curious Censure, censure me vnfit
the moderne eye of learning & of witt
Yet for in pietie your worthy hartes
haue borne for Henrys loss of woe yor partes
And y^t I doubt not but in gentle gree
you will accepte, these tymeles births from me

[fo. 5^r]

On dead Prince Henries Altars loe I bynde
these sad oblations of a troubled mynde
as sacrifizd to his vnhappie fate
You are the Priests y^t must them consecrate

Ad criticos.

Haud Italso, ego, sublimiores
Hispanos, gallosque, superbiores,
Nec imitor Anglos vberiores
Atqui plane Planus, hosce dolores
Lugentes, Lugeo, inter olores,
Haud Criticorum metuens Colores.

Englished thus.

The stately Tuskan I will imitate,
the lofty French, or proud Hiberian,
Nor flowing English, ripned much of late,
But plainly as a grieud plaindealing man,
Powre forth these plaints although no singing Swan,
Nor do I dread the Criticks spotted hate.

[fo. 5ᵛ]

Cestria Lugens   Muses wonder
Epitaphe. 1.

Schollers cast away yoʳ bookes Soldiers no more let Armes awake you
Courtes, Contreys, States, vaile yoʳ high lookes, ladies to rufull teares
    betake you
The calme alas of peacefull Arts, of dreary war yᵉ hoped Thunder
Commander of great Brittains harts; of bounty, youth, & love yᵉ wonder

Henry our Prince Prince best belou'd; earths heauy loss heauens delight.
from earth to heauen is remov'd through cruell fortune deaths despight,
There rest swete Prince wᵗ glory crown'd, ladies to rufull teares betake
    you,
Arts, Spirits, harts, yoʳ selues confounde, Soldieʳˢ no more let Armes
awake you

Epitaph. 3.

As full of vertues as of Royall bloud
of our newe Monarch Rose first Springinge Bud
Though not of worlds, a Conqueror of harts
Lyes here diuided into many partes.

Scotlande his birth, his manhood England claymes
His body Brittaine great maym'd with his maymes
Heauen his Soule, sterne fate his youthfull prime
His death the present & succeedinge Tyme.

His memory the worlde, his graces fame
And his victorious Grandsires his great name

Amongst whom sleepe; & daigne thy heauy herse
Some bottom nooke for this abortive verse
Tymeless begott, twixte greefe & wofull payne
else had it songe thy prayse in higher strayne.

[fo. 6^r]

Epitaph. 4.

Tyme thou nere iniur'dst Monarchy till nowe
In breakinge many an honorable vowe
To princely Henry made, but Tyme since thou
and death have thus of hope vncrowned his browe
The fates haue vow'd, despeight of death & thee
Hencefurth great Brittaines Geme he shalbe

Epitaph. 6.

Thou trauayler from whence so ere thou come
Aproch with Reuerence this sacred vrne
Which doth containe a farr more pretious gom
Than euer did in Egiptes Memphis burne
Nowe if thou arte desirous for to knowe
The matter whence this Soueraigne substance springs
It only doth in Brittaines Bowells growe
Dust from ye dust of many mightie kings
If more? behoulde it is a Phaenix nest
Wherein alone the only Phaenix fyres,
Breathinge his Balmy odours from the East
As far as Titans weary Carr retyres
It is the Bed of honor & of loue
Wherein interred lies the Sonne of Joue

[fo. 6^v]

Epitaph 7.

Never in Prince Had Subiectes greater store
Then of thy liuinge hopes Henrie Diuine
Sone of great Brittayne, while thy Sun did shyne
Oh hadst thou liu'd we wolde have wish't noe more
But since the fates thos hopes in sunder tore

Our harts we breake as Sacrifize to thine
And yelde our selues in willinge death to pine.
for thy wept death vnhappie we therefore
Nore we alone, but fforaigners deplore
Thy heauy loss, & their sad eares incline
To our laments, & theirs with ours combine
Boundinge their plaints, along our British shore
which meeting ours, we thus together singe
Tis tyme to die, since dead is Englands Springe

Epitaph 8.

Religious, Valiant, liberall, Just & wise
Death of all harts & deludge of all Eyes
Vntymeley dead here Princely Henry lies
And thus can death ore Kingdoms Tyrranise.

[fo. 7^r]

Epitaph. 9.

Within this weeping Niobe doth lie
The noble dust of Princelie Henries Bones
But not Prince Henry, whose perfections hye
Canot be clos'd w^thin a heape of stones.
for they with him to heauen vp are fled
as ouer good for this base Orbe of oures
where his great Spirit, though his body dead
pertakes the ioyes of Angells, Saincts, & Powers,
Where he attends in Triumph to fulfill
The Hest of Gods inuiolable will.

Epitaph. 8.

It is not true as men do saie
Dead & aliue, both on a daie
for tell me can that life decaie
which is opos'd to death allway?
Life of the Soule endureth aye
Though bodie dead be wrapt in claye
So part of man dies for a season
But not y^t parte endude with reason
So I confess good reason why
That here Prince Henries Corpes doth lye
But not Prince Henries Spirit high
which ever liues & canot dye

And though to duste his Body fall
In his great vertues liue he shall.

[fo. 7ᵛ]

Epitaph. 9.

Wonder not Reader at a Princes fall
vnder full loue, yᵗ here is layde deathes thrall
for had I bin as vicious as good
Nor death, or fate, as yet had suckt my blood
How god decrees why, whom, & when to call
Thou canst good frend noe reason geue at all

Epitaph. 10.

He that could loade his Canon Pike aduaunce
At Barries fire his sworde, at Tilt his Lawnce
Learne loue to Caper, & the Graces daunce

Discourse make use of learnîgs & of Armes
Councell of fforaigne and domestick Harmes
And wisely stop his eares at Circes charmes

Loe here Prince Henry youthfull though his yeres
Entombd within a cloude of sighes & teares,
Of lordly death, the frightfull standard beares.

Epitaph. 11.

In vayne the Macedon deaths triumphs spurnde
Earth must to earth & I to earth am turnde
A Prince as much, as he bewailde, & mornde.

[fo. 8ʳ]

Epitaph 12.

The fading Rose, which doth full quicklie waste
Or beawties flowre, yᵗ nips at euery blaste
Do not impale this monument of mine
In steed thereof the gnawing wormes do twine
Yet loe bespangled with the lights of heauen
& glittringe brightness of the Planetts Seauen

My vertues crownd, for euer fayrly shine
And I of earthly Scepters base bereauen
Immortalizd inioy a crowne diuine
By Gods aeternall finger artely cast
& he himself vpon my browes it plas't

Epitaph 13.

Further example seeke thou none
Of deaths spoile, then vnder this stone
Where lies a Prince of matchles fame
Great in his Parents great in name——
And when thou hast seene all thou can
thou canst but see the dust of man

or thus

Wherein a mightie Prince is laide
By spightfull fate & death betrayde.

[fo. 8ᵛ]

Epitaph. 14.

When after tymes shall in this marble Booke
Of mortall course yᵉ fatall stars orelooke
And therein see, what now I am & was
Ne sooner toucht but yᵗ to dust I pas

Oh let them then no greater trust repose
On humane hopes, then whilom were on myne
A Prince who young, & louely as the Rose
had set my Suñ before it furth did shine

For then when euery eye my youth admyrde
And euery ear attentiue heard my prayse
Before I knew of life the pathles wayes
Into this Cell of death I was retyrde
      Where I the shaking laborinth do treade
      Of black Corrupcõn, & of Lustiheade.

Epitaph. 15.

How happy Sleepes this Prince within his chest
Whose spotles youth, nere blemisht was with vice,
Who euer did earthes flattering ioyes detest,
And euer held his honor at high Price,
Vpon whose Tombe here writt w^t fam's brass Pen,
Mens generall loue to him, & his to men.

[fo. 9^r]

Epitaph 16.

I list not paint vpon my Tombe my fame
Suffice it Brittaine lost, death got the game.

Epitaph. 17.

And hast thou thus oh more than cruell death
Fetcht venom'd Ayres from darkest nooke in hell
To stop the passage of Prince Henries Breath?
What has thou got therby, death canst thou tell?
Prince Henry lives, thoug Seard his youthfull spring
his glory far Surmounts thy wastfull gaine
That at Joves foote, doth sit a crouned Kinge
Neglecting Earths designments, base & vayne
And peerlesse Prince since we thy loss sustaine
& that the heauens our heauy loss have founde
Wounded by thy dead woundes we will complaine
Of trustless death the loue to thee I bore
Henceforth of mirth, my muse shall sing no more

[fo. 9^v]

Epitaph. 18.

If with my teares it may not lawfull be
Dead Prince to water this wept herse of thine
In apprehendinge our great losse of thee
Oh let me weepe ore natiue England mine
That weeping vowes aeternally to pine.

ffor thou ye Hector wert of her new Troye
of Armes her Mars, her Mercury of State
of Emprey her Joue her Neptuns ioy
Phoebus & Phoebe on thy Eyebrowes sate
And now vntymely slayne by enuious fate.

The eies of Europe at thy hopefull sight
Blinded & dwelkt, stood gazing, ech at other
But dead alas, vnhappy, happy plight
Thou queath'st thos hopes to Princly Charles thy brother
Weepe Brittons weepe this loss exceeds all other

[fo. 10^r]

Epitaph. 19.

Admir'd of euery harte & eye
Mirror of Princes here am I
vntymely laide in graue full lowe
fortune & death wold have it soe
And if thou aske a reason why
Kings are but men & men must die
More of my death I may not showe
The cause thereof god best doth knowe.

Epitaph. 20.

This Doly monument doth here containe
More hopes then bin in Europe left againe
To nomber them a Poets labor were
nor could I, wold I, name them all I feare
Only here lies I dare reporte so much
A Prince the world, hath not another such
for fame, for name, for Parents, honors hye
Belou'd, admir'd, wayled, wept of every eye
What would you more? He was for Soveraingtee
More then a man, if more then man can be.

[fo. 10ᵛ]

Epitaph. 21.

Of my sad death striue not to finde yᵉ reason
Death neuer coms to men but out of season
& when he coms men clamor at his rage
Whether it be to Infancy, or age
When the starud wretch impartially doth strike
Beggers & Kings, the high & lowe alike
Only observe that god perhaps on me
Inflicts the woundes Brittayne ordainde for thee
& that on me the Punishments betyde
Of thy Ingratitude & careless Pride
And by my loss learne to take heede
The while thy neighboʳˢ wounds yet freshly bleed

Epitaph. 22.

Vaine are their ioyes in mortall things yᵗ trust
Or seate their hopes on brittle sand & Slyme
Which in ech aduerse tempest fall to Dust
Witnes this Prince dead in his youthfull prime
Nor can I title death herein vniust
Deaths but the Executioner of Tyme.

[fo. 11ʳ]

Epitaph. 23.

He was as fresh as is yᵉ Rose in May
    Whie was he nipt the english say?
He was yᵉ pearly daysy of our Springe
    Now welladay yᵉ Scottish singe
Active he was, & younge, why did he dye?
    Oh hone oh hone the Irish Crie
And thus dead Prince thy loss they all complaine
    Oh could they geue thee life againe
But heauy case since twill noe better be
    they offer vp theire vowes to thee
And in their loues, buyld unto thee a Tombe
    more durable then brass or Niobs wombe

Epitaph. 24.

A heauy spectacle for euery eye
Of Conscience pittie & humanity
A prince vntymely dead, lo here doth lye
The spoile of fortune & mortalitie
Henry his name, y^t name my Sences Charmes
Henry ye Prince of men, & Mars of Armes.

[fo. 11^v]

Epitaph. 25.

Deare Brittaine mine blinde not with teares thine eies
greater I am then earth cold euer make me
what if to dust my fading bodye flyes?
My Spirit liues and neuer will forsake thee
In all thy deedes of Rusty peace & war
Ile crowne thy browes w^t my eternall bayes
Ile be thy guyde & fyrd Idean Star
To light thy paths in forraigne home assaies
And though I neu^{er} did my armes aduance
In bloody field, yet name but Henry thine
and as fifth Henries was to conquerd Fraunce
So shall thy foes astonied stand at myne
I am not dead as Mortalls thinke I was
My spirit exchangd did but to heauen pass.

[fo. 12^r]

Epitaph. 26.

What we haue lost in Henrys loss
   no tonge can fully tell
for neuer yet so great a cross
   vnto the state befell
On him next to his father kinge
   Our Brittayne hopes relyde
He was the Primerose of our Springe
   & girlhand of our pride
About whos lamentable Herse
   the waylfull sisters nyne

Do tune in euerlastinge verse
    theire Elegies diuine
And while the skies uncessant weepe
    the Sun denyes to shine
The earth dame natures course to keepe
    & creatures all repine
Heroyick Spirits astounded sit
    the Comons howle & crie
The Surly Rocks for Sorow split
    & Sees in sunder flie
The elements deuided rent
    beasts, birds, & fishes droope
And with the winde of this event
    the lofty Cedars stoope
Nothing there is, but mournes, & lowres,
    only the heauens smyle
And haue in their Olympick bowres
    buylt him a strong Azile |

[fo. 12ᵛ]

Epitaph. 27.

Tyme, & sterne death late stroue wᶜʰ of them twoe
could through their Cheuisance most mischeif doe
Death vow'd to make the greatest harte to bleede
& tyme to wound yᵉ greatest state decreede
So furth they went. death in vnlucky stowre
his shaftes into Prince Henries brest let powre
Which blowe no soonᵉʳ tyme espied but hee
wounds half to death the Brittish Monarchye
whereat all seeing heauens wᵗ pitty mou'd
for Heavens this Prince, & Kingdom dearly lou'd
Exhale him vp vnto their Cristall Sphere
from deaths achiue; whence to his brother heyre
younge Springing Charles, this lyuing grace they geve
That drooping Brittaine in his hopes shall liue.
Since when agreeu'd Tyme in sickbed lyes,
And death in Tymes Agreuance lingering dies.

[fo. 13ʳ]

Epitaph. 28.

Princes that in my deaths perspectiue glass
May see afar, what now I am & was
A Sometyme springing Rose now withered gras
as myne be sure so shall your beawties pas
And while the awfull crowne your browes doth twyne
Learne you wᵗ me your spirits to refine
with lyuing vertues wᶜh foreuᵉʳ shine
Making the dead becom in them diuine
Ells litle boots the sworde of Rule <war> to weare
or in your hands the peacefull Scepter beare
Yf that by noble prowes, wisdom cleare
You brighten not the rest of Empire here.
The hatefull name of Nero lives defam'de
Better for him, it had been neuer nam'de

Epitaph. 29.

Loe here I finde within this lothsome graue
        Such ioyes as lyuing, I could neuer haue
Content of mynde, & peace deuoyde of strife
the blessed fruits of a well govᵉʳn'd life.

[fo. 13ᵛ]

Epitaph. 30.

Nor dead, nor lyuing, sleeping nor awake
Man & no man & yet of man partake
Dust, & no dust, but all of them am I
Prince & no Prince yᵗ here interred lye
Henry I was, and am the night & day
of Brittaines hopes; of life & death the waie
The welked sun yᵗ shineth in the darke
of tyme the Ruine, & of tyme yᵉ Arke
About whose Snaky Pinacles the fates
haue wreath'd deaths Trophaes ouᵉʳ kingdoms States
On Top whereof (the heauens so thought it fitt)
No Monarch I, aboue the Monarchs sitt.

Epitaph. 31.

Here vnder lies Prince Henry wrapt in lead
and yet Prince Henry liues, nor is he dead
dead & aliue how sauors y^t of Reason
his Spirit liues though body, sleepe a season
Nor do his vertuous hopes die in his graue
In his young brother Charles new life they haue

[fo. 14^r]

Epitaph. 32.

Behoulde the Prince of Princes, soe renown'd
Whilom on whom soe many Spirits depended
that here in claye full lowe laid vnder ground
Spoyl'd of his earthly trayne lies vnattended
Ay me y^t death should geue so fell a wound
As w^t ye blowe thereof of harts maks millions bleed
Where are the Crownets y^t his Temples bounde.
Whers now his manly lawnce & martiall steed?
To euerlasting rust they are decreed
And in theire place a Cipress bough & graue
And hungry wormes deuouringlie do feede
Vpon his noble bones, & body braue
Mourne Brittons morne, & steepe in teares your eies
Henry alas you^r Prince, here buried lies

[fo. 14^v]

Epitaph. 33.

Scarce was my spring w^t her fresh flowrs adornd
When seard, & dried for wante of feeding dewe
My mounting tree of life y^t Topless grew
By cruell death vntymly was oretornde
Weepe Brittaine weepe for thou hast cause to rewe
Full well the fates, my great designem^{nts} knewe
And I y^t at their threatning thunder spurnd
am with the shame thereof consumd & burnd

Brittaine for euermore, Armes, Arts adewe
Your teares sufficient haue you morn'de
Prince Henry doubles his farwell to you
My earthly woes to heauenly ioyes are turnde

Epitaph. 34.

Within this Tombe slaine by vntimely death
Vnto the Mayden Queene Elizabeth
The seconde hiere to James my Father King
Henry the first, first blossom of his spring
Loe here I lie a sometyme Prince of fame
great now in nothing, but my Princly name.

Loe here I lie a somtyme Prince esteem'd
great now in nothing but in which I seem'd

[fo. 15^r]

Epitaph. 34.

Now was ye tyme when winters wrath seem'd calme
& Tellus wombe grewe lauish of her balme
When euery little birde new cheerd could singe
Our winters now becom a seconde Springe
& Pallas sonns prepar'd in verse diuine
Paeans to singe to the Count Palatine
That now hath chang'd for Thams his fruitfull Rhyne
When heauy fate, I faint in spirit to tell
Death in a cloud more black then blackest hell
(for neu^{er} cloude so black mongst mortalls fell)
Embrac't Prince Henry, as hee did aduance
aboue the rest his foaming steed to Praunce
Chaunging ye gladsom Spring of our delight
into ye blasted winter of despight
Since when; there cease till from the Rauens winge
A Pen to thee, black as her selfe she flinge
To write withall———

[fo. 15ᵛ]

Conclusion

Thus though no Maro, yet an Ennius rude
Whose Browes in Castally were nere embrude
I do betake my heauy Muse to rest
Griefe will not let me write, Plaindealings best
My Sorowe is the guerdon I pursude
fforbeare my eies with teares to drench yᵉ chest
Of this great Prince on Earth in heauen blest

G.B.

[fo. 16ʳ]

Epigramma ad Jacobum Regem
& Carolum Principem

Manca diu, tandem perfecta Brittannia Membris
    Sub triplici Sceptro Magne Jacobe Nitens,
Nunc iterum Mortis, laethali vulnere Fixa
    Principis Henrici, Funere, Manca maneat.
Spes tamen alma tuis, licet imperfecta Salutis
    Germinat Auspiciis, Carole Die tuis.

[fo. 16ᵛ *blank*]

APPENDIX B

Four elegies by Edward Radcliffe:
A group of elegies from Oxford in the 1620s

Bodley MS Don. d. 58 is a folio volume dated 1647.[1] The compiler classified his material neatly within sections, and his uniformly tidy work suggests that the book was copied over a comparatively brief period.[2] Many pieces have Oxford connections, such as Corbett's attack on Price's *Anniversaries* (fo. 45), and the epitaphs on Prick of Christ Church (fo. 16ᵛ) and Jupp of Lincoln (fo. 17ʳ), while there are some more 'courtly' poems, such as 'When to her lute Corrinna sings' (fo. 36ᵛ) and laments for Queen Elizabeth and Queen Anne (fo. 15ʳ). In common with many other miscellanies of the period, this manuscript is notable for lack of interest in contemporary affairs, for a general air of nostalgia.[3] It has none of the frantic anti-Puritanism of more explicitly Royalist anthologies.[4]

The compiler included works, many of them occasional, by poets of the academic generation of King and Corbett and was generally sparing in his attributions. Yet four elegies are attributed to a hitherto unknown poet, Edward Radcliffe, whose work was evidently valued sufficiently still to be copied twenty years after composition.[5] His poems are reproduced here as an example of academic elegies at the end of the period covered by this study; their indebtedness to the traditions presented earlier will be evident.

Radcliffe, a Lancastrian, matriculated from University College 23 June 1621 (age 19), proceeding BA 1622 and MA in 1624.[6] It is not clear how, if at all, the poet was related to the many Radcliffes connected with the College in the seventeenth century. The first elegy, however, on Jonas Radcliffe, is subscribed 'Hec maerens posuit cognatus obseruantissimus' (fo. 3ᵛ), but this may be the scribe's speculation. Jonas Radcliffe was born in Todmorden, matriculated from University College 23 November 1592 (age 22), proceeding BA 1595, MA 1598 (when he became a Fellow), and BD 1615. His death is recorded on 27 August 1626 and his will was

---

[1] The title-page reads, 'Miscentur seria iocis. 1647. Elegies, Exequies, Epitaphes, Epigrams, Songs, Satires and other Poems'.

[2] The sections are: 'ffuneral Exequies Elegies and Epitaphes' (fos. 1–14ʳ); 'Epitaphes' (fos. 15ʳ; 19ᵛ): 'Songs' (fos. 21ʳ–30ᵛ); 'Epigrams' (fos. 31ʳ–40ʳ); 'Satires and poems of diuers subiects' (fos. 41ʳ–61ᵛ).

[3] See T. R. Davis, 'Materials for an Edition of the Poems of Thomas Randolph', B.Litt. thesis (Oxford, 1969), 30–1.

[4] See e.g. BL MSS Harley 1221 and 3511.

[5] D. C. Kay, 'A Univ. Poem of 1626', *University College Record* 7 (1976), 75–8.

[6] Foster, *Alumni Oxonienses* iii. 1227, notes a herald's visitation to Ratcliffe in Lancashire which reported that Edward, son of Robert Radcliffe, was aged 60 in 1664.

proved in November of the same year.[7] The personal details of the elegy are satisfyingly corroborated by a memorial tablet in the College ante-chapel; each mentions Radcliffe's disability and suggests that he was held back thereby from advancement, to the College's benefit (ll. 35–50).[8] After the second poem, on an unknown but evidently exemplary physician, comes an elegy on John Stanhope, son and heir of Philip Stanhope, 1st Earl of Chesterfield. He matriculated among a group of titled persons 11 November 1622 from Christ Church (with his brother Henry); he was buried at Shelford 27 July 1625.[9] The text of the elegy survives in two full-length versions, one that is wanting two lines, and a further fragment of eight lines.[10] The fourth of Radcliffe's poems is on the death of Sir Thomas Bamburgh, Bart., son of William Bamborough of Howsham (Yorks.), who was knighted in 1603 and created a Baronet in 1619. He died 18 July 1623 and was succeeded by his son (age 16) who died 3 June 1624 (the will dated 13 May was proved 4 October at York). He was in turn succeeded by his 11 year old brother who died unmarried in 1631, when the baronetcy became extinct. Radcliffe refers to himself as Bamborough's friend, but there is nothing to corroborate this.[11]

[fo. 3ʳ]

Vpon the death of Mr Jonas Radclyffe of Oxford.[12]

yett dost thou ever live to me; nor must
thy name soe soone be scattered wᵗʰ thy dust,
Thoughe hid, though vaulted: though my eye haue quite
lost the, my teares shall keepe the still in sight
Death well might plucke the hence, but though thou dye   5
itt cannot roote the from our memorye:
Oh lett itt not vnto our shame be said
that Radclyffe was soe soone forgott as dead!
They that soe soone can loose the, lett them bee
loosers of all good that they gott by the   10
When if wee iustlye weighe our cause to greiue
our teares wold longer last then thou didst liue.

---

[7] Details from Foster, *Alumni Oxonienses*, iii. 1228.

[8] The tablet has lost its arms since it was described in Anthony Wood, *The history and antiquities of the colleges and halls in the university of Oxford, publ. with a continuation to the present day by the ed., J. Gutch* (Oxford, 1786), 63. I am indebted to Mr A.D.M. Cox and Dr C.B.R. Pelling of University College for their generous assistance.

[9] Foster, *Alumni Oxonienses* iv. 1408; see also DNB.

[10] The other Bodley MSS are Ashmole 47, CCC 327, CCC 328, and Douce f 5.

[11] *Complete Baronetage*, i. 131.   [12] Line numbers are editorial.

O coldst thou dye? and are not wee withall
the sadd partakers in this funerall?
Is not our Colledge wounded? Dost not find   15
itt selfe (not meanely) in thy fate declind?
Thou that vpheldst itt wth a surer hand
and (though thy selfe vnable) madst itt stand.
Such was thy strickter course, such thy graue care
thy Judgement & thy knowledge alike rare: 20
What one amongst vs not to the in debt?
how many owe the all their goodnes yett
That can noe reason of their vertue giue
but their blest fortune vnder the to liue
Of whom even Tutors selues might learne to knowe   25
what heedye care vnto their chardge they owe
And not indulgent to the nobler breed
cherish their vice, by killing not the seed:
Thou wast alike to all: or if there were
any that felt thy temper lesse severe   30
Itt was their industrie their fauour wanne
not to the gentler, but the better mann
Thus all encourag'd were: since they cold tell
The way to meritt the, to merritt well:
Thus fortune in thy hurt to vs was kind,   35
that she soe longe wth in our walls confind
Itt was a providence that here she staid
lest if thou further, we had alsoe stray'd.

[fo. 3^{v}]

Thy weaknes was our prop, and who cold tell
but that thy staffe held vp the howse as well   40
as the; wch els p^{r}rchance had sunke downe quite
had not thy lamenes made itt stand vpright,
Noe more reproach to the, then Jacobs hault
wch was to him a blessing not a fault:
Gods voice itt was that warnd the goe not hence   45
that we might all reape by thy impotence
Till he sent for the to a place indeed
worth a remoue: for wch thou didst not need
A legge to carrye the: since he cold spare
An Angell for the, or Eliahs chaire   50

    Hec maerens posuit cognatus obseruantissimus: E.
Radclyffe

Vpon a good Phisitian:

Wert but a single death, or but one warse
borne to the graue, itt had not been of force
To haue caus'd a generall mourning? we might then
haue well compounded wth our griefe: and beene
lesse prodigall vpon one tombe, and kept   5
some teares instore new funeralls to haue wept:
But when Phisitians feele the envious knife
tis not a liues losse, but a losse of life
And when we mourne for them we mourne wth all
our owne healths ruine wch wth them does fall   10
Then he's a churle of's teares that now denies
the iust exhausture of his drye wept eyes,
Att this sadd worke of fate; that murthering the
hath causd noe death but a mortalitie:
Now wth more freedome may she vse her power   15
Vpon poore helplesse bodyes whose last howre
Soe often was p^rvented by thy skill
wherby deaths bounded rage did slowlier kill:
Thou wast none of that Patient tortureing brood
whose arte is best in letting purses blood   20
whose gripeing hands the Proverbe loaths as much
as lawyers or the hangmans stretching touch
That are soe farr from yeilding any ease
as their Extorcions doubles the disease

[fo. 4^r]

By their vnsavorye drugs excessive rate   25
bringing a poore consumption on his state
That can p^rlong a sicknes till they haue
left the poore mann quite naked fitt for's graue:
Then wth a demure countenance at last
can say he's none of this world, he's past   30
All hope of recouerye, when indeed tis they
haue made his substance past recouerye
And now they thinke that they may well deserue
in killing him that shold but liue to starve:
I doe but speake of these to sett out the   35
whose honest hand nere gript a thancklesse fee
Thou were a true Phisitian, coldst repaire
even wth thy speech a heart halfe broke wth care

Appollos both skills were well knowne to the
that wth his drugs imbracted poetry: 40
But phisicke in thy sickness lost her heart
because thy nature was aboue thy art
Uerses more gratefull wold not leaue the here
but stay to attend thy bodye on the beare.|

E. Radclyffe.

[fo. 7^r]

Vpon the death of Mr John Stanhope:

And hast thou left vs then (deare soule) must wee
comfort our eyes we were beholding the?
Woldst thou be soe much a proficient here
to learne to dye soe soone in thy first yeare?
woldst thou be thus a graduate to shine   5
in heauen already & there turne devine?
Such a degree whose luster quite defaces
all our silke hoods, and Academicke graces
Sure death mistooke the, measureing the a man
by thy soules ell, not by thy bodies spann: 10
hadst thou bene duller thou p^rchance mightst haue
gone but a slowe & foote pace to the graue:
The inke of fate had not bene stird! the skies
wold not so greedlye snatch so mean a prize
Thy quicknes kild the: ripenes was thy deathe   15
running to goodnes thou runne out of breathe.
How didst thou pitche beyond thy yeares! how sage!
how wise! how staid! how older then thy age!
what manly gravitie was knowne to house
more in thy smooth then others wrinkled browes,   20
ffar different from the common nobler sort
that here for fashion, onely come & sport:
To weare a gawdye gowne: and then wth ease
pervse the streets and learne the colledges:
Scrape some few ends of iests wherewith hereafter   25
to branch discourse & entertayne a laughter
That nere reacht further then the misticall
science of Tennis (and their spheare) a ball.

Or else to wield some fencers wooden toole
or sweate a nightcappe in the danceing schoole   30
To cracke a lute stringe, & such worthy arts,
in others complements, in great menn parts.
Thy studies were more serious as thy lookes
Whilst others bandied thou wast tossing bookes,
Busied in papers & collecting there   35
geṁs to sticke in thy mind not in thy eare.
Me thincks I see the yett close by thy selfe
reaching some choice booke, from thy furnisht shelfe

[fo. 7ᵛ]

loose the silke strings: and wᵗʰ a willing paine
to read, & thinke, and write, & read againe.   40
Thus didst thou spend thy lives short day till night
Deaths night ore tooke the & putt out thy light.
This sable curtaine was too soone ore spread
Thy day taskes done to bringe the to thy bedd.
Rest happy soule whose first night did beginne   45
in death: vndarkned wᵗʰ the night of sinne.

                                          E. Radclyffe.

Vpon the death of Sʳ Thomas Bamburghe Barronᵗ.

Adiewe blest soule! yett take my teares wᵗʰ thee
take my last sighes to beare the companie
Not to thy graue, but heauen; my griefe shall liue
iṁortall as thy sould: what this can giue.
What my distracted spiritt may now breath forth   5
to the deare memorie of thy deceased worthe
I giue, & wold my soule, wold heauen soe please:
Life is not life, when such are carkasses:
Behold our teares for our owne ruines shedd
ours is the funerall, wee the mourners dead   10
we are enterrd! and all this spacious roome
of earth, wᵗʰout the, seems a ghostlye tombe
Thy tombe the world! since itt may iustlye vaunt
itt holds the world richest in habitant
A coarse beyond some spiritts! happy stone   15
honored to bee those reliques mansion

whom that soule shall revisite when itt must
Resume these bones & reinspire that dust
Meane tyme our eyes haue lost the, & looke on
thy marble, & thy poore inscripcōn   20
That speakes our miserie, and onely showes
how iust our griefe is, how deserv'd our woes
When we read here soe gracious & soe good
was vanisht ere he well was vnderstood:
Scarce had he gone the twentith yeare his staye   25
was envy'd as to longe: he must awaye!
his vertue was his crime, itt was confest
he had deserv'd death, by deserveing best.
Why shold he liue to outshame the world? why shold
goodnes keepe house here & liue uncontrold: 30

[fo. 8^r]

As wth thy father whose heroicke minde
did hold vp worth yett, though itt were declind
Amongst whose best Acts, I doe number this
that to haue begott the for a future blisse:
To seed the world wth a greene pietie   35
when himselfe withered, who seem'd to dye
or leaue his losse behind him leaveing the
his vertues heire, his soules posteritie.
T'had beene the course of nature, t'had bene right
t'haue followed after in a hardier flight   40
And staid some yeares behinde, nor seated there
even iumpe wth him & striue to be ioynt heire,
Or if thou hadst condemn'd the world as vile
thou mightst haue liu'd for pittye yett a while
ffor thy friends sake? whose eyes but late suckt drye 45
in thy deare fathers mourned obsequie
Requir'd some respite for a fresh lament
our eyes are taskt now when their moystures spent:
Our sorrowes too much racke vs & inforce
(th'old debt vnpaid) teares for a second course,   50
Take grones, take sobs, take sighes sad funerall
if those can murther take our lives & all:

ffor cold we into this losse but throughlye diue
wee'd thincke a man hard hearted to survive
And not embrace thy companie in deathe   55
deare shape of goodnes, thou whose yeilded breathe
was the last gaspe of vertue! that did even
expire wth the, and wth the make for heauen.
whose life was our lifes miracle, & the best,
Patterne & cannonn to direct the rest   60
To square out theirs: who when they all haue done
may well come nere indeed, but like the none:
Thy death shall teach to die: & even this storye
shall more availe then the gravest oratorye
Of an assistant doctor! soe wast thou   65
to thy devines a doctor: taught them how
They might dye well! soe did thy soule drawe on
thy heart died last wth itt religion
    Againe (deare soule) lett me my farewell giue
    left here to waile, & wch is worse to liue.   70

                                        E. Radclyffe.

APPENDIX C

Three versions of Henry King's elegy on Prince Henry

Like other Christ Church men, Henry King (then aged 20), contributed to *Iusta Oxoniensium* (1612). It was perhaps at that time he composed the first version of his elegy on the Prince. My text is from Bodley MS Malone 21, fo. 11^r: (i) below. There is another copy of this version in Bodley MS Eng. Poet. e. 14, fo. 46. The earliest text appears to reflect the span of Henry's life in its length of 18 lines. But despite its stress on the eloquence of the plain fact of the Prince's death, King nevertheless embarked on revision and expansion. Version (ii) is given from Bodley MS Rawl. Poet. 209, fo. 8^v, a manuscript from the 1620s, and it is notable that King's expansion begins with the line 'Here then breake of my Muse' and ends with a somewhat trite couplet. It is as if he were seeking to qualify or soften the terseness of his original conception. The third text, version (iii), is from Margaret Crum's edition of *The Poems of Henry King* (Oxford, 1965), 65–6, textual notes 194–5, based on King's *Poems* of 1657 (p. 95). It was this final version, which may have attained its last state close to the author's sixty-fifth birthday, that Ruth Wallerstein dismissed as the work of a 'youth' (*Studies in Seventeenth-Century Poetic*, 86). It will be apparent that King's elegy in its various stages is an index of literary history; we can observe, as we can over a shorter span with a text such as Drayton's *Idea*, a poet responding to changing tastes and fashions.

For a fuller account of King's poem, see my unpublished D.Phil thesis, 'The English Funeral Elegy', pp. 198–206.

(i) On Prince Henry's Death

Keepe station nature, and rest heauen sure
On thy supporters shoulders, least past cure
Thou dasht by ruine fall by a great weight
Twill make thy Basis shrinke, & lay thy height
Low as ye Center. Death and horrour wed
To vent their teemeing mischiefe: Henry's dead.

It is enough, who seekes to aggravate
One strayne beyond this proves more sharpe his fate
Then o^r sad doome: ye world dares not survive
To parallell this woes superlative
Compendious eloquence of death, two words
Breath stronger terrour, then plague, fier or sword

Ere conquered: why 'tis Epitaph and verse
Able to be fixt on Natures hearse
At Earthes last dissolution, whose fall
Will be lesse greivous though more generall
  For all the woe ruine ere buried
  Lyes in this narrow compasse
                    Henrye's Dead.

(ii) On Prince Henries death.

Keepe station Nature: & rest heaven sure
On thy supporter shoulders, least past cure
Thou dash't in ruine fal by a griefes weight
Wil make thy bases shrinke & lay thy height
Low as ye Center: Hear & feele it read
Through th'astonisht world y^t Henries dead
It is enough who seekes to agravate
One straine beyond this: prove more sharpe his fate
Then sad our doome ye world dar not survive
To paralel, this was superlative
O murthering eloquence of death! two words
Breacke stronger than plague, fire, or swords
Ere conquerd: these were Epitaph & verse
Worthy to be prefixt on Natures herse
On Earths sad dissolution; whose fal
Wilbe lesse greivous, though more general
For all ye woe ruine ere buried
Throngs in this narrow Compasse. Henries dead
Here then breake of my Muse, thy love & Phrase
Is hoarse & dul to strike vs in Amaze
worthy thy vaster subiect: let none dare
To coppy this sad hap but W^{th} dispaire
Hanginge on his quils pointe, for not a streame
Of Inke Can write, much lesse improve this theame
  Suffice we learne by this mortalitie
  The sun rose but to set fraile man to die.

(iii) An Elegy Upon Prince Henryes Death

Keep station Nature, and rest Heaven sure
On thy Supporter's shoulders, least past cure
Thou dash't in ruine fall, by a griefe's weight
Will make thy bases shrink, and lay thy height

Lowe as the Center! Heark, and feele it read
Through the astonish't Kingdom, Henry's dead.
It is enough. Who seekes to aggravate
One straine beyond this, prove more sharp his fate
Then sad our doome. The World dares not survive
To parallel this Woe's superlative.
Oh Killing rhetorick of Death! Two words
Breath stronger terrours, then Plague, Fire, or Swords
Er're conquer'd. This were Epitaph and Verse
Worthy to be praefixt on Nature's Hearse,
Or Earth's sad dissolution; whose fall
Will be lesse grievous, though more generall.
For all the woe ruine e're buryed,
Sounds in these fatal accents, Henry's dead.
Cease then unable Poetry; Thy Phrase
Is weak and dull to strike us with amaze
Worthy thy vaster Subject. Let none dare
To coppy this sad happ, but with despaire
Hanging at his quill's point. For not a Streame
Of ink can write, much less improve this Theame.
Invention highest wrought by Grief or Witt
Must sink with Him, and on his Tombstone splitt.
Who, like the Dying Sunne, tells us the Light
And glory of our Day sett in His Night.

APPENDIX D

Elegies on Prince Henry
by Sir Walter Aston and William Juxon

(i) The poem reproduced here from Bodley MS Eng. Poet. e. 37 is attributed by the scribe to 'Sir W: A:'. The poem accompanies two other pieces on Prince Henry's death, the elegies by Hugh Holland (not attributed in the MS) and by Sir Henry Goodyer (attributed to 'Sir H: G:'), both of which appear in Joshua Sylvester's anthology *Lachrimae lachrimarum*.

I have rehearsed the arguments for Aston's authorship and set out what is known about his writing generally in an article, 'Poems by Sir Walter Aston, and Date for the Donne/Goodyer Verse Epistle *"Alternis Vicibus"* ', *RES* NS 37 (1986), 198–210.

(ii) Few of Juxon's writings, outside official papers, have survived. The text of the poem reproduced here is from Bodley MS Douce f. 5. fo. 34ᵛ. It enjoyed a wide circulation, and copies include BL MSS Add. 30982 (fo. 32ᵛ); Add. 3399 (fo. 85ᵛ); Harl. 1221 (fo. 70ᵛ); Harl. 6038 (fo. 11ʳ); Sloane 1792 (fo. 10ʳ), and the Bodley MSS Ashmole 47 (fo. 39ʳ); CCC 328 (fo. 27ᵛ); Eng. Poet. e. 14 (fo. 99ᵛ (*rev.*)); Malone 21 (fo. 3ᵛ); Rawl. Poet. 212 (fo. 151ᵛ (*rev.*)). Some of these MSS are quite obviously Royalist collections from the Civil War period, and the appearance of Juxon's poem may say as much about Juxon's status at the time as about Henry's remarkable posthumous metamorphosis from the hero of militant Puritanism into a Laudian saint. For more detail, see my article, 'William Juxon's Elegy on Prince Henry (1612)', *N&Q*, NS 32 (1985), 60–1.

(i) Sr: W.A.

Weepe, weepe, even mankinde weepe, so much is dead
That teares in soe iust greefe wear never shed,
So publicke is the loss yᵗ to express
It to the sadnes, makes teares manlyness.
Lett our swolne brest & eyes themselues present
As though each weare of him a monument.
Let vs morne like repentance: Let it bee
held Not to weepe for him an infamie
He yᵗ hath losses had & no releife
& liud still in a full expence of greefe:
That hath decayd his sorrowes to a teare
& keept yᵗ for his sinns, yet spend it heare,

Alas what are we now y^t he is gone?
Though we are number still we are alone.
And soe astonisht, from our selues remayne
That few know wheare to meete themselues againe,
To some vast statue formed for a height
We are climbd vp to looke on, & doe fright
Make the eyes stare & nose & mouth displace
as though we had ill manners taught ye face
ffor by thy death we all are sett awrye
& by our faulse positions we belye
& mishape goodnes so, y^t pure & cleare
to there late shrine, no vertues doe appeare
All lesser things some way deformed bee
Health now is sicknes & infirmitie
Physitions soone must glory in there wealth
for physick now is taken to cure health
Rather then dead; is he not gone away
As beinge advised from heaven not to stay
Wth vs? or had it not much mercy bene
Y^t we example of his life had seene?
Thy death is more then fathers; for tis they
Y^t we doe liue againe another way
The death of children meaner greifes begett
There losse is but our sciences ill sett,
By this even death of freinds is overcome
And seemes a foreiner retourned home
What swells not greefe to heare? Y^e loss of thee
is our owne death wch we doe liue to see
But y^t it were vncivill to grow wise
(where we owe greefe) what learninge would arise
Out of thy death? O who did ever see
So much before of mans mortalitie?
No selfe care can remove vs from thy death
We still are at this Now we lose his breath
This, now hath time in't & will faulsly last
Till we wth the same cloude be overcast
Noe more then this shall our gray children say
Hee's dead, hee's dead, & he dide yesterday.

(ii) On Prince Henryes death. Dr. Juxon

Nature waxeing old beganne
  this to desire
Once to make vp such a man
  man might admire;
And so wth too fine a thred
  she rues it since
In 18 yeares she perfected
  a peerelesse prince.
Death ye moth of natures art
  This danger spied.
For his sight reviu'd each heart
  And noe man died.
Soe in time amends to make
  And helpe this error
Remorselesse death vntimelie brake
  This louelie mirrour.
    But death beware a surfett, for 'tis sed
    That noe man cares to liue now Henrie is dead.

WORKS CITED

PRIMARY SOURCES

MANUSCRIPTS

British Library MSS

Harley MSS: 1221, 2129, 6038, 6243, 6758, 7007. Add. MSS: 3399, 10308, 22118, 30982.

MS Sloane 1792.

Bodley MSS

Ashmole 47; Ashmole 53; Aubrey 6; CCC 327; CCC 328; Don. d. 58; Douce 170; Douce f 5; Eng. Poet. e.14; Eng. Poet. e.37; Malone 21; Malone 238; Rawl. Poet. 26; Rawl. Poet. 85; Rawl. Poet. 116; Rawl. Poet. 160; Rawl. Poet. 209; Rawl. Poet. 212.

Henry E. Huntington Library

MSS EL 34/B/56; 34/B/19; 34/B/57; MS Ellesmere 1130; MS HN 904.

PRINTED BOOKS

Alexander, Sir William, *An elegie on the death of Prince Henrie* (Edinburgh, 1612).
—— *The Works of Sir William Alexander*, ed. H. B. Charlton and L. E. Kastner (Edinburgh and London, 1921).
Allyne, Robert, *Funerall elegies* (1613).
—— *Teares of joy at the happy departure of Frederick and Elizabeth, prince and princesse Palatine* (1613).
Anon. *Alcilia* (1595).
Anon. *The French herald, summoning all true christian princes to a generall croisade* (1611).
Ariosto, Lodovico, *Orlando Furioso*, tr. Sir John Harington (1591).
Aubrey, John, *Brief Lives*, ed. A. Clark, 2 vols. (Oxford, 1898).
B[addily], R., *The Life of Dr Thomas Morton* (1669).
Barnfield, Richard, *Poems in diuers humours* (1598).
Basse, William, *Three pastoral elegies* (1602).
—— *Great Brittaines sunnes-set bewailed* (Oxford, 1613).
Baxter, Nathaniel, *Sir Philip Sidney's Ouránia, that is Endimions song and tragedie* (1606).
Blennerhasset, Thomas, *A direction for the plantation in Ulster* (1610)
The Book of Common Prayer 1559, ed. J. E. Booty (Charlottesville, 1976).

Braithwait, Richard, *Remains after death: including divers memorable observances* (1618).

Breton, Nicholas, *Poems by Nicholas Breton (not hitherto reprinted)*, ed. J. M. Robertson (Liverpool, 1952).

—— *Brittons bowre of delights* (1591).

Brooke, Christopher, *Two elegies consecrated to the memorie of Henry, prince of Wales*, 2 pts. (1613).

Bryskett, Lodowick, *Lodowick Bryskett: Literary Works*, ed. J. H. P. Pafford (1972).

Bucer, Martin, *De obitu . . . Martini Buceri . . . Epistolae duae* (1551).

Cambridge University, *Epicedium cantabrigiense in obitum Henrici principis Walliae* (Cambridge, 1612).

Camden, William, *Remaines of a greater worke concerning Britaine* (1605).

—— *The historie of the princesse Elizabeth*, tr. R. Norton (1630).

Campion, Thomas, *Songs of mourning bewailing the death of prince Henry. Worded by T. Campion* (1612).

—— *The Works of Thomas Campion*, ed. P. Vivian (Oxford, 1909).

Carew, Thomas, *The Poems of Thomas Carew with his Masque 'Coelum Brittanicum'*, ed. R. Dunlap (Oxford, 1949, corr. edn., 1957).

Castiglione, Baldassare, *The Book of the Courtier*, tr. Sir Thomas Hoby, Everyman edn. (1928).

Chamberlain, John, *Letters*, ed. N. E. McLure, 2 vols. (Philadelphia, 1939).

Chapman, George, *An epicede or funerall song* (1612).

—— *The memorable mask of the Middle Temple and Lyncolns Inne* (1613).

—— *Eugenia: or true nobilities trance, for death of William Lord Russell* (1614).

—— *The whole works of Homer in his Iliads and Odysses* (1616).

—— *The Poems of George Chapman*, ed. P. B. Bartlett (New York, 1941).

—— *Bussy d'Ambois*, ed. N. Brooke (Manchester, 1964).

Chaucer, Geoffrey, *The Complete Works of Geoffrey Chaucer*, ed. F. N. Robinson (2nd edn., Boston, 1957).

Chettle, Henry, *Englandes mourning garment: worne here by plaine shepherdes; in memorie of their mistresse Elizabeth* (1603).

Churchyard, Thomas, *The epitaph of the Honorable Earle of Penbroke* (1570).

—— *A generall rehearsall of warres* (1579).

—— *A pleasant laborinth called Churchyardes chance* (1580).

—— *The epitaph of Sir Philip Sidney* (1587).

—— *A sparke of frendship and warme goodwill* (1588).

—— *A reuyuing of the deade by verses that foloweth* (1591).

—— *A feast full of sad cheere* (1592).

—— *Churchyards challenge* (1593).

—— *Churchyards good will* (1604).

Cleland, James, *The institution of a young noble man* (Oxford, 1607).

Coleridge, S. T., *Specimens of the Table Talk of Samuel Taylor Coleridge*, ed. H. N. Coleridge, 2 vols. (1835).

Cooper, John, *Funeral teares for the death of the Earle of Devonshire. Figured in seaven songs* (1606).

Corbett, Richard, *The Poems of Richard Corbett*, ed. J. A. W. Bennett and H. R. Trevor-Roper (Oxford, 1955).

Cornwallis, Sir Charles, *A Discourse of the most illustrious Prince Henry* (1641).

Coryate, Thomas, *Coryates crudities: hastily gobled up in five moneths travels* (1611).

Dallington, Sir Robert, *A booke of epitaphes made vpon the death of Sir W. Buttes* (1583/4).

Daniel, Samuel, *Delia: Contayning certayne sonnets* (1592).

—— *Delia and Rosamond augmented* (1594).

—— *A funerall poeme uppon the death of the late noble Earle of Deuonshire* (1606).

—— *The whole workes of S. Daniel Esquire in poetrie* (1623).

—— *Samuel Daniel: The Brotherton Manuscript*, ed. J. Pitcher, Leeds Texts and Monographs, NS 7 (Leeds, 1981).

Danyel, John, *Songs for the lute, viol and voice* (1606).

Davies, Sir John, *The Poems of Sir John Davies*, ed. R. Krueger (Oxford, 1975).

Davies, John, of Hereford, *The Muses-teares for the losse of Henry Prince of Wales* (1613).

—— *The Muses sacrifice, or divine meditations* (1612).

Day, Angel, *The English secretorie* (1586).

—— *Vpon the life and death of Sir Phillip Sidney* (1587).

Digby, Sir Kenelm, *Loose Fantasies*, ed. V. Gabrieli (Rome, 1968).

Donne, John, *Poems. With elegies on the author's death* (1633).

—— *LXXX Sermons* (1640).

—— *Letters to Several Persons of Honour* (1651).

—— *The Poems of John Donne*, ed. H. J. C. Grierson, 2 vols. (Oxford, 1912).

—— *Essays in Divinity*, ed. E. M. Simpson (Oxford, 1952).

—— *The Sermons of John Donne*, ed. G. R. Potter and E. M. Simpson, 10 vols. (Berkeley, 1953–62).

—— *The Elegies and the Songs and Sonnets of John Donne*, ed. H. Gardner, (Oxford, 1965).

—— *John Donne: The Satires, Epigrams and Verse Letters*, ed. W. Milgate (Oxford, 1967).

—— *John Donne: The Epithalamions, Anniversaries and Epicedes*, ed. W. Milgate (Oxford, 1978).

—— *John Donne: Paradoxes and Problems*, ed. H. Peters (Oxford, 1980).

Drayton, Michael, *The Works of Michael Drayton*, ed. J. W. Hebel, 5 vols. (Oxford, 1931–51).

Drayton, Michael, *Idea. The Shepheards Garland* (1593).

—— *Poemes lyrick and pastorall* (1606).

—— *The Poems of Michael Drayton*, ed. J. Buxton, The Muses' Library, 2 vols. (1953).

Drummond, William, *The Poetical Works of William Drummond of Hawthornden. With 'A Cypresse Grove'*, ed. L. E. Kastner, 2 vols. (Edinburgh, 1913).

—— *William Drummond of Hawthornden. Poems and Prose*, ed. R. M. Macdonald (Edinburgh, 1976).

—— *Teares on the death of Meliades* (Edinburgh, 1613).

Elizabeth, Queen, *The Poores Lamentation for the death of Elizabeth* (1603).

Elyot, Sir Thomas, *The Boke Named the Governor*, ed. S. G. Lehmberg, Everyman edn. (1962).

Erasmus, Desiderius, *The Colloquies of Erasmus*, tr. C. R. Thompson (Chicago, 1965).

Faral, E., *Les Arts Poétiques du XIIe et du XIIIe siècle* (Paris, 1923).

Ferrabosco, Alfonso, *Ayres* (1609).

Fletcher, Robert, *A briefe and familiar epistle shewing his maiesties title to all his kingdomes* (1603).

Ford, John, *Fames memoriall, or the Earle of Devonshire deceased* (1606).

Fugitive Tracts written in verse, etc., 2nd ser., *1600–1700*, ed. W. C. Hazlitt, 2 vols. (1875).

Fuller, Thomas, *The Worthies of England* (1662).

Googe, Barnabe, *Eglogs, epytaphes, and sonnettes* (1563).

Gorges, Sir Arthur, *The Poems of Sir Arthur Gorges*, ed. H. E. Sandison (Oxford, 1953).

Greville, Fulke, *The Life of Sir Philip Sidney*, ed. Nowell Smith (Oxford, 1907).

Habington, William, *Castara* (1635).

—— *The Poems of William Habington*, ed. K. Allott (Liverpool, 1948).

Hakewill, George, *Scutum regium* (1612).

Hall, Joseph, *The Poems of Joseph Hall*, ed. A. Davenport (Liverpool, 1969).

—— *The King's prophecie: or weeping joy* (1603).

Hamor, Ralphe, *A true discourse of the present estate of Virginia* (1615).

Hannay, Patrick, *A happy husband. To which is adjoyned the Good Wife, by R. Braithwait* (1618).

Harleian Miscellany: or a collection of scarce . . . tracts, etc., ed. W. Oldys, 8 vols. (1744–6), ed. T. Park, 10 vols. (1808–13).

Harrison, T. P. jun., ed., and Leon, H. J., tr., *The Pastoral Elegy: An Anthology* (Austin, 1939).

Harvey, Gabriel, *Smithus, vel musarum lachrymae pro obitu T. Smithu, equitis Britanni* (1578).

Henry, Prince of Wales, *Mausoleum: or the choisest flowres of the epitaphs on the death of Prince Henrie* (Edinburgh, 1613).

Henryson, Robert, *The Poems of Robert Henryson*, ed. D. Fox (Oxford, 1981).

Herbert, Edward, *Poems, English and Latin*, ed. G. C. Moore Smith (Oxford, 1923).

Heywood, Thomas, *A funerall elegie upon the death of Henry, prince of Wales* (1613).

—— *The brazen age* (1612).

—— *The iron age* (1632).

James I, *Englands welcome to James* (1603).

—— *The Poems of James VI of Scotland*, ed. J. Craigie, 2 vols. (Edinburgh, 1955, 1958).

Jonson, Ben, *Jonsonus virbius: or, the memorie of Ben: Jonson revived* (1638).

—— *Ben Jonson*, ed. C. H. Herford, P. and E. Simpson, 11 vols. (Oxford, 1925–52).

—— *Poems*, ed. I. Donaldson (Oxford, 1975).

Kendall, Timothy, *Flowers of epigrammes, out of sundrie the most singular authors* (1577).

King, Edward, *Iusta Edouardo King Naufrago, ab amicis moerentibus, amoris* (Cambridge, 1638).

King, Henry, *The Poems of Henry King, Bishop of Chichester*, ed. M. Crum (Oxford, 1965).

Lachrymae Musarum, ed. R. B. (1649).

Lane, John, *An elegie upon the death of Elizabeth* (1603).

—— *Tom Tel-Troths message, and his pens complaint* (1600).

Lant, Thomas, *Sequitur celebritas & pompa funeris* (1587).

Latimer, Hugh, *Sermons by Hugh Latimer*, ed. G. E. Corrie, Parker Society (1844).

Leigh, Edward, *Annotations on Five Poetical Books of the Old Testament* (1657).

Leighton, Sir William, *The tears or lamentations of a sorrowfull soule* (1613).

Lescarbot, Marc, *Nova Francia; or the description of that part of New France wh. is one continent with Virginia Tr. P. E.* (1609).

Lewkenor, Sir Edward, *Threnodia in obitum D. Edouardi Lewkenor equitis. Funerall verses* (1606).

Lipsius, Justus, *Sixe bookes of politickes or civil doctrine*, tr. W. Jones (1594).

Lovelace, Richard, *The Poems of Richard Lovelace*, ed. C. H. Wilkinson (Oxford, 1930).

Lyly, John, *The Complete Works of John Lyly*, ed. R. W. Bond, 3 vols. (Oxford, 1902).

Machyn, Henry, *The Diary of Henry Machyn, Citizen and Merchant-Taylor of London, from A.D. 1550 to A.D. 1563*, ed. J. G. Nichols, Camden Society, os 42 (1848).

Marcelline, George, *The triumphs of King James* (1609–10).

Marlowe, Christopher, *Christopher Marlowe, The Complete Poems and Translations*, ed. S. Orgel (Harmondsworth, 1971).

Maxwell, James, *The laudable life, and deplorable death, of prince Henry* (1612).

—— *The imperiall and princely pedegree of . . . Friderick . . . and Elizabeth* (1613).

——*A monument of remembrance, erected in Albion, in honor of the departure from Britannie, and honorable receiving in Germany of Fredericke, and Elizabeth* (1613).

Menander Rhetor, ed. D. A. Russell and N. G. Wilson (Oxford, 1981).

Milton, John, *Milton, Complete Shorter Poems*, ed. J. Carey (1968).

—— *The Complete Prose Works of John Milton*, ed. D. M. Wolfe, *et al.*, 8 vols. (New Haven, 1953–).

Montaigne, Michel de, *The essayes or morall, politike and millitarie discourses. Done into English by [J. Florio]* (1603).

More, George, *Principles for young princes* (1611).

Mornay, Phillippe du, *The mysterie of iniquitie: that is to say the historie of the papacie* (1612).

Nashe, Thomas, *Works*, ed. R. B. McKerrow, rev. F. P. Wilson, 5 vols. (Oxford, 1966).

Neville, Alexander, ed., *Academiae cantabrigiensis lacrymae tumulo P. Sidneij sacratae* (1587).

Newton, Thomas, *Atropoïon.Delion, or, the death of Delia* (1603).

Niccols, Richard, *Expicedium. A funeral oration, vpon the late deceased princesse Elizabeth queen of England. By Infelice Academico Ignoto, . . . etc.* (1603).

——*A winter nights vision* (1610).

—— *The Cuckow* (1607).

—— *The three sisters teares. Shed at the funeral of Henry, prince of Wales* (1613).

—— *Sir Thomas Overburies vision. With the ghoasts of Weston, Mrs Turner* (1616).

——*Monodia, or Walthams complaint, upon the death of the lady Honor Hay* (1615).

Nichols, J. G., *The Progresses and Public Processions of Queen Elizabeth*, 3 vols. (1823).

Nixon, Anthony, *Elizaes memoriall. King James his arrivall. And Romes downefall* (1603).

Oxford University, *Luctus posthumus sive erga defunctum Henricum Walliae principem, Magdalensium officiosa pietas* (Oxford, 1612).

—— *Eidyllia in obitum fulgentissimi Henrici Walliae principis* (Oxford, 1612).

——*Justa Oxoniensium. (Lachrymae Oxonienses stillantes in tumulum principis Henrici)* (1612).

——*Musarum Oxoniensium Charisteria pro serenissima regina Maria, recens e nixus laboriosi discrimine recepta* (Oxford, 1638).

Pallavicino, Sir Horatio, *An Italians dead bodie, stucke with English flowers: Elegies, on the death of Sir Oratio Pallavicino* (1600).

Peacham, Henry, *The period of mourning. Disposed into sixe visions. Together with nuptiall hymnes* (1612).

—— *Minerva Britanna, or a garden of heroical devises* (1612).

—— *Prince Henrie revived. Or a poeme* (1615).

Petowe, Henry, *Elizabetha quasi vivens, Eliza's funerall* (1603).

—— *Englands Caesar. His maiesties most royall coronation* (1603).

Pett, Phineas, *The Autobiography of Phineas Pett*, ed. W. G. Perrin, *Publications of the Navy Records Society*, 51 (1918).

Phillips, John, *A commemoration of the Ladye Margrit Duglasis good grace* (1578).

—— *The life and death of Sir Philip Sidney* (1587).

—— *A sommon to repentance* (1584).

—— *Vt hora, sic fugit vita; a commemoration of Sir C. Hatton* (1591).

The phoenix nest, ed. H. E. Rollins, 2 vols. (Cambridge, Mass., 1931).

—— intr. D. E. L. Crane (Menston, 1970).

A Poetical Rapsody 1602–21, ed. H. E. Rollins, 2 vols. (Cambridge, Mass., 1931).

Poliziano, Angelo, *Angeli Politiani Operum* (Lyons, 1546).

Price, Daniel, *Lamentations for the death of prince Henrie* (1613).

—— *Prince Henry his first anniversary* (Oxford, 1613).

—— *Prince Henry his second anniversary* (1614).

Price, Sampson, *Londons warning by Laodicea's lukewarmnesse. A sermon* (1613).

Pricket, Robert, *A souldiers wish unto his soveraigne Lord king James* (1603).

—— *A souldiors resolution* (1603).

—— *Honors fame in triumph riding* (1604).

Puttenham, George, *The Arte of English Poesie*, ed. G. D. Willcock and A. Walker (Cambridge, 1936).

Quin, Walter, *Sertum poeticum, in honorem Jacobi sexti* (Edinburgh, 1600).

Ralegh, Sir Walter, *The Works of Sir Walter Raleigh*, eds. T. Birch and J. Oldys, 8 vols. (Oxford, 1829).

—— *The history of the world* [Anon.] (1614).

—— *The Poems of Sir Walter Ralegh*, ed. A. Latham (1951).

Robbins, R. H., *Historical Poems of the XIV and XV Centuries* (New York, 1959).

Rogers, Thomas, *Gloucesters myte, delivered with the mournefull records of Great Brittaine, into the worlds register. For the remembrance of prince Henrie* (1612).

Ronsard, Pierre, *Œuvres complètes*, ed. P. Laumonnier (Paris, 1946).

Rutter, Joseph, *The shepheards holy-day* (1635).

Sandys, G., *Paraphrase upon the Divine Poems* (1638).

Sannazaro, Jacopo, *Arcadia*, ed. M. Scherillo (Turin, 1888).

—— *Arcadia and Piscatorial Eclogues*, tr. R. Nash (Detroit, 1966).

Sidney, Sir Philip, *Syr P.S. his Astrophel and Stella. To the end of which are added, sundry other rare sonnets of diuers gentlemen* (1591).

—— *Arcadia* (1590), ed. A. Feuillerat: vol. i of *The Complete Works of Sir*

Philip Sidney, 4 vols. (Cambridge, 1912–26; reissued as *The Prose Works of Sir Philip Sidney* (Cambridge, 1962)).

—— *The Countess of Pembroke's Arcadia (The Old Arcadia)*, ed. J. Robertson (Oxford, 1973).

—— *The Poems of Sir Philip Sidney*, ed. W. A. Ringler (Oxford, 1962).

—— *The Countess of Pembroke's Arcadia (The New Arcadia)*, ed. V. Skretkowicz (Oxford, 1987).

—— *Sir Philip Sidney. Selected Poems*, ed. K. Duncan-Jones (Oxford, 1973).

—— *Miscellaneous Prose of Sir Philip Sidney*, ed. K. Duncan-Jones and J. van Dorsten (Oxford, 1973).

—— *Peplus*, ed. J. Lloyd (Oxford, 1587).

—— *Exequiae illustrissimi viri D. Philippi Sidneaei . . . etc.*, ed. W. Gager (1587).

Skelton, John, *Pithy, pleasant and profitable workes of Maister Skelton* (1568).

Smith, G. G., *Elizabethan Critical Essays*, 2 vols. (Oxford, 1904).

Spenser, Edmund, *The Works of Edmund Spenser: A Variorum Edition*, ed. E. Greenlaw, C. O. Osgood and F. M. Padelford (Baltimore, 1932–49).

—— *The Poetical Works of Edmund Spenser*, ed. J. C. Smith and E. de Selincourt (Oxford, 1912).

—— *A View of the Present State of Ireland*, ed. W. L. Renwick (Oxford, 1970).

Stock, Richard, *The Churches lamentation for the losse of the godly* (1614).

Stow, John, *The annales of England, . . . etc. Continued unto 1631* (1631).

Suckling, Sir John, *The Works of Sir John Suckling. The Non-Dramatic Works*, ed. T. Clayton (Oxford, 1971).

Surrey, Earl of, *Henry Howard, Earl of Surrey: Poems*, ed. E. Jones (Oxford, 1964).

—— *Songes and sonettes, written by Henry Howard late Earle of Surrey, and other* (1557) ('Tottel's Miscellany').

Sylvester, Joshua, *Lachrimae lachrimarum or the distillation of teares shede for the death of prince Panaretus* (1612), STC 23576.

—— *[Lachrimae lachrimarum . . .]*, Anr. edn. (1612), STC 23577.

—— *[Lachrimae lachrimarum . . .] Third edition, with addition of his owne, and other elegies* (1613), STC 23577.5.

—— *The Divine Weeks and Works of Guillaume de Salluste, Sieur du Bartas*, ed. S. Snyder, 2 vols. (Oxford, 1979).

Tasso, Torquato, *Discourses on the Heroic Poem*, tr. M. Cavalchini and I. Samuel (Oxford, 1973).

Taylor, John, *Great Brittaine, all in blacke. For the incomparable losse of Henry, our late worthy Prince* (1612).

—— *Heavens blessing, and earths joy. Or a true relation, of the al-beloved mariage, of Fredericke & Elizabeth, . . . etc.* (1613).

Tilley, M. P., *A Dictionary of Proverbs in England in the Sixteenth and Seventeenth Centuries* (1950).

Tooker, William, *Duellum siue singulare certamen cum Martino Becano Jesuita* (1611).

Tottell, Richard, *Songes and sonettes, written by Henry Howard late Earle of Surrey, and other* (1557) (Menston, 1970).

—— *Tottel's Miscellany (1557–1587),* ed. H. E. Rollins, 2 vols. (Cambridge, Mass., rev. edn., 1965).

Tourneur, Cyril, *A griefe on the death of prince Henrie* (1613).

—— *A funerall poeme. Upon the death of Sir Francis Vere* (1609).

—— *Three elegies on the most lamented death of prince Henrie, by C. Tourneur. J. Webster and T. Heywood* (1613).

—— *The Atheist's Tragedy,* ed. I. Ribner (1964).

Turberville, George, *Epitaphes, epigrams, songs and sonets . . . etc.* (1567).

Unton, Sir Henry, *Funebria nobilissimi equitis D. H. Untoni . . . etc.* (Oxford, 1596).

Vinsauf, Geoffrey de, *Poetria Nova,* in E. Faral, *Les Arts Poétiques du XIIe et du XIIIe siècle* (Paris, 1923).

W. T., *The lamentation of Melpomene, for the death of Belphaebe our late Queene* (1603).

Walton, Izaak, *The Lives of John Donne, Sir Henry Wotton, Richard Hooker, George Herbert and Robert Sanderson* (1675; World's Classics edn., Oxford, 1927).

Watson, Thomas, *Meliboeus* (1590).

—— *An eclogue vpon the death of Sir F. Walsingham* (1590).

Webster, John, *The Complete Works of John Webster,* ed. F. E. Lucas, 4 vols. (1927).

—— *A monumental columne, erected to the memory of Henry, late prince of Wales* (1613).

Weever, John, *Ancient funerall monuments within the united monarchie of Great Britaine, Ireland, and the islands adjacent* (1613).

Whetstone, George, *A Remembraunce of the life, death, and vertues of Thomas, late erle of Sussex* (1583).

—— *A mirror of treue honnour and christian nobilitie* (1585).

—— *A remembrance of the wel imployed life, & godly end, of George Gaskoigne, esquire* (1577).

—— *A Remembraunce of the worthie and well imployed life, of . . . Sir Nicholas Bacon* (1579).

—— *A remembraunce of the precious vertues of the right Honourable and reuerend Iudge, Sir James Dier* (1582).

—— *Sir Philip Sidney, his honorable life, his valiant death, and his true vertues* (1587).

Willymat, William, *A princes looking glasse excerpted out of Basilikon Doron* (1603).

——*A loyal subjects looking-glasse, or a direction, to the duties of an honest and obedient subject to his king* (1604).

Wilson, A., *The History of Great Britain* (1653).

Wilson, Thomas, ed., *Vita et obitus duorum fratrum Suffolciensum, Henrici et Caroli Brandoni* (1551).

Wither, George, *Prince Henries obsequies or mournefull elegies upon his death* (1612).

——*Abuses stript, and whipt. Or satirical essayes* (1613).

—— *Wither's motto. Nec habeo, nec careo, nec curo* (1621).

Wotton, Sir Henry, *The Life and Letters of Sir Henry Wotton*, ed. L. Pearsall Smith, 2 vols. (Oxford, 1907).

Wright, Thomas, *The passions of the mind in generall* (1604).

SECONDARY SOURCES

Alexiou, M., *The Ritual Lament in Greek Tradition* (Cambridge, 1974).

Alpers, P., 'Lycidas and Modern Criticism', *ELH* 49 (1982), 468–96.

Aries, P., *Western Attitudes Towards Death*, tr. P. N. Ranum (1974).

—— *The Hour of Our Death*, tr. H. Weaver (Harmondsworth, 1983).

Atkins, J. W. H., *English Literary Criticism: The Medieval Phase* (Cambridge, 1943).

Attridge, D., *Well-Weighed Syllables: Elizabethan Verse in Classical Metres* (Cambridge, 1974).

Axton, M., *The Queen's Two Bodies* (1977).

Baker-Smith, D., 'Great Expectations: Sidney's Death and the Poets', in J. Van Dorsten, D. Baker-Smith, and A. F. Kinney, eds., *Sir Philip Sidney: 1586 and the Creation of a Legend*, 83–103.

Bald, R. C., *John Donne: A Life* (Oxford, 1970).

Barker, F., *The Tremulous Private Body* (1984).

Barton, A., 'Harking back to Elizabeth: Ben Jonson and Caroline nostalgia', *ELH* 48 (1981), 701–31.

—— *Ben Jonson: Dramatist* (Cambridge, 1984).

Bayley, P., *Edmund Spenser: Prince of Poets* (1972).

Beal, P., ed., *Index of English Literary Manuscripts*, 1. 1450–1625, 2 vols. (1980).

Bellette, A. F., 'Art and Imitation in Donne's *Anniversaries*', *SEL* 15 (1975), 83–96.

Bennett, A. L., 'The Principal Rhetorical Conventions in the Renaissance Personal Elegy', *SP* 51 (1954), 107–26.

Bentley, G. E., *The Profession of Dramatist in Shakespeare's Time* (Princeton, 1970).

Berger, H., jun., 'Mode and Diction in *The Shepheardes Calender*', *MP* 67 (1969), 140–9.

——*Revisionary Play: Studies in the Spenserian Dynamics*, with an introductory essay by L. A. Montrose (Berkeley, 1988).

Bergeron, D. M., *English Civic Pageantry, 1558–1642* (1971).

Berry, P., *Of Chastity and Power. Elizabethan Literature and the Unmarried Queen* (London, 1989).

Binns, J. W., 'William Gager on the death of Sir Philip Sidney', *Humanistica Lovaniensia*, 21 (1972), 221–38.

Birch, T., *The Life of Henry, Prince of Wales* (1760).

Black, L. G., 'Some Renaissance Children's Verse', *RES*, NS, 24 (1973), 1–16.

Bloomfield, M. W., 'The Elegy and the Elegiac Mode: Praise and Alienation', in B. K. Lewalski, ed., *Renaissance Genres: Essays on Theory, History and Interpretation* (Cambridge, Mass., 1986), 147–57.

Bondanella, P. E., and J. Canaway, 'Two Kinds of Renaissance Love: Spenser's "Astrophel" and Ronsard's "Adonis"', *ES* 52 (1971), 311–18.

Bos, S., M. Lange-Meifers, and J. Six, 'Sidney's Funeral Portrayed', in J. Van Dorsten, D. Baker-Smith and A. F. Kinney, eds., *Sir Philip Sidney: 1586 and the Creation of a Legend*, 38–61.

Boswell, J., and H. R. Woudhuysen, 'Some Unfamiliar Sidney Allusions', in J. Van Dorsten, D. Baker-Smith, and A. F. Kinney, eds., *Sir Philip Sidney: 1586 and the Creation of a Legend*, 221–37.

Bradbrook, M. C., *John Webster: Citizen and Dramatist* (1980).

Brennan, M. G., *Literary Patronage in the English Renaissance: The Pembroke Family* (1988).

——'The Literary Patronage of the Herbert Family, Earls of Pembroke, 1550–1640', D.Phil. thesis (Oxford, 1982).

Brown, C. C., *John Milton's Aristocratic Entertainments* (Cambridge, 1985).

——'The Death of Righteous Men: Prophetic Gesture in Vaughan's *Daphnis* and Milton's *Lycidas*', *George Herbert Journal*, 7 (1983–4), 1–24.

Burnley, J. D., 'Some Terminology of Reception in *The Book of the Duchess*', *ELN* 23 (1986), 15–22.

Bush, D., *English Literature in the Earlier Seventeenth Century* (2nd edn., Oxford, 1962).

Butler, C., *Number Symbolism* (1970).

Buxton, J., 'Shakespeare's *Venus and Adonis* and Sidney', in J. Van Dorsten, D. Baker-Smith, and A. F. Kinney, eds., *Sir Philip Sidney: 1586 and the Creation of a Legend*, 104–10.

——*Sir Philip Sidney and the English Renaissance* (3rd edn., 1988).

Cain, T. H., *Praise in 'The Faerie Queene'* (Lincoln, Nebr., 1978).

Carey, J., ed., *English Renaissance Studies Presented to Dame Helen Gardner in Honour of her Seventieth Birthday* (Oxford, 1980).

——*John Donne: Life, Mind and Art* (1981).

Cave, T., ed., *Ronsard the Poet* (1973).

——*The Cornucopian Text: Problems of Writing in the French Renaissance* (Oxford, 1979).

Caws, M A., *The Eye in the Text: Essays in Perception, Mannerist to Modern* (Princeton, 1981).

Chambers, E. K., *William Shakespeare: A Study of Facts and Problems*, 2 vols. (Oxford, 1930).

Chaudhuri, S., *Infirm Glory: Shakespeare and the Renaissance Image of Man* (Oxford, 1981).

Cheney, D. R., 'Spenser's Fortieth Birthday and Related Fictions', *Spenser Studies*, 4 (1984), 3–31.

Colaianne, A. J., and W. L. Godshalk, eds., *Elegies for Sir Philip Sidney (1587)*, (Delmar, 1980).

Colie, R. L., ' "All in Peeces": Problems of Interpretation in Donne's Anniversary Poems', in P. A. Fiore, ed., *Just So Much Honor: Essays Commemorating the 400th Anniversary of the Birth of John Donne* (University Park, 1972), 189–218.

——*Paradoxica Epidemica* (Princeton, 1969).

——*The Resources of Kind: Genre Theory in the Renaissance* (Berkeley, 1973).

——*Shakespeare's Living Art* (Princeton, 1974).

Collinson, P., *The Religion of Protestants: the Church in English Society 1559–1625* (Oxford, 1982).

Cooper, H., *Pastoral* (Ipswich, 1977).

Corbin, P. F., 'A Death and a Marriage: An Examination of the Literature Occasioned by the Death of Henry Prince of Wales and the Marriage of His Sister Princess Elizabeth, 1612–1613', Ph.D. thesis (Birmingham, 1966).

Courthope, W. S., *A History of English Poetry*, 6 vols. (1895–1910).

Crawshaw, E., 'Hermetic Elements in Donne's Poetic Vision', in Smith, ed., *Donne: Essays in Celebration*, 324–48.

Creaser, J., '*Lycidas*: The Power of Art', *Essays and Studies*, 34 (1981), 123–47.

Cummings, R. M., *Spenser: The Critical Heritage* (1971).

Curtius, E. R., *European Literature and the Latin Middle Ages*, tr. W. R. Trask (1953).

Dana, M. A., 'The Providential Plot of the *Old Arcadia*', *SEL* 17 (1977), 39–57.

Davis, T. R., 'Materials for an Edition of the Poems of Thomas Randolph', B.Litt. thesis (Oxford, 1969).

Davis, W. R., 'Narrative Methods in Sidney's *Old Arcadia*', *SEL* 18 (1978), 13–33.

Deneef, A. L., *Spenser and the Motives of Metaphor* (Durham, NC, 1982).

Dime, G. T., 'The Difference Between "Strong Lines" and "Metaphysical Poetry" ', *SEL* 26 (1986), 47–57.

Doebler, B. A., *The Quickening Seed: Death in the Sermons of John Donne* (Salzburg, 1974).

Duncan-Jones, K., 'Ford and the Earl of Devonshire', *RES*, NS, 39 (1978), 447–52.

—— 'Sidney, Stella and Lady Rich', in J. Van Dorsten, D. Baker-Smith, and A. F. Kinney, eds., *Sir Philip Sidney: 1586 and the Creation of a Legend*, 170–92.

Edmonds, J. P., 'Elegies and Other Tracts on the Death of Prince Henry', *Publications of the Edinburgh Bibliographical Society*, 6 (1906), 141–58.

Evans, J. M., 'Lycidas, Daphnis, and Gallus', in J. Carey, ed., *English Renaissance Studies*, 228–44.

Farmer, N. K., jun., 'A Theory of Genre for the Seventeenth Century', *Genre*, 3 (1970), 293–317.

Febvre, L., *Au cœur religieux du XVIe siècle* (Paris, 1957).

Fineman, J., *Shakespeare's Perjured Eye. The Invention of Poetic Subjectivity in the Sonnets* (Berkeley, 1986).

Fish, S. E., 'Author-Readers: Jonson's Community of the Same', *Representations*, 7 (1984), 26–58.

—— '*Lycidas*: A Poem Finally Anonymous', *Glyph*, 8 (1981), 1–18.

Fitzmaurice, J., 'Carew's Funerary Poetry and the Paradox of Sincerity', *SEL* 25 (1985), 127–44.

Fogle, F. R., ' "Such a Rural Queene": The Countess Dowager of Derby as Patron, in F.R. Fogle and L. A. Knafla, *Patronage* in *Late Renaissance England*, William Andrews Clark Memorial Library (Los Angeles, 1983), 3–29.

Forster, L., *The Icy Fire: Five Studies in European Petrarchism* (Cambridge, 1969).

Foster, J., ed., *Alumni Oxonienses, being the Matriculation Register of the University 1500–1714*, 4 vols. (Oxford, 1891–2).

Fowler, A., *Triumphal Forms* (Cambridge, 1970).

—— ed., *Silent Poetry: Essays in Numerological Analysis* (1970).

—— *Conceitful Thought* (Edinburgh, 1975).

—— *Kinds of Literature: An Introduction to the Theory of Genres and Modes* (Oxford, 1982).

Frank, M. H., 'Milton's Knowledge of Music: Some Speculation', in J. M. Patrick and R. H. Sundell, ed., *Milton and the Art of Sacred Song*, (Madison, Wisconsin, 1979), 83–98.

Friis, A., *Alderman Cockayne's Project and the Cloth Trade* (1927).

Frye, N., *Anatomy of Criticism: Four Essays* (Princeton, 1957).

Fumerton, P., ' "Secret" Arts: Elizabethan Miniatures and Sonnets', in S. Greenblatt, ed., *Representing the English Renaissance*, 93–133.

Galpern, A. N., *The Religions of the People in Sixteenth-Century Champagne*, Harvard Historical Studies, 92 (Cambridge, Mass., 1976).

Garland, R., *The Greek Way of Death* (1985).

Gearin-Tosh, M., 'Marvell's "Uppon the Death of the Lord Hastings" ', *Essays and Studies*, 34 (1981), 105–22.

Giesey, R., *The Royal Funeral Ceremony in Renaissance France* (Geneva, 1960).

Gillman, E. B., *The Curious Perspective: Literary and Pictorial Wit in the Seventeenth Century* (New York, 1978).

Gittings, Clare, *Death, Burial and the Individual in Early Modern England* (1984).

Goldberg, J., *Voice Terminal Echo: Postmodernism and English Renaissance Texts* (1986).

Goldwyn, M. H., 'Notes on the Biography of Thomas Churchyard', *RES*, NS, 17 (1966), 1–15.

—— 'A Note on Thomas Churchyard's Pension', *N&Q*, NS, 21 (1974), 89.

Gordon, D. J., 'Chapman's *Memorable Masque*', in D. J. Gordon, *The Renaissance Imagination*, ed. S. Orgel (Berkeley, 1975), 194–202.

Gottlieb, S., '*Elegies upon the Author*: Defining, Defending and Surviving Donne', *John Donne Journal*, 2 (1982), 23–38.

Gouws, J., 'Fact and Anecdote in Fulke Greville's Account of Sidney's Last Days', in J. Van Dorsten, D. Baker-Smith, and A. F. Kinney, eds., *Sir Philip Sidney: 1586 and the Creation of a Legend*, 62–82.

Gray, D., *Themes and Images in the Medieval English Religious Lyric* (1972).

Greenblatt, S., *Sir Walter Ralegh. The Renaissance Man and his Roles* (New Haven, 1973).

—— *Renaissance Self-Fashioning: From More to Shakespeare* (Chicago, 1980).

—— *The Forms of Power and the Power of Forms* (Norman, Oklahoma, 1982: special issue of *Genre*, 15 (1982)).

—— *Representing the English Renaissance* (Berkeley, 1988).

—— 'Invisible Bullets: Renaissance Authority and its Subversion', *Glyph*, 8 (1981), 20–61.

—— *Shakespearian Negotiations* (Oxford, 1988).

Greene, T. M., *The Light in Troy: Imitation and Discovery in Renaissance Poetry* (New Haven, 1982).

Greenfield, S. B., 'The Old English Elegies', in E. G. Stanley, ed., *Continuations and Beginnings* (1966), 142–75.

Griffin, J., *Homer on Life and Death* (Oxford, 1980).

Gross, K., *Spenserian Poetics: Idolatry, Iconoclasm, and Magic* (Ithaca, 1985).

Grundy, J., *The Spenserian Poets* (1969).

Gurr, A., *Playgoing in Shakespeare's London* (Cambridge, 1987).

Hagar, A., 'The Exemplary Mirage: Fabrication of Sir Philip Sidney's Biographical Image and the Sidney Reader', in D. Kay, ed., *Sir Philip Sidney*, 45–60.

Hannaford, R., ' "Express'd by mee": Carew on Donne and Jonson', *SP* 84 (1987), 61–79.

Hardin, R. F., *Michael Drayton and the Passing of Elizabethan England* (Lawrence, Manhattan, Wichita, 1973).

Hardison, O. B., jun., *The Enduring Monument* (Chapel Hill, 1962).

Harris, D., and N. L. Steffen, 'The Other Side of the Garden: An Interpretative Comparison of Chaucer's *The Book of the Duchess* and Spenser's *Daphnaida*', *JMRS* 8 (1978), 17–36.

Helgerson, R., *Self-Crowned Laureates: Spenser, Jonson and the Literary System* (Berkeley, 1983).

—— 'The Land Speaks: Cartography, Chorography, and Subversion in Renaissance England', *Representations*, 16 (1986), 51–85; repr. in S. Greenblatt, ed., *Representing the English Renaissance*, 326–61.

Heninger, S. K., *Touches of Sweet Harmony: Pythagorean Cosmology and Renaissance Poetics* (San Marino, 1974).

—— 'The Typographical Layout of Spenser's *Shepheardes Calender*', in K. J. Höltgen, P. M. Daly, and W. Lottes, eds., *Word and Visual Imagination: Studies in the Interaction of English Literature and the Visual Arts* (Nürnberg, 1988), 33–51.

Hill, C., *Intellectual Origins of the English Revolution* (Oxford, 1965; repr. 1972).

—— *Milton and the English Revolution* (1977).

—— 'George Wither and John Milton', in J. Carey, ed., *English Renaissance Studies*, 212–27.

Himelick, R., 'Samuel Daniel, Montaigne, and Seneca', *N&Q*, NS, 3 (1956), 61–4.

Hodges, D. L., *Renaissance Fictions of Anatomy* (Amherst, 1985).

Hollander, J., *The Figure of Echo* (Berkeley, 1981).

Horace, *The Third Book of Horace's Odes*, ed. G. Williams (Oxford, 1969).

Hudson, H. H., *The Epigram in the English Renaissance* (Princeton, 1947).

Huebert, R., *John Ford, Baroque English Dramatist* (Montreal, 1977).

Huizinga, J. L., *The Waning of the Middle Ages*, tr. F. Hopman (Harmondsworth, 1972).

Hume, A., *Edmund Spenser, Protestant Poet* (Cambridge, 1984).

Hunt, C., *Lycidas and the Italian Critics*, ed. I. Samuel (New Haven, 1979).

Huntingdon, R., and P. Metcalf, eds., *Celebrations of Death: The Anthropology of Mortuary Ritual* (Cambridge, 1979).

Iser, W., 'Spenser's Arcadia', in P. Steiner *et al.*, *The Structure of the Literary Process* (Amsterdam and Philadelphia, 1982), 211–41.

—— 'Spenser's Arcadia: The Interrelation of Fiction and History', in M.

Spariosu, ed., *Mimesis in Contemporary Theory: An Interdisciplinary Approach*, i. *The Literary and Historical Debate* (Philadelphia, 1984), 109–40.

Jack, R. D. S., *The Italian Influence on Scottish Literature* (Edinburgh, 1972).

Jentoft, C. W., 'Surrey's Five Elegies: Rhetoric, Structure, and the Poetry of Praise', *PMLA* 91 (1976), 23–32.

Jones, D., *Thomas Lodge and Other Elizabethans*, ed. C. J. Sisson (Cambridge, Mass., 1933).

Jones, E., *The Origins of Shakespeare* (Oxford, 1977).

Jordan, W. K., *Edward VI: The Threshold of Power* (Cambridge, Mass., 1970).

Jungman, R., 'Greville as a Source for *Lycidas*, lines 8–9', *Sidney Newsletter*, 4 (1983), 14–15.

Kantorowicz, E. H., *The King's Two Bodies: A Study in Medieval Political Theology* (Princeton, 1957).

Kay, D., 'The English Funeral Elegy in the Reigns of Elizabeth I and James I, with Special Reference to Poems on the Death of Prince Henry (1612)', D.Phil. thesis (Oxford, 1982).

—— 'Gonzalo's "Lasting Pillars": *The Tempest*, v i. 208', *Shakespeare Quarterly*, 35 (1984), 322–4.

—— '"To Hear the Rest Untold": Shakespeare's Postponed Endings', *RQ* 37 (1984), 207–27.

—— 'Poems by Sir Walter Aston, and a Date for the Donne/Goodyer Verse Epistle "*Alternis Vicibus*"', *RES*, NS, 37 (1986), 198–210.

—— ed., *Sir Philip Sidney: An Anthology of Modern Criticism* (Oxford, 1987).

Kennedy, W. J., *Jacopo Sannazaro and the Uses of Pastoral* (Hanover, 1983).

Keynes, G., *A Bibliography of John Donne* (4th edn., Oxford, 1973).

King, J. N., *English Reformation Literature* (Princeton, 1982).

—— 'Spenser's *Shepheardes Calender* and Protestant Pastoral Satire', in B. K. Lewalski, ed., *Renaissance Genres*, 369–98.

Kirkconnell, W., *Awake the Courteous Echo* (Toronto, 1973).

Klause, A. L., 'Donne and the Wonderful', *ELR* 17 (1987), 41–66.

Kolin, P. C., 'Donne's "Obsequies to the Lord Harrington": Theme, Structure, and Image', *Southern Quarterly*, 13 (1974), 65–82.

Kreider, A., *English Chantries: The Road to Dissolution*, Harvard Historical Studies, 97 (Cambridge, Mass., 1976).

Kuhn, U., *English Literary Terms in Poetological Texts of the Sixteenth Century* (Salzburg, 1974).

Laborsky, R. S., 'The Allusive Presentation of *The Shepheardes Calender*', *Spenser Studies*, 1 (1980), 29–67.

Lambert, E. Z., *Placing Sorrow: A Study of the Pastoral Elegy Convention from Theocritus to Milton* (Chapel Hill, 1976).

Lanham, R. A., 'Sidney: The Ornament of His Age', *Southern Review* (Adelaide), 2 (1967), 319–40.

Lebans, W. M., 'A Critical Edition of the "Epicedes and Obsequies" of John Donne', B.Litt. thesis (Oxford, 1964).

—— 'The Influence of the Classics in Donne's *Epicedes and Obsequies*', *RES*, NS, 23 (1972), 127–37.

—— 'Donne's *Anniversaries* and the Tradition of Funeral Elegy', *ELH* 39 (1972), 545–59.

—— Review of B. K. Lewalski, *Donne's Anniversaries*, *RES*, NS, 27 (1976), 346–50.

Lederer, J., 'John Donne and the Emblematic Practice', *RES* 22 (1946), 185–200.

Lee, S., *The French Renaissance in England* (1910).

Le Huray, P., 'The Fair Musick that All Creatures Made', in C. A. Patrides and R. B. Waddington, eds., *The Age of Milton: Backgrounds to Seventeenth-Century Literature* (Manchester, 1980), 241–72.

Lewalski, B. K., *Donne's Anniversaries and the Poetry of Praise: The Creation of a Symbolic Mode* (Princeton, 1973).

—— 'Donne's Epideictic *Personae*', *Southern Quarterly*, 14 (1976), 195–202.

—— *Protestant Poetics and the Seventeenth Century Religious Lyric* (Princeton, 1979).

—— *Renaissance Genres: Essays on Theory, History and Interpretation* (Cambridge, Mass., 1986).

—— 'Lucy, Countess of Bedford: Images of a Jacobean Courtier and Patroness', in K. Sharpe and S. Zwicker, eds., *The Politics of Discourse*, 52–77.

Lewis, C. S., *English Literature in the Sixteenth Century Excluding Drama* (Oxford, 1954).

Lindley, D., *Thomas Campion* (Leiden, 1986).

Lloyd, M., 'Justa Edouardo King', *N&Q*, NS, 5 (1958), 432–4.

Loewenstein, J., *Responsive Readings: Versions of Echo in Pastoral, Epic, and the Jonsonian Masque* (New Haven, 1984).

—— 'Echo's Ring: Orpheus and Spenser's Career', *ELR* 16 (1986), 287–302.

Lyall, R. J., 'Tradition and Innovation in Alexander Barclay's "Towre of Vertue and Honoure"', *RES*, NS, 23 (1972), 1–17.

Macdonald, R. M., *The Library of Drummond of Hawthornden* (Edinburgh, 1971).

Macfarlane, I., *Buchanan* (1981).

MacLean, H., 'Ben Jonson's Poems: Notes on the Ordered Society', in M. MacLure and F. W. Watt, eds., *Essays in English Literature from the Renaissance to the Victorian Age.* (Toronto, 1964), 43–68.

Mallette, R., *Spenser, Milton and Renaissance Pastoral* (Lewisburg, 1981).

Marotti, A. F., *John Donne, Coterie Poet* (Madison, Wis., 1986).

—— 'John Donne and the Rewards of Patronage', in G. F. Lytle and S. Orgel, eds., *Patronage in the Renaissance* (Princeton, 1981), 207–34.

Martz, L. L., *The Poetry of Meditation* (rev. edn., New Haven, 1962).

—— *Poet of Exile* (New Haven, 1980).

Maurer, M., 'The Real Presence of Lucy Russell, Countess of Bedford, and the Terms of John Donne's "Honour is so sublime perfection" ', *ELH* 47 (1980), 205–34.

—— 'Samuel Daniel's Poetical Epistles, Especially Those to Sir Thomas Egerton and Lucy, Countess of Bedford', *SP* 74 (1977), 418–44.

McCanles, M., *Dialectical Criticism and Renaissance Literature* (Berkeley, 1975).

—— 'The *Shepheardes Calender* as Document and Monument', *SEL* 22 (1982), 5–19.

McFarlane, K. B., *Lancastrian Kings and Lollard Knights*, ed. G. L. Harriss (Oxford, 1972).

McLane, P., *Spenser's Shepheardes Calender: A Study in Elizabethan Allegory* (Notre Dame, 1961).

Mercer, E., *English Art, 1553–1625*, Oxford History of English Art, 7 (Oxford, 1962).

Milgate, W., 'Donne and the Roman Triumph', *Parergon*, 1 (1971), 18–23.

Miller, D., 'Spenser's Vocation, Spenser's Career', *ELH* 50 (1983), 197–231.

Miner, E., 'Milton and the Histories', in K. Sharpe and S. Zwicker, eds., *The Politics of Discourse*, 181–203.

Montrose, L. A., ' "The Perfect Paterne of a Poete": The Poetics of Courtship in *The Shepheardes Calender*', *TSLL* 21 (1979), 34–67.

—— ' "Eliza, Queene of Shepheardes", and the Pastoral of Power', *ELR* 10 (1980), 153–82.

—— 'The Elizabethan Subject and the Spenserian Text', in P. Parker and D. Quint, eds., *Literary Theory/Renaissance Texts*, (Baltimore, 1986), 303–40.

—— *In Mirrors More than One: Elizabeth I and the Figurations of Power* (Chicago, forthcoming).

—— ' "Shaping Fantasies": Figurations of Gender and Power in Elizabethan Culture', in S. Greenblatt, ed., *Representing the English Renaissance*, 31–64.

Muir, E., *Civic Ritual in Renaissance Venice* (Princeton, 1981).

Mulryne, J. R., ' "Here's Unfortunate Revels": War and Chivalry in Plays and Shows at the Time of Prince Henry', in Mulryne and M. Shewring, eds., *War, Literature and the Arts in Sixteenth-Century Europe* (1989), 165–89.

Murphy, A. J., 'The Critical Elegy of Earlier Seventeenth Century England', *Genre*, 5 (1972), 75–105.

Newdigate, B. H., *Michael Drayton and his Circle* (1941).

Nohrnberg, J., *The Analogy of 'The Faerie Queene'* (2nd edn., Princeton, 1980).

Norbrook, D., 'Panegyric of the Monarch, and its Social Context under Elizabeth I and James I', D.Phil. thesis (Oxford, 1978).

—— *Poetry and Politics in the English Renaissance* (1984).

Novarr, D., *The Disinterred Muse: Donne's Texts and Contexts* (Ithaca, 1980).

O'Connell, M., *'Astrophel*: Spenser's Double Elegy', *SEL* 11 (1971), 27–35.

Oman, Sir Charles, *The History of the Art of War in the Sixteenth Century* (1937).

Oram, W., *'Daphnaida* and Spenser's Later Poetry', *Spenser Studies*, 2 (1981), 141–58.

Parker, D. H., 'The Literary Epitaph in the Seventeenth Century', B.Litt. thesis (Oxford, 1970).

Parker, M. R., 'Diamond's Dust: Carew, King and the Legacy of Donne', in C. J. Summers and T.-L. Pebworth, eds., *The Eagle and the Dove: Reassessing John Donne* (Columbia, 1986), 191–200.

Parmenter, M. H., 'Spenser's "Twelve Aeglogues Proportionable to the Twelve Monethes"', *ELH* 3 (1936), 190–217.

Parrish, P. A., 'Donne's "A Funerall Elegie"', *PLL* 11 (1975), 83–7.

—— 'Poet, Audience, and the Word: an Approach to the *Anniversaries*', in G. A. Stringer, ed., *New Essays on Donne* (Salzburg, 1977), 110–39.

—— ' "A Funerall Elegie": Donne's Achievement in Traditional Form', *Concerning Poetry*, 19 (1986), 55–66.

Parry, G., *The Golden Age Restor'd: The Culture of the Stuart Court 1603–1642* (Manchester, 1981).

Partridge, E., 'Johnson's *Epigrammes*: The Named and the Nameless', *SLI* 6 (1973), 153–98.

Patterson, A., *Censorship and Interpretation* (Madison, Wis., 1984).

—— *Pastoral and Ideology. Virgil to Valery* (Oxford, 1988).

Pearsall, D. A. *John Lydgate* (1970).

Peck, L. L., *Northampton: Patronage and Policy at the Court of James I* (1982).

—— ' "For a King not to be Bountiful were a Fault": Perspectives on Court Patronage in Early Stuart England', *Journal of British Studies*, 25 (1986), 31–61.

Peck, R. A., 'Theme and Number in Chaucer's *Book of the Duchess*', in A. Fowler, ed., *Silent Poetry* (1970), 73–115.

Perosa, A., and J. Sparrow, eds., *Renaissance Latin Verse: An Anthology* (1979).

Peter, J., *Complaint and Satire in Early English Literature* (Oxford, 1956).

Peterson, D.L., *The English Lyric from Wyatt to Donne* (Princeton, 1967).

Pigman, G. W., III, 'Imitation and the Renaissance Sense of the Past: The Reception of Erasmus' *Ciceronianus*', *JMRS* 9 (1979), 155–77.

—— 'Versions of Imitation in the Renaissance', *RQ* 33 (1980), 1–32.

—— *Grief and English Renaissance Elegy* (Cambridge, 1985).

Pitcher, J., 'Samuel Daniel's Occasional and Dedicatory Verse: A Critical Edition', D.Phil. thesis, 2 vols. (Oxford, 1978).

—— ' "In those figures which they seeme": Samuel Daniel's *Tethys' Festival*', in D. Lindley, ed., *The Court Masque* (Manchester, 1984), 33–46.

Plomer, H. R., and T. P. Cross, *The Life and Correspondence of Lodowick Bryskett* (Chicago, 1927).

Pollock, Z., ' "The Object, and the Wit": The Smell of Donne's *First Anniversary*', *ELR* 13 (1983), 301–18.

Pope-Hennessy, J., *The Portrait in the Renaissance* (Princeton, 1966).

Pratt, S. M., 'Jane Shore and the Elizabethans: Some Facts and Speculations', *TSLL* 11 (1970), 1293–1306.

Prestwich, M., *Cranfield: Politics and Profits under the Stuarts. The Career of Lionel Cranfield Earl of Middlesex* (Oxford, 1966).

Prince, F. T., *The Italian Element in Milton's Verse* (Oxford, 1954).

Pullan, I., *The History of the Book of Common Prayer* (1900).

Quint, D., *Origin and Originality in Renaissance Literature* (New Haven, 1983).

Rees, J., *Samuel Daniel: A Critical and Biographical Study* (Liverpool, 1964).

—— *Fulke Greville, Lord Brooke, 1554–1628* (1971).

Reeves, M., *The Influence of Prophecy in the Later Middle Ages* (Oxford, 1969).

Ribiero, A., 'Sir John Roe: Ben Jonson's Friend', *RES*, NS, 24 (1973), 153–64.

Ringler, W. A., 'The Myth and the Man', in J. Van Dorsten, D. Baker-Smith and A. F. Kinney, eds., *Sir Philip Sidney: 1586 and the Creation of a Legend*, 3–16.

Robertson, D. W., '*The Book of the Duchess*', in B. Rowland, ed., *A Companion to Chaucer Studies* (rev. edn., New York, 1979), 403–13.

Roche, T. P., jun., '*Astrophil and Stella*: A Radical Reading', *Spenser Studies*, 3 (1982), 139–91.

Rooney, A., '*The Book of the Duchess*: Hunting and the "ubi sunt" Tradition', *RES*, NS, 38 (1987), 299–314.

Rosenberg, D. M., *Oaten Reeds and Trumpets: Pastoral and Epic in Virgil, Spenser, and Milton* (Lewisburg, 1981).

Rosenberg, E., *Leicester, Patron of Letters* (New York, 1955).

Rosenmeyer, T. G., *The Green Cabinet: Theocritus and the European Pastoral Lyric* (Berkeley, 1969).

Roston, M., *The Soul of Wit* (Oxford, 1974).

Røstvig, M.-S., *The Hidden Sense* (Oslo, 1963).

Sacks, P. M., *The English Elegy: Studies in the Genre from Spenser to Yeats* (Baltimore, 1985).

Sargent, R., 'Poetry and the Puritan Faith: The Elegies of Anne Bradstreet and Edward Taylor', in W. Haslauer, ed., *A Salzburg Miscellany. English and American Studies 1964–84* (Salzburg, 1984), 149–60.

Sargent, R. M., *At the Court of Queen Elizabeth: The Life and Lyrics of Sir Edward Dyer* (1935).

Scattergood, V. J., *Politics and Poetry in the Fifteenth Century* (1971).

Schoell, F. L., 'Chapman and the Neo-Latinists of the Quattrocento', *MP* 13 (1915), 215–38.

Schoenbaum, S., *William Shakespeare: A Compact Documentary Life* (Oxford, 1977).

Schutte, W., 'Thomas Churchyard's "Dollfull Discourse" and the Death of Lady Katherine Grey', *Sixteenth Century Journal*, 15 (1984), 471–87.

Shapiro, I. A., 'The Date of a Donne Elegy, and its Implications', in J. Carey, ed., *English Renaissance Studies*, 141–50.

Sharpe, K., *Sir Robert Cotton, 1586–1631: History and Politics in Early Modern England* (Oxford, 1979).

Sharpe, K., and S. Zwicker, eds., *The Politics of Discourse* (Berkeley, 1986).

Sharpe, K., *Criticism and Compliment* (Cambridge, 1987).

Sheavyn, P., *The Literary Profession in the Elizabethan Age* (2nd edn., rev. J. W. Saunders, Manchester, 1967).

Sherwood, P. G., 'Reason in Donne's Sermons', *ELH* 39 (1972), 353–74.

—— 'Reason, Faith and Just Augustinian Lamentation in Donne's Elegy on Prince Henry', *SEL* 13 (1973), 53–63.

—— *Fulfilling the Circle: A Study of John Donne's Thought* (Toronto, 1984).

Smith, A. J., ed., *John Donne: The Critical Heritage* (1975).

Smith, B. R., 'Ben Jonson's *Epigrammes*: Portrait-Gallery, Theater, Commonwealth', *SEL* 14 (1974), 91–109.

Smith, H., *Elizabethan Poetry* (Cambridge, Mass., 1952).

Stannard, P. G., *The Puritan Way of Death: A Study in Religion, Culture and Social Change* (Oxford, 1977).

Stanwood, P. G., '"Essential Joye" in Donne's *Anniversaries*', *TSLL* 13 (1971), 227–38.

Stein, A., *The House of Death: Messages from the English Renaissance* (Baltimore, 1986).

Sternfeld, F. W., 'Repetition and Echo in Renaissance Poetry and Music', in J. Carey, ed., *English Renaissance Studies* (Oxford, 1981), 33–43.

Stillman, R. E., *Sidney's Poetic Justice: The Old Arcadia, its Eclogues, and Renaissance Pastoral Traditions* (Lewisburg, 1986).

Stone, D., *French Humanist Tragedy* (Manchester, 1974).

Stone, L., *An Elizabethan: Sir Horatio Pallavicino* (Oxford, 1956).

Stone, L., *The Crisis of the Aristocracy, 1558–1641* (Oxford, 1965).

Strong, R., *The Cult of Elizabeth* (1977).

—— *Henry Prince of Wales and England's Lost Renaissance* (1986).

Tennenhouse, L., 'Sir Walter Ralegh and the Literature of Patronage', in G. F. Lytle and S. Orgel, ed., *Patronage in the Renaissance* (Princeton, 1981), 235–58.

Thomas, Keith, *Religion and the Decline of Magic* (2nd edn., Harmondsworth, 1973).

Thompson, J., *The Founding of English Metre* (1961).

Thomson, P., 'John Donne and the Countess of Bedford', *MLR* 44 (1949), 329–40.

—— 'Donne and the Poetry of Patronage', in A. J. Smith, ed., *John Donne: Essays in Celebration* (1972), 308–23.

Tourney, L. D., 'Convention and Wit in Donne's *Elegie* on Prince Henry', *SP* 71 (1974), 473–83.

Tromley, F. B., 'Lodowick Bryskett's Elegies on Sidney in Spenser's *Astrophel* Volume', *RES*, NS, 37 (1986), 384–8.

Turner, A. T., 'Milton and the Convention of the Academic Miscellanies', *YES* 5 (1975), 86–93.

Turner, M., ' "Where Rooted Moisture Failes": Sidney's Pastoral Elegy (OA75) and the Radical Humour', *ELN* 15 (1977), 7–10.

Tuve, R., *Elizabethan and Metaphysical Imagery* (Chicago, 1947).

—— *Allegorical Imagery* (Princeton, 1966).

Vale, M., *War and Chivalry: Warfare and Aristocratic Culture in England, France and Burgundy at the End of the Middle Ages* (1981).

Van Dorsten, J., D. Baker-Smith, and A. F. Kinney, eds., *Sir Philip Sidney: 1586 and the Creation of a Legend* (Leiden, 1986).

Van Velzen, A., 'Two Versions of the Funeral Elegy: Henry King's "The Exequy" and Thomas Carew's " . . . Elegies Upon . . . Donne" ', *Comitatus*, 15 (1984), 45–57.

Vickers, B., 'Epideictic and Epic in the Renaissance', *New Literary History*, 14 (1982–3), 497–537.

—— *In Defence of Rhetoric* (Oxford, 1988).

Vovelle, M., *Mourir autrefois* (Paris, 1974).

Wallerstein, R., *Studies in Seventeenth-Century Poetic* (Madison, Wis., 1950).

Walters, M., 'Epistolary Verse and its Social Context, 1590–1640', B.Litt. thesis (Oxford, 1972).

Weitzmann, F. W., 'Notes on the Elizabethan "Elegie" ', *PMLA* 50 (1935), 435–43.

Welsby, P. A., *George Abbott: The Unwanted Archbishop* (1962).

West, D., and T. Woodman, eds., *Creative Imitation and Latin Literature* (Cambridge, 1979).

Whigham, F., 'Interpretation at Court: Courtesy and the Performer–Audience Dialectic', *New Literary History*, 14 (1982–3), 623–39.

Williams, N., *Elizabeth, Queen of England* (1967).

Williams, P., *The Tudor Regime* (Oxford, 1979).

Williamson, G., 'Mutability, Decay, and Seventeenth Century Melancholy', *ELH* 2 (1935), 121–50.

Williamson, J. W., *The Myth of the Conqueror, Prince Henry Stuart: A Study of 17th Century Personation* (New York, 1978).

Willson, D. H., *King James VI and I* (1956).

Wilson, E. C., *England's Eliza* (Cambridge, Mass., 1939).

—— *Prince Henry and English Literature* (New York, 1946).

Wittreich, J. A., 'From Pastoral to Prophecy: The Genres of *Lycidas*', *Milton Studies*, 13 (1979), 59–80.

—— *Visionary Poetics: Milton's Tradition and His Legacy* (San Marino, 1979).

Wood, A., *The History and antiquities of the colleges and halls in the University of Oxford, publ. with a continuation to the present day by the ed., J. Gutch* (Oxford, 1786).

Woodhouse, A. S. P., 'Milton's Pastoral Monodies', in M. E. White, ed., *Studies in Honour of Gilbert Norwood* (Toronto, 1952), 264–74.

—— and D. Bush, eds., *A Variorum Commentary on the Poems of John Milton*, vol. ii (New York, 1972).

Wood-Legh, K. L., *Perpetual Chantries in Britain* (Cambridge, 1965).

Woolf, R., *The English Religious Lyric in the Middle Ages* (Oxford, 1968).

Wordsworth, C., *Memoirs of William Wordsworth, Poet-Laureate, DCL*, 2 vols. (1851).

Woudhuysen, H. R., 'Leicester's Literary Patronage: A study of the English Court 1577–82', D.Phil. thesis (Oxford, 1981).

Wright, L. B., *Middle-Class Culture in Elizabethan England* (1935; repr. Washington, 1958).

Yates, F. A., *Astraea: The Imperial Theme in the Sixteenth Century* (1975).

INDEX